Date Due

Centralia

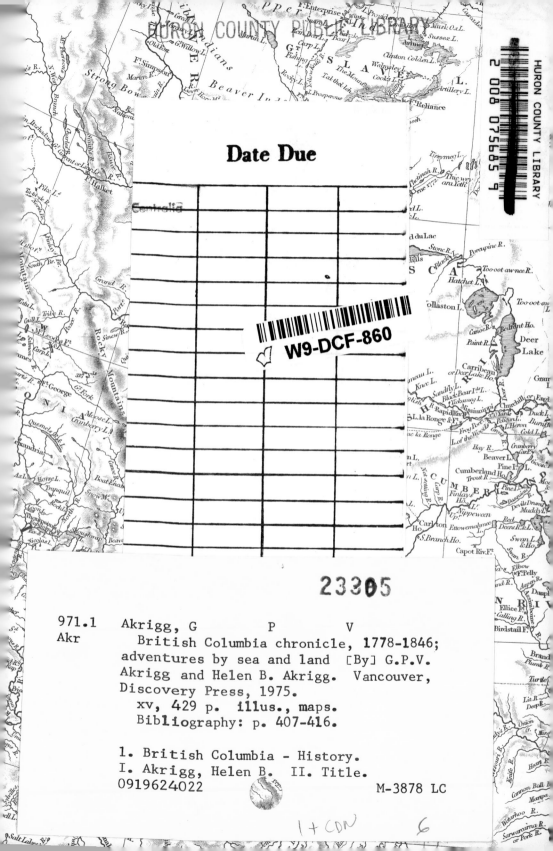

W9-DCF-860

1 + CDN   6

British Columbia
CHRONICLE
1778-1846

CAPTAIN JAMES COOK, R.N.

British Columbia
CHRONICLE
1778-1846

ADVENTURERS
BY SEA AND LAND

G. P. V. Akrigg and Helen B. Akrigg

DISCOVERY PRESS
1975

I.S.B.N. NUMBER 0-919624-02-2

Published by
DISCOVERY PRESS
P.O. BOX 46295
VANCOUVER, BRITISH COLUMBIA V6R 4G6

First printing September 1975
Second printing November 1975

Canadian Shared Cataloguing in Publication Data

Akrigg, George Philip Vernon, 1913-
    British Columbia chronicle, 1778-1846: adventurers by
sea and land/by G. P. V. Akrigg & Helen B. Akrigg. —

    1. British Columbia — History.   I. Akrigg,
Helen Brown (Manning), 1921-   II. Title.
FC   971.1
[LC: F1088.A]
[UBC: F5811.A597]

By G. P. V. Akrigg
Jacobean Pageant or The Court of King James I
Shakespeare and the Earl of Southampton
HARVARD UNIVERSITY PRESS & HAMISH HAMILTON LTD.

By G. P. V. Akrigg & Helen B. Akrigg
1001 British Columbia Place Names
DISCOVERY PRESS

Designed and printed in Canada by
MORRISS PRINTING COMPANY LTD.
Victoria, British Columbia

DEDICATED

TO THE MEMORY OF

THE OFFICERS AND MEN

OF

The North West Company

AND

The Honourable Hudson's Bay Company

WHO THROUGH THEIR COURAGE AND ENDURANCE

WON FOR BRITAIN

HER DOMAIN IN THE PACIFIC NORTH-WEST

List of Illustrations

Maps and Diagrams

Abbreviations

BCHQ	*British Columbia Historical Quarterly*
HBC	Hudson's Bay Company
HBCA	Hudson's Bay Company Archives
HBRS	Hudson's Bay Record Society
H.M.S.	His (Her) Majesty's Ship
OHQ	*Oregon Historical Quarterly*
PABC	Provincial Archives of British Columbia
PAC	Public Archives of Canada
PRO	Public Record Office (London, England)
PSAC	Puget's Sound Agricultural Company
R.N.	Royal Navy
UBC	University of British Columbia Library
U.S.S.	United States Ship
WHQ	*Washington Historical Quarterly*

Acknowledgements

The writing of history is a continuing process, with each generation of historians indebted to those who went before. It is, then, fitting to begin this chronicle with recognition of those whose work has preceded our own, beginning with that first *History of British Columbia* by H. H. Bancroft in 1887 and concluding with Professor Margaret Ormsby's *British Columbia: A History*, commissioned by the Province of British Columbia to mark its 1958 centennial. (Professor Martin Robin's two volumes, since they deal with the period 1871-1972, lie outside our area.)

Looking back over the work that has been done, one is immediately impressed by the very important achievement of two men. One is the late Judge F. W. Howay. Between 1902 and his death in 1943, Judge Howay produced some 286 articles and books dealing with the history of British Columbia and the Pacific North-west, maintaining always an impeccable standard of scholarship. His achievement is the more amazing in that most of it was accomplished during the busy years previous to his retirement from the bench. The other major figure in the field of British Columbia history is Dr. W. Kaye Lamb, originally Provincial Archivist and Librarian for British Columbia, then Librarian of the University of British Columbia, and finally both Dominion Archivist and National Librarian in Ottawa. Perhaps because the later stages of Dr. Lamb's career have been spent far from British Columbia, this province has been insufficiently aware of its debt to him. While writing numerous and substantial articles, Dr. Lamb has made his great contribution in the self-effacing labour of providing succeeding British Columbian historians with authoritative editions of the foundation works. The present authors were assisted greatly by Dr. Lamb's editions of Mackenzie, Fraser, Harmon, Franchère, and the three-volume edition of McLoughlin's letters to which Dr. Lamb provided the introductions. Finally we are all in his debt for founding and initially editing the *British Columbia Historical Quarterly*, which so unfortunately was allowed to lapse under a later editor. It is a measure of Judge Howay and Dr. Lamb that both men received the ultimate recognition of being elected President of the Royal Society of Canada.

So many individuals have assisted us with our inquiries and research that it is impossible to list them all. Mention must be made, however, of the assistance that we have received from Mrs. Anne Yandle and Miss Frances Woodward of the Special Collections Division of the library of our home institution, the University of British Columbia. Special mention must be made also of Rear-Admiral P. W. Brock, C.B., D.S.O., for his helpful suggestions and assistance in guiding us to valuable sources in England. We recall with pleasure our discussions with Dr. Dorothy Blakey Smith, known through long association in the English Department at U.B.C. and the Provincial Archives in Victoria. We recall other friends: the late Doug. Stevenson and his wife Anne, at Williams Lake, and the late Gordon Bowes and his wife Stephanie, in Vancouver, who by their own zeal added to our enthusiasm for British Columbia history.

A special word of appreciation must be said for the Hudson's Bay Company, which not only gave us access to its archives (now happily transferred to Winnipeg), but assisted us with pictures. We are indebted to Shirlee Anne Smith, the Company's Archivist, for checking our references to manuscripts in that great and invaluable collection.

It remains to list other institutions which welcomed us and assisted us with our research. The chief of these are the Public Archives of Canada and the Provincial Archives of British Columbia. Other Canadian repositories in which we worked include the University of British Columbia's Special Collections, the Vancouver Public Library's Northwest Room, the Provincial Archives of Ontario, the Metropolitan Toronto Central Library, and the Library of McGill University.

In the United States we visited the Huntington Library, Pasadena; the Bancroft Library of the University of California, Berkeley; and the Library of the Oregon Historical Society, Portland. We were welcomed at the Turnbull Library in Wellington, New Zealand; and the Mitchell Library and Dixson Library in Sydney, Australia, and the National Library of Australia in Canberra.

A great amount of material relating to the history of early British Columbia is, of course, to be found in Britain, and we wish to thank the following for letting us examine their holdings: the Public Record Office, London, and the Scottish Record Office; the British Library (formerly the Library of the British Museum); the Navy Library (formerly the Admiralty Library); the National Maritime Museum; the Office of the Hydrographer of the Navy, Taunton; the Botany Library of the Natural History Museum, Kensington; the Library of the Royal Botanical Gardens at Kew; the India Office Library; and the Library of the University of Cambridge.

Celista, B.C.   G.P.V.A.

                                                   H.B.A.

The Beginning

When did men first walk through the valleys of British Columbia, paddle their canoes on her broad lakes, her swift rivers and deep fiords, paint in red ochre their signs upon her rock faces, make their trails, establish their habitations, and leave their artifacts? How did these first British Columbians, the Indians, come to be?

Various tribes reply with legends passed on from generation to generation. Typical of these genesis myths is that of the Nootka Indians. First there was a god named Qua-utz. And Qua-utz created a woman and left her to live alone and lamenting in the dark forests of Yucuatl (Nootka Sound). And with her in the forest were deer created by Qua-utz, but they had as yet no antlers. And there were dogs, but they had as yet no tails. And there were ducks, but they had as yet no wings. Then Qua-utz took pity on the loneliness of the maiden. He came to her over the ocean in a gleaming canoe made all of copper. Swiftly the copper canoe came towards the shore, with young men plying copper paddles. One of the handsome young men spoke to the desolate maiden from the copper canoe and told her that Qua-utz, to whom all things are possible, had come to supply her with company of her own kind. At these words the maiden wept and her tears fell upon the ground. Then Qua-utz himself bade her look where her tears had fallen, and she saw that they had formed the body of a tiny baby. And Qua-utz told her to place it in a small seashell and then, as it grew in size, in a larger shell, and later a still larger shell. Then Qua-utz extended his bounty to the deer, the dogs, and the ducks. The deer sprouted antlers, the dogs wagged tails and the ducks, growing wings, soared into the air. Qua-utz and his men departed in their great canoe of copper, but the little baby remained.

He grew into a sturdy boy and then into a strong young man. Then he took the maiden to be his wife and they begat children. From their first-born son descended the tyees (chiefs), and from their other sons the common people.

Such is the tale that the Nootka Indians told early Spanish visitors;[1] but in time the white men, with their sciences, explained differently the origin not only of the Nootkas but of all the Indians. From his original home in Africa man, hundreds of thousands of years in the past, spread into Europe and Asia. Between 25,000 and 30,000 years ago descendants of the first hunting bands that crossed from Siberia into North America penetrated southward through what would one day be British Columbia. Migration within the area ceased with the onset of the last great ice age which began about 25,000 years ago and lasted for some 12,000 years. During the height of this ice age nearly all of British Columbia lay under a vast ice sheet, thousands of feet in depth. Needless to say, all the campsites, artifacts or other traces of this earliest human occupation of the province were destroyed by the enormous weight of the ice sheet, or lie deeply buried under the sediment left by the continental glacier.

When the climate warmed and the glaciers receded, man once more entered British Columbia. About 7500 B.C. newcomers from south-western Yukon found their way down the coast, or pushed through the corridor separating the Rocky Mountains from the ranges to the west. About one or two thousand years earlier other men, whose ancestors had survived in areas south of the ice front, began moving northward into the valleys and coastlands left clear by the receding glaciers. Thus, from both north and south, came the ancestors of the Indian peoples who still play an important role in the life of our province. Oldest of the known archaeological sites of the returning human population is one in the Fraser Canyon near Yale, dating from about 7050 B.C.[2] Other evidence suggests that the first arrivals from the south may have come to the south-western mainland around 10,500 years ago.

---

[1] [José Cardero], *A Spanish Voyage to Vancouver and the North-West Coast of America*, trans. C. Jane (London, 1930), pp. 108-109.

[2] Known as the Milliken Site, this was excavated by Professor C. E. Borden, of the University of British Columbia, between 1958 and 1963.

No history survives for the millenia which followed, for none of the native tribes ever evolved a system of writing sufficient to provide a history. The earliest events preserved by the memory of the Indians probably do not extend more than a couple of centuries before the coming of the white man.

1579-1777

Drake sails north from California — The mystery of Juan de Fuca — The Russians cross Bering Straits — Juan Perez sights British Columbia but does not land — Perez off Nootka — Smallpox strikes the Indians.

For the purposes of this chronicle, British Columbia's history began in 1778 when Captain Cook and his crews became the first white men to set foot upon her territory. But before that notable event there were other happenings, some apocryphal but others historical, which form a necessary prologue to our annals.

We begin then in June 1579, with a little English ship of only 100 tons, the *Golden Hind*, sailing under cloudy skies along the North-west Coast of North America. Twenty months earlier she had sailed from Plymouth Ho, proud flagship of a squadron of five vessels. By the time she entered the Straits of Magellan she had only two consorts left. Hardly were the three little ships through into the Pacific than an appalling storm lasting some fifty-two days struck them. Amid the "mountains of the sea" one of the three little ships, the *Marigold*, sank with all her crew. Another, the *Elizabeth*, became separated from the *Golden Hind* and, after waiting in vain at an appointed rendezvous, returned to England. Alone with his *Golden Hind*, Captain Francis Drake, the first Englishman ever to round the southern tip of South America, sailed northwards along the coasts of Chile and Peru. Behind him he left a trail of looted ships, striking consternation into the hearts of the Spaniards who never had thought to find this famous English corsair within their western ocean. Drake's great moment came off the shores of Nicaragua when he captured the treasure-ship *Nuestra Señora de la*

Concepcion. From her he transferred to his little ship 26 tons of silver (which served as ballast for the rest of her incredible journey), thirteen chests filled with pieces of eight, and a quantity of gold, jewels and plate.

With this fortune stowed beneath his decks, Drake was chiefly concerned to get his loot safely home to England. But how? The route by which he had come was impossible — Spanish warships, patrolling both the western and eastern shores of South America, would be sure to intercept him. But in theory, at least, two other routes were available for Drake. By the first he could follow Ferdinand Magellan's course across the Pacific and Indian Oceans, then round the Cape of Good Hope and so return to England, becoming the first English captain ever to circumnavigate the world. But that route would indeed be long and dangerous. Another way, should it prove to exist, might be safer and shorter. This was the much discussed "North-west Passage" around the northern end of North America. In 1574 the famous geographer Abraham Ortelius had published a map showing a kingdom named Anian, very approximately where Alaska is, with a passage between Anian and Asia leading into a long open channel to the North Atlantic. Drake made his decision: he would look for the North-west Passage. Accordingly, the *Golden Hind* turned north.

Farther and farther northwards Drake and his seamen sailed. The blue skies of the south gave way to the rainstorms of the Pacific North-west. Francis Drake, short, stocky and red-bearded, limping from his old wound received on the Spanish Main, stared ahead with piercing blue eyes as storms gave way to fog, and yet more storms. Had he decided aright? Finally the ship made a landfall, but the coast stretched north-westerly, not north-easterly towards the Atlantic. Here we may quote from the nearest thing we have to an official account of the voyage, *The World Encompassed by Sir Francis Drake*, published in 1628 by a nephew of Drake: [1]

---

[1] Unfortunately Drake's richly illustrated official journal and his maps, which he presented to Queen Elizabeth upon his return, have been lost. Accordingly, we have to fall back upon this book which carries upon its title page a note, "carefully collected out of the notes of Master Francis Fletcher, preacher in this imployment [voyage], and diuers others his followers in the same."

The land in that part of America, bearing farther out into the West then [than] we before imagined, we were neerer on it then wee were aware; and yet the neerer still wee came vnto it, the more extremitie of cold did sease vpon vs. The 5 day of *Iune*, wee were forced by contrary windes to runne in with the shoare, which we then first descried, and to cast anchor in a bad bay, the best roade we could for the present meete with, where wee were not without some danger by reason of the many extreme gusts and flawes that beate vpon vs, which if they ceased and were still at any time, immediately upon their intermission there followed most uile, thicke, and stinking fogges, against which the sea preuailed nothing. . . .

In this place was no abiding for vs; and to go further North, the extremity of the cold (which had now vtterly discouraged our men) would not permit vs; and the winds directly bent against vs, hauing once gotten vs under sayle againe, commanded vs to the Southward whether we would or no.

From the height of 48 deg., in which now we were, to 38, we found the land, by coasting alongst it, to bee but low and reasonable plaine, euery hill (whereof we saw many, but none verie high), though it were in *June*, and the sunne in his neerest approch vnto them, being couered with snow.[2]

Thus it was that, before fog, wind and cold drove him back, Captain Francis Drake from Devon apparently reached some point in the vicinity of the 48th parallel, tantalizingly close to the Strait of Juan de Fuca and the land that would one day be British Columbia.

The suggestion has been made that, in fact, Drake sailed considerably further north. The continuous storms and fog probably prevented him taking any bearings from the sun, and he presumably calculated his position by dead reckoning. Captain R. P. Bishop, carefully weighing possible errors in dead reckoning and studying the ocean currents which would have been carrying Drake north in that season of the year, concluded that Drake may have made his landfall anywhere up to 50 degrees north, finding his "bad bay" somewhere on Vancouver Island. Others, however, have felt that Drake never got farther north than the 43rd parallel.[3] In any event

---

[2] W. S. W. Vaux, ed., *The World Encompassed by Sir Francis Drake*, Hakluyt Society (London, 1854), p. 115.

[3] Of Drake's contemporaries, Richard Hakluyt says variously that Drake reached the 42nd or 43rd parallel and John Stow says the 47th parallel.

Drake, after turning south, overhauled his ship in a bay a little north of where San Francisco now rises. Then he headed west to the Spice Islands, committed to circumnavigating the globe and leaving us with an unanswerable question: did he or did he not sight the shores of British Columbia?

When Drake was sailing up the coast of Chile in December 1578, he had captured off Valparaiso a small Spanish vessel carrying a Greek pilot named Juan. Born Apostolos Valerianos on one of the Greek islands, this pilot was known to the Spaniards as Juan de Fuca. He had the misfortune in 1587 to be captured again by an English raider, this time Captain George Cavendish, who put Juan de Fuca and various other captives ashore at Cape St. Lucas at the southern tip of Lower California. Apparently de Fuca remained in Mexico about seven years longer, but in 1596 he was in Italy, a man of sixty returning to spend his declining years in his Greek home-land. At Venice he was introduced to Michael Lok, an English merchant with an obsessive belief in the existence of the North-west Passage. Surviving for us is Lok's own account of what he learned from Juan de Fuca concerning the latter's discovery, between the 47th and 48th degrees of latitude, of the western entrance to the North-west Passage, commonly known as the Strait of Anian:

... the said Viceroy of *Mexico*, sent him out againe *Anno* 1592, with a small *Carauela*, and a Pinnace, armed with Mariners onely, to follow the said Voyage, for discouery of the same Straits of *Anian*, and the passage thereof, into the Sea which they call the North Sea, which is our North-west Sea. And that he followed his course in that Voyage West and North-west in the South Sea, all alongst the coast of *Noua*

Hondius notes on a map of 1586 that Drake turned back at "lat.42". On the other hand, an anonymous manuscript of the period says Drake reached the 48th parallel. On the voyage with Drake was his young cousin John Fletcher, and when he was captured by the Spaniards in 1582, at two separate examinations he testified that the *Golden Hind* reached the 48th parallel. John Davis, the Arctic navigator, spoke in 1595 of Drake having reached the 48th parallel. The references to the extreme cold encountered by Drake in June have inspired at least one writer to wonder if Drake did not reach "some point closer to the Arctic Circle" (G. M. Thomson, *Sir Francis Drake* (London, 1972), p. 141). The whole vexed question is canvassed with the greatest detail and fairness in R. P. Bishop, "Drake's Course in the North Pacific", *British Columbia Historical Quarterly* [hereafter referred to as *BCHQ*] 3 (1939):151-182.

Spania, and *California*, and the *Indies*, now called North *America* ...
vntill hee came to the Latitude of fortie seuen degrees, and that there
finding that the Land trended North and North-east, with a broad
Inlet of Sea, betweene 47. and 48. degrees of Latitude: hee entred
thereinto, sayling therein more than twentie dayes, and found that
Land trending still sometime North-west and North-east, and North,
and also East and South-eastward, and very much broader Sea then
was at the said entrance, and that hee passed by diuers Ilands in that
sayling. And that at the entrance of this said Strait, there is on the
North-west coast thereof, a great Hedland or Iland, with an exceeding
high Pinacle, or spired Rocke, like a piller thereupon.

Also he said, that he went on Land in diuers places, and that he saw
some people on Land, clad in Beasts skins: and that the Land is very
fruitfull, and rich of gold, Siluer, Pearle, and other things, like *Noua
Spania*.

And also he said, that he being entred thus farre into the said Strait,
and being come into the North Sea already, and finding the Sea wide
enough euery where, and to be about thirtie or fortie leagues wide
in the mouth of the Straits, where hee entred; hee thought he had now
well discharged his office, and done the thing which he was sent to doe:
and that hee not being armed to resist the force of the Saluage people
that might happen, hee therefore set sayle and returned homewards
againe towards *Noua Spania*, where hee arriued at *Acapulco*, *Anno*
1592. hoping to be rewarded greatly of the Viceroy, for this seruice
done in this said Voyage.[4]

According to Lok, Juan de Fuca told him also that the Viceroy,
despite repeated petitions, had failed to reward him but had advised
him to go to the court of the King of Spain with his request; that in
Spain also he had failed to win recompense, and that in his consequent bitterness he was ready to give the English the advantage of
his experience. Greatly excited, Lok kept in touch with Juan de Fuca
by letters while he vainly tried to raise financial support in England
for an expedition on which Juan de Fuca would go as pilot. Finally
in 1602, while himself in the Greek islands, he received word that
Juan de Fuca was dying, if not already dead.

Late in the 18th century an English sea captain, Charles Barkley,
discovered on the North-west Coast a broad passage sweeping

---

[4] *Purchas His Pilgrimes* (London, 1625), Book III, Part iv, p. 850 (fol.
Aaaa2v).

inland, just where Juan de Fuca claimed to have found one almost two centuries before. Not surprisingly Barkley named this waterway the Strait of Juan de Fuca. But had the adventurous Greek with his Spanish ship ever sailed these waters? Or was Juan de Fuca an astute old scoundrel who had invented the whole story of his voyage as a means of getting money out of a credulous Englishman who had already made up his mind that the Strait of Anian, a navigable North-west Passage, did in fact exist?

Those who accept Juan de Fuca's story point out that he is absolutely correct in his location of the entry to the strait leading to that "very much broader sea" which is the Strait of Georgia. They believe that Juan de Fuca's amazing range of directions reflects his experiences as he threaded his way possibly down into Puget Sound, and up along the waterways north of it. They believe that his "divers islands" are the Gulf Islands. Chief of those who believe de Fuca's story is Captain John Walbran who, in his many years as captain of the *Quadra* around the end of the last century, came to have an unparalleled knowledge of the British Columbia coast. He was convinced that "De Fuca's pillar" off Tatooche Island is Juan de Fuca's "high Pinacle, or spired Rocke".[5]

On the other hand, Henry R. Wagner, one of the most authoritative historians of the Spanish voyages in the Pacific, was totally convinced that, while de Fuca undoubtedly spent many years on the Pacific coast of Spanish America, he never made the voyage he described to Lok. Supporting Wagner are a number of other scholars[6] who have pointed out apparent discrepancies in de Fuca's account. The last word seems to remain with Warren L. Cook, who recently has re-examined the whole controversy, advanced possible answers to the objections of Wagner and his fellow sceptics, and concluded:

The archives of Spain and Spanish America are far from plumbed and may yet provide evidence to confirm or disprove Fuca's claims. Until

---

[5] John T. Walbran, *British Columbia Coast Names 1592-1906* (Ottawa, 1909), p. 274.

[6] See Henry R. Wagner, "Apocryphal Voyages to the Northwest Coast of America", *Proceedings of the American Antiquarian Society*, 41 (1931):179-90. Sharing Wagner's disbelief are H. H. Bancroft, George Davidson and Judge F. W. Howay.

such a time, the old Greek's curious tale cannot be left out of any account of early voyages to the northwest coast.[7]

The years rolled on. For over a century and a half no European was even reputed to have sailed into the waters of the North-west Coast. But the veils were soon to begin to lift from this part of the world. On 16 July 1741 Vitus Bering, a Danish officer in the service of the Russians, saw the clouds part before him and there, magnificent in the sunshine, glittered the mountains of the St. Elias Range. Tragedy lay ahead for Bering on this his final voyage. Caught in a tremendous gale, his ship the *Saint Peter* was wrecked on Bering Island where he died in December. The survivors at the end of the winter built a new vessel out of the wreckage of the old and, clad in long robes which they had made out of sea otter skins, safely landed at Petropavlovsk in Siberia. They had been preceded by Captain-Lieutenant Aleksei Chirikov and the crew of their sister ship the *Saint Paul*, who had safely returned after exploring the Aleutians. Chirikov's crew had brought word of the great abundance of sea otters off Alaska. Sea otters meant wealth, real wealth, for those who could procure them for the Chinese market. Russian adventurers lost little time in heading for Alaska. In 1745 Chevaevskoi and Trapeznikov outfitted the first fur trading expedition to the Aleutians. The following years saw the Russian fur traders gradually moving farther and farther down the Alaskan coast.

Fearing involvement with Spain, which claimed the entire western coast of the Americas, Russia tried to keep secret Bering's voyage of 1741 and the subsequent development of Russian trade off northwestern Alaska. The Spanish government, however, soon learnt what was happening. Briefed by the Spanish ambassador at St. Petersburg, the councillors of the King of Spain conferred about these Russian interlopers in an area which, even if unknown and unexplored, they regarded as theirs by right of the Bull of Pope Alexander VI, issued in 1493, which had divided the New World between Spain and Portugal. Obviously something would have to be done — a Spanish expedition would have to be sent into the

---

[7] Warren L. Cook, *Flood Tide of Empire: Spain and the Pacific Northwest, 1543-1819* (New Haven, 1973), p. 29. Cook's book is now the definitive one on the Spanish voyages along the North-west Coast.

North Pacific to see what the Russians were up to, and to establish Spanish possession in a manner that would prevent further encroachment. Accordingly early in June 1774 Juan Perez set sail from Monterey, California, in command of the frigate *Santiago* with instructions to sail to latitude 60°, there to make a landing and take possession of the territory in the name of the King of Spain. With him he took two friars, Crespi and Peña, whose journals inform us about this voyage.

The little ship made a slow passage north. By July 15th Perez had only reached the latitude of 51°42′. Here, on the advice of his officers, Perez decided to turn eastward and seek land so that he might replenish his supply of fresh water. The *Santiago*'s carpenters began making a great wooden cross, over twelve feet high, bearing on its length the inscription "Carolus III Hispaniarum rex" and along its arm the date "año de 1774". When they came to land this would be planted to mark Spanish sovereignty. The Spaniards did not have long to wait. On Monday, July 18th, about 11:30 a.m., after sailing through rain showers and fog, the *Santiago* sighted land. They were off the Queen Charlotte Islands and had become the first white men known to have sighted any part of British Columbia.[8]

Under grey skies the *Santiago* sailed slowly northward. On July 20th, after the heavy morning fog had lifted, the Spaniards ventured within a few miles of the shore where bonfires made them aware that the inhabitants of this new land had seen their coming. That afternoon a Haida canoe put out for the Spanish ship:

While they were still some distance from the bark we heard them singing. . . . They drew near the frigate and we saw that there were eight men and a boy in the canoe, seven of them rowing, while the eighth, who was painted, was standing up in the attitude of dancing, and, throwing feathers on the water.[9]

[8] F. W. Howay, "Discovery of the North West Coast," *Annual Report of the Canadian Historical Association*, 1926, p. 89. Howay thinks that the snowy mountains the Spaniards saw were the San Christoval Range, Queen Charlotte Islands. On the whole, these seem to be too far south.

[9] H. E. Bolton, *Fray Juan Crespi, Missionary Explorer on the Pacific Coast 1769-1774* (Berkeley, 1927), p. 323. The feathers were a traditional Indian way of expressing compliment and goodwill.

Although the Spaniards held out handkerchiefs, beads and biscuits and lowered a rope, the Indians did not venture aboard, though they travelled some distance in company with the *Santiago*. By gestures the Indians seemed to invite the Spaniards ashore and to indicate that they would find fresh water at a safe anchorage. The *Santiago* however continued on her course northwards along the coast. Some trading was done with one of the other canoes which put out to the ship, trinkets being exchanged for dried fish. The Spaniards noted with interest that the Indians had an iron head on one of their harpoons.

Leaving the canoes behind, Perez sailed on until he approached Langara Island, at the north-west tip of the Queen Charlotte Islands. Here for four days he vainly waited for a wind which would carry him into Dixon Entrance. While the Spaniards were becalmed on July 21st, no less than twenty-one canoes came out, containing some two hundred men and women, boys and girls.

All those canoes came toward the side of the frigate, some singing and strumming wooden instruments like a drum or timbrel, and some in the attitude of dancing. They drew near the frigate, surrounding it on all sides, and a fair was opened at once between them and our people, for we understood that they came to trade with our folks and exchange their little trinkets for ours. Our people gave them some knives, cloth, and beads, in exchange for very well tanned skins of beaver and other animals not known to us, quilts of beaver skins cut in pieces and sewed together so skillfully that no tailor could have done it better; other quilts or blankets of fine wool, or hair of animals which resembled fine wool, woven and worked with thread made of the same hair in several colors, principally black, white and yellow. It is so closely woven that it seems to have been made on a loom. . . . [10]

The Spaniards also received in trade conical cedar hats, carved wooden platters, spoons made of wood and horn, and two carved wooden boxes ornamented with inset pieces of seashell.

Both the Spanish chaplains were impressed by the good looks of the Indians. Friar Crespi noted "they were well formed Indians, with good faces, rather fair"; Friar Peña, speaking of the females,

[10] *Ibid.*, p. 329.

declared, "They are as fair and rosy as any Spanish woman."[11] Both were shocked, however, by the hideous appearance caused by labrets, the large discs which the women inserted in their lower lips.

Two Indians mustered the courage to go aboard the *Santiago* and two of the Spanish seamen went down into the canoes where the Indians gave "great expressions of joy . . . giving it to be understood by the sign of placing their hands on their breasts that they liked them very much."[12] Unfortunately, just when the Spaniards felt that they might safely go ashore and get resupplied with fresh water, the fog came in and, because of a dangerous current, the Spaniards took leave of the Haidas and put out to sea. The following days were spent in attempts to get into Dixon Entrance but fogs, currents and adverse winds made the task impossible and, on July 23rd, Perez abandoned the endeavour and turned his ship southwards, heading towards Mexico.

The *Santiago*, however, was not to depart without a second brief meeting with the Indians of British Columbia. On August 8th, sailing along the coast of Vancouver Island, she put into the entrance to Nootka Sound. Here Perez and his seamen met with a reception strangely different from the friendly welcome of the Haidas. Only nine men came out in three small canoes, and these raised strange cries and shouts of lamentation while gesturing that the ship should go away. When the Spaniards made signs that they wanted fresh water, the nine Indians ignored their appeals and turned back to the shore. In the evening Indians again approached the Spanish frigate.

About eight o'clock at night three canoes, with fifteen pagans in them, came to us; but they remained at a distance from the ship, their occupants crying out in a mournful tone of voice. We called to them, and they drew near. Shortly afterward they went away again, but, until after eleven o'clock, they remained at a distance of about a musket-shot from the ship, talking among themselves and sometimes crying out.[13]

The Spaniards would have understood the strange behaviour of

---

[11] *Ibid.*, p. 331; and Fray Tomas de la Peña, "Diary of the Voyage . . . in His Majesty's Ship called the *Santiago*," *Publications of the Historical Society of Southern California*, Vol. 2, Part 1 (1891):123.

[12] Bolton, *Crespi*, p. 332.

[13] Peña, "Diary", p. 132.

the natives if they had realized the effect of their coming on the watchers on the shore. Eighteen years later this was recounted vividly to the Spanish scientist José Mariano Moziño, who was stationed at Nootka and had learned the Nootkan tongue. Moziño was told that the Indians had been seized with terror when they saw this huge object coming in from the sea. They decided that it must carry their god Qua-utz, the same who in a wonderful canoe of copper had arrived on this shore to found their race.

They believed that Qua-utz was coming to make a second visit, and were fearful that it was in order to punish the misdeeds of the people. As many as were able hid themselves in the mountains, others closed themselves up in their lodges, and the most daring took their canoes out to examine more closely the huge mass that had come out of the ocean.[14]

Next morning the Indians had apparently recovered from the shock of the Second Coming. While the Spaniards were preparing to go ashore in their longboat and, at long last, get water and raise the great cross that they had been lugging around the coast, they found no less than fifteen canoes, bearing a hundred men and women, coming out from the shore. With them they brought skins and cedar hats which they traded with Perez's seamen for knives, cloth and seashells from Monterey. The trading continued but, just when the longboat was ready to leave for the shore, a sudden west wind sprang up driving the *Santiago*, her anchor dragging, towards the shore. Hastily Perez hoisted his sails, let slip his anchor, and began to tack out towards the open sea. Relieved, he and his crew resumed their voyage southward. Perez gave the name of San Lorenzo to the roadstead where he had made so brief a halt, the promontory at its southern end he named Punta San Estevan after Esteban José Martinez, one of his officers. Estevan Point is on our maps to this day.

And so Perez returned to California, still carrying his cross with him. The Spanish authorities, disappointed at his failure, sent out a second expedition the following year. This one was commanded by

---

[14] José Mariano Moziño, *Noticias de Nutka*, trans. I. H. Wilson (Seattle, 1970), p. 66.

Bruno de Hezeta aboard the *Santiago*, on which Perez now served as second in command. Accompanying the *Santiago* this year was a second ship, the *Sonora*, commanded by Lieut. Juan Francisco de Bodega y Quadra, with Francisco Antonio Mourelle as *piloto* or mate. Although Hezeta's instructions were to proceed to latitude 65°, he got no farther north than some unascertainable point off the west coast of Vancouver Island, where he made no attempt to land. Quadra, who had become separated from Hezeta, did considerably better. With the *Sonora* he pushed up to Alaskan waters. In August, when their calculations placed them in latitude 55°17′ (which would put them in the vicinity of the Nass River), they experienced unusual heat, which they believed came from violent volcanic action inland:

They suffered somewhat from the heat, which they attributed to the great flames which issued from four or five mouths of a volcano and at night-time lit up the whole district, rendering everything visible.[15]

Geologists tell us that around this time there was volcanic action near the Nass. Quadra and his men may have witnessed one of the last eruptions of a volcano in British Columbia.

Two Spanish exploring expeditions had now sailed into the waters of British Columbia, but as yet no Europeans had made any recorded landing on her shores. Her natives had, however, already experienced the first baleful effects of contact with the whites — smallpox! It was just around the time of these Spanish voyages that this appalling plague struck the Indians of the North Pacific coast for the first time. It was not Perez or Hezeta who brought the smallpox. Rather there was a tremendous epidemic which swept through the Indian population of the western half of the continent. Some said the disease was deliberately introduced by Americans who wanted to clear the Indians from lands which they coveted, others laid the blame on the French, or on the Spaniards.[16] All we can say is that the smallpox

---

[15] "Diary of Padre Miquel de la Campa" (trans.), Cambridge University Library, Add. MS. 7278 (7), p. 54.

[16] For the first mention of this smallpox see Nathaniel Portlock, *A Voyage Round the World; But More Particularly to the North-West Coast of America* (London, 1789), p. 272. On the origins and area see Ross Cox, *The Columbia River*, ed. E. I. & J. R. Stewart (Norman, Okla., 1957), p. 169.

began among the Indians of the Missouri basin, swept across the
Rockies and on to the Pacific, where it spread like wildfire up the
coast. The smallpox epidemic remained a terrible memory among
survivors, pitted by the disease, who later were to be encountered by
Vancouver's crews.

1778

Early life of Captain Cook — His discoveries in the Pacific Ocean — He lands at Nootka on his "Third Voyage" — Musical entertainments — Grisly items offered in trade — Furs and women — Thievery — Cook's tour of Nootka Sound — His departure.

The abortive voyage of Juan Perez signifies little in the history of British Columbia, that of Hezeta and Quadra even less. That history really commenced in March 1778 when Captain James Cook, R.N., and his crews became the first white men known to have set foot upon the soil of British Columbia.

This landing could not have been made by a more distinguished captain than Cook, who vies with Columbus for recognition as the world's most famous maritime explorer and navigator. Born in 1728 in a two-room Yorkshire farm cottage, Cook, the son of an agricultural day labourer, was to attain fame and renown throughout the civilized world. Always he was the quintessential Yorkshireman, compounded of common sense, courage and integrity. His career was founded upon those qualities.

Educated at the expense of his father's employer at a little village school, Cook at the age of seventeen became a grocer's assistant at Staithes, a village on the North Sea coast. The sea called, and at eighteen he shipped aboard the collier *Freelove* as an apprentice. At twenty-three, due to his industry and flair for navigation, he was promoted mate; in prospect for him was command of a new ship to be built by his employers. He never accepted that command. Instead, in 1755, James Cook, seeing a war with France in prospect, sacrificed both money and rank to join the Royal Navy as an able seaman. Later he said simply, "I had a mind to try my fortune that way." Posted to H.M.S. *Eagle*, Cook within a month was promoted to master's mate. Seven months later he was acting as boatswain.

Two years after entering the Navy, Cook was sailing master (navigator) of H.M.S. *Pembroke*, a warship of 64 guns. In 1759 Cook and H.M.S. *Pembroke* sailed to the St. Lawrence River where Cook became engaged in discovering and marking the navigable channel that General Wolfe used in bringing his army up to Quebec for the Battle of the Plains of Abraham. After that great victory, Cook's skill in charting the lower St. Lawrence won him appointment as master of H.M.S. *Northumberland*, the flagship of Commodore Lord Colville. Cook's reputation had become such that when the French war ended in 1763 he was not demobilized. Instead he was given command of a little schooner and sent to survey the waters off Newfoundland. Each year he visited England to attend to the publication of his charts. A paper he wrote on an eclipse of the sun was published by the Royal Society whose editor introduced him as "Mr. Cook, a good mathematician, very expert in his business".

The Royal Society had a special interest in eclipses. Many years previously Edward Halley had predicted, on the basis of his astronomical calculations, that in 1769 Venus would pass between the sun and the earth. The Royal Society urged that the observations of the transit of Venus should include ones made in the South Pacific from the recently discovered island of Tahiti. The Admiralty agreed to undertake the necessary expedition. Accordingly in 1768 James Cook, the ploughman's son, was summoned to the Admiralty, made for the first time a commissioned officer (something extraordinary in an age when commissions were normally reserved for persons who were gentlemen by birth) and placed in command of H.M.S. *Endeavour*.

Cook's famous "First Voyage" lasted from August 1768 to July 1771. On it he rounded Cape Horn, arrived at Tahiti and, with complete success, carried out the observation of the transit of Venus. Sailing westward, Cook discovered New Zealand and charted the entire 2400 miles of its coastline. Resuming his voyage westward, Cook reached the hitherto undiscovered eastern coast of Australia. Sailing northward along that coast, he put in at Botany Bay, close to modern Sydney. Then he proceeded into the infinitely treacherous waters of the Great Barrier Reef. Grounding on some coral heads the *Endeavour* suffered terrible damage but, after temporary repairs,

Cook nursed her through the Torres Strait to the nearest shipyard, one in the Dutch East Indies. From there he sailed for home via the Cape of Good Hope.

Upon his return James Cook, in recognition of his great achievement, was presented to the King and promoted by the Admiralty. The latter in fact had a further mission for Cook. That irascible geographer Alexander Dalrymple dogmatically maintained that a vast southern continent extended from Tasmania to the general vicinity of Chile. Another voyage would have to be taken to silence Dalrymple's clamour that Cook had been negligent in not finding this southern continent. Accordingly, in 1772 Cook sailed with H.M.S. *Resolution* and H.M.S. *Adventure* on his "Second Voyage".

This time Cook rounded the Cape of Good Hope, sailed farther into the Antarctic than any previous navigator, and in the process totally destroyed Dalrymple's fiction. New Zealand and Tahiti were revisited, then Cook was off again into unexplored waters, discovering the Cook Islands and New Caledonia and making important new discoveries among the Tonga Islands, the New Hebrides and the Marquesas. He arrived back in England in 1775 by way of Cape Horn.

Cook returned home to find himself famous. He was received in audience twice by His Majesty the King, promoted to the rank of post-captain, and elected a Fellow of the Royal Society. At the age of forty-seven, he could enjoy the end of the incredible demands made upon his powers of physical endurance by the two great voyages. The Admiralty appointed him Fourth Captain of Greenwich Hospital, the almost palatial building which served as a retreat for old sailors. Here Cook would have a splendid apartment for himself, his wife and their two sons, and a secure income as well. His duties at Greenwich would be almost nominal, leaving him free to participate in the life of science and the formulation of exploration policies.

The quiet life did not last long. Russian discoveries off Alaska had got England interested anew in that fascinating but elusive goal, a north-west passage around the top of North America. The Admiralty resolved to send an expedition under a Lieut. Pickersgill, R.N., to find if Bering Straits led into the long-sought waterway. But Cook changed all that. He hankered for the great waters and the thrill of unknown shores. Declaring that he could not endure to be "confined within the limits of Greenwich Hospital", he suddenly volunteered to lead the search for the North-west Passage. Thus it was that, in July 1776, Captain James Cook embarked upon his "Third Voyage", the one which was to bring him to the shores of British Columbia.

On this voyage Cook had with him once more H.M.S. *Resolution*, 460 tons, 112 men, and an armament of twelve 12-pounder cannons. For his consort he had H.M.S. *Discovery* (Captain Clerke), a smaller ship of less than 300 tons. Rounding the Cape of Good Hope, Cook made first for Tasmania, and then for New Zealand. Travelling onward he revisited Tahiti. Leaving that delectable island behind him, he sailed towards the north-east. On January 18th he discovered a cluster of hitherto unknown islands just within the tropics and named them the Sandwich Islands, after the Earl of Sandwich, recently First Lord of the Admiralty. Today we refer to them collectively as Hawaii.

Cook did not linger long among these new islands. At the beginning of February he resumed his voyage to the north-east. Finally, on March 7th, he reached the coast of modern Oregon and turned north. Dangerous westerly gales, mixed with rain and sleet, made him keep some distance from the continental shore which he saw only intermittently. On March 22nd he discovered and named Cape Flattery, but the coming on of night and a new succession of storms kept him from finding the entrance to the Strait of Juan de Fuca.

On Sunday, March 29th, Cook was off Vancouver Island, examining through his telescope a rocky coast behind which snowy mountains rose inland. The shoreline here seemed to form a very long bay of no great indentation. He named it Hope Bay. The promontory at its northern limit was later to be known as Cape Cook, but Cook himself named it Woody Point. At the bay's southern end stood Perez's Punta San Estevan, a name unknown to Cook since the Spaniards had never informed the world of Perez's expedition. Because of the surf breaking along its rocks, Cook gave Estevan Point the name of Point Breakers. Within Hope Bay Cook saw at least two inlets. The wind prevented him from entering the more northerly (probably Kyuquot Sound) so he set his course for the more southerly. Thus it was that, at around 5 o'clock in the afternoon, H.M.S. *Resolution* and H.M.S. *Discovery* entered Nootka Sound, or King George's Sound to give it the name bestowed by Cook.

Indians put out from the shore as the British ships stood in, and by the time that the latter had anchored within the Sound some thirty or forty canoes were accompanying them. The appearance of the occupants gave Cook and his sailors something of a shock. Lieut. James King has left us a description:

> It will require the assistance of ones imagination to have an adequate Idea of the Wild, savage appearance & Actions of these first Visitors, as it is difficult to describe the effect of gestures & motions. Their dark coppery coloured bodies were so cover'd over with filth as to make it a doubt what was really the proper Colour; their faces were bedaub'd with red & black Paint & Grease, in no regular manner, but as their fancies led them; their hair was clott'd also with dirt, & to make themselves either fine, or frightful, many put on their hair the down of young birds, or platted it in sea weed or thin strips of bark dyed red; the Dress of some was a loose skin thrown round their Shoulders, & which was not seemingly intended to hide their private parts, which in many were expos'd. . . . [1]

Midshipman Riou described the Indians as "a set of the dirtiest beings ever beheld — their faces and Hair being a lump of red and black Earth and Grease".[2] Captain Clerke of H.M.S. *Discovery* said flatly, "These are the dirtiest set of People I ever yet met with".[3] Subsequently he noted that their long hair was full of dirt and lice, "the pulling these Lice & eating them passes away (seemingly very agreeably) many a leisure Hour".

After the warships had anchored, most of the Indians returned to the shore. Some remained and joined in a rather remarkable musical entertainment:

---

[1] J. C. Beaglehole, ed., *The Journals of Captain James Cook*, 3 vols. Vol. III, "The Voyage of the *Resolution* and *Discovery* 1776-1780", Hakluyt Society (Cambridge, 1967) : 1393-94.

[2] *Ibid.*, III: 295.

[3] *Ibid.*, III: 1326. Subsequent explorers were almost invariably appalled by the filthiness of the Indians on the West Coast. However, for a justification of their dirtiness see R. E. McKechnie, *Strong Medicine* (Vancouver, 1972), p. 12.

Night coming on they all paddled ashore except five or six Canoes which drew in a Cluster together at a small distance from the Ship, and as it were to bid us a good night the people in them sang in concert in no disagreeable Stile; this Mark of their Attention to us we were unwilling to pass over unnoticed & therefore gave them in return a few tunes on two french Horns after their Song was ended, to these they were very attentive, not a word to be heard among them during the time of playing; this salutation was returned by another Song from the Indians, after which we gave them a Tune on the Drum & Fife to which they paid the same attention as they had done to the Horns. These Canoes staid by the Ship most part of the Night seemingly with no other View but that of gratifying their Curiosity.[4]

The next day the Indians flocked to the ships to trade. Obviously they knew the use of iron, and it was this that they chiefly desired, showing little interest in cloth or beads. In exchange for iron they offered skins of the sea otter and of beaver, deer, wapiti, bear and other animals. Also offered in barter were fish, both fresh and dried, hummingbirds and a wide range of curios such as masks and weapons. The British were taken aback however when the Indians offered them human skulls, amputated hands and a human arm. William Bayly, astronomer with the expedition, noted:

We bought 3 or 4 Human hands which they brought to sell, they appeared to have been lately cut off as the flesh was not reduced to an horny substance but raw — they made signs that they were good eating, & seemed to sell them us for that purpose or at least all of us understood them in that light.[5]

A minority doubted that the Indians were cannibals, particularly since one of them vehemently refused to eat one of the hands when urged to do so. Subsequent explorers were also to be offered hands.

Captain Cook was not particularly interested in trading with the Indians. Now, at the threshold of his voyage into Arctic waters, he was concerned to get his ships into good shape before entering that dangerous stage of his voyage. Having failed to understand the gestures of Indians who apparently had sought to direct him to the safe anchorage in Friendly Cove, he moved his ships into a decidedly

[4] *Ibid.*, III : 1088.
[5] *Ibid.*, III : 297.

inferior harbour, Ship Cove (now known as Resolution Cove) on Bligh Island. Cables were put out fore and aft to moor the ships to the shoreline.

Four weeks of toil followed. The ships had to be caulked. The foremast had to be taken out from H.M.S. *Resolution*, brought ashore and repaired by the carpenters. A new mizzenmast had to be provided out of a tree felled on the island. Water casks had to be filled and extra spars cut for future use. A brewery had to be set up to manufacture the anti-scorbutic spruce beer needed for the crews in the months ahead. New sets of rigging had to be fitted. Close by, on Observatory Rock, tents were set up and here the astronomers, by repeated observations, tried to fix their exact latitude and longitude, check the accuracy of their chronometers, and establish compass deflection.

Meanwhile the Indians continued to flock to the ships. Custom dictated that at first arrival each canoe should paddle at top speed around one, other, or both of the ships. Only after that initial gesture could they come up alongside for trade. Lieut. Burney has left us a vivid little account of the canoes' leave-taking:

... in the evening, several of the larger Canoes saluted us, by making a Circuit round the ships and giving 3 Halloos at their departure, they paddle in most excellent time, the foremost man every 3^d or 4th Stroke making flourishes with his paddle, the halloo is a single note in which they all join, swelling it out in the middle and letting the Sound die away. in a Calm with the hills around us, it had an effect infinitely superior to what might be imagined from any thing so simple.[6]

The crews of the *Resolution* and *Discovery* knew that they were heading up to very cold climes — some seemed to think that they were bound for the North Pole. Certainly, with a commander of Cook's determination, they would be going very far north indeed and into a region of intense cold. Accordingly, officers and men secured from the Indians a copious stock of furs. Bear skins and sea otter pelts, especially when cunningly sewn into robes, were in particular demand.

There was also another article of trade — women. The free

[6] *Ibid.*, III: 299.

women of Nootka were chaste, but for a price the men of Nootka were ready to make their female slaves available. Many of the sailors apparently were so put off by the filth of these poor creatures that they kept away from them. Others, including it would seem some of the junior officers, found pleasure with the women — after they had been thoroughly washed and deloused. The irrepressible David Samwell, surgeon aboard the *Resolution* who seems not to have been very squeamish, has an interesting passage in his journal for April 6th:

Hitherto we had seen none of their young Women tho' we had often given the men to understand how agreeable their Company would be to us & how profitable to themselves, in consequence of which they about this time brought two or three Girls to the Ships; tho' some of them had no bad faces yet as they were exceedingly dirty their Persons at first sight were not very inviting, however our young Gentlemen were not to be discouraged by such an obstacle as this which they found was to be removed with Soap & warm water, this they called the Ceremony of Purification and were themselves the Officiators at it, & it must be mentioned to their praise that they performed it with much piety & Devotion, taking as much pleasure in cleansing a naked young Woman from all Impurities in a Tub of Warm Water, as a young Confessor would to absolve a beautiful Virgin who was about to sacrifice that Name to himself.

Subsequently Samwell comments upon the unexpected aesthetic pleasures which the Ceremony of Purification could yield. After noting that courage and perseverance were needed to "refine this ore", he added:

... it must be confessed we sometimes found some Jewels that rewarded our trouble, Namely two sparkling black Eyes accompanied with a beautiful Face, & when such was our fortune we never regretted the time & trouble it had cost us in digging through loads of red Oaker [ochre], Soot & other Dirt to get at them.[7]

Lieut. Burney found that the Nootka Indians, under all their dirt, were "a white people" and some of their women to be "Jolly, likely Wenches".[8]

---

[7] *Ibid.*, III : 1094-95 & 1100.

[8] *Journal of the Proceedings of his Majys. Sloop Discovery* [10 Feb. 1776 - 11 Oct. 1777] (typescript U.B.C. Library), p. 34.

There was, of course, the problem of finding metal with which to pay the Indians who supplied the women. The crews of both the *Resolution* and the *Discovery* had been pretty well "stripped of all our Hatchets & iron trade by the beautiful Nymphs of the South Sea Islands"; however, there were other resources. Men took to giving away their pewter dishes in return for their nights spent with the slave women of Nootka. For the rest of the voyage, being without any plates, they would have to eat their salt beef and pork off tables and sea-chests, but that was a hardship which the more amorous could bear.

Having obtained iron enough, the Indians began to cast covetous eyes upon brass. Captain Cook in his own journal for April 18th recorded the consequences:

Nothing would go down with them but metal and brass was now become their favourate, So that before we left the place, hardly a bit of brass was left in the Ship, except what was in the necessary instruments. Whole Suits of cloaths were striped of every button Bureaus &c. of their furniture [fittings] and Copper kettle[s], Tin canesters, Candle sticks, &c all went to wreck.[9]

The Indians did not secure all their metal by honest means, for the British soon became aware that the Indians at Nootka were expert and ruthless thieves. The small boats were stripped of their metal fixtures. When a boat guard was posted, one Indian would keep him "amused" while his fellows made off with metal fittings from the other end of the boat. Even the great iron hook, weighing between twenty and thirty pounds, used for helping to raise the anchor, was stolen from one of the ships. One Indian managed to get into Captain Cook's cabin and steal his gold watch, though a speedy pursuit recovered this. The British found two things to the credit of the Indians amid all these thefts: first, (unlike the South Sea Islanders who stole anything no matter how useless to them), the Nootka Indians took only those things for which they had a use; secondly, when they were caught they handed over the stolen articles without making trouble. There was one exception. Late during the ships' visit a canoe was seen making off with a stolen piece of iron.

[9] Cook, *Journals*, Vol. III:302.

When the thieves refused to return it, Captain Cook lost his patience and "fired a Musquet (loaded with small shot), into the Canoe which wounded three or 4 men in their Backs & backsides."[10]

Actually this was about the only case of conflict between Cook and the Indians, though earlier there had been one major alarm. On April 4th the Nootkas, either bearing weapons or hurriedly supplying themselves with sticks and stones, had assembled on the shore close to where Cook's men were cutting wood and filling their water casks. Muskets were rushed to the men in the working parties, and they were sent up to Observatory Rock the better to undertake their defence. Meanwhile Cook brought cannon to bear on the shore. Seeing that the British anticipated an attack, the Nootkas hastened to explain that their warlike preparations were solely on account of an approaching band of Indians who were their enemies. The hostile canoes came into sight. Insulting gestures and fervent harangues followed, but the battle which seemed to be inevitable did not occur.

The newcomers who had caused such agitation were Indians from another part of the coast who, learning of Cook's arrival, had come to trade. Their arrival infuriated the Nootkas who were determined to monopolize all bartering with the white men. Finally the newcomers were allowed to trade with the British but only under the close supervision of the Nootka Indians, who were determined that the interlopers must not reduce the tariff which they had established. Gradually Cook's men became aware that the local Indians were, in fact, developing a major industry reselling to other tribes much of the metal which they obtained from the sailors, and obtaining from these other tribes fresh supplies of skins and artifacts with which to replenish their own exhausted stock of items for trade.

By April 20th most of the hard work on the ships had been completed. The weather after a rainy spell had turned fine again, and Captain Cook decided to take the day off and do a little sightseeing. Setting off with two small boats he first visited Friendly Cove and its adjacent Indian village of Yuquot, where he was received with the utmost hospitality and the inhabitants did not

10 *Ibid.*, III:307.

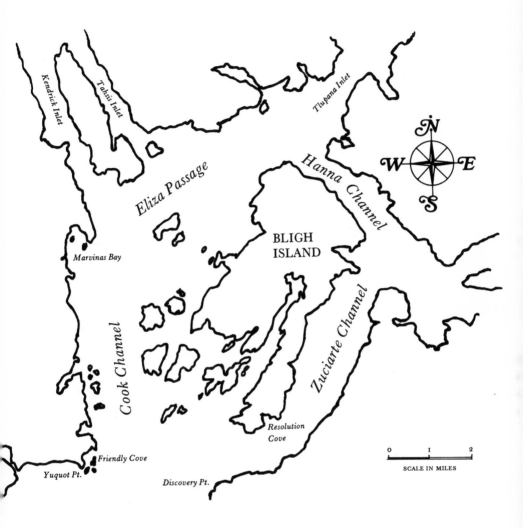

Map 1.

Nootka Sound

attempt to steal anything. Then he swung up Cook Channel, passed the mouths of Kendrick Inlet, Tahsis Inlet and Tlupana Inlet, turned southwards through Hanna Channel and Zuchiarte Channel, and ended up at Resolution Cove, having proved himself right in his guess that it was an island (Bligh Island) off which he had moored his ships. Along the way he had passed several Indian villages and fishing weirs, and had marvelled at the enormous trees, over forty feet in circumference, growing along the shores.

When Cook had sailed from England he had on board, rather to his annoyance, an assortment of livestock (a bull and two cows, pigs, sheep and goats) wished on him by a benevolent George III intent upon introducing such useful animals into the new lands which Cook would visit or discover. By the time Cook reached Nootka all that remained of this menagerie were a few goats and sheep. Having noticed grass growing by Yuquot village, Cook revisited it a few days later to obtain grass for his livestock. In his journal he has preserved for us a somewhat amusing account of that second visit:

The Inhabitants of this village received us in the same friendly manner they had d[o]ne before, and the Moment we landed I sent some to cut grass not thinking that the Natives could or would have the least objection, but it proved otherways for the Moment our people began to cut they stoped them and told them they must *Makook* for it, that is first buy it. As soon as I heard of this I went to the place and found about a dozen men who all laid cla[i]m to some part of the grass which I purchased of them and as I thought liberty to cut where ever I pleased, but here again I was mistaken, for the liberal manner I had paid the first pretended pr[o]prietors brought more upon me and there was not a blade of grass that had not a seperated owner, so that I very soon emptied my pockets with purchasing, and when they found I had nothing more to give they let us cut where ever we pleased.

Here I must observe that I have no were [sic] met with Indians who had such high notions of every thing the Country produced being their exclusive property as these; the very wood and water we took on board they at first wanted us to pay for. . . . [11]

On Sunday, April 26th, Cook was ready to resume his voyage and his crews took their leave of the Nootkas. All things considered, their relationship had been a happy one, and their trading had gone

[11] *Ibid.*, III:306.

without trouble. One of the last items acquired from the Indians had been a pair of Spanish silver spoons filched from one of Perez's officers four years earlier, although right to the end the British remained ignorant of the fact that the Spaniards had earlier sailed into the entrance of Nootka Sound. Cook's small boats put out their oars and, providing what the seamen called an "ash breeze", towed the *Resolution* and *Discovery* out into the open Pacific.

As we hove up the Anchor, all the Canoes in the Cove assembled together and sung us a parting song, flourishing the Saws, Swords, hatchets and other things they had got from us. One man was mounted on a stage of loose boards supported by the Indians nearest it, and danced to the Singing, with different masks on; at one time resembling a man, and at others a bird or beast.[12]

Captain Cook's visit to Nootka was at an end. Within less than a year he would be slain on a Hawaiian beach.

[12] *Ibid.*, III:307.

1779

Cook's sailors learn the value of their furs.

In December of this year Cook's ships, now under the command of Lieut. John Gore, put in at Macao. The rigours of their cruising in Arctic waters now behind them, the sailors no longer needed the furs which they had bought in Nootka and Alaska for clothing and bedding in the icy North. Going ashore in China, they began to peddle these furs and found that they brought the most amazing prices. Furs obtained at Nootka for a trifle of iron would bring from the Chinese the equivalent of a dozen English golden guineas. The tars were incredulous at their luck. Enthusiastically they sold their furs and bought tea, china and silk to take home to England as gifts for their women. Not that all of them were any longer in a hurry to return — Gore almost had a mutiny when he refused to let the ships return to Nootka and Alaska to get more furs.

1780

Cook's ships return home.

On October 4th H.M.S. *Resolution* and H.M.S. *Discovery* arrived home in England after a voyage which had lasted four years, two months and twenty-two days. With them they brought artifacts from Nootka and journals which would inform the world of an area which the secrecy of the Spaniards had hitherto kept unknown. Soon word was spreading of fortunes which could be made in the fur trade between Nootka and China.

1781

Unauthorized accounts of Cook's last voyage — William Bolts' unsuccessful Nootka venture.

When H.M.S. *Resolution* and H.M.S. *Discovery* arrived back in England in 1780, the whole country was impatient for an account of the last voyage of the famous Captain Cook. The British government was determined, however, that no book on the subject should appear prior to its own officially sponsored publication of Cook's journal, whose sales would supply funds for Cook's widow. Accordingly everything possible was done to keep other accounts out of print. Nevertheless there were leaks. The bookseller Newbery managed to get hold of the journal of Lieut. John Rickman and, with this as a basis, had a hack prepare a romantic, melodramatic *Journal of Captain Cook's Last Voyage*. Published this year with all its flagrant shortcomings, this was the first book to deal with any part of British Columbia. It expresses a favourable opinion of the Indians of Nootka: "a more open and communicative people does not live under the sun".[1] A second unauthorized account to appear this year was Heinrich Zimmermann's *Reise um die Welt, mit Captain Cook*, published in Mannheim in Germany. Zimmermann, a German volunteer serving as a seaman on the *Resolution*, devoted only half a sentence to Captain Cook's visit to Nootka. His entire little book was only a matter of a hundred or so pages.

These books and talk by Cook's crews made men aware of the lucrative markets in China awaiting furs from the shores of Northwest America. The first entrepreneur to seek wealth from this trade was an interesting rogue, William Bolts, who this year had a ship and tender ready to sail for Nootka from Trieste. Here he had registered his ship under Austrian colours so as to evade the juris-

---

[1] [John Rickman], *Journal of Captain Cook's Last Voyage to the Pacific Ocean* (London, 1781), p. 237.

2. A Native of King George's Sound
   (Nootka) - by W. Ellis

3. Maquinna, Chief of Nootka

4. Tetacú, Chief of the Entrance
   of the Strait of Juan de Fuca

5. Maria, Wife of Tetacú

6. Puberty Ceremony for Maquinna's Daughter

7.   Callicum and Maquinna

8. Interior of an Indian House, Nootka

9. Indian Encampment near Fort Colvile

diction of the East India Company and the South Sea Company, which held official monopolies as far as trading in the Pacific by British subjects was concerned.

Bolts never sailed to Nootka. Eight years later Captain Portlock contemptuously observed that "this feeble effort of an imprudent man failed prematurely, owing to causes which have not yet been sufficiently explained".[2] The whole Bolts affair remains pretty much a mystery.

[2] Nathaniel Portlock, *A Voyage Round the World*, p. 2. For more on Bolts see Vincent T. Harlow, *The Founding of the Second British Empire 1763-1793* (London, 1964), II:495.

1782

William Ellis' indiscretion.

Late in 1781 collectors of engravings had been able to purchase in the London printshops a plate entitled "A Native of King George's Sound". Reproduced from a sketch by William Ellis, an assistant surgeon on Cook's final expedition, this engraving gave people back in Britain their first chance to see what a British Columbia coastal Indian looked like.

Now, in 1782, this same William Ellis published in two elegant quarto volumes *An Authentic Narrative of a Voyage Performed by Captain Cook and Captain Clerke*. This proved to be a decidedly readable and accurate account of the voyage, although it only occasionally goes into detail. Instructing his readers concerning the Nootka Indians' fondness for painting their faces, Ellis had this to say:

> Some black their face entirely, and then sprinkle small particles of white or black talc (which they have here in abundance) upon it; others make one half of their face black and the other red; in short, there is no end to their fancy. One of their greatest beaux frequently was on board the ships; and in order to observe the manner of painting their faces, a looking-glass was shewn him; which he no sooner found the use of than he set down to dress his face, which employed him full two hours; for he no sooner put on one face than he disliked it, and demolished the whole, and continued rubbing out and painting, till he made one that pleased him.[1]

The previous year's violations of the government's ban on unauthorized accounts of Cook's final voyage were minor compared with that now committed by Ellis. If Rickman had knowingly been

---

[1] W. Ellis, *An Authentic Narrative of a Voyage Performed by Captain Cook and Captain Clerke* (London, 1782), I: 213.

involved in the book based on his journal, he had carefully concealed that fact. Ellis, proud of his writing, let his name appear on the title page of his two volumes, and by so doing ruined his career in the Navy.

1783

Sergeant Ledyard's account of Nootka.

This year saw the publication of a fourth unauthorized account of Cook's final voyage. One of the two corporals of marines with Cook had been John Ledyard, born in the British North American colony of Connecticut. At the end of the voyage he was given a promotion like almost everybody else, and became a sergeant. Posted in 1782 to the Navy's North American station, Ledyard deserted and returned to his birthplace, about to become a part of the new United States of America. Here, in Hartford, he supplied a printer with an account of Cook's last voyage. Ledyard took much of his material verbatim from the Rickman book of a couple of years earlier but did provide some things of his own. Appealing to American patriotism, he dwelt on what a comfort it was to him at Nootka to be once more upon the soil of the continent of his birth. He had something to say to his countrymen also about the lucrative fur business which had begun in Nootka:

We purchased while here about 1500 beaver besides other skins, but took none but the best, having no thoughts at that time of using them to any other advantage than converting them to the purposes of cloathing, but it afterwards happened that skins which did not cost the purchaser sixpence sterling sold in China for 100 dollars. Neither did we purchase a quarter part of the beaver and other furr skins we might have done, and most certainly should have done had we known of meeting the opportunity of disposing of them to such an astonishing profit.[1]

---

[1] John Ledyard, *A Journal of Captain Cook's Last Voyage to the Pacific Ocean* (Hartford, 1783), p. 70.

1784

Publication of Cook's journal.

In June of this year, the official account of Cook's final voyage was published, at long last, in three thick folio volumes. Two consisted of Cook's own journal as edited by Dr. John Douglas, Canon of Windsor and St. Paul's. The third volume, covering the period following Cook's murder, was written by Captain James King who had been one of Cook's lieutenants. Within three days the edition was sold out. King's portion of the work was not unworthy of the preceding volumes. Especially interesting for British merchants were his comments upon the bonanza that the sailors had found when selling their furs in China:

When, in addition to these facts, it is remembered, that the furs were, at first, collected without our having any idea of their real value; that the greatest part had been worn by the Indians, from whom we purchased them; that they were afterward preserved with little care, and frequently used for bed-clothes, and other purposes, during our cruize to the North; and that, probably, we had never got the full value for them in China; the advantages that might be derived from a voyage to that part of the American coast, undertaken with commercial views, appear to me of a degree of importance sufficient to call for the attention of the Public.[1]

[1] *A Voyage to the Pacific Ocean. Undertaken, by the Command of His Majesty for Making Discoveries in the Northern Hemisphere* (London, 1784), III:437.

37

1785

Captain Hanna, first of the fur traders.

Only a little more than a year after the publication of King's report, the first fur trading vessel put in at Nootka Sound. She was the *Harmon*, a brig of sixty tons, commanded by the bold and domineering James Hanna, who had sailed from the China coast on April 15th of this year. On August 9th Hanna arrived off Nootka, and his journal for this part of the expedition survives in the Provincial Archives of British Columbia. Under this date he recorded:

At nine o'clock in the evening three canoes approached; as the night was dark, the arms were got up. And they hallowed at a distance 'Maakook' — this was asking to trade. We soon got them alongside.[1]

And then suddenly, when we most want to read further, the journal kept by Captain Hanna comes to an abrupt end. Presumably from there on he was too busy trading for sea otter pelts to keep up a journal.

From other sources we can pick up a few details about this first mercantile venture to Nootka. Martinez, at Nootka a few years later, got the story of a stupid and dangerous practical joke which Hanna's crew played on Chief Maquinna. When the tyee was visiting their ship, they invited him as a particular honour to sit in a chair. Once he was seated, a sailor performed a ritual of placing a small quantity of "black sand" under the seat, with a thin trail leading away from it. When the train was ignited, the whole went off with a flash and a blast that blew Maquinna right into the air. Later he was to exhibit to the Spaniards the scars on his posterior left by this sudden elevation.[2]

---

[1] Provincial Archives of British Columbia [hereafter referred to as PABC] A-A-20.5-Sel H.

[2] Martinez, "Diario" cited in Cook, *Flood Tide of Empire*, p. 101.

Perhaps in consequence of this idiotic affront to their chief, the Nootkas launched an attack on the *Harmon*, one which Hanna repelled with considerable slaughter. Peace was somehow restored and trading resumed. After a stay at Nootka of some five weeks, Hanna sailed back to China with no less than 560 sea otter skins which he sold in Canton for 20,600 Spanish dollars.[3]

In the course of his trading, Hanna, following an Indian custom, had ceremoniously exchanged names with one of the Indian chiefs. Consequently, other traders repeatedly mention "Captain Hanna" as one of the Indians with whom they dealt. Other chiefs were similarly to exchange names with the captains of various trading vessels. Thus "Captain Hanna" was joined in time by "Captain Douglas" and a number of other "captains".

[3] George Dixon, *A Voyage Round the World; But More Particularly To the North-West Coast of America* (London, 1789), pp. 315-16.

1786

Hanna's second voyage — The Captain Cook *and* Experiment *arrive from India — The first white man to live among the Indians — Meares, Portlock and Dixon, La Pérouse.*

This year Captain Hanna made his second voyage to Nootka from China, this time with the *Sea Otter*, a vessel of 120 tons, just twice the size of his tiny ship of the previous year. Hanna's trading was much less successful this year for, when he put into Nootka Sound in August, he found two other ships had already been there and obtained just about all the skins the Indians had to offer.

The newcomers were the *Captain Cook* (Captain Laurie) and the *Experiment* (Captain Guise), two fine ships which had set out from Bombay late the previous year. Their owners were James Strange (on leave from the East India Company, who accompanied the two ships to supervise the enterprise) and David Scott (who remained in India looking after his other ventures). The chief event of Strange's stay at Nootka was his decision to leave ashore a young man named John Mackay. Some ambiguity surrounds the circumstances and the motives for this unexpected proceeding. Strange says he felt that it would be a very good idea to have somebody at Nootka when he came back the following year (which he failed to do) who would have obtained an expert knowledge of the language and customs of the Indians. He reported:

To this end therefore, I was glad to avail myself, of the Offer of Service made me by a young man, named Mackay, who acted as Surgeon on Board the Experiment. No description of Person could so well have answered the Purposes I had in View, in leaving somebody behind me; & no one was so likely to establish his Consequence among the Natives, & secure to himself as Comfortable an Existence, as it was possible such a situation to admit of. I placed him in the Family of a Chief named Maquilla; whose friendship I had secured by repeated acts of Liberality, and who assured me in the presence of Enkitsum (The God of Snow) that my Doctor should eat the Choicest Fish, the Sound produced; and that on my return, I should find him, as fat as a Whale.[1]

At the request of Maquilla (better known as Maquinna), a musket and pistols were left with the *Experiment*'s surgeon. Suspicious that Maquinna might intend to use these arms himself, Strange told him that they could be used effectively only by a white man, and that if any Indian were to meddle with a gun he would hurt himself. Perceiving that the Indians received this information with visible scepticism, Strange asked if one of them would like to fire a gun. Maquinna himself volunteering, Strange loaded it, putting in much more than the proper charge of powder. When Maquinna pulled the trigger he was lucky that the musket did not explode and kill him. As it was, he received a tremendous kick from the weapon, and other Indians had to rush to hold him up. Having thus impressed the Nootkas with "dread and terror" at the consequence of using the arms left with Mackay, Strange had his ships raise anchor and sail to Prince William Sound in Alaska, leaving behind him British Columbia's first white resident.

In Alaska, Strange found competitors in his quest for furs. From India, sailing as consorts, had come the *Nootka* (Captain Meares) and another ship named, like Hanna's, the *Sea Otter* (Captain Tipping). Moreover, there had arrived from England two ships sent out by the newly formed King George's Sound Company, the *King George* (Captain Portlock) and her consort the *Queen Charlotte* (Captain Dixon). In September, at the end of the Alaskan trading season, Portlock and Dixon sailed south to winter in Hawaii. En route they arrived off Nootka Sound. The unwieldy nature of the ships of that day was such that, though for four days they vainly tried to get into the Sound, storms, adverse winds and currents made it impossible for them to get through the two-mile-wide entrance to Nootka Sound. At the end they just gave up and sailed on to Hawaii or, as they were known then, the Sandwich Islands.

[1] *James Strange's Journal and Narrative of the Commercial Expedition from Bombay to the North-West Coast of America* (Madras, 1928), p. 22.

Not all the ships to visit the coast this year were British. In 1785 there had sailed from Brest, under a commission from Louis XVI, a French expedition of discovery commanded by Jean François de Galaup, Comte de La Pérouse. This expedition was, in effect, France's reply to Captain Cook, and La Pérouse's instructions specifically directed him to examine that part of the coast of Northwest America which had not been seen by Cook. Early in August of this year La Pérouse's ships, *Astrolabe* and *Boussole,* arrived off the north end of the Queen Charlotte Islands, discovering Dixon Entrance a year before Dixon himself. Coasting down the Queen Charlotte Islands, La Pérouse rounded their southern tip and gave to Cape St. James the name of Cape Hector. After sailing eastward, he ranged the mainland coast from Milbanke Sound southwards. Later, from Kamchatka, he sent to France his journal for this part of his voyage. The action was providential for, after sailing from Australia in 1788, he and his ships disappeared and became one of the mysteries of the sea. About 1828 the wrecks of his ships were finally discovered in the Solomon Islands. He and all his men had been massacred by the natives.

1787

Meares' ghastly winter on the coast — Imperial Eagle *discovers Barkley Sound* — *Rich returns for Portlock and Dixon.*

In April of this year Portlock and Dixon, back from Hawaii, were once more off the Alaskan coast. Here they met Indians who repeatedly muttered the word "Nootka" while pointing in the direction of King William Sound. To solve the mystery, Dixon took the *Queen Charlotte* up the Sound and discovered Captain Meares with his ship the *Nootka*. Meares, lingering late on the Alaskan coast the previous season, had most unwisely decided to winter there. He had spent a ghastly winter. Reported Dixon:

> He had wintered in the creek where now I found him, and his vessel was still fast in the ice. The scurvy had made sad havock amongst his people, he having lost his Second and Third Mates, the Surgeon, Boatswain, Carpenter, Cooper, Sail-maker, and a great number of the foremast men, by that dreadful disorder. . . .
>
> On our enquiring whether the scurvy, unattended with any other complaint, had made such fatal havock amongst the people belonging to the Nootka, we were informed, that a free and unrestrained use of spirits had been indiscriminately allowed them during the extreme cold weather, which they had drank to such excess about Christmas, that numbers of them kept their hammocks for a fortnight together; . . . surely it was ill-judged in Captain Meares to suffer such hurtful excesses amongst his people. . . . [1]

Portlock and Dixon in fact felt no great sympathy for the abject Meares. According to British law, the South Sea Company enjoyed a monopoly of all trade along the western shores of North America, and the East India Company a similar monopoly off the China coast. For a British vessel lawfully to engage in trade across the

---

[1] Dixon, *Voyage*, pp. 155-57.

Pacific it must have licences from both these companies. Such licences had been procured by the King George's Sound Company but only under stringent conditions, the East India Company requiring a bond of £20,000 that its conditions would be met. Meares by a shifty subterfuge had entered into the trade without either of these expensive licences. Thus, he was an illegal interloper, very capable of spoiling the market for Portlock and Dixon. Nevertheless, they supplied him with desperately needed food and two able-bodied seamen to help him sail his ship to Hawaii once it was clear of the ice. Portlock took the precaution, however, of making Meares give a bond that he would indeed head straight for Hawaii and not hang around the coast illicitly competing with them for furs.

While Portlock set about trading along the Alaskan coast, Dixon set a course southwards and arrived off the Queen Charlotte Islands which he named after his ship. Along the way Dixon's men traded to good effect with the Haidas, getting an abundance of pelts (over three hundred sea otter skins in half an hour's trading at Cloak Bay) in return for such commodities as pewter basins, tin kettles and knives. Sailing southward near Nootka Sound, Dixon met two other ships sent out from England by his employers, the King George's Sound Company. These were the *Prince of Wales*, 171 tons and 14 cannon (Captain Colnett) and the tiny *Princess Royal*, 65 tons and 4 cannon (Captain Duncan). Both officers were on leave from the Royal Navy.

Another newcomer on the coast this year was Captain Barkley with the *Imperial Eagle*. This was a fine smart ship which had set out from Ostend, sailing under Austrian colours to avoid the stringent conditions imposed by the East India and South Sea Companies. Aboard the *Imperial Eagle* was Frances Barkley, the seventeen-year-old bride of the ship's captain and the first white woman to visit British Columbia. Upon putting in at Nootka Captain Barkley met John Mackay, left there by Captain Strange the previous year. Mackay's condition was truly wretched for " . . . the natives had stripped him of his cloaths, and obliged him to adopt their mode of dress and filthiness". Joyfully he accepted Captain Barkley's invitation to join the *Imperial Eagle*, and proved most useful to him in carrying on his trade with the Indians.

Ranging in quest of furs Barkley discovered, south of Nootka and Barkley Sound, a great waterway leading inland. Equating it with the inland passage reported in just this latitude by Juan de Fuca, he called it the Strait of Juan de Fuca.

After giving his successors Colnett and Duncan information about the rich supplies of furs to be found around the Queen Charlotte Islands, Dixon gave up his plan to visit Nootka, having learned that Captain Barkley had exhausted the natives' store of furs. Fortunately he had already made a most satisfactory cruise and, turning westward, he headed for Hawaii. Failing to find Portlock there at their designated rendezvous, Dixon sailed on to China where he finally was rejoined by Portlock with the *King George*. When the furs off the *King George* and *Queen Charlotte* were offered on the Canton market, they brought in the unprecedented price of 52,662 Spanish dollars, truly a fortune.[2]

We know very little of the adventures this year of Portlock and Dixon's associates, Captains Colnett and Duncan. We do know, however, of one rather charming episode at Nootka. With Colnett, aboard the *Prince of Wales* as surgeon, was a dedicated botanist Archibald Menzies, commissioned by the great Sir Joseph Banks to make botanical collections and investigations. Ashore at Nootka, Menzies plunged into the forest, eager to set about his collecting but unaware of the dangers to which he was exposing himself. He probably owed his survival to a group of little Indian girls:

... they frequently shewed so much solicitude for my safety, that they often warned me in the most earnest manner of the dangers to which my Botanical rambles in the Woods exposed me, & when they found me inattentive to their entreaties, they would then watch the avenue of the Forest where I enterd, to prevent my receiving any insult or ill usage from their Countrymen. But it was not till after I left them that

---

[2] According to the figures supplied to the East India Company, which was considering entering the fur trade directly itself, Hanna on his first trip got furs worth 20,400 Spanish dollars, the *Captain Cook* and the *Experiment*, got furs worth Sp. $24,000. La Pérouse's two ships obtained furs worth Sp. $9,000. Hanna on his second venture only realized Sp. $8,000, Meares with the *Nootka* sold his furs for Sp. $14,000, and Barkley with the *Imperial Eagle* received Sp. $29,000. *v.* India Office Library, Home Misc. Series, Vol. 494, p. 431.

I became sensible how much I owed to their disinterested zeal for my welfare by knowing more of the treacheries & stratagems of the Natives on other parts of the Coast.[3]

[3] C. F. Newcombe, ed., *Menzies' Journal of Vancouver's Voyage, April to October 1792*, PABC Memoir No. 5 (Victoria, 1923), p. 118.

1788

Meares returns with the Felice *and* Iphigenia — *He builds a base at Nootka* — *Arrival of first Americans.*

After the grim experiences of Captain Meares in wintering in Alaska, nobody was likely to repeat that procedure. The *Prince of Wales* and *Princess Royal* of the King George's Sound Company spent the winter of 1787-88 in the balmy climate of Hawaii. In the spring they appeared back on the North-west coast. Colnett in the *Prince of Wales* worked the Alaskan coast, while Duncan with the valiant little *Princess Royal* traded for furs along the coast of British Columbia. Off Nootka in May she passed a new ship, the *Felice*, freshly arrived from China and commanded by that same John Meares whom Portlock and Dixon had first succoured and then booted off the coast the year before.

John Meares is one of the most incredible persons in the history of the North-west Coast. Though slight and sensitive in appearance, he obviously had a constitution of iron. A good man of business in one sense, he was also completely shifty and dishonest. During his years in the maritime fur trade, all with whom he dealt learned that he was an inveterate liar. Mrs. Barkley, from whose husband he tried to filch the credit for discovering the Strait of Juan de Fuca, is vehement in her declaration about him "inventing lies of the most revolting nature".[1] No competent historian can accept without supporting evidence anything which Meares says in his vast *Voyages Made in the Years 1788 and 1789 from China to the North-West Coast of America.*

This second venture of Meares in the American-China fur trade was admirably planned and executed. In partnership with John Henry Cox, a merchant of Macao, he fittted out two ships, the

---

[1] PABC, A-A-30B-24A, p. 47.

Felice (230 tons and 50 men) and the *Iphigenia* (200 tons and 40 men). On 22 January 1788, the two ships set sail from Macao. At their mastheads fluttered the flag of Portugal, partly to evade the control of the British East India and South Sea Companies, and partly to escape the fees which the Portuguese at Macao levied on foreign shipping. The *Iphigenia*, commanded by Captain Douglas, headed for Alaskan waters to acquire all the furs she could in that region before heading south to rendezvous at Nootka with the *Felice*, commanded by Meares himself.

Meares at the outset sailed straight for Nootka to establish a base there. Having arrived and anchored in Friendly Cove, Meares arranged with Maquinna for a piece of land on which he could build. A few years later one of his officers, Robert Duffin, in a sworn deposition, declared that Meares bought the whole of the land forming Friendly Cove for eight or ten sheets of copper and several trifling articles.[2] Having once obtained his land, Meares set about building a house. Elevated some five feet above the ground this, the first European building to be erected in British Columbia, contained a mess hall, three private chambers for the officers, and sleeping quarters for the other men assigned to shore duty. Under the house there was room for stores and provisions, and a space where coopers, sailmakers and other workmen could carry on their labours during bad weather. Adjacent was a shed where the blacksmith set up his forge. As soon as this establishment was completed and surrounded by a defensive breastwork, Meares pushed ahead with the project which had required its construction, the building of a sloop.

Early in June, when his shore party including his Chinese carpenters (the first Oriental labourers to be imported into British Columbia) were well started on the little ship, Meares left for a trading cruise to the south. On this trip Meares visited Wickaninnish, the paramount chief of Clayoquot Sound, put into Barkley Sound, encountered the particularly savage subjects of Chief Tatooche at the entrance of the Strait of Juan de Fuca, and proceeded some distance down the Washington coast. He arrived back at Nootka on July 25th. Early in August Meares was off on a second visit to

[2] Public Record Office, London [hereafter referred to as PRO], Adm. 1/2628, f.640r.

10. H.M.S. *Resolution* and H.M.S. *Discovery* at Nootka Sound

11. Launching of the *North West America* at Nootka Sound

12. The Spanish Fort at Friendly Cove

13.   Portrait of a Gentleman, for long assumed to be Capt. George Vancouver
(National Portrait Gallery, London, now doubts this identification)

14. H.M.S. *Discovery* on Rocks in Queen Charlotte's Sound

15. The *Columbia* Attacked by Indians

Wickaninnish. Before departing, he supplied Maquinna with fire-arms for a raid on the latter's enemies to the north. On August 26th, back at Nootka, Meares with his men witnessed both the safe arrival of their consort, the *Iphigenia*, laden with Alaskan furs, and the victorious return of Maquinna from his raid. September 16th was another notable day for it saw the totally unexpected arrival of a ship flying the flag of the fledgling United States of America.

The accounts of the riches to be made in the fur trade with China had not gone unnoticed by the shrewd Yankee merchants of New England. The previous year a syndicate of six Boston merchants had acquired two ships and outfitted them for the North-west Coast trade. They were the *Columbia Rediviva* or *Columbia* (Captain Kendrick) of just over 212 tons, and the *Lady Washington*, usually referred to as the *Washington* (Captain Gray) of 90 tons. In a gale off Cape Horn the two got separated. First to put in at Nootka was the *Washington*, which arrived in time for the festivities of September 19th when the small ship which Meares' men had built that summer was ready for launching. The historic nature of that moment was not lost on Meares:

As soon as the tide was at its proper height, the English ensign was displayed on shore at the house, and on board the new vessel, which, at the proper moment, was named the North West America, as being the first bottom ever built and launched in this part of the globe.[3]

With the launching of his new vessel safely attended to, Meares moved into the next phase of his operation. Loading the *Felice* with all the furs which the season had so far yielded her and the *Iphigenia*, he prepared for a speedy departure to China and the Canton market. Entertained at dinner aboard the *Washington* before his departure, Meares and his officers did everything they could to discourage their unwelcome American competitors from engaging in the sea otter trade. Haswell, one of the *Washington*'s officers, records:

All the time these Gentlemen were onboard they fully employed themselves fabricating and rehursing vague and improvable tales

[3] John Meares, *Voyages Made in the Years 1788 and 1789 from China to the North West Coast of America* (London, 1790), p. 220.

relative to the coast of the vast danger attending its navigation of the Monsterous Savage disposition of its inhabitants adding it would be maddness in us so week as we were to stay a winter among them. Capt. Mears protested both vessells ever since they had been on the coast had not collected fifty skins; on our smileing (for we had been differently informed) he said it was a fact upon his sacred word and honour, so intent was this Gentleman in deceiving us that he hesatated not to forfit his word and Honour to what we were convinced was a notorious falsity. The fact was they wished to frighten us off the Coast that they alone might menopolise the trade but the debth of there design could be easily fathemed. They very polightly offered to aford us every asistance that lay in their power.[4]

On September 23rd, the same day that the second American vessel, the *Columbia*, arrived at Nootka, Meares sailed with the *Felice* and her rich cargo of furs. According to Meares' master plan, the *Iphigenia* and the *North West America* remained until late October, gathering what furs were still to be acquired. Finally they sailed to winter in Hawaii, leaving the disgruntled Americans to spend the season at Nootka. The latter noted that as long as the English had been in Friendly Cove, "they menopelized all the skins nor could we get intercourse with one of the Natives even for the purchace of fish or deer".[5]

[4] F. W. Howay, ed., *Voyages of the "Columbia" to the Northwest Coast 1787-1790 and 1790-1793*, Massachusetts Historical Society (Boston, 1941), p. 49.

[5] *Ibid.*, p. 52.

1789

The Spaniards establish a base at Nootka — "The Nootka Incident" — British ships are taken to Mexico as Spanish prizes.

This was the year of the famous "Nootka Incident" which brought Britain and Spain to the very brink of war. Although no Spanish ships had been at Nootka since Perez had briefly anchored offshore in 1774, the Spaniards had not abandoned their claims to the entire North-west Coast. Late in 1789 two ships of the Spanish navy had returned from an Alaskan cruise with news not only of the recent British trading activity at Nootka but, more alarming, of Russian intentions of coming down from Alaska and taking possession of the area for Catherine the Great. Confronted with this double threat, the Spanish authorities moved swiftly to establish their own sovereignty at Nootka. From their base at San Blas in Mexico, two Spanish warships headed north this February — the frigate *Princesa* (26 guns) commanded by Don Esteban José Martinez, and her consort the *San Carlos* (16 guns) commanded by Don Gonzalo Lopez de Haro. Martinez's orders instructed him to assert Spain's sovereignty "with prudent firmness, but without being led into harsh expressions which may give serious offense and cause a rupture".[1] Unfortunately, as we shall see, Martinez was a truculent bully who went directly against the spirit of his instructions.

Off Nootka on May 3rd, Martinez with the *Princesa* encountered Gray with the *Washington*, just as the latter was setting forth on a fur collecting expedition. Firing a shot across the bow of the American ship, Martinez forced her to heave to, then interrogated Gray and his officers. Blandly they concealed their involvement in the fur trade, declaring that they were merely in quest of barrel

[1] W. R. Manning, "The Nootka Sound Controversy", *American Historical Association Annual Report, 1904*, p. 304.

staves. They informed the Spanish captain, however, that if he entered Nootka Sound he would find not only their own consort the *Columbia* but also the pseudo-Portuguese *Iphigenia*.

After wintering in Hawaii, the *Iphigenia* and the *North West America* had arrived back at Nootka some ten days earlier. Almost at once the *North West America* had left on a trading mission to the north but, as Gray had said, Martinez found the *Iphigenia* still at anchor when he himself entered Nootka Sound. For a few days there was no trouble. Captain Douglas kept the Portuguese flag flying on the *Iphigenia* and pretended to be a mere supercargo, subordinate to the figurehead Portuguese commander "Captain" Viana — fictions which Martinez was content for the moment to accept.

The situation changed abruptly on May 12th with the arrival of Lopez de Haro with the second Spanish warship, the *San Carlos*. Confident now that he had the superior force needed to make an arrest, Martinez took Douglas and Viana into custody, put a prize crew aboard the *Iphigenia* and replaced her Portuguese flag with a Spanish ensign. Second thoughts followed this precipitant action. After a couple of weeks Martinez restored her to Captain Douglas but, according to the English, so stripped of trade goods and provisions that they were forced to purchase fresh supplies from the Spaniards. Glad to get away from this fire-eating Spaniard, Douglas swiftly put to sea. For a month he successfully traded for furs, all the while vainly watching for his little consort the *North West America* to warn her of the dangerous situation at Nootka. In the end he headed for Macao.

On June 8th the unsuspecting *North West America* with her furs returned to Nootka just as Martinez was completing Fort San Miguel and Fort San Rafael,[2] which commanded the entrance of Nootka Sound and the anchorage at Friendly Cove. Martinez promptly seized the little English vessel, maintaining he did so to repay himself for supplies provided for the *Iphigenia*. After thoroughly reconditioning the *North West America* and renaming her the *Santa Gertrudis la Magna* (later she was to become the

[2] Cook, *Flood Tide of Empire*, p. 154.

Santa Saturnina), Martinez sent her to explore the entrance to the Strait of Juan de Fuca and, incidentally, to do a bit of fur trading for his own benefit. An interpreter being needed to deal with the Indians during this little cruise, David Coolidge, a mate aboard the *Washington*, accepted this service — having seen what had happened to the *Iphigenia*, the Americans were obviously on edge about the Spaniards and did everything they could to ingratiate themselves with them.

Had Meares' plans of the previous year been carried through, he himself should by now have arrived at Nootka with the *Felice* to join the *Iphigenia* and the *North West America* in obtaining furs along the coast. Important developments during the past winter had, however, led to a complete change of his plans.

In December 1788 Meares had got to Canton with the *Felice* a few crucial days ahead of the *Prince of Wales* and *Princess Royal* of the King George's Sound Company, thus securing an advantage in marketing his furs. Later Meares and his associates held conversa-tions with Captain Colnett of the *Prince of Wales* and John Etches, who was not only the ship's supercargo but a partner in the King George's Sound Company. All parties agreed that, with American competitors already on the North-west Coast, the English would be fools to compete among themselves in the 1789 season. In short order they merged to form a new company, the Associated Merchants of London and India. The *Felice* was sold, and the *Prince of Wales* chartered to the East India Company. In their place the Associated Merchants acquired a new ship, the *Argonaut*, and placed her under Captain Colnett's command. Early this year the *Argonaut* and the veteran *Princess Royal* sailed for Nootka. Aboard were European artificers and Chinese labourers who were to build at Nootka a permanent trading post.

First of the two ships to arrive at Nootka was the *Princess Royal*. She had little trouble with Martinez. Indeed her captain, Thomas Hudson, was one of the little group of British and American witnesses who on June 24th attended the elaborate ceremony with which Martinez took possession of Nootka for Carlos III.[3] On July

---

[3] *Ibid.*, p. 164.

2nd Spanish launches obligingly towed the *Princess Royal* out of the Sound when she left, ostensibly for the Orient but in fact to collect furs along the North-west Coast.

The very day that the *Princess Royal* left Nootka, Captain Colnett arrived with the *Argonaut*. The newcomer was by no means of the discreet and diplomatic character of his colleague Hudson who had just saved his ship from Spanish seizure. Colnett, in fact, was as truculent and headstrong a man as Martinez. Indeed a few years later a Spaniard at Nootka made the observation, "It is likely that the churlish nature of each one precipitated things . . . since those who sailed with both complained of them equally and condemned their uncultivated boorishness."[4] The day following the *Argonaut's* arrival saw mounting tension, with Colnett declining to recognize Spanish sovereignty and maintaining his intention to build a fortified trading post on the land which his new partner Meares had bought the previous year. That evening matters reached a climax with a furious argument aboard the *Princesa*, which ended with Martinez placing Colnett under arrest and refusing to let him leave the ship.

Colnett was mad to have allowed himself this sort of confrontation since the *Argonaut* was moored directly under the Spanish guns. Understandably there was no resistance the following day when the Spaniards boarded the *Argonaut*, forced her officers to lower the British flag and exultantly hoisted the Spanish ensign in its stead.

Transferred back to his own cabin aboard the captured *Argonaut*, Colnett became more and more agitated as he realized how his own folly had brought to ruin the expensive venture of the Associated Merchants of London and India. Going out of his mind, he attempted suicide.

On July 12th, looking for Colnett, Captain Hudson and the *Princess Royal* reappeared off Nootka. By bad luck they came too close inshore. A racing tide sucked the ship into the Sound, and in short order she too was captured by Martinez.

While Colnett, Hudson and the crew of the *Princess Royal* were kept imprisoned on the latter ship, the crew of the *Argonaut* was

[4] Moziño, *Noticias de Nutka*, p. 74.

placed ashore pending deportation to Mexico. Once ashore, the *Argonaut*'s men with their lamentations and tears so moved the Indians that they turned against the Spaniards. On the afternoon of July 13th, Maquinna's kinsman Callicum (or "Ke-le-kum") went aboard the *San Carlos* to denounce to Lopez de Haro the actions of his commander. Returning to the shore, the Nootka tyee passed Martinez where the latter stood by the rail of the *Princess Royal*. Disdainfully refusing Martinez's invitation to come aboard and receive presents, Callicum shouted "Martinez Pisec! Martinez Capsil!" Infuriated at hearing his name coupled with the native words for rogue and thief, Martinez grabbed a musket and fired at Callicum. He missed his mark, but one of his sailors fired also and his shot killed the Indian chief.

On July 14th a Spanish prize crew started for San Blas with the *Argonaut*, taking Colnett and his crew with them as prisoners. Martinez kept Colnett's Chinese with him to work on further construction of the base he had established at Nootka. Two weeks later Lopez de Haro headed south with the *San Carlos*, having in custody the *Princess Royal* and her crew. Meanwhile the commanders of the American vessels, the *Columbia* and the *Washington*, had exchanged ships and prepared to depart. Martinez persuaded Gray to carry the crew of the *North West America* to China with him aboard the *Columbia*. Only when Gray reached China in November did Meares learn of the catastrophic failure of the venture of the Associated Merchants.

Meanwhile there had been an ironic development at Nootka. Martinez had fully expected to maintain a permanent Spanish base there but, when his supply ship *Aranzazu* arrived, it brought orders from the Viceroy of Mexico that Nootka was to be abandoned. Glumly Martinez set about demolishing his fortifications. By the end of the year all the Spaniards and their British prisoners were back in Mexico. No white man remained to look across the waters of Nootka Sound, for a while once more occupied solely by Maquinna and his people.

1790

Meares arrives in England — Imminent war with Spain over Nootka — The Nootka Convention — Colnett released by the Spaniards — Lieut. Eliza refortifies Nootka.

On the first day of this year the Royal Navy commissioned for a voyage of exploration along the coast of North-west America H.M.S. *Discovery*, 340 tons, and fresh from the builder's yard. The preceding years had brought reports from the fur trading skippers, many of them on leave from the Royal Navy, that a deeply indented coast extended along those hundreds of miles unseen by Captain Cook when he had sailed from Nootka to Alaska. Speculation had mounted that one of these inlets might lead to the North-west Passage, or might at least connect with Lake Athabasca to provide an easy water route across North America. Since merchant ships, intent on furs and profits, had little time for surveying and charting all these inlets, the Royal Navy had been given this task. Assigned to the command of the *Discovery* was Lieut. Henry Roberts. Second in command of the ship as she lay at Deptford taking on supplies and equipment was Lieut. George Vancouver. Then instructions arrived to stop the work — Britain, it appeared, was going to war with Spain and all the energies of the Royal Navy must go into preparations for the coming hostilities.

This sudden prospect of war had been caused by news of seizure of the British ships at Nootka. Hastening home from China, John Meares had brought with him not only a deposition sworn by various men off the *North West America* but one of them in person, William Graham. Graham swore before Sir Sampson Wright, Justice of the Peace for Middlesex, an "information" relating how the Spaniards had ordered Captain Hudson aboard the warship *Princesa*, "and threw said Hudson down the after hatchway of the said frigate, saying 'Get down, you English dog'." He carefully recorded how the Spaniards had put his shipmates in irons and "fed them with horse-beans and water for the space of about three weeks, and beat and otherwise ill-treated several of them". Meares himself drafted a "Memorial" setting forth alleged indignities and injustices heaped upon the British. This he presented to the House of Commons on May 13th.[1] The Commons had no way of knowing that Meares' "Memorial" was in many respects a thoroughly dishonest document. Accepting it at face value, the government ordered it published to prepare public opinion for the anticipated war.

At stake was much more than ownership of a tiny patch of land in a remote corner of North America, and the return of two or three petty vessels. Britain was using the Nootka affair to challenge Spain's pretensions to reserve for herself all trans-Pacific trade, and also her assumption that mere proclamations of sovereignty (with no subsequent permanent settlements) were sufficient to give Spain sovereignty along the North-west American coast. On May 5th Parliament voted £1,000,000 to prepare for war with Spain. Seeing that Britain was determined upon action, the Spaniards commenced negotiations which finally resulted in the Nootka Convention of October 28th. This gave Britain all that she wanted, not only generous compensation for Meares and his associates, but restitution of all the seized property and, more significantly, a declaration that British subjects were free to carry on their commerce anywhere in the Pacific Ocean, except within ten leagues of areas occupied by Spain.[2]

With the crisis passed, work was resumed readying H.M.S. *Discovery* for her voyage to the Pacific North-west. Roberts now being absent on service in the West Indies, Vancouver on November 17th was summoned to the Admiralty and informed that he was being given command both of the *Discovery* and of her consort, the smaller armed tender *Chatham*. He was instructed to survey the mainland coast of North America from the 30th to the 60th degrees

---

[1] Meares' "Memorial" and Graham's "Information" will be found among the unpaginated appendices to Meares' voluminous *Voyages* published this same year.

[2] For the terms of the Nootka Convention see Manning, "Nootka Sound Controversy", pp. 454-56.

of latitude, and to enter Nootka Sound to receive from the Spaniards restitution of the territory there. The year ended with Vancouver carefully supervising the readying of his ships.

Meanwhile, what was going on in the Pacific? In the spring the Viceroy of Mexico received instructions from Madrid to restore to Colnett the *Argonaut* and the *Princess Royal*. Unfortunately the latter had already been sent north in the Spanish service. However, Colnett was given back the *Argonaut*, informed that he could pick up his other ship at Nootka, and blandly invited to bring action against Martinez in the courts. Anxious to get back to the sea otter regions, Colnett waived the invitation. Having provisioned the *Argonaut*, he left Mexico for the North-west in July. Once clear of the Spaniards, Colnett decided not to risk any more encounters with them in Nootka. Instead he made his base in Clayoquot Sound, wintered there, and next year arrived in Macao with a lucrative harvest of 1200 sea otter pelts.

And what of the Spaniards? Never guessing that some months later his home government would back down in the face of Britain's threat of war, the Conde de Revilla Gigedo, the newly appointed Viceroy of Mexico, ordered the reoccupation of Nootka, this time on a permanent basis. On February 3rd, in obedience to the Viceroy's orders, Don Francisco de Eliza sailed from San Blas for Nootka with the *Concepcion*, the *San Carlos* and the *Princesa Real* (the captured *Princess Royal*).

At Nootka, Eliza proceeded to rebuild the fort of San Miguel which he garrisoned with seventy-five Catalonian troops under the command of Don Pedro Alberni. Barracks and supply buildings were erected, also a residence for the governor, a church and even a hospital. Gardens were laid out and enclosures provided for cattle.[3] Expecting to remain at Nootka over the years, the Spaniards were concerned to make themselves comfortable.

Once Eliza had settled in at Nootka, he sent off Manuel Quimper and Gonzalo Lopez de Haro (known to the English as "Captain Arrow") with the *Princesa Real* to explore and chart the coast to the south. Sailing up the Strait of Juan de Fuca, Quimper and Haro

<hr>

[3] F. W. Howay, "The Spanish Settlement at Nootka", *Washington Historical Quarterly* [hereafter referred to as *WHQ*] 8 (1917):167-68.

stopped at Sooke and Royal Roads where they went ashore, erected crosses, and proclaimed Spanish sovereignty. Pushing on, they went as far as Rosario Strait and Whidbey Island (now in the United States) before their allotted time ran out and they had to return to Nootka.[4]

[4] Henry R. Wagner, *Spanish Explorations in the Strait of Juan de Fuca* (Santa Ana, 1933), pp. 15-25.

1791

Vancouver sails from England — American fur traders —
Gray winters at Fort Defiance — Kendrick attacked by
Haidas — Ballad of the "Bold Northwestman" — Spanish
explorations in the Strait of Georgia.

On March 20th, in Falmouth harbour, Captain George Vancouver received his final instructions from the Admiralty. On April 1st he set sail for North-west America with the *Discovery* and the *Chatham*, choosing the long route around the Cape of Good Hope.

Since Vancouver was to play so prominent and illustrious a role in the history of British Columbia, it is proper to give at this point something of his biography. Born at King's Lynn in Norfolk on 22 June 1757, he came of a prominent local family of Dutch descent. King's Lynn was a busy seaport in those days and obviously young George Vancouver early responded to the excitement of the seafaring life. Joining the Royal Navy as an able-bodied seaman at the age of fourteen, he shipped with Captain Cook on his second great voyage of exploration (1772-1775). Probably Vancouver's family had arranged his enlistment with Cook on the understanding that, if he shaped up, he would be in line for a commission. When Cook sailed on his final voyage, the one which brought him to Nootka Sound, he again had Vancouver with him, this time advanced to the rank of midshipman.

Two months after the return of Cook's ships from that fatal voyage, young George Vancouver was commissioned a lieutenant in the Royal Navy. The next few years saw Vancouver down in the Caribbean serving on H.M.S. *Fame*. In 1783 the Peace of Paris turned Vancouver into one of the thousands of semi-retired, half-pay officers whiling away their time ashore. Fortunately Vancouver's reputation was such that in 1784 he managed to get back on active service. Serving on H.M.S. *Europa*, he sailed once more for the

Caribbean. Here he made a very favourable impression on Captain Alan Gardner, one of the most progressive officers in the Royal Navy. Gardner, by 1791 one of the Lords of the Admiralty, was probably largely responsible for Vancouver being given command of this expedition to the Pacific North-west.

This summer of 1791 there was no dearth of shipping in the remote region towards which Captain Vancouver was bound. As many as a dozen ships may have been engaged in the fur trade along the coast. The newcomers included, for the first time, a French vessel *La Solide* from Marseilles, and the *Gustavus III* flying the Swedish flag (though only nominally Swedish). Most of the trading vessels were American.[1]

Chief among the American ships were our old acquaintances the *Columbia* and the *Washington*. Their commanders, Captains Gray and Kendrick, were an interesting pair. Later Joseph Barrell, head of the Boston syndicate which had employed them, was told bluntly that each was both fool and rogue.[2] Certainly the two were hard men who could be tyrannical when dealing with the Indians, but there the similarities ceased. Kendrick was a lazy, dilatory, middle-aged man spinning grandiose schemes but achieving little. One-eyed Gray was a reckless package of energy, forever flitting from inlet to inlet, and recklessly taking chances along the uncharted coast.

Gray with the *Columbia*, on a second venture from Boston, arrived on the coast first. Despite the financial failure of his earlier voyage in 1789, he had persuaded Barrell to finance him for a second time though Barrell, suspecting that Gray may have been cheating him, this time sent along an honest young fellow, John Hoskins, to keep the accounts. The *Columbia* spent an active season trading from the Queen Charlotte Islands to the Strait of Juan de Fuca. One tragedy marred the season. One morning in mid-August when the ship was trading along the coast of northern British Columbia, her second mate, Caswell, went off with two seamen in the jolly boat to do some fishing. A signal gun having failed to recall

[1] *v.* F. W. Howay, "A List of Trading Vessels in Maritime Fur Trade, 1785-1794", *Transactions of the Royal Society of Canada* (Section II, 1930), pp. 120-23.

[2] Howay, *Voyages of the "Columbia"*, p. 491.

the party, the *Columbia* sent her pinnace to investigate. Hoskins in his journal records that shortly thereafter the *Columbia*'s crew:

... saw the pinnace returning with the jolly boat in tow without any person in her and soon discovered they had a flag hoisted halfmast with this melancholy token they approached the ship and when they came alongside I saw my worthy friend Mr. Caswell laying dead in the bottom of the boat stripped perfectly naked and stabbed in upwards of twenty places   this was a sight too shocken [*sic*] ever to be effaced from my memory. . . .

Mr. Smith reported when he entered the cove he saw the jolly boat laying at anchor a small distance from the shore but no person in her supposing they had gone into the woods a gunning but he soon found himself mistaken for ere he had gone far he saw the body of Joseph Barnes laying dead on the beach stripped of everything but his trouses [*sic*] but saw nothing of John Folger   fearing least the natives might be laying in ambush he dare not land to take of[f] the corps[e] but took the jolly boat in tow with Mr. Caswell as he found him and came on board.[3]

It may well be that these unfortunate men were not the first whites to be murdered by the Indians. The previous year, when Colnett had lost two officers and four seamen after their small boat struck a reef, the Spaniards strongly suspected that they had in fact been murdered by the Hesquiat Indians.

At the end of his trading season Captain Gray prepared to winter at Clayoquot Sound. On Meares Island in a sheltered cove (recently conclusively identified by Kenneth Gibson of Tofino on the basis of archaeological excavations),[4] he built a shore establishment which he named Fort Defiance and, following Meares' precedent with the *North West America*, began building the *Adventure*, a sloop.

As for Captain Kendrick, he arrived on the coast from China in mid-June. Unwisely he made for Barrell's Sound (Houston Stewart Channel) in the Queen Charlotte Islands. Trading there two years earlier, he had indulged in coercive tactics of the kind which speedily made the Indians hate the "Boston men", as they called all Americans. Removing a small cannon from its wooden carriage, he had

3 *Ibid.*, pp. 221-22.

4 Jack Fry, "Fort Defiance", *The Beaver* (Summer 1967), pp. 18-21.

taken two Indian chiefs and clamped a leg of each where the arms of the gun barrel had rested. He had then declared that he would kill the two chiefs unless their fellow tribesmen let him have all their skins at the price he had set for them. The pretext for this outrageous behaviour was that the Indians had stolen laundry off Kendrick's lines and had not restored all of it. The Haidas had not forgotten this episode when Captain Kendrick came sailing once more into their harbour. Obtaining possession of the *Washington*'s arm chests, they soon succeeded in driving the Americans below decks. Fortunately for Kendrick, his officers were able to arm themselves with their own private firearms. A short and bitter battle followed in which the Indians were unavailingly urged from flight by a heroic woman who had already had one of her arms slashed off by an American cutlass. Finally driven from the ship, she was killed in the water by a shot. Kendrick's revenge was merciless:

... a constant fire was kept up as long as they could reach the natives with cannon or small arms after which they chased them in their armed boats making the most dreadfull havock by killing all they came across.[5]

Such was the account recorded by Hoskins after he had spoken with Kendrick's men later that summer. But Kendrick's actions were not exceptional. Various of the fur trading captains, British as well as American, made hostages of chiefs or used their cannon to force the Indians to sell all their furs to them, at whatever price they offered, so that none would be left for their competitors.

On September 29th, after a touching farewell with Gray at Clayoquot, Kendrick sailed back to China. Fortunately he never returned to British Columbia waters.

One interesting consequence of Kendrick's massacre of the Haidas was the writing of the earliest extant piece of British Columbia literature, a ballad composed almost certainly by one of Kendrick's crew and published some years later in New England under the title of "Bold Northwestman". It commences:

Come all ye bold Northwestmen who plough the raging main,
Come listen to my story, while I relate the same;

[5] Howay, *Voyages of the "Columbia"*, p. 241.

'Twas of the Lady Washington decoyed as she lay
At Queen Charlotte's Island, in North America.*

On the sixteenth day of June, boys, in the year Ninety-One,
The natives in great numbers on board our ship did come,
Then for to buy our fur of them our captain did begin,
But mark what they attempted before long time had been.

Abaft upon our quarter deck two arm chests did stand,
And in them there was left the keys by the gunner's careless hand;
When quickly they procuring of them did make a prize,
Thinking we had no other arms for to defend our lives.[6]

[*Given the old pronunciation of "North Amerikay".]

Generally the fur trading ships gave a wide berth to the little
Spanish fort and settlement at Nootka. When the Americans did put
into Nootka Sound they went up to Marvinas Bay, out of sight of
the Spaniards and some miles north of Friendly Cove. Stuck in their
lonely outpost, the Spaniards at least got some useful work done by
surveying the coast for His Catholic Majesty. Sailing from Nootka
on May 4th (with the *San Carlos* under his own command and the
smaller *Santa Saturnina* under that of José Maria Narvaez), the
commandant Eliza explored Clayoquot Sound and Barkley Sound
before pushing on to the Strait of Juan de Fuca and picking up
where Quimper had left off the previous year. Mid-June found
Eliza's men close to Saturna Island. Narvaez with the *Santa Saturnina*
got as far north as Texada Island. En route he possibly entered
Burrard Inlet; certainly he did some exploring around Howe Sound.
Returning south, Narvaez skirted the eastern shore of Vancouver
Island; thus he discovered Nanaimo harbour which the Spaniards
named Bocas de Winthuysen. Reunited, the *Santa Saturnina* and
the *San Carlos* made slow progress against headwinds as they sought
to beat their way out of the Strait of Juan de Fuca. The consequence
was a disappointment for Eliza. When he arrived back at Nootka at
the end of August, he found that he had missed, by just two days, a
visit by the Malaspina expedition.

[6] For the full text of this song see F. W. Howay, " 'The Ballad of the Bold
Northwestman', An Incident in the Life of Captain John Kendrick", *WHQ*
20 (1929):114-23.

Malaspina with his ships was Spain's reply to Britain's Cook and France's La Pérouse. Belatedly regretting the secrecy with which she had so long concealed her own discoveries, Spain had decided to mount a superb expedition of exploration and research which would garner her a belated share of international recognition and acclaim. Two warships, the *Descubierta* and the *Atrevida*, were splendidly outfitted at Cadiz, provided with a whole corps of scientists and placed under the command of Don Alejandro Malaspina, one of the most brilliant officers in the Spanish navy. Setting out from Cadiz in 1789, Malaspina, pausing for frequent scientific studies along the way, reached Alaska from Acapulco late in June of this year. Retracing his course to Mexico, he decided to put in at Nootka, entering the harbour there on August 13th.

Almost immediately Malaspina's scientists had their tent observatories erected on the shore. There were exchanges of hospitality. Possibly Alberni and Saavedra, commanding at Nootka during Eliza's absence, were entertained at a recital played on the harpsichord which was part of the furnishings of the *Descubierta*'s principal cabin. On the whole, Malaspina's people were very favourably impressed by Nootka. Certainly they were appreciative of the vegetables from Alberni's gardens and the fresh bread from the bakery. True, they noted in the Indians "a timid and cautious attitude toward our settlement",[7] fully attributable to what they had suffered from Martinez, though Eliza had begun to win back their confidence. The process of reconciliation was notably hastened when Malaspina presented Maquinna with four panes of window glass for his house, along with other gifts. Before Malaspina sailed on August 28th, Maquinna had confirmed the cession of the site on which the Spaniards had erected their base.

[7] p. 282 of the typescript translation in UBC Library by Carl Robinson of *Politico-Scientific Voyage Round the World by the corvettes "Descubierta" and "Atrevida" under the command of the Naval Captains Don Alexandro Malaspina and Don José de Bustamente y Guerra from 1789-94* (Madrid, 1885).

1792

Columbia *attacked at Clayoquot — Gray's revenge —*
Quadra arrives at Nootka — Explorations of Galiano and
Valdes — Vancouver commences his survey and meets
Spaniards — Discovery *and* Chatham *run on rocks but escape*
— Vancouver meets Quadra — Negotiations at Nootka —
An excursion to Tahsis — Vancouver leaves for California.

The numerals of this year should be printed in red, for it was truly a
notable one for British Columbia. For one thing, 1792 saw a
tremendous increase in the number of ships coming in quest of furs.
For another, it saw the last manoeuvres by which the Spaniards
sought to keep Nootka. Finally, it saw the beginning of Captain
Vancouver's great achievement in surveying and mapping the
mainland coast.

First the fur trading ships. Their names make an impressive roll-
call: the *Adventure, Butterworth, Columbia, Fenis and St. Joseph,*
Felice Adventurer, Florinda, Grace, Gustavus III, Hancock, Hope,
Jenny, Jackal, La Flavie, Margaret, Prince Lee Boo, Phoenix, Prince
William Henry, Three Brothers and *Venus.* According to one count,
if warships as well as merchantmen were included, no less than
thirty ships visited the North-west Coast this year.[1] The increasing
number of ships brought fierce competition in trade; and the Indians,
becoming more aware of the value of their furs, held out for higher
prices — nails and blue beads no longer sufficed; copper sheets and
blue coats were demanded and, increasingly, firearms and ammunition. For their sea otter skins the Indians demanded twenty times as
much copper as they had once accepted. Some of the ships' captains,
especially those new to the trade, paid the higher prices; but some of
the older captains retained the prices of earlier years and, when the

[1] Archibald Menzies to Sir Joseph Banks, Jan. 1-14, 1793, MSS in Botany
Library of the Natural History Museum, London, D.T.C., Vol. 8:142-55.

Indians refused to sell at them, seized hostages, and cannonaded and burned the Indian villages.

Most important among the fur traders was Gray, whom we left building his sloop *Adventure* while wintering with the *Columbia* in Clayoquot Sound. With him on the *Columbia* was a ship's boy, Ottoo, a young Hawaiian who, unhappy in Gray's service, slipped away and joined the Indians. By holding prisoner Tootiscoosettle, brother of their chief, Gray forced the Clayoquot Indians to send the boy back. Angered by the insult to the family of their chief, as well as inflamed by desire for the white men's goods and ship, the Indians began to plot revenge while keeping up a show of friendly intimacy with the Americans. Their attack would be no simple bow-and-arrow affair. As Haswell the first mate on the *Columbia* noted:

> The natives of this place and the villages nigh had by barter become possessed of more than two hundred stands of arms, and a large quantity of ammunition, and were now become skilled in the use of them.[2]

The suspicions of the Americans were aroused in mid-February when Ottoo was seen in secretive conversation with one of the Indians. Under sustained grilling, the boy broke down and confessed that the Indians had offered to make him a great chief if he would wet the gunpowder in the guns which the Americans kept constantly loaded in case of surprise attack. According to the unhappy Ottoo, the Indian onslaught could be expected almost at once. The Americans hurriedly moved the *Columbia* from her berth, where she almost touched a bank on shore, and worked through the night making their position as defensible as possible. In the darkness howls from the Indians revealed that the attackers had come and were frustrated to find that their plot had been discovered.

From this point on Gray and his men worked as quickly as possible getting the *Columbia* ready for sea and completing their work on the *Adventure*. A month later Captain Gray was ready to sail from Clayoquot Sound, but before he left he had one final piece of business to attend to. This he entrusted to young John Boit, his fifth mate. In his journal for March 27th Boit wrote:

---

[2] Howay, *Voyages of the "Columbia"*, p. 312.

I am sorry to be under the nessescity of remarking that this day I was *sent* with three boats, all well man'd and arm'd, to destroy the Village of Opitsatah   it was a Command I was no ways tenacious off, and am grieved to think Capt. Gray shou'd let his passions go so far. *This* Village was about half a mile in Diameter, and Contained upwards off 200 Houses, generally well built for *Indians*   ev'ry door that you enter'd was in resemblance to an human and Beasts head, the passage being through the mouth, besides which there was much more rude carved work about the dwellings some of which was by no means *innelegant*. This fine Village, the Work of Ages, was in a short time totally destroy'd.[3]

Clayoquot left behind, the *Columbia* and the *Adventure* parted company, the former heading south and the latter north to work the Queen Charlottes. For the rest of the season the two vessels operated more or less separately except for the occasional rendezvous. Gray's great moment came on May 12th when he rediscovered the long reported "River of the West", earlier discovered by the Spaniards in 1775 and named by them the Rio de San Roque. To this noble river he gave the name of Columbia's River, after his ship. Gray's rediscovery of the Columbia was to provide the cornerstone for future American claims to possession of the Pacific North-west.

When Gray returned north he found the Indians increasingly hostile. Occasionally to cow them, he opened fire with his cannon. One such incident occurred on May 29th in Esperanza Inlet. Here, according to the Americans, the Indians were preparing an attack. Accordingly, when a war canoe insisted upon approaching despite warnings to keep away, Captain Gray opened fire, killing or wounding all its occupants. A few days later the Spaniards at Nootka received a very different account:

This day [June 3rd] there came a canoe from outside the harbour with various natives asking help from the commandant Don Juan de la Bodega against a ship which was in the Buena Esperanza Inlet and had there attacked an Indian settlement, killing seven men and wounding others, and robbing the rest of the otter skins which they had. They brought one wounded man for the surgeon to heal, and Macuina interceded with the commandant that care should be taken of this man

---

[3] *Ibid.*, pp. 390-91.

and that he should proceed to chastise the aggressors. As far as could be understood the ship was the American frigate *Columbia*, Captain Gray, whom the Indians indicated by making signs that he was one-eyed, which we knew to be a characteristic of that captain.[4]

It must have been a matter of relief for the Indians when Gray left the coast for good at the beginning of October, sailing for China to market his furs. A few days before his departure, he sold the little *Adventure* to the Spaniards, who renamed her the *Orcasitas*.

For the Spaniards this was an active and crucial year. The Viceroy of Mexico had decided that, if they had to evacuate Nootka, they must secure recognition of the Strait of Juan de Fuca as their northern boundary. Accordingly late in May the warship *Princesa* under the command of Don Salvador Fidalgo took up station in Bahia de Nuñez Gaona (Neah Bay) and began establishing a base there. A garden was cleared and planted, enclosures were built for livestock, and a barracks was erected for a Spanish detachment posted there.

Just a little earlier, on April 29th, the frigate *Santa Gertrudis* had arrived at Nootka, bearing Don Juan Francisco de la Bodega y Quadra, the officer commanding Spain's naval forces on the west coast of North America. Conducting an inspection, he was pleased to find "indisputable proof of the efficiency, diligence, and activity"[5] with which Eliza and Alberni had attended to matters at Nootka, but he found the principal house in very poor repair and lost no time in making it into a residence where he could fittingly entertain the representatives of Great Britain when they should arrive to receive restitution under the terms of the Nootka Convention.

In mid-May Quadra was joined by two officers whom Malaspina had detached from his own command — Don Dionisio Alcala Galiano and Don Cayetano Valdes, with the little schooners *Sutil* and *Mexicana*. Galiano and Valdes were to continue the explorations conducted by Quimper and Eliza in the two previous years. Although both schooners needed repairs, Quadra lost no time in getting them off on their mission. A week later he despatched Jacinto Caamaño

---

[4] [Cardero], *A Spanish Voyage*, p. 22.

[5] Quadra, *Voyage to the North West Coast of North America*, trans. V. D. Webb, typescript in UBC Library, pp. 16-17.

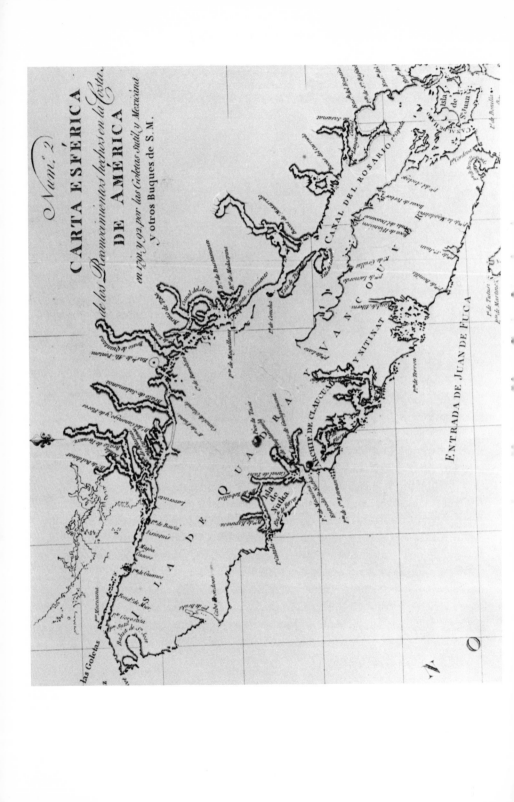

with the frigate *Aranzazu* on an exploratory cruise of the northern coast. Daily expecting the arrival of Captain Vancouver, he was mindful of his instructions from the Viceroy of Mexico to keep the English commander negotiating at Nootka as long as possible, unable to start his own explorations, while the Spanish navigators pushed ahead finding as much new country as they could and claiming it for Spain.[6]

Captain Vancouver, in fact, had already arrived on the coast and since mid-April had systematically been working his way north from Cape Mendocino. Unfortunately, in making his survey, he had failed to recognize the mouth of the Columbia which Gray was to enter just a few weeks later. Somewhere off the Washington coast he encountered the *Columbia* sailing southwards and sent aboard Lieut. Puget and Archibald Menzies, the botanist. They returned with news of the unreliability of Meares. In one of his maps Meares had boldly shown the "Track of the American Sloop Washington in the autumn of 1789". This had shown the vessel entering, by way of the Strait of Juan de Fuca, a great inland canal which rejoined the Pacific north of the Queen Charlotte Islands. Gray informed them the whole thing was a fabrication. He had never sailed more than fifty miles into the Strait of Juan de Fuca, and quite obviously Kendrick had not done so after he took over command of the *Washington*.

Perturbed by this strange new light on Meares, Vancouver arrived off Cape Flattery. Here he had to make a decision. Should he continue north to Nootka and attend to his diplomatic business? Or should he stick to his other task of tracing the continental shore? He had, of course, no way of knowing if the Spanish representative had arrived at Nootka and he could waste a lot of time there waiting for him. Moreover, he badly needed the summer months for his survey. Turning to the starboard, he entered the Strait.

In delightful spring weather Vancouver sailed along the southern shore of the Strait, enchanted by the beautiful scenery that unfolded. At the end of the Strait he found a safe anchorage in Port Discovery. Now began the hard work of the survey, and a routine to which the

[6] Wagner, *Spanish Explorations*, p. 50.

Map 3.
Portion of Vancouver's Map, showing Burrard Inlet and Howe Sound

men of the *Discovery* and *Chatham* would become inured over the next few years. Leaving the ships anchored "at station", detachments from the crews would take to the small boats and then, sailing when there was a breeze, and rowing when there was not, they would range anywhere up to a hundred miles, in all sorts of weather, investigating winding inlets and narrow passages where it would be folly to risk the *Discovery* and *Chatham*. When soaking rainstorms swept in, the officers slept in tents while they camped ashore for the night, but the common seamen "had no other shelter but what they formed by the Boat Sails which were found very inadequate to screen them from the inclemency of such boisterous weather & such deluge of rain".[7]

Vancouver that May thoroughly explored Puget Sound, then moved back into waters traversed by the Spaniards during the past two years, though he was unaware of this prior discovery. On June 4th (birthday of King George III) Vancouver named these waters "the Gulf of Georgia". Going ashore, he took possession in the name of His Majesty of all the lands bordering upon this inland sea. A few days later, with the *Discovery* and *Chatham* at station in Birch Bay, Captain Vancouver with the *Discovery*'s yawl, and Lieut. Puget with her launch, set out to explore northwards. After strangely failing to notice the Fraser River, Vancouver, on June 13th, coming ashore on Point Grey, for the first time set foot on the soil of the future province of British Columbia. The next week saw him exploring and naming Burrard Inlet, Howe Sound and Jervis Inlet. Finally, eighty-four miles from his ships, he started home. En route he discovered, anchored at Spanish Banks, the *Sutil* and the *Mexicana* which a few days before had exchanged salutations and news with the *Chatham*. Vancouver's mortification at learning that the area he had just surveyed had already been visited by previous Spanish explorers was matched only by his amazement at the inadequacy of the Spanish vessels:

... having partaken with them a very hearty breakfast, [I] bad them farewell, not less pleased with their hospitality and attention, than astonished at the vessels in which they were employed to execute a

[7] Menzies, *Journal*, p. 101.

service of such a nature. They were each about forty-five tons burthen, mounted two brass guns, and were navigated by twenty-four men, bearing one lieutenant, without a single inferior officer. Their apartments just allowed room for sleeping places on each side, with a table in the intermediate space, at which four persons, with some difficulty, could sit, and were, in all other respects, the most ill calculated and unfit vessels that could possibly be imagined for such an expedition; notwithstanding this, it was pleasant to observe, in point of living, they possessed many more comforts than could reasonably have been expected.[8]

Before leaving to rejoin the *Discovery* and *Chatham*, Vancouver invited the Spaniards to join forces with him in exploring the unknown coast to the northwards, an invitation which the Spaniards accepted.

June 26th saw the combined British and Spanish vessels taking up station in Desolation Sound. From here the small boats explored around Cape Mudge and up Bute Inlet while James Johnstone, the master of the *Chatham*, travelling up the coast for 120 miles by open boat, discovered Johnstone Strait leading northward to the open waters of the Pacific. Upon Johnstone's return Vancouver made haste to take his ships up this newly discovered passage. The Spaniards had by now realized that, with their slower vessels and more limited resources, they could not keep up with the British as the latter made their rapid, comprehensive, surveying sweeps. Accordingly, they decided to let Vancouver proceed, and follow him at their own slower pace. With mutual expressions of regard, the Spaniards remained behind when Vancouver sailed from Desolation Sound on July 13th.

After passing through Johnstone Strait, Vancouver worked his way towards Queen Charlotte Sound, an area already well-known to the maritime fur traders. Along the way, Vancouver and his officers indulged in some fur trading of their own. Thomas Manby preserves for us the jaundiced view with which the men on the lower deck regarded this activity:

On the 20th [of July] we anchored off a very extensive Village.

---

[8] George Vancouver, *A Voyage of Discovery to the North Pacific Ocean and Round the World* (London, 1798), I:313-14.

Upwards of one hundred Canoes came off and a vast quantity of all kinds of skins were purchased: those people who were intrusted with the various articles sent out by Government made to their disgrace an amazing harvest. Bales of Cloth and blankets were sold with a lavish hand for skins, when many of our persevering Tars in our own Crew were shivering with cold for the want of wollen cloathing.[9]

Continuing on, through complex passages studded with rocks and reefs, both ships nearly met disaster. On August 6th the *Discovery* grounded on sunken rocks. Attempts to lighten her by throwing overboard part of her ballast achieved nothing. As the tide fell, she leaned over at a more and more precarious angle while the crew tried to shore her up with spars and masts.

In this melancholy situation, we remained, expecting relief from the returning flood, which to our inexpressible joy was at length announced by the floating of the shoars, a happy indication of the ship righting. Our exertions to lighten her were, however, unabated, until about two in the morning; when the ship becoming nearly upright, we hove on the stern cable, and, without any particular efforts, or much strain, had the undescribable satisfaction of feeling her again afloat, without having received the least apparent injury.[10]

Later on the day of the *Discovery*'s escape the *Chatham* struck a reef in the same treacherous waters. She too was floated free at the next high tide, but only after being pounded by heavy surf and suffering damage which would require extensive repairs, though she did remain fairly seaworthy.

August 17th found the two ships once more taking up station, this time in Safety Cove on Fitzhugh Sound. Here they met the British trading vessel *Venus* from Bengal which had news for them. Vancouver had already learned from Galiano and Valdes of Quadra's arrival at Nootka. Now he learned that his own supply ship, the *Daedalus*, was also there. The *Venus* had tragic news about the *Daedalus*. Passing the Hawaiian Islands, the supply ship had landed, at Waikiki Bay on Oahu,[11] a small party to obtain fresh

---

9 Thomas Manby, "Journal" (Pacific North-west portion, p. 24). MS in Public Archives of Canada [hereafter referred to as PAC].

10 Vancouver, *Voyage*, I:364.

11 Menzies to Banks, Jan. 1-14 (letter previously cited). He calls it "Whyteetee Bay on the South side of Woahoo".

water. Suddenly the natives attacked, killing not only one of the seamen but Lieut. Hergest, a personal friend of Vancouver, and Mr. Gooch, an astronomer coming out to join the expedition. In view of the *Venus*'s tidings Vancouver, who had intended to work northward for another month, headed immediately for Nootka. On August 28th, conducted by a pilot sent out by Quadra, he brought his ships to anchor in Friendly Cove. Three days later he was followed by the *Sutil* and *Mexicana*, which paused only briefly before returning to Mexico. These tiny Spanish schooners had endured many perils while threading their way through the innumerable islands off the mainland inlets. At times the Indians had turned ugly. For a while their launch had lost her way. The incredible currents and tiderips had given them nerve-shaking experiences. Caught in one whirlpool, the *Sutil* had been spun around three times with such velocity as to giddy her crew.

The negotiations at Nootka were carried on in an atmosphere of meticulous protocol and eighteenth century urbanity. At the outset Captain Vancouver sent Lieut. Puget ashore to inform Quadra that he was prepared to salute the Spanish flag if he could be assured that the compliment would be returned. Quadra promptly agreeing, thirteen volleys were discharged from the British cannon and answered by thirteen volleys from the Spanish guns. Thereafter visits of the British to the Spaniards or the Spaniards to the British were accompanied by salutes from the artillery. Each arrival of a trading vessel called for additional salutes. Menzies, the botanist, wryly noted the consequences:

... there was scarcely a day past without puffings of this kind from some Vessel or other, & we too followed the example, & puffed it away as well as any of them, till at last we were obligd to get supplies of Powder from both the Spaniards & Traders before we left the Coast.[12]

Meanwhile the transfer of territory was being discussed by the two commissioners. Quadra had used his idle months in Nootka in collecting, from captains who had been trading on the coast in 1789, depositions contradicting Meares' account of what had happened.

[12] Menzies, *Journal*, p. 127.

He also secured a deposition from Maquinna, witnessed by seven
Spaniards, Portuguese and Americans (including an M.A. from the
University of Cambridge), declaring that the chief had never sold
any land to Meares. Confronted with these documents, Vancouver
replied that he had not come to negotiate a settlement, that having
been done in Madrid. He was here simply to receive possession of
Nootka according to the terms laid down by the Convention.
Quadra then agreed to hand over Nootka but stipulated that, since
there was a Spanish settlement at Neah Bay, the Strait of Juan de
Fuca must be recognized as a boundary for Spain, and that the seas
to the south of it must be recognized as closed to British commerce.
Vancouver retorted that he was aware that this "settlement" had
been founded only a few months before. Pointing out that San
Francisco was the most northerly Spanish settlement at the time of
the Nootka Incident, he declared that he could not view anything
north of San Francisco as being Spanish.

Quadra now found himself confronted with a very serious situation. Whereas he construed the Nootka Convention as giving the
British free access to the coast only as far south as Clayoquot Sound,
the British were declaring that the same convention permitted them
settlements right up to within ten leagues of San Francisco.[13] The
more Quadra thought about the British claim, the more he became
convinced that at this point Spain should not relinquish her title to
Nootka. Finally he informed Vancouver that, although the British
could have the use of the base which the Spaniards had built at
Nootka, with all its houses, gardens and miscellaneous facilities, the
actual title to all of these must remain with the King of Spain. The
only transfer of actual sovereignty that Quadra would make was
limited to one little cove with its shores, a triangle measuring little
more than a hundred yards on each side, the site where Meares had
had his house and built the *North West America*. Some of the
British had their own theory as to the cause of Quadra's hardened
position. They attributed it to Captain Joseph Ingraham, who at
this point in the negotiations had put into Nootka with his ship, the
Hope of Boston. It was all a matter of malevolence on the part of

---

[13] Cook, *Flood Tide of Empire*, p. 374. Cook discusses in great detail the negotiations between Vancouver and Quadra.

the Yankees, so recently their enemies during the American Revolution. The British suspicions about Ingraham being the troublemaker were recorded by Thomas Manby, whom Vancouver promoted at Nootka to be master of the *Chatham*. Says Manby:

> The arrival of an American Brig stopped the intended plans: the Master of her having sufficient influence with the Spaniards persuaded them that the treaty between the two nations only gave the English the spot which they were dispossessed of by Senr. Martinez.[14]

Manby is right about the influence Ingraham enjoyed with the Spaniards. Quadra, in his own record of the proceedings at Nootka, refers to him in glowing terms as "an active young man with great experience on the coast, and of great talent".[15]

It was, of course, absurd to expect that the British, after spending one million pounds in armaments to force Spain to yield Nootka, would be content with a single cove. For Vancouver to accept the offered acre could well be subsequently construed as acceptance of Quadra's interpretation of the Nootka Convention. Vancouver replied that either he must receive title to Nootka *in toto* or he would refuse to take any part of it. And here matters became hopelessly deadlocked. Fortunately the Nootka Convention had provided for just such a contingency by saying that, should the commissioners be unable to agree, they were to refer the disputed points to their home governments for renewed negotiation. Quadra and Vancouver agreed to do just that.

During the weeks spent on these troublesome negotiations, the civilized code of manners of the eighteenth century was never more punctiliously observed than on the savage shores of Nootka Sound. A personal friendship had developed between the two commanders. The benefits were almost wholly Vancouver's for Quadra lived in a manner befitting a grandee of Spain, even though the tiny Spanish settlement may not have numbered more than sixteen houses. The commanders of the ships which put in at Nootka were invariably invited to dine at Quadra's table. One of Gray's officers describes the sort of "grand entertainment" at the commandant's residence:

[14] Manby, "Journal", p. 35.
[15] Quadra, *Voyage*, p. 31.

... fifty four persons sat down to Dinner, and the plates, which were *solid silver*, was shifted five times, which made 270 Plates. the Dishes, Knifes and forks, and indeed evry thing else, was of Silver and always replaced with spare ones. There could be no mistake in this as they never carried the dirty plates or Dishes from the Hall where we dined (as *I thought*, on purpose to let us see the quantity of plate used by the Spaniards in South *America*).[16]

Captain Vancouver and his officers dining with Quadra had a similar experience: "A dinner of five courses, consisting of a superfluity of the best provisions, was served with great elegance." Almost every day British officers were guests at Quadra's table. For Vancouver's crews, Quadra sent vegetables from his gardens and fresh bread from his bakery.

One of the things which most impressed Vancouver about Quadra was the splendid relationship which he had established with the Indians. In part this was a result of the meticulous courtesy with which Quadra treated Maquinna. As one of the Spanish officers has recorded, "Macuina was endowed with remarkable ability and quickness of intelligence, and knew very well his rights as a sovereign."[17] Quadra scrupulously respected those rights, receiving him with honour when he joined white officers as a guest at his board. On the other hand the British, upon their first arrival, got off to a very bad start with Maquinna. The duty officer on the deck of the *Discovery*, not recognizing him as a chief, refused to allow him to come on board. Quadra at once set himself to reconcile the insulted Maquinna who, though he made it plain he would not like to see the British take the place of the Spaniards, gradually came to accept them as his friends also. A high point was reached early in September when Quadra and Vancouver paid a visit of compliment to Maquinna at his residence at Tahsis.

Archibald Menzies, surgeon and botanist with the Vancouver expedition, has left us a lively account of that occasion. The scene springs to life for us as Menzies describes how the English and Spaniards rowed up the smooth waters of the inlet under sunny skies, "with drums beating & Fifes playing to the no small entertain-

---

[16] Howay, *Voyages of the "Columbia"*, p. 411.

[17] [Cardero], *A Spanish Voyage*, p. 17.

ment of the Natives". And he tells us how at Tahsis, after the Indians had entertained their guests with a show "in imitation of various characters of different Countries, some represented Europeans armed with Muskets & Bayonets, others were dressed as Chinese & others as Sandwich Islanders",[18] Captain Vancouver reciprocated by having some of his British tars dance a reel or two to the music of the fife.

After the final deadlock over the transfer of Nootka, there was no point in Quadra remaining absent any longer from his headquarters in Mexico. On September 22nd he set sail for the south, pausing en route to evacuate the abortive Spanish colony at Neah Bay. A week later Captain Vancouver sent Lieut. Mudge to England aboard a trading vessel which was sailing for China. With him Mudge carried despatches fully acquainting the British government of the failure to secure possession of Nootka Sound. In mid-October Vancouver set sail with the *Discovery*, *Chatham* and *Daedalus*, enjoying further Spanish hospitality at San Francisco and Monterey before sailing to spend the rest of the winter in Hawaii. While the British had been en route down coast, Lieut. Broughton had explored the Columbia River for about eighty-four miles upstream. This was a considerably greater distance than Gray had gone, but it could not eliminate the fact that the Americans had been the first actually to enter the river. However, at the highest point he reached on the Columbia, Broughton "formally took possession of the river, and the country in its vicinity, in His Britannic Majesty's name".[19] From Monterey Captain Vancouver sent Broughton to England by way of Mexico City, to make sure of despatches reaching the Admiralty should any misadventure overtake Mudge.

One of the letters Broughton carried with him to England was an interesting one by Joseph Whidbey, master of the *Discovery*. In it Whidbey urged that a British trading company be created with its main base on Barkley Sound, and subordinate bases in the Queen Charlotte Islands and at the mouth of the Columbia River. He also felt that Britain should lose no time in getting part of the country

[18] Menzies, *Journal*, pp. 116-19.
[19] Vancouver, *Voyage*, II:66.

settled and agriculture begun. Whidbey thought it would be a good idea for Britain to establish a convict colony "at the Head of Fuca Straights" — presumably in the area of Port Discovery, Washington.[20]

[20] "A Letter from the Vancouver Expedition", ed. Hardin Craig, Jr., *Pacific North West Quarterly* 41 (1950) : 352-55.

1793

Sir Alexander Mackenzie — Early life and entry into fur trade — Journey to the Arctic — His second quest for the Pacific — Difficulties of the journey — Down the Fraser — The West Road River route to the Pacific Ocean — Inscription at Dean Channel — Mackenzie's return journey — Previous arrival at Dean Channel of Captain Vancouver — Vancouver's men see first totem poles — Women wearing labrets — Poisonous mussels — Alaskan waters — Vancouver sails for California.

Thus far in our chronicle we have spoken of Spain and Britain, Russia and the United States but now, for the first time, we have the name of a nation yet unborn. This year, with an added significance which he surely never suspected, a young Scot aged about twenty-nine painted upon a rock near Bella Coola, "ALEX MACKENZIE FROM CANADA BY LAND 22d JULY 1793".[1] The "Canada" whose name he wrote was a British colony comprising parts of Quebec and Ontario, populated largely by an unlikely combination of French peasants who had remained after France lost Quebec and British loyalists who had recently emigrated from the United States of America. Due in part to the words painted that day on the rock rising above the Pacific at Bella Coola, Canada would become one day a splendid nation with the proud motto, *"A mari usque ad mare"*, from ocean to ocean.

Born in Scotland probably in 1764, Alexander Mackenzie was a boy about ten when his widower father took him to the Colony of New York in 1774. When the American Revolution broke out,

---

[1] Such is the inscription as it appears today on Mackenzie's Rock. See, however, footnote 10 and the passage to which it refers.

Alexander Mackenzie's father and uncle fought for the King as officers in the Royal Regiment of New York, while the young boy was sent to Montreal to receive his schooling. Montreal was of course the base for the Canadian fur trading firms which were increasingly competing with the Hudson's Bay Company. Young Mackenzie's first job was in the Montreal office of a fur trading merchant. In 1785 he was off on his first fur trading expedition into the "Indian Country". Two years later he was a partner in that most important of all the Montreal-based fur concerns, the famous North West Company. Increasingly Mackenzie became aware that the fur trade, ever extending westward, must at length outrun its lines of supply from Hudson Bay or Montreal. Bases should be established on the Pacific, from which the most westerly posts could be serviced. But how did one reach the Pacific? Nobody had ever crossed North America north of Mexico.

In 1789 young Mackenzie set out from Fort Chipewyan to find the Pacific. He returned 102 days later, having travelled about 3000 miles and reached salt water. Unfortunately the river down which he had travelled, one which today bears his name, emptied into the Arctic, not the Pacific.

In 1792 Mackenzie was ready for a second attempt. Setting out from Fort Chipewyan that fall, he established an advance base near the junction of the Peace River and the Smoky, and wintered there. On 9 May 1793 he set out for a second time in search of the Pacific. In his journal for that day Mackenzie wrote:

. . . the canoe was put into the water: her dimensions were twenty-five feet long within, exclusive of the curves of stem and stern, twenty-six inches hold, and four feet nine inches beam. At the same time she was so light, that two men could carry her on a good road [trail] three or four miles without resting. In this slender vessel, we shipped provisions, goods for presents, arms, ammunition, and baggage, to the weight of three thousand pounds, and an equipage of ten people; viz. Alexander Mackay, Joseph Landry, Charles Ducette, François Beaulieux, Baptist Bisson, François Courtois, and Jacques Beauchamp, with two Indians as hunters and interpreters.[2]

2 W. Kaye Lamb, ed., *The Journals and Letters of Sir Alexander Mackenzie*, Hakluyt Society (Cambridge, 1970), p. 257.

They also had with them Mackenzie's dog which accompanied them all the way to the Pacific.

The journey upon which Mackenzie had now embarked was the greatest and most heroic venture in the whole history of the exploration of British Columbia. Nobody can begin to appreciate the hardships of Mackenzie and his little band unless he himself has shot down one of British Columbia's raging rivers in a canoe, and laboured by tow-line and pole to make headway upstream, has experienced the sudden dangers of unknown rapids, rocks, snags or "sweepers" or, most dangerous of all, huge barriers of jammed drift-wood which totally obstruct the channel while the swift current flowing beneath the log jams can, in an instant, suck under canoe and canoeists. Really to know what Mackenzie's men endured, one must oneself have hacked portages along mountain sides and dragged heavy canoes across them then, back in the stream, have waded for hours through icy waters "siwashing" one's canoe through shallow boulder-strewn channels, until all feeling is lost in the feet and at night, by the campfire, one's skin turns black. One must have had the experience of backpacking, for days on end, loads of ninety pounds amid heat, flies and mosquitoes. Only those who have done all these things can truly appreciate what Mackenzie and his men went through as, without maps and relying upon uncertain directions from the Indians, they plunged deeper and deeper into the mountains, forests, muskegs and plateaus of the nameless land.

There is not space here to trace in detail Mackenzie's progress. Anyone with a feeling for British Columbia's history owes it to himself to read Mackenzie's account of that great journey. All that can be offered here is the briefest of summaries with a few illustrative quotations.

Ten days after setting out, Mackenzie and his men reached the Peace River Canyon. With no idea of the insurmountable obstacle it constituted, they decided to try to take their canoe through it. As the current got worse and worse, they had to rely almost entirely upon lining it upstream. Watching his men pulling at the rope by which they laboriously hauled their canoe up the rapids, Mackenzie was anything but happy:

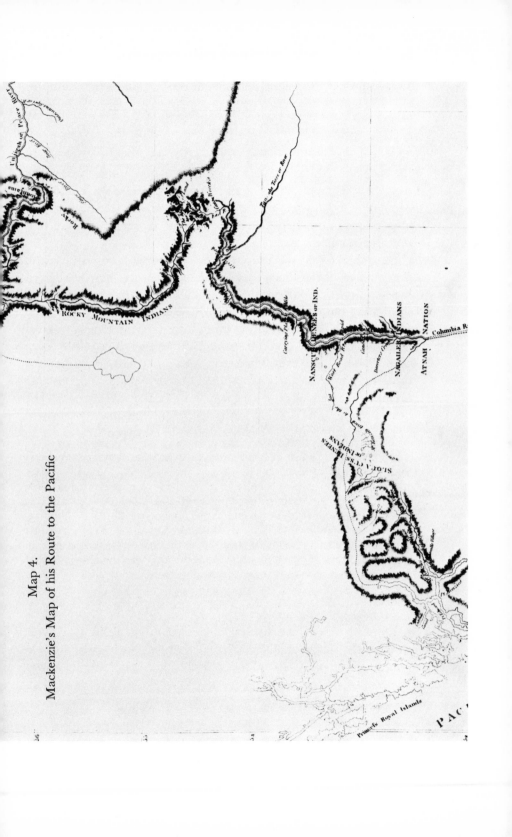

Map 4.

Mackenzie's Map of his Route to the Pacific

... I could not but reflect, with infinite anxiety, on the hazard of my enterprize: one false step of those attached to the line, or the breaking of the line itself, would have at once consigned the canoe, and every thing it contained, to instant destruction. .... [3]

They would be left stranded in the wilderness, totally destitute. In the end, even Mackenzie had to admit that to continue through the canyon was impossible. A trail was cut up the slope of Portage Mountain and down to the head of the canyon. Sweating and straining, his men portaged their canoe and all its freight a distance of some seven miles.

Re-embarked on the Peace, Mackenzie worked his way up it to the junction of the Finlay and the Parsnip Rivers (now submerged beneath artificial Williston Lake). All his inclinations were to go up the Finlay but, relying upon the advice he had received from an Indian, he went up the Parsnip instead. By June 7th their canoe had been so battered on rocks, snags and shallows as to be "little better than a wreck" and even Mackenzie who drove his men relentlessly, breaking camp as early as 3 a.m. and travelling until 7 p.m., decided that they must pause for half a day and make repairs. The next day they saw a small group of Sekani Indians, who showed every sign of distrust as Mackenzie brought his canoe ashore:

They, however, laid aside their weapons, and when I stepped forward and took each of them by the hand, one of them, but with a very tremulous action, drew his knife from his sleeve, and presented it to me as a mark of his submission to my will and pleasure. On our first hearing the noise of these people in the woods, we displayed our flag, which was now shewn to them as a token of friendship. They examined us, and every thing about us, with a minute and suspicious attention. They had heard, indeed, of white men, but this was the first time that they had ever seen an human being of a complexion different from their own.[4]

From the Sekanis they learned of a great river (the Fraser) to the south, and one of the Indians consented to go along as a guide through the tangle of lakes and small streams which lay ahead. On June 12th the party crossed the watershed into the Fraser basin and

[3] *Ibid.*, p. 267.
[4] *Ibid.*, p. 286.

for the first time in over a month found themselves travelling with the current. Amid the hideous difficulties of James Creek (or Bad River, as Mackenzie named it), disaster came. The canoe hit an obstruction and spun at right angles to the torrent, which broke the canoe on a bar. Swept onwards again, Mackenzie's craft shattered its stern on a rock, and the steersman could no longer direct it. Striving to bring it ashore, one of the men caught a branch of a tree. The canoe was swept relentlessly downstream and the man found himself suddenly catapulted ashore by the backlash of the branch. Plunging onward, the canoe entered a cascade where two large holes were smashed in its bottom. The wreck settled flat with the water. Responding to Mackenzie's peremptory commands, the men stayed with the ruined craft and finally managed to get it ashore.

The Indians, when they saw our deplorable situation, instead of making the least effort to help us, sat down and gave vent to their tears. I was on the outside of the canoe, where I remained till every thing was got on shore, in a state of great pain from the extreme cold of the water; so that at length, it was with difficulty I could stand, from the benumbed state of my limbs.[5]

Amazingly, very little had been lost in the wreck. The next day was spent drying ammunition and repairing the canoe. Then they were on their way again, but the strains were beginning to tell and one of the stoic French-Canadians refused to continue until, by a mixture of ridicule and flattery, Mackenzie brought him around. Two days later their Sekani guide deserted them. Pushing on as best they could without him, on June 18th Mackenzie's party reached the broad-flowing waters of the Fraser River.

Sweeping down the Fraser they came to Fort George Canyon, where they found the waters impassable:

We had therefore no alternative but to widen the road [trail] so as to admit the passage of our canoe, which was now carried with great difficulty; as from her frequent repairs, and not always of the usual materials, her weight was such, that she cracked and broke on the shoulders of the men who bore her. The labour and fatigue of this undertaking, from eight till twelve, beggars all description. . . . [6]

5 *Ibid.*, p. 298.
6 *Ibid.*, p. 307.

Taking to the Fraser again, on June 21st they passed Quesnel River. Later this same day they met Indians on the river who uttered threats and shot arrows at the canoe. Mackenzie, however, desperately needed directions from these Indians as to where the river ran, and how he might best make a route to the Pacific:

I therefore formed the following adventurous project, which was happily crowned with success. I left the canoe, and walked by myself along the beach, in order to induce some of the natives to come to me, which I imagined they might be disposed to do, when they saw me alone, without any apparent possibility of receiving assistance from my people. . . . [7]

The gambit worked. Unaware that Mackenzie was covered by one of his own Indians placed in hiding, two Indians finally came ashore and accepted the offered beads. Soon friendly communications were established and Mackenzie was receiving the information he desired. The river down which he was travelling continued south a very great distance going through canyons which no canoe could pass in safety. On the other hand, if he would retrace his route for a considerable distance upstream he would reach a point where Indian trails would take him to the coast in a week or so.

Working his way back up the Fraser with his discouraged men, who now wanted to abandon the expedition, Mackenzie found that the Indians, though previously friendly, had turned panicky and hostile. On June 24th a recently acquired guide deserted them. Providentially he returned five days later when Mackenzie was having his men build a new canoe on an island near Cottonwood Canyon. Resuming his journey upstream Mackenzie, whose provisions were running low, had to put his men on half-rations. On July 3rd they reached a stream which Mackenzie named the West Road River, since it was the beginning of the trade route by which the local Indians trafficked with tribes living on the Pacific Coast.

At this point Mackenzie laid the whole situation before his semi-mutinous followers. His candour and unique aura of leadership carried the day. Unanimously they agreed to follow him westwards. After making a cache of part of their pemmican, gunpowder and

[7] *Ibid.*, p. 313.

trade goods under the ashes of their fire, and leaving their canoe in a place safely out of the sun, they prepared for their march to the Pacific.

We carried on our back four bags and a half of pemmican, weighing from eighty-five to ninety pounds each; a case with my instruments, a parcel of goods for presents, weighing ninety pounds, and a parcel containing ammunition of the same weight. Each of the Canadians had a burden of about ninety pounds, with a gun, and some ammunition. The Indians [the two he had recruited at Fort Chipewyan the previous year] had about forty-five pounds weight of pemmican to carry, besides their gun, &c. with which they were very much dissatisfied, and if they had dared would have instantly left us. They had hitherto been very much indulged, but the moment was now arrived when indulgence was no longer practicable. My own load, and that of Mr. Mackay, consisted of twenty-two pounds of pemmican, some rice, a little sugar, &c. amounting in the whole to about seventy pounds each, besides our arms and ammunitions. I had also the tube of my telescope swung across my shoulder, which was a troublesome addition to my burthen.[8]

The next two weeks saw the heavily burdened men pushing onward towards the Pacific. By and large the Indians were friendly and provided them with guides. Finally after crossing the 6000 foot high Mackenzie Pass, they descended into the valley of the Bella Coola River. Never were they more warmly greeted than by the Bella Coola Indians who welcomed them with embraces, feasted them, and presented Mackenzie with a splendid robe of sea otter skins. On July 19th Mackenzie reached another village and recorded, in the most anti-climactic of statements, his first view of the Pacific: "From these houses I could perceive the termination of the river, and its discharge into a narrow arm of the sea."[9]

Mackenzie was not content merely with sighting the Pacific — he wished to explore some distance along its shore. Guided by a young chief, he and his party started along the coast of North Bentinck Arm on July 21st. But now they encountered increasing hostility and truculence on the part of the Indians they met. Their guide entreated them to turn back if they wished to preserve their

8 *Ibid.*, p. 339.
9 *Ibid.*, p. 372.

lives. Finally, coming to a great rock on Dean Channel, Mackenzie decided he had reached his journey's end:

I now mixed up some vermilion in melted grease, and inscribed, in large characters, on the South-East face of the rock on which we had slept last night, this brief memorial — "Alexander MacKenzie, from Canada, by land, the twenty-second of July, one thousand seven hundred and ninety-three."[10]

A month later, on August 24th, their flag flying, volleys echoing from their muskets, Mackenzie and his men arrived back at Fort Forks from which they had set out that May. They had reason to celebrate. Without the loss of a single man, they had completed one of the world's greatest expeditions of inland exploration.

Mackenzie, when he had embarked briefly upon the waters of the Pacific, had encountered Indians who, as already noted, met him with open hostility:

One of them in particular made me understand, with an air of insolence, that a large canoe had lately been in this bay, with people in her like me, and that one of them, whom he called *Macubah*, had fired on him and his friends. . . . [11]

"Macubah" was Captain George Vancouver, who had in fact been surveying Dean Channel at the beginning of June. After wintering in Hawaii, H.M.S. *Discovery* and H.M.S. *Chatham* had made for Nootka. There they found a notable change. Lieut. Salvador Fidalgo, partly to keep his men occupied over the winter, had greatly strengthened the Spanish fortifications:

When we were here last year, there was only a platform on Hog Island, off which Mr. Quadra took the few remaining Guns we saw at our first coming in, but we now found on the same spot a regular Fort, forming a Square, having 12 Embrasures in three sides of it, at present 11 Guns were only mounted here, four of which were pointed to the Southward, four to the Eastward, and the other 3 to command the

---

[10] *Ibid.*, p. 378. Actually this journal survives only as revised and given literary elegance by William Combe. It seems most unlikely that Mackenzie, daubing his famous message on the rock, would have observed the niceties of punctuation and the extreme formality of spelling out the dates.

[11] *Ibid.*, p. 375.

North side of the Cove, the Parapet was built of thick Plank, fill'd with earth. . . . [12]

After the two British ships rendezvoused at Restoration Bay on Burke Channel at the end of May, they resumed their survey of the continental shore north of where they had left off the previous year. Once more the ships periodically moved from station to station, always anchoring at nightfall as they edged their way along the incredibly intricate coast with its perils of fog, storm, rock and reef, as well as currents which could at times make even the *Discovery* "totally ungovernable". Each time the two ships anchored at a new station it was back to the old routine with the small boats being away from seven to ten days at a time, the men generally sleeping in the boats at night, starting out rowing or sailing at 4 a.m. and continuing until 7 p.m. The work was hard enough when the weather was fine and food adequate. But sometimes the rain poured down for days on end, while the men tried to keep dry under the canopies they raised over the open boats. At other times the zeal of their officers took them so far from the ships that food ran low and they could be down to half a pint of peas per man for their day's ration. With profound relief the men in the small boats came back from these surveys to the comparative luxury of life aboard the *Discovery* and the *Chatham*.

Various diversions broke the monotony. Vancouver's men had learned the year before of the great value that the Indians attached to abalone shell and, while they were at Monterey, had laid in a stock of the commodity. Now, trading with the Indians, they gave four shells for a sea otter pelt. As the ships moved northward new sights were seen. At one of the villages Vancouver saw totem poles, apparently for the first time:

. . . near one or two of the most conspicuous mansions were carved figures in large logs of timber, representing a gigantic human form, with strange and uncommonly distorted features.[13]

Now that Vancouver and his crew were entering the area of the

[12] Edward Bell, *Journal of Voyage on H.M.S. "Chatham" 1791-94*, p. 121. MS in Alexander Turnbull Library, Wellington, New Zealand.

[13] Vancouver, *Voyage*, II: 272.

northern Indians, forever warring against each other, they found a
new kind of fortified village built on piles on a rock. And for the first
time they saw women with labrets in their lower lips. Until the use
of the labret died out in the later part of the next century, practically
every white visitor to the north coast had some appalled comments
to make on the resulting appearance of the women. Typical is the
comment of Edward Bell, clerk aboard H.M.S. *Chatham*, who this
year wrote in his journal:

Here we saw some of the American Women for the first time this Year,
and here for the first time we saw in them the horrid & frightful
ornament of the Lip-piece of which I had before heard a great deal;
But all that I had heard, had given me but a faint idea of the reality.
— I never beheld any thing in man or woman half so disgusting. An
orifice is made in the thick part of the Lower Lip parrallel with the
mouth, into which is fitted a piece of wood of an eliptical form about
the thickness of an Inch or an Inch and a half in the edge or sides
of this, all round, is a groove that admits the lips of the Orifice — it
stands Horizontal from the mouth, and the upper and lower sides of
the wooden piece are excavated, or in plaine language hollowed in the
shape of the inside of a Saucer. This operation is performed on the
women when about 11 or 12 years of age for the first time; — it is then
made very small and stretched with either a bit of wood, or a piece of
Copper Wire, from time to time according to the rank of the woman,
or as she advances in years — the orifice is enlarged, and a fresh
wooden piece put in. — till at last they stretch the orifice in the lip to
an Extent of three inches in common — but more particularly in the
aged women & women of rank, and I am sure I do not exagerate when
I say that I have seen some of their diabolical ornaments of wood three
inches & a half in length, and upwards of two & a half in breadth. As
may readily be supposed, this beauteous ornament affects their Speech
— or rather their articulation in a very great degree, and it is droll to
observe this enormous Trencher, wagging up and down at every word
the wearer says. . . . Besides the unnatural and frightful appearance this
thing makes in itself, it is rendered still more disgusting from the
quantity of dirt & Filth about it, for from its size, its Horizontal
position, and hollowed shape it is calculated to, and does receive every
filth that comes from the parts above it. . . . [14]

Grim and dour though Captain Vancouver might be, a tyrant to
his high-spirited young midshipmen, he nonetheless took very good

[14] Bell, *Journal*, pp. 143-45.

care of his men. Not a single man came down with scurvy during the long voyage out from England. On June 15th, however, while surveying the coast near Princess Royal Island, he did have the misfortune to lose a man, but the circumstances were entirely beyond his control. Cutters from the *Discovery* and *Chatham* were out on a routine survey of one of the inlets when some of the men, for their breakfast, roasted mussels which were abundant on the beach where they had landed. Back in the boats they were seized with numbness and giddiness. Landing as soon as he realized the trouble, Lieut. Johnstone ordered water warmed and gave it to the afflicted men to drink as an emetic. Unfortunately one of the men was too far gone to take the warm water and died a little more than five hours after eating the poisonous mussels. That night he was buried on the shore of the bay where the boats had put in and camped. When the boats finally rejoined the ships, the episode was reported to Captain Vancouver, who subsequently recorded:

To this bay I gave the name of CARTER'S BAY, after this poor unfortunate fellow; it is situated in latitude 52°48', longitude 231°42': and to distinguish the fatal spot where the muscles [*sic*] were eaten, I have called it POISON COVE, and the branch leading to it MUSCLE CANAL.[15]

The names of Carter Bay, Poison Cove and Mussel Inlet appear on the maps to this day. For the rest of their cruise Vancouver's men had to deny themselves the pleasures of their frequent mussel and clam bakes.

By late July Vancouver's men were thoroughly tired of this "dismal unfriendly coast". One evening the *Discovery* and *Chatham*, amid gloom, fog and impending gale, were anxiously feeling their way through the "intricate inhospitable labyrinth" of islets and rocks when to their amazement they saw a whaleboat rowing towards them. It had been sent out by Captain Brown of the British trading ship *Butterworth* which, with its consorts *Prince Lee Boo* and *Jackal*, was at anchor nearby. Led by the whaleboat, the British warships joined them in a snug and commodious harbour. Vancouver records:

[15] Vancouver, *Voyage*, II: 286.

Soon after we had anchored, Mr. Brown visited the Discovery, and I believe I may venture to assert, that the satisfaction arising from meeting with our fellow countrymen in such distant regions of the globe was very mutual on this occasion.[16]

Brown informed Vancouver that no great distance off was "a village of the natives, whose improper conduct made it necessary to fire upon them from the vessels, which was attended with some slaughter".[17] The next day Brown lent Vancouver the *Jackal* to pilot him through the tricky waters leading to Observatory Inlet.

At the beginning of August, after surveying Observatory Inlet and Portland Canal, Vancouver and his men crossed into Alaskan waters and out of the purview of this book, though we may note that up in Alaska Vancouver very narrowly escaped the fate of Captain Cook, and two of his men were grievously injured with spears, when Indians who had seemed completely friendly launched a murderous attack upon one of the detached small boats.

On September 22nd, well up into Alaskan waters, Captain Vancouver decided to end his explorations for the season and turn south. En route to Nootka he took the opportunity to make a fleeting survey of the west coast of the Queen Charlotte Islands. This completed his work for the season. Much of the area which Vancouver had surveyed this summer had been examined superficially the previous year by Caamaño, and Vancouver had Caamaño's charts with him. The British, doggedly working up to the end of each inlet, at one point travelling 700 miles in order to carry their survey 60 miles up the coast, viewed the Spanish surveys both here and elsewhere with little professional respect:

But indeed the Spaniards seem to be but very bad surveyors, and in all their Charts of this Coast that I have seen, their work has been very imperfectly done; I have scarcely observed in any of them any of the extensive openings, or Inlets of the Sea finished, they seem to be content with laying down the entrances of the places on the outside side (and even those with no great degree of accuracy) — without ever

16 *Ibid.*, II:324.
17 *Ibid.*, II:325.

penetrating any farther, or endeavouring to trace these formidable openings to their head.[18]

Vancouver had hoped to find his supply ship *Daedalus* back from Australia awaiting him at Nootka. Continuing on, he finally met her south of San Francisco. After calling at San Francisco, Monterey, Santa Barbara and San Diego, Vancouver sailed once more to Hawaii and spent the winter in that delectable clime.

[18] Bell, *Journal*, p. 155.

1794

*Vancouver surveys from Cook Inlet to Port Conclusion —
General Alava at Nootka — Vancouver sails for home — The
Haidas capture an American schooner.*

On March 15th Captain Vancouver left Hawaii for his third year
of surveying the North-west Coast of America. This year he made
for Cook's River in Alaska, the point at which Captain Cook had
begun his detailed study of the coast running northwards. Vancouver
found Cook's River not to be a river at all, and accordingly renamed
it Cook's Inlet. This was the northern boundary set for his own
surveying, and he began to work his way south, after taking his leave
of Russians who assured him that he had reached territory belonging
exclusively to the Russian Empire.

On August 19th, the small boats doing the inshore surveying
returned from their final trip with news that they had reached the
point at which they had discontinued their survey the previous year.
Captain Vancouver joyfully gave the name of Port Conclusion to
the bay where H.M.S. *Discovery* and H.M.S. *Chatham* were
anchored during this final exploration. And he gave his men a
chance to celebrate:

> In order that the valuable crews of both vessels, on whom great
> hardships and manual labour had fallen, and who had uniformly
> encountered their difficulties with unremitting exertion, cheerfulness
> and obedience, might celebrate the day, that had thus terminated their
> labours in these regions; they were served such an additional allowance
> of grog as was fully sufficient to answer every purpose of festivity on
> the occasion. This soon prompted a desire for mutual congratulations
> between the two vessels, expressed by three exulting cheers from each;
> and it may be easily conceived that more heart-felt satisfaction was
> scarcely ever more reciprocally experienced, or more cordially
> exchanged.[1]

[1] Vancouver, *Voyage*, III:272.

His great task completed, Vancouver lost no time in starting south. On September 2nd he arrived at Nootka to find no fewer than three Spanish warships and three fur trading vessels anchored in Friendly Cove. One of the Spanish ships had arrived only the previous day with Brigadier-General Don José Manuel de Alava, who was both the new governor of Nootka and the new Spanish commissioner for carrying out the terms of the Nootka Convention. Unfortunately he had not yet received any word as to how Britain and Spain had resolved the matters referred to them by Vancouver and Quadra. Similarly no letter dealing with this matter had yet arrived for Vancouver. The two commissioners decided to wait at Nootka until mid-October for these long-delayed instructions from their home governments. Meanwhile there was plenty of work for Vancouver's men in getting their battered ships readied for the long voyage back to England by way of Cape Horn. The British were anxious to get away, long tired of the North Pacific and eager to see action in the war which they knew now existed between Britain and France.

Writing from Nootka to a friend, Vancouver declared:

... I expected no farther detention in this hemisphere not doubting but the business respecting these territories must have been settled a sufficient length of time for a vessel to have arrived by whome we might be relieved and proceed on our route towards Old England in hopes to partake of some shair in the glorious and honorable cause her Fleets and Armies are at present engaged in, but in these espectations [sic] we are disappointed no vessel having arrive[d] from England to that effect nor have I received any information in answer to my dispatches sent home by Mudge and Broughton. . . .

Thus you see my good friend I am once more entrapped in this infernal ocean. . . . [2]

Menzies, the naturalist, wrote to Sir Joseph Banks in the same vein:

... Captain Vancouver does not conceive himself authorized to leave this coast, untill he has some further orders from home; so that we do not know how long we may still remain in this dreary Country, of which we are all heartily tired. . . . [3]

[2] "Original Vancouver Letters", *WHQ* 18 (1927):55-56.
[3] Letter of 1 Oct. 1794. Botany Library of Natural History Museum, London, D.T.C., Vol. IX:105-108.

In mid-October Vancouver moved his ships down to the sunnier skies of Monterey. After lingering here for another month, still vainly awaiting instructions, Vancouver had had enough. At the beginning of December he sailed for home.

Vancouver's three summers on the coast had given him ample opportunity to observe the activities of the fur trading ships, both British and American. Vancouver did not like what he had seen. The traders' readiness to sell arms to the Indians seemed to him reprehensible, and he had more than that to lay against them:

> ... I am extremely concerned to be compelled to state here, that many of the traders from the civilized world have not only pursued a line of conduct, diametrically opposite to the true principles of justice in their commercial dealings, but have fomented discords, and stirred up contentions, between the different tribes, in order to increase the demand for these destructive engines.[4]

It was a dangerous game that the traders were playing. Little was needed, under the best conditions, to provoke the Indians to attack. Sometimes mere human cupidity, a desire to acquire free all the goods in a trading vessel, was enough to cause an attempted coup. In one instance the natives attempted to seize a ship because of a naive belief that possession of a ship would make them the match of the newcomers. Such motives were strongly augmented when savage desires for revenge were aroused by the tactics of the traders. The skippers who commanded these vessels knew, of course, the risks that they ran. Whenever an Indian attack seemed possible, standard procedures were followed — all guns were loaded, riflemen were sent to stations high on the masts, and great boarding nets were swung into position, from bow to stern, denying access to the deck to any attackers. Nevertheless there were successful attacks. This year in the Queen Charlotte Islands, Chief Cumshewa and his Haidas captured the American schooner *Resolution*, massacring all but one of her crew.

[4] Vancouver, *Voyage*, II:364.

1795

*Alava and Pearce carry out provisions of Nootka Convention
— Nootka abandoned — Vancouver's voyage home — Captain Bishop and the* Ruby *— His meeting with Chief Shakes.*

On March 28th of this year a brief ceremony took place in Friendly Cove at Nootka. Into the bay had sailed the Spanish warship *Activa*. From it had landed Brigadier-General Alava and a newly-appointed British commissioner, Lieut. Thomas Pearce[1] of the Royal Marines. The two commissioners exchanged documents, and the British flag was raised in sign of restored possession of the area where Meares had built his house back in 1788. Then Pearce lowered the flag and handed it to Maquinna with directions to hoist it whenever a ship put in at Nootka. Everything from the shore establishment that could be carried away had been put aboard ship. All that was left was abandoned to the Indians, who soon tore down the houses in their quest for nails, and once more built their lodges on the village site which the Spaniards had taken from them.

Under the revision of the Nootka Convention, signed in Madrid in January of the previous year, both Britain and Spain had bound themselves not to maintain any permanent base in Nootka, though the ships of each could put in there on temporary visits. Both countries had also pledged themselves to keep any other country from establishing sovereignty there.

At the moment when the British flag was hoisted at Nootka, Captain Vancouver was off the coast of Chile on his homeward voyage. Entering the Atlantic he had a special anxiety, fear of being

---

[1] The name is frequently given as Pierce. The files of the Royal Marines show no Lieut. Pierce serving in 1795, but do list a 1st Lieut. Thomas Pearce. (Letter of 3 June 1971, from Royal Marines Historian.)

For Pearce's account of the proceedings, see J. Forsyth, "Documents Connected with the Final Settlement of the Nootka Dispute", *B.C. Historical Assn. Second Annual Report* (1924), pp. 33-35.

intercepted by one of the French warships on the prowl for British ships. H.M.S. *Discovery*, lightly armed as a survey ship rather than a man-of-war, and worn out by four and a half years of voyaging, could not hope to defend herself successfully against a French cruiser. Vancouver's great voyage could end all too possibly with him and his crews rotting in a French prison. At St. Helena he received very welcome news: the French National Assembly, recognizing the contribution to human knowledge rendered by the Vancouver expedition, had instructed its warships not to molest the *Discovery* and the *Chatham* on their homeward journey. Separated from the *Chatham*, Vancouver decided to take no chances and, meeting with a British convoy, joined it. On September 13th the *Discovery* dropped anchor in the mouth of the Shannon River in Ireland and, leaving her there, Captain Vancouver hastened to London.

Back on the British Columbia coast there was a new arrival this year, the *Ruby*, a British ship from Bristol. Her journal survives and is of considerable interest. These eighteenth century visitors were far from being impressed by the beauty and grandeur of British Columbia's inlets. Captain Bishop of the *Ruby* is typical when he declares: "The amazing high mountains hanging over us, their Tops covered with Snow, and the water gushing down in Perpendicular streams formed a Cold, rude, and unpleasant scene."[2]

Like other traders, Bishop was impressed by the dominance the women held among the Haidas, ordering the men about, making the final trading decisions, and actively participating in the fighting. Another trader noted that the Haida women did not hesitate to beat their men if they displeased them.[3]

At this period the most powerful Indian chief on the northern British Columbia coast was the famous Shakes. Bishop offers a vivid picture of his meeting with Shakes and the subsequent trading:

In the Afternoon, Shakes in a large Cannoe Paddled by 20 men with his two Wives, his Son, and Several Other chiefs, Attended by 2 Large

[2] Michael Roe, ed., *The Journal and Letters of Captain Charles Bishop on the North-West Coast of America, in the Pacific and in New South Wales 1794-1799*, Hakluyt Society (Cambridge, 1967), p. 75.

[3] F. W. Howay, "The Voyage of the *Hope*: 1790-1792", *WHQ* 11 (1920):16.

cannoes full of Arm'd Men ... came Paddling down to the Ship, Singing, with Great Melody, in which every voice but the chief joined, the Song of Peace. Being arrived alongside they lay on their Paddles some time viewing the Hu'en Clue (GREAT SHIP). Shakes appear'd to be about 40 years of age and was of a respectable Figure, but the Small Pox with which he was Covered, though it appeared to be in the latest stages of the disorder, rendered him a Piteous object: nevertheless after some invitation he came on board and Giving me a Fraternal Embrace, (a ceremony I thought Proper not to decline) Presented a dress of those Skins I have before spoke of — a Laced Hatt and a Silver hilted sword were Presents suitable in return, and highly Gratifying to the Chief, who after being regaled with Biscuit and Butter and a few Glasses of wine retired to his Cannoe, and the Trade commenced, an old good Humered Blind (but cunning Man) conducting the whole of it, for all the Cannoes, who whould sell nothing, till the Goods had been put into his hands, and his Assent given. It was a matter of astonishment to us, to see how readily he would find a Flaw in the Iron &c and by feeling the Furs, the Price they ought to fetch.[4]

4 Bishop, *Journal*, pp. 70-71.

1796

Broughton returns with H.M.S. Providence — *Fur trade in decline.*

In March of this year there sailed into Nootka Sound, fresh from England, H.M.S. *Providence,* commanded by William Broughton, with Zachary Mudge as his first lieutenant. Since they had become acquainted with the coast while serving under Vancouver, they had been sent hither with credentials to accept Nootka from the Spaniards. To their disgust they found their mission pointless, Alava and Pearce having attended to the business the previous year. Since the *Providence* was leaking badly, Broughton spent a couple of months at Nootka repairing his ship. Then he left to survey the islands off Japan.

The usual fur trading ships were off the coast again this year, but their number was reduced to six, probably because of a slump in the prices being paid in the Canton market.[1]

[1] Bishop, *Journal,* p. 176.

1797

John Finlay explores lower Finlay River.

Created by Bennett Dam, the debris-strewn waters of Williston Lake now lie where once two notable rivers met. These were the Finlay and the Parsnip, which formerly converged at Finlay Forks to form the Peace River. In 1793 when Mackenzie had arrived at these forks he had wisely followed the advice of the Indians rather than his own inclination, and turned southwards up the Parsnip on his way to the Pacific. The suspicion lingered, however, that perhaps an easier way to the Pacific might be found by going up the Finlay River. This year, to decide the matter, the North West Company sent John Finlay up the Peace River with directions to follow the northerly tributary. Little is known of this expedition. Possibly Finlay got up the river (subsequently named for him) as far as its junction with the Ingenika. In any event, he was able to report that navigation of the Finlay River was blocked by impassable rapids and waterfalls. It was fortunate that Mackenzie had not gone that way.

1798

Vancouver's death — Publication of his Voyage of Discovery.

Captain Vancouver had not been in robust health when he set out on his great voyage and during its course he had periodically required treatment by Menzies who, besides being the expedition's botanist, was qualified as a surgeon. Vancouver's appearance when he returned to England in 1795 must have been something of a shock to those who met him:

> Ever since Captain Vancouver's last return to England, his health has been in a very debilitated state, and his constitution was evidently so much impaired by the arduous services in which, from his earliest youth, he had been constantly engaged, that his friends dared to indulge but little hope that he would continue many years amongst them.[1]

Probably he was suffering from tuberculosis.

Despite his failing health, Vancouver devoted himself to his final task, preparing for publication an account of his famous expedition. Vancouver had almost completed writing this work and had received the great part of it in proof from the printers when, stopping at the Star and Garter Inn in Richmond, he died in May of this year.

He was buried in the churchyard of the nearby village of Petersham. His grave, carefully tended at the expense of the Province of British Columbia, is a modest one. Its headstone reads simply:

CAPTAIN GEORGE VANCOUVER
Died in the Year 1798
Aged 40

Above that headstone rises a British Columbia dogwood tree. By a happy coincidence, it is in blossom each spring on the anniversary of

[1] John Vancouver, "Advertisement", prefaced to Vancouver, *Voyage.*

104

Vancouver's death when the Agent-General of British Columbia comes from nearby London with a party to attend the annual memorial service.

After Vancouver's death his brother John Vancouver, with the help of Captain Puget, attended to the completion of the book. Later that year it was published in three thick folio volumes.

A

VOYAGE of DISCOVERY

TO THE

NORTH PACIFIC OCEAN,

AND

ROUND THE WORLD;

IN WHICH THE COAST OF NORTH-WEST AMERICA HAS BEEN CAREFULLY
EXAMINED AND ACCURATELY SURVEYED.

Undertaken by HIS MAJESTY's *Command,*

PRINCIPALLY WITH A VIEW TO ASCERTAIN THE EXISTENCE OF ANY
NAVIGABLE COMMUNICATION BETWEEN THE

North Pacific and North Atlantic Oceans;

AND PERFORMED IN THE YEARS

1790, 1791, 1792, 1793, 1794, and 1795,

IN THE

DISCOVERY SLOOP OF WAR, AND ARMED TENDER CHATHAM,

UNDER THE COMMAND OF

CAPTAIN GEORGE VANCOUVER.

IN THREE VOLUMES.

VOL. I.

LONDON:
PRINTED FOR G. G. AND J. ROBINSON, PATERNOSTER-ROW;
AND J. EDWARDS, PALL-MALL.

1798.

1799

Growing activities of Russians and Americans.

This year saw both the Russians and the Americans entering more fully into the North Pacific fur trade. On July 8th the Czar signed the charter of the Russian American Company. This same year the Russians founded their fort at Sitka. True, in 1802 the Tlingits were to burn the settlement, massacre almost four hundred of its occupants (mostly Aleuts), and set their heads on the points of the palisades. However in 1804 the Russians re-established the fort, though on a new site. As for the Americans, two-thirds of the ships engaged in the fur trade this year flew the Stars and Stripes.[1]

[1] One of the numerous services which the late Judge F. W. Howay rendered to B.C. historians was compiling annotated lists of the trading vessels in the fur trade from 1785 to 1814. These will be found printed in the *Transactions of the Royal Society of Canada*, Section II, for 1930 (pp. 111-34), 1931 (pp. 117-49) and 1932 (pp. 43-86).

1800

The first overland fur traders.

So far all the fur trading carried on between white men and Indians had been conducted from ships cruising off the coast. Now the North West Company was contemplating entering the trade, coming in overland from the east. This year a reconnaissance of sorts was made by two French-Canadians, La Gassi and Le Blanc, in the Company's employ. Each summer, hunting the buffalo, the Kootenay Indians ventured into the Blackfoot country east of the Rockies. This year when the Kootenays returned to their own country, they were accompanied by La Gassi and Le Blanc, who apparently penetrated into the country around the headwaters of the Columbia River.

1801

Maritime fur trade reaches zenith — Publication of Macken-zie's Voyages.

This year the maritime fur trade reached its peak with perhaps as many as twenty-three vessels active along the coasts of British Columbia and Alaska. That number would never be matched again, and would gradually shrink to just two ships in 1830.[1]

Alexander Mackenzie now re-enters our chronicle. Ever since his great journey to the Pacific, he had been anxious to publish an account of his expeditions to the Arctic and the Pacific. Unfortunately subsequent time spent as a fur trader in the Indian Country, a period of nervous depression, and years of complicated business negotiations kept him from making a suitable draft of his journal. At last he managed to attend to the job. Feeling that he lacked literary ability, Mackenzie turned over his script to William Combe, a professional author, who had already rendered more elegant the works of Meares and Colnett. With purple passages added by Combe, Mackenzie's journals were published in London in December of this year under the title *Voyages from Montreal on the River St. Laurence, through the Continent of North America, to the Frozen and Pacific Oceans; In the years, 1789 and 1793 ... by Alexander Mackenzie, Esquire.*

[1] F. W. Howay, "An Outline Sketch of the Maritime Fur Trade", *Annual Report of the Canadian Historical Association, 1932,* p. 14.

1802

Mackenzie knighted — His plans for the fur trade.

Mackenzie was to remain Alexander Mackenzie, Esquire, very little longer, for on February 10th of this year he received the accolade and became Sir Alexander Mackenzie, Knight. Dr. Kaye Lamb has suggested that Mackenzie may, in part, have owed this distinction, so soon after the successful launching of his book, either to the Duke of Kent, with whom he is said to have travelled in Canada, or Lord Hobart, Secretary of State for War and the Colonies.[1] Writing to Hobart on January 7th, Mackenzie had set before him a scheme to limit the monopolies of the Hudson's Bay Company and the East India Company, and to license a new company to which all the Montreal merchants involved in the fur trade could belong. This new company would organize the trade on a truly transcontinental basis. The first article in the document that Mackenzie submitted to Hobart set forth a major purpose:

> To form a Supreme civil and Military Establishment, on the centrally situated and Navally defencible Island of Nootka, at King Georges Sound Lat. 50° North, with two subordinates, one in the River Columbia Lat. 46° and the other on *Sea Otter Harbour* Lat. 55 North.[2]

Nootka would never acquire a British fort, but the rest of this clause foreshadows the days when the Hudson's Bay Company would have its depots at Fort Vancouver and Fort Simpson.

[1] Mackenzie, *Journals*, p. 36.
[2] *Ibid.*, p. 504.

1803

President Jefferson and Mackenzie's book — Capture of the
Boston and massacre of her crew — Survival of John Jewitt.

Mackenzie's *Voyages* enjoyed an immediate success. Napoleon had
it published in French and this year, when a second American
edition was published, one of its purchasers was the President of the
Republic, the imaginative and far-sighted Thomas Jefferson. At the
end of his book Mackenzie, after eloquently pointing out the
strategic importance of the Columbia River, had urged that the
British establish a base there as well as a string of interior forts, thus
obtaining for Britain command of a fur trade conducted on a transcontinental scale. The scheme was far-sighted and practical but, if
conducted by the British, was hardly likely to commend itself to a
President of the United States, especially one who already had a
vision of his country extending westwards to the Pacific. Jefferson
pondered the chances of bringing that vision to fulfillment. Gray's
"discovery" of the Columbia, and the fact that he had been the first
navigator actually to enter the river, had given the Americans some
sort of claim to the area, and the score or so of American ships which
had traded off the North-west Coast had established a minimal
American presence. But obviously more than this was going to be
required. Jefferson decided that an American expedition should
cross the continent and establish a base, even if only a temporary
one, at the mouth of the Columbia.

While President Jefferson was thinking long thoughts and getting
congressional approval for his projected expedition, a tragedy had
overtaken an American vessel at Nootka. On March 22nd the ship
Boston, while anchored in the Sound, was captured by Maquinna
and his followers, and all but two of its crew murdered. The
survivors were John Jewitt, a young Englishman who was the ship's
blacksmith or armourer, and an older man named Thompson, the
ship's sailmaker.

During their captivity, young John Jewitt, at the prompting of the illiterate Thompson, set himself to keep a journal, using an empty account book salvaged from the ship and writing with ink made out of blackberry juice and charcoal. About twelve years later, drawing on this journal and his memories, Jewitt provided one Richard Alsop with the material contained in the *Narrative of the Adventures and Sufferings of John R. Jewitt*, a book full of vivid detail of life as a prisoner of the Nootkas. From it comes the following account of the capture of the *Boston*:

On the morning of the 22d [of March] the natives came off to us as usual with salmon, and remained on board, when about noon Maquina came along side with a considerable number of his chiefs and men in their canoes, who, after going through the customary examination were admitted into the ship. He had a whistle in his hand, and over his face a very ugly mask of wood representing the head of some wild beast, appeared to be remarkably good humoured and gay, and whilst his people sung and capered about the deck, entertaining us with a variety of antic tricks and gestures, he blew his whistle to a kind of tune which seemed to regulate their motions. As Capt. Salter was walking on the quarter deck amusing himself with their dancing, the king came up to him and enquired when he intended to go to sea? — he answered, to-morrow. — Maquinna then said, 'you love salmon — much in Friendly Cove, why not go then and catch some?' — The Captain thought that it would be very desirable to have a good supply of these fish for the voyage, and on consulting with Mr Delouisa [the first mate] it was agreed to send part of the crew on shore after dinner with the seine in order to procure a quantity — Maquina and his chiefs staid and dined on board, and after dinner the chief mate went off with nine men in the jolly boat and yawl to fish at Friendly Cove, having set the steward on shore at our watering place to wash the captain's clothes. Shortly after the departure of the boats I went down to my vice-bench in the steerage, where I was employed in cleaning muskets. I had not been there more than an hour when I heard the men hoisting in the long boat, which, in a few minutes after, was succeeded by a great bustle and confusion on deck. I immediately ran up the steerage stairs, but scarcely was my head above deck, when I was caught by the hair by one of the savages, and lifted from my feet; fortunately for me, my hair being short, and the ribbon with which it was tied slipping, I fell from his hold into the steerage. As I was falling, he struck at me with an axe, which cut a deep gash in my forehead, and penetrated the skull, but in consequence of his losing his hold, I luckily escaped the full force of the blow; which, otherwise, would have cleft my head in two. I fell, stunned and senseless upon the floor — how long I continued in this situation I know not, but on recovering my senses the first thing that I did, was to try to get up; but so weak was I, from the loss of blood, that I fainted and fell. I was however soon recalled to my recollection by three loud shouts or yells from the savages, which convinced me that they had got possession of the ship. . . . Having at length sufficiently recovered my senses to look around me after wiping the blood from my eyes, I saw that the hatch of the steerage was shut. This was done, as I afterwards discovered, by order of Maquina, who, on seeing the savage strike at me with the axe, told him not to hurt me, for that I was the armourer, and would be useful to them in repairing their arms; while at the same time to prevent any of his men from injuring me, he had the hatch closed. But to me this circumstance wore a very different appearance, for I thought that these barbarians had only prolonged my life in order to deprive me of it by the most cruel tortures. I remained in this horrid state of suspense for a very long time, when at length the hatch was opened, and Maquina, calling me by name, ordered me to come up. I groped my way up as well as I was able, being almost blinded with the blood that flowed from my wound, and so weak as with difficulty to walk. The king, on perceiving my situation, ordered one of his men to bring a pot of water to wash the blood from my face, which having done, I was able to see distinctly with one of my eyes, but the other was so swollen from my wound, that it was closed. But what a terrific spectacle met my eyes; six naked savages, standing in a circle around me, covered with the blood of my murdered comrades, with their daggers uplifted in their hands, prepared to strike. I now thought my last moment had come, and recommended my soul to my Maker. — The king, who, as I have already observed, knew enough of English to make himself understood, entered the circle, and placing himself before me, addressed me nearly in the following words — "John — I speak — you no say no — You say no — daggers come!" He then asked me if I would be his slave during my life — If I would fight for him in his battles — If I would repair his muskets and make daggers and knives for him — with several other questions, to all of which I was careful to answer, yes. He then told me that he would spare my life, and ordered me to kiss his hands and feet to show my submission to him, which I did. . . . he led me to the quarter deck, where the most horrid sight presented itself that ever my eyes witnessed — the heads of our unfortunate Captain and his crew, to the number of twenty-five, were all arranged in a line, and Maquina ordering one of his people to bring a head, asked me whose it was: I answered, the Captain's; in like manner the others were showed me, and I told him the names, excepting a few that were so horribly mangled that I was not able to recognize them. I now discovered that all our unfortunate crew [except the sailmaker who was subsequently found in hiding] had been massacred, and learned that after getting possession of the ship, the savages had broke open the arm chest and magazine, and supplying themselves with ammunition and arms, sent a party on shore to attack our men who had gone thither to fish, and being joined by numbers from the village, without difficulty overpowered and murdered them, and cutting off their heads, brought them on board, after throwing their bodies into the sea. On looking upon the deck, I saw it entirely covered with the blood of my poor comrades, whose throats had been cut with their own jack-knives, the savages having seized the opportunity while they were busy in hoisting in the boat to grapple with them and overpower them by their numbers; in the scuffle the captain was thrown overboard and despatched by those in the canoes, who immediately cut off his head: What I felt on this occasion, may be more readily conceived than expressed.[1]

Later Jewitt was to learn what had made the Indians resolve upon this attack. Partly it was the carefully concealed fury of Maquinna when he had heard Captain Salter's contemptuous remark upon receiving back from Maquinna a borrowed fowling-piece which the chief had damaged. Partly it was a desire to even old scores with the whites: among them a Captain Tawnington who (when only the women were at home) had raided the village at Friendly Cove and carried off all the furs; also Martinez who, they claimed, had murdered not one but four of their chiefs; and finally Hanna who, they alleged, had killed twenty of their tribe when he opened fire after the theft of a chisel. All of which led Jewitt to remark:

... I cannot but indulge a reflection that has frequently occurred to me on the manner in which our people behave towards the natives. For though they are a thievish race, yet I have no doubt that many of the melancholy disasters have principally arisen from the imprudent conduct of some of the captains and crews of the ships employed in this trade, in exasperating them by insulting, plundering, and even killing them on slight grounds.[2]

[1] *Narrative of the Adventures and Sufferings of John R. Jewitt* (New York, n.d.), Galleon Press facsimile 1967, pp. 25-29.

[2] *Ibid.*, p. 93.

1804

Union of the XY Company and the North West Company.

As Sir Alexander Mackenzie had for years been aware, the British North American fur trade was seriously handicapped by needless competition between rival companies based in Montreal. The largest of the Montreal concerns was the North West Company, but the most energetic was the younger XY Company. Late this year the two companies united. The benefits of this merger became evident during the next few years as the North West Company, stronger in both its financial and human resources, moved into a more dynamic period.

1805

Rescue of John Jewitt — Attack on the Atahualpa *— Simon Fraser crosses the Rockies and establishes post at McLeod Lake — The Americans Lewis and Clark reach the mouth of the Columbia River.*

Early in July this year the brig *Lydia* of Boston was trading with the Indians off the village of Kla-iz-zart on the west coast of Vancouver Island when the local chief handed its captain a letter. Written by John Jewitt in his blackberry ink, it was one of sixteen which he had smuggled out of Nootka by means of visiting Indians, charging them to hand these over to any white officers whom they might meet. News of the capture and subsequent destruction of the *Boston* and of the survival of two of her crew had quickly spread up and down the coast, but rather than risk the *Boston*'s fate other trading ships had been giving Nootka a wide berth. Nevertheless, reading Jewitt's appeal for rescue, Captain Hill decided to make for Nootka.

The arrival of the *Lydia* created a crisis among the Nootka Indians. They all wanted to trade with her, rather than secure the white man's goods at much greater cost from other tribes which could procure them directly from the trading vessels. On the other hand, they feared revenge for the capture of the *Boston* and the massacre of her crew. And what should be done about Jewitt and Thompson? Many of the Nootkas clamoured for their immediate death so that they could not tell their compatriots of the horrible fate of the *Boston*'s crew. Maquinna however refused to kill them. Over the intervening two years something which could almost be called friendship had developed between the chief and Jewitt, a young man of an attractive good-natured disposition — Maquinna had even bought the young man a wife who, Jewitt declared, exhibited "sweetness of temper and modesty" and would be considered "very pretty" in any country. In the face of the dilemma posed by the

Lydia's arrival Maquinna sought Jewitt's advice. Jewitt, according to his later account, played his hand perfectly. Professing not the slightest desire to go aboard the *Lydia* himself, he declared that Maquinna might do so with perfect safety since he would supply him with a letter certifying that Maquinna had used Thompson and himself well and deserved a good reception. According to Jewitt, he now wrote a letter advising Captain Hill to seize Maquinna as a hostage for the release of Thompson and himself.[1] Having read the letter, Captain Hill blandly invited Maquinna into his cabin to partake of some biscuits and a glass of rum. Once the chief had entered, he found the door barred and himself a prisoner.

Wailing and lamentation swept through the Nootkan village when the Indians found their Maquinna a prisoner on board the *Lydia*. Needless to say, it did not take long for Jewitt and Thompson to obtain their release in return for that of Maquinna.

Fascinating as is the story of the trick that Jewitt played on Maquinna with his letter, it may be quite untrue, a colourful bit of embroidering by Jewitt to help add to the interest and sales of his book. The captain of the *Lydia* made no mention of any such letter in the account of the rescue which he later supplied to a newspaper, the *Columbian Centinel*.[2]

The attack on the *Boston* was only one of many such made on trading vessels during these years. Only a month before Jewitt's rescue the American ship *Atahualpa* was attacked in Milbanke Sound when Indians, apparently friendly, were coming aboard for trade. The assault began when the local chief, Calete or Kaiete, called Captain Porter to the side of the ship to look down at some furs in one of the canoes. As soon as the captain leaned over the bulwark, the chief threw his coat over the captain's head, stabbed him twice between the shoulders and threw him overboard. With that, the attack was on. Left and right the seamen fell before the onslaught, then four men managed to break free, got below, and secured loaded muskets. Resolutely returning, they cowed the Indians, drove them from the ship, and turned a swivel gun on a

---

[1] Jewitt, *Narrative*, p. 148.

[2] For this report see F. W. Howay, "An Early Account of the Loss of the *Boston* in 1803", *WHQ* 17 (1926) : 280-87.

canoe which was attempting to cut the *Atahualpa*'s anchor cable. Looking about them, the survivors found that ten of the ship's complement of twenty-three were dead, including the captain and the first and second mates. Two more men died of their wounds shortly thereafter, including the ship's cook who had desperately defended himself, as long as he could, by throwing boiling water on the attackers. The four or five able-bodied men left took the ship to a harbour where additional crew members were supplied by other trading ships, sufficient to get the *Atahualpa* to Hawaii where the crew was brought up to strength.

We must turn now to those who came not by sea but by land. This was the year that the North West Company, strengthened by its union with the XY Company, began extending its fur trade into the country west of the Rocky Mountains, an area which for years had been known to be prime beaver country. The partner chosen to lead the Company into this new area was Simon Fraser. Like Sir Alexander Mackenzie, Fraser was the son of a United Empire Loyalist. His father, Captain Fraser, had died in an American prison, leaving his widow to take their children to Canada where young Simon received a minimal education. In 1792, at the age of sixteen, Simon Fraser became an apprentice clerk in the employ of the North West Company. Nine years later he became a partner in the Company, entitled to one forty-sixth of its profits. By 1805 experience in the Athabasca country as well as personal qualities of stamina, determination and leadership, had made Fraser a fit person to undertake this new expansion of the Company's activities into the lands west of the Rockies.

In the absence of any contemporary description of Simon Fraser, we cannot do better than fall back on that given by E. O. S. Scholefield after a close study both of his writings and of the surviving portraits:

... a well-built, active, man, with a heavy, almost dour, face, whose distinguishing features are a determined chin, firm, large-lipped mouth, prominent somewhat snubbed nose, light blue-grey eyes, broad receding brow, overhung with a mass of tousled hair of reddish tinge — a strong, honest face, indeed, but one giving more the idea of determination and physical robustness than of intellectuality or refinement. A man inured to hardship; versed in woodcraft and the lore of the savage; strong in danger; of inconquerable will and energy; unlettered, not polished, it may be, but true to his friends and honourable in his dealings. . . . [3]

In the autumn of 1805 Fraser with some twenty men travelled up the Peace River and, just below the Peace River Canyon, established Rocky Mountain Portage House, which was to serve as the base for their expedition. Leaving some of his men to complete construction of the buildings here, Fraser pushed on with the rest, taking Mackenzie's route up the Parsnip but departing from that route to turn up the Pack River. This brought him to a lake where he built the first of his transmontane trading posts, Trout Lake Post, soon to be renamed Fort McLeod. The founding of this post completed Fraser's program for this year. Now known simply as McLeod Lake, this is possibly the oldest permanent white settlement in British Columbia, though a challenge for this distinction is posed by Fort Nelson, which appears to have been founded by the North West Company in this same year.

Meanwhile another overland approach into the Pacific Northwest was being made from the east. President Jefferson's long-planned expedition was at last in the field. It consisted chiefly of men from the United States Army under the command of Captain Meriwether Lewis and Captain William Clark, not to mention the indispensable Sergeant Ordway. The military men needed the better part of two years to get from St. Louis to the Pacific, even though they had a fairly good route which led them up the Missouri to its headwaters, over the continental divide, and down streams and rivers leading to the Columbia. Even that ardently patriotic American historian Bancroft noted that "army captains and soldiers were no match for Scotch fur traders and Canadian voyageurs in forest travel".[4] Nevertheless, on November 7th of this year, Lewis and Clark and their party, almost thirty in all, arrived at the mouth of the Columbia where they built a cluster of log cabins, surrounded it with a stockade, and hoisted the Stars and Stripes above Fort Clatsop.

---

[3] *Westward Ho! Magazine*, 3 (1908) : 222.

[4] H. H. Bancroft, *History of the Northwest Coast* (San Francisco, 1886), II : 1.

1806

Lewis and Clark depart — Fraser establishes posts at Stuart Lake and Fraser Lake.

On March 23rd, Lewis and Clark with their men evacuated Fort Clatsop and commenced their long journey back to the United States. Just as Mackenzie had made no claim of sovereignty for Britain when he reached the Pacific near Bella Coola, so Lewis and Clark made no proclamation of American sovereignty at the mouth of the Columbia. However, they did leave posted on Fort Clatsop a declaration which read:

> The object of this last is, that through the medium of some civilized person, who may see the same, it may be made known to the world, that the party consisting of the persons whose names are hereunto annexed, and who were sent out by the government of the United States to explore the interior of the continent of North America, did penetrate the same by the way of the Missouri and Columbia rivers, to the discharge of the latter into the Pacific Ocean, where they arrived on the 14th day of November 1805, and departed the 23rd day of March 1806, on their return to the United States, by the same route by which they had come out.[1]

The Lewis and Clark expedition returned safely to St. Louis on September 23rd.

Meanwhile, up north, Simon Fraser was engaged in the second phase of opening up the territory which seems to have received from him the name of New Caledonia, since it reminded him of his mother's description of the Scottish Highlands. Early this spring James McDougall, the clerk in charge of the tiny post at McLeod Lake, had sent word that he had visited a large lake, which the Indians called Nakazeleh, some distance to the south-west. He also informed Fraser that a river, reputedly navigable, flowing out from

---

[1] Bancroft, *Northwest Coast*, II:59-60.

this lake joined the "Columbia". Supplied with this information, Fraser planned his own explorations and fur trading for this year.

Late in May, the ice at long last being out of the Peace River, Fraser and John Stuart, his ever-faithful friend and clerk, set out with their men from Rocky Mountain Portage House. Up the Peace they went, and then up the Parsnip, following Mackenzie's route. Along the way they made a side trip up the Pack River to visit the recently established post on McLeod Lake. The first furs had already been shipped from there, many of them superior to anything Fraser had ever seen in the Athabasca district. At McLeod Lake Fraser built new canoes, his old ones being already terribly damaged.

Retracing his way to the Parsnip, Fraser again followed Mackenzie's route. He found most of it just as bad as Mackenzie had, full of snags, log jams and rapids — moreover, he was plagued with bad weather, and all sorts of ailments afflicting his crews. "Saucier is sick, Gagnon complains of his side, Blais of having a pain, and a lump upon his stomach, and Gervais is not well, and La Londe is not able to steer his canoe".[2] Moreover, La Malice, an ugly surly brute, had some mysterious ailment which made him delirious at times. On July 10th, after a thoroughly miserable trip along various wild streams, lakes and portages, they at last reached the broad waters of the "Columbia" [i.e. Fraser] River. Fraser had one somewhat dubious consolation. Along the way he had learned from the Indians that a much easier route (today followed by the John Hart Highway) via Summit Lake and Crooked River, could be used to get from the Parsnip River to the "Columbia". A day's travel brought them to the junction of the Fraser and Nechako Rivers, site of the modern city of Prince George. For two weeks they fought their way up the swift Nechako and the Stuart Rivers, sometimes unable to use paddles, poles or towlines, and pulling themselves upstream by grabbing at the overhanging branches of trees.

The Indians at Nakazeleh Lake, although prepared in advance by McDougall for the coming of Fraser's trading party, had a few frightening experiences when they met the newcomers. When some of Fraser's voyageurs lit their pipes and began to smoke, the Indians,

---

[2] W. Kaye Lamb, ed., *The Letters and Journals of Simon Fraser 1806-1808* (Toronto, 1960), p. 209.

who knew nothing of tobacco, were appalled. These they decided must be ghosts and the smoke coming out of their mouths must come from their cremation fires (the Carriers regularly cremated their dead). When cakes of soap were given to the women they mistook them for fat, began chewing them and, to their amazement, started to foam at the mouth while bubbles floated away in the air. Such events passed with no bad consequences and here, on the shore of Nakazeleh Lake, which would become known as Stuart Lake, Fraser built a little post which in time grew into Fort St. James, the fur trading capital of New Caledonia.

Fraser had planned, once he had established this post, to get a supply of salmon, head back to the "Columbia" and, continuing beyond the point where Mackenzie had turned back, to follow it to the Pacific. Unfortunately the salmon were six weeks late this year and, when they belatedly arrived in September, it was too late for Fraser to attempt his dash to the Pacific.

To make what use he could of the rest of the season, Fraser sent Stuart to look at a lake farther to the south, one known to the Indians as Natleh. When Stuart brought back an encouraging report, Fraser went to the lake himself and established another trading post there. This post on Natleh or Fraser Lake received in time the name of Fort Fraser. The onset of winter found Fraser settled in at the new Fraser Lake post and John Stuart established at the Stuart Lake post.

1807

Simon Fraser's native "courtship" — A lost year — David
Thompson enters the scene — His early career — He crosses
the Rockies and builds Kootenae House.

The opening months of this year found Fraser still appositely at
Fraser Lake and Stuart at Stuart Lake. Fraser had found female
consolation during the bleak winter season with all its loneliness. In
a letter to Stuart dated February 1st, he wrote: "Yes my friend I
have once more entered upon the matrimonial state and you would
have a hearty laugh if you heard of our Courtship, this I will inform
you of if you have not heard of it already. . . . "[1] Unfortunately the
story of the courting of Simon Fraser has not been preserved, and
British Columbia history is probably the poorer for the loss of a very
good story. The robust Simon Fraser clearly had a penchant for
"matrimony". He must have been referring to the fruits of a previous
venture when, just at this time, in a letter to McDougall at McLeod
Lake he added a postscript: "N.B. Anything that the Children are
in want of and that can be had please give it to them & Charge the
same to my acct."[2]

There was a double standard in these matters. While the gentlemen of the North West Company allowed themselves native women,
they usually disapproved of the voyageurs acquiring "wives" and
begetting children who would be an added charge on the Company.
Almost a year before, Fraser had made St. Pierre give up an Indian
woman, consoling him with the promise that at least no other
voyageur would be permitted to have her. Now he was furious to
learn that the irresponsible McDougall had allowed another of the
Company's men to acquire the woman. In his letter to McDougall,
just mentioned, he fired off a broadside:

[1] Fraser, *Journals,* p. 250.
[2] *Ibid.,* p. 248.

Your conduct at T[rout] Lake [McLeod Lake] is highly blamable and your character as a Trader much blasted which you can only recover, but by your future assiduity and attention to your business. . . .[3]

Fraser had counted on travelling down the "Columbia" to the Pacific this spring. Unfortunately the winter months had so reduced his supplies (especially of trade goods needed to purchase the friendship of Indians) that he had to await the arrival of new shipments already ordered from east of the mountains. Pending the arrival of these supplies, Fraser drew up plans for a third post, Fort George, at the confluence of the Nechako and the "Columbia". This would be his advance base for his journey to the sea. As luck would have it, autumn had come this year before the canoes arrived with reinforcements of men and supplies for Fraser. Yet another year had been lost. He would have to wait until 1808 for his great adventure.

Now for a while we must leave a frustrated Fraser and turn our eyes in a different quarter. The North West Company's drive into the country west of the Rockies had two prongs. The northern one was headed by Simon Fraser, the southern by David Thompson. In Thompson we have one of the most ambivalent and controversial figures in the history of British Columbia. Born in England in 1770 of Welsh parents, David Thompson arrived in British North America in 1784 as an apprentice in the service of the Hudson's Bay Company. While stationed at Cumberland House he received a thorough training in surveying, and in the years that followed became the most accomplished surveyor and mapmaker in the British territories. Thompson's distinction as a geographer has never been questioned. At the end of his apprenticeship he accepted a three year contract with the Company. In 1794, at the end of this contract, the Hudson's Bay Company quadrupled his salary when signing him up for another three year term. Obviously Thompson was a bright young man, and the Company fully appreciated his services. Furnishing him generously with equipment, the Company encouraged him to take time off from routine fur trade life so that he could conduct surveys and make maps.

In 1796 Malcolm Ross, the Hudson's Bay Company's Master to

[3] *Ibid.*, p. 246.

the Northward, was engaged in one of the Company's repeated efforts to discover a practicable route into the Athabasca country, that extraordinarily rich beaver territory which heretofore had been the preserve of the competing North West Company. Ross, only a year from retirement, had for his second in command David Thompson, already designated as his successor. Returning from a reconnaissance, Thompson was emphatic that he had found a practicable route for Ross' party. Against his own inclination, Ross accepted Thompson's recommendation. Too late the party found Thompson's route impracticable for their canoes. As a result, they had to turn back and spend the winter half-starving at Bedford House which, despite its grandiose name, was merely a shack measuring twenty feet by twenty-six. Being cooped up through months of winter cold with fourteen famished men who knew that he was to blame for their predicament obviously placed a great strain on Thompson. Moreover, he knew that, once Ross left, he would have to take command of these embittered men.

As spring approached Alexander Fraser, a partner in the North West Company, visited Bedford House. Apparently Fraser had some private conversation with Thompson for, on the morning of May 21st, Thompson told Ross that he was forthwith leaving to enter the service of the North West Company. The outrageous aspect of this action was that Thompson, like every other employee of the Company, was bound to give a year's notice before leaving. The Hudson's Bay Company, with its sparse and widely scattered force and slow communications, needed a full year to arrange replacements. Men in its service just could not opt for out, and leave. But Thompson did. Two days after breaking the news to Ross, he left. Fortunately for the Company, Ross, out of a sense of loyalty, agreed to postpone his retirement to Britain and stayed on as Master to the Northward. A flaw had become apparent in the character of David Thompson.

The North West Company rejoiced to obtain the services of so outstanding a surveyor. Affluent as they were at this period, they could afford to release him entirely from fur trading and permit him to devote himself for some years to making explorations and surveys for them. In 1801, with a party led by James Hughes, Thompson was engaged in an unsuccessful attempt to cross the Rockies. In

1806 at Fort William he received instructions to make another attempt to penetrate the Rockies and open up the area for trade. That autumn Thompson based himself at Rocky Mountain House, ready for a major expedition in the coming spring.

Now, in 1807, David Thompson headed west. Travelling up to the headwaters of the North Saskatchewan River, he discovered Howse Pass (named after a Hudson's Bay Company man who used it several years later), and, having crossed the Rockies, followed the Blaeberry River down to the Columbia. Travelling up the Columbia, he arrived at Lake Windermere. At the end of July, just north of this lake and close to where Toby Creek flows into the Columbia, Thompson built Kootenae House. It was in fact a fort since it was equipped with palisades and bastions. Here he settled with his men, plus his wife and family whom he had brought with him over the mountains. He commenced trading with the Indians, while devoting time also to his astronomical, meteorological and topographical observations.

Thompson, apparently, had left for the succeeding year the carrying out of his real mission. That mission had been reported by James Bird of the Hudson's Bay Company in a letter from Edmonton House on 23 December 1806: "Mr. David Thompson is making preparations for another attempt to cross the Mountains, pass through [the Kootenay country] and follow the Columbia River to the sea."[4]

---

[4] A. S. Morton, "The North West Company's Columbian Enterprise and David Thompson", *The Canadian Historical Review* [hereafter referred to as *CHR*] 17 (1936) :282.

1808

Fraser starts down the "Columbia" — Canyons and portages — A friendly Atnah chief — Fraser reaches Thompson River — Hell's Gate — Indians turn hostile — The Pacific at last — Fraser's river is not the Columbia — David Thompson follows the Kootenay River to Kootenay Lake — He turns back instead of pushing on to the Pacific — He travels east with his furs — Return to Kootenae House.

This year is a major one in the exploration of British Columbia. Its opening months saw Fraser and Thompson both poised for their main ventures: Fraser at the junction of the Nechako and Fraser, and Thompson at the headwaters of the Columbia.

Simon Fraser was a man aged thirty-two when, at five o'clock in the morning of Saturday, May 28th, he put his four canoes into the water at the advance base he had established at the confluence of the Nechako and the Fraser, and started down what he believed was the Columbia River. With him were two clerks — the faithful John Stuart, quiet, sensitive, patient, a bit of a philosopher and an expert canoe-builder, aged twenty-nine; and Jules Quesnel, more ebullient and less experienced, aged twenty-two. Fraser also had nineteen voyageurs and two Indians, making up a party of twenty-four in all.

The first few days saw them safely through the white water of Fort George Canyon and Cottonwood Canyon and past a river which Fraser named after young Quesnel. "This country," wrote Fraser, "which is interspersed with meadows and hills, dales & high rocks, has upon the whole a *romantic* but *pleasant* appearance."[1] Things began to look less pleasant on May 31st when they had to portage part of their load around Soda Creek Canyon, run some very bad rapids near Williams Lake River, and camped for the

---

[1] Fraser, *Journals,* ed. Lamb, p. 63. All brief, unfootnoted quotations that follow are from this edition.

night at the head of dangerous rapids near Chimney Creek. From
here on, the river would get worse and worse. They had, however,
one great piece of good fortune — the Indians were proving friendly
and helpful. This day when they entered into the Atnah (Shuswap)
country, an old chief agreed to accompany them as their guide. On
June 1st Fraser's party attempted to run the rapids which lay ahead
of them but gave up the endeavour when they realized it could cost
them their lives. Portaging, they had a very bad time slithering along
the steep banks. At times only by plunging their daggers into the
bank could they keep from sliding into the tumultuous river.

Fraser had chosen the very worst season, that of the spring freshets,
to make his descent of the river; thus, on June 2nd, he noted that
the river had risen eight feet in twenty-four hours. Pressing on, he
passed Riske Creek and the Chilcotin River. In the Iron Canyon he
noted that the whirlpools and eddies surpassed anything that he had
seen before. Somewhere along the way a whirlpool wrenched the
stern off one of the canoes. Increasingly the men had to portage
around the canyons and rapids.

On June 6th the old Atnah chief, their guide, joined other Indians
in telling Fraser that further navigation was out of the question.
(Obviously they thought that the white men were mad to stick to
the river instead of striking westward, overland to the Pacific.) The
Indians' advice was ignored, and Fraser with his men continued
downstream. The constant portages began to tell on their feet — in
this terrain a pair of shoes could be worn out in a single day. They
stopped for a day to rest, while they repaired their shoes and other
equipment and made a reconnaissance ahead. Then they went on
down the river again, travelling now in excessive heat. They had a
terrible time in French Bar Canyon, the water shooting with
incredible velocity between high perpendicular cliffs which, Fraser
estimated, towered 1200 feet above the water. So far the Indians
had been friendly, even helping Fraser's people across the portages,
but now they joined in rebuking him for not having heeded the old
chief's advice and abandoned navigation earlier. Further scouting
made it clear even to the indomitable Fraser that he could not hope
to take his canoes farther. On June 10th and 11th, near Leon Creek
(north of Lillooet), the party put their canoes under shelter and

cached everything that could not be carried. Then, each bearing a pack of eighty pounds, they started walking. From here on they would travel mostly on foot, using horses or Indian canoes when and where they could.

On June 14th there was the first sign of trouble with the Indians. They were now in the territory of the Lillooets and these angrily told Fraser's guide, the old Atnah chief, that the men he was leading were not white men but enemies. Peace was established, but Fraser and his ragged company took the hint, shaved, and put on their best apparel.

On June 15th their faithful guide, the old chief, left them, having seen them safely into the Lillooet territory. They continued on their way, feeling curiously vulnerable and insecure without him as their conductor. Three days later they met their first Thompson Indians and were fortunate to find another friend in the Thompson chief, who went ahead to prepare a welcome for them. On June 19th they arrived at the junction of their river with another almost its equal in size, to which Fraser gave the name it still carries: "From an idea that our friends of the *Fort des Prairies* department are established upon the sources of it, among the mountains, we gave it the name of Thomson's [Thompson's] River."[2] Here at Camchin, the great centre of the Thompson Indians (now the site of Lytton) he was ceremoniously greeted:

... the principal chief invited us over the river. We crossed, and He received us at the water side, where, assisted by several others, he took me by the arms and conducted me in a moment up the hill to the camp where his people were sitting in rows, to the number of twelve hundred; and I had to shake hands with all of them.[3]

On the morning of June 20th Fraser started on the most difficult stretch of his journey, that down the Fraser Canyon. Fortunately the principal chief of the Thompson Indians and another Indian, known to them only as "The Little Fellow", accompanied them. Despite help received at various portages from the Indians, the health of Fraser's men was beginning to deteriorate under the

[2] *Ibid.*, p. 88.
[3] *Ibid.*, p. 87.

tremendous physical strains. Near Jackass Mountain a canoe purchased from the Indians was lost and one of Fraser's men had a
miraculous survival, having been carried "three miles among rapids,
cascades, whirlpools, &c., all inconceivably dangerous." On June
25th the Thompson chief returned home, leaving with them the
Little Fellow who was to go all the way down to the mouth of the
river and back with them. Soon they had to pass the very worst place
in all their journey, Hell's Gate, where the Fraser River, with
incredible force, hurls itself through a narrow opening between the
rocky cliffs. Without the complete cooperation of the Indians, Fraser
and his men would have had to abandon their journey here. Fraser
wrote:

> I have been for a long period among the Rocky Mountains, but have
> never seen any thing equal to this country, for I cannot find words to
> describe our situation at times. We had to pass where no human being
> should venture. Yet in those places there is a regular footpath
> impressed, or rather indented, by frequent travelling upon the very
> rocks. And besides this, steps which are formed like a ladder, or the
> shrouds of a ship, by poles hanging to one another and crossed at
> certain distances with twigs and withes [tree boughs], suspended from
> the top to the foot of precipices, and fastened at both ends to stones
> and trees, furnished a safe and convenient passage to the Natives —
> but we, who had not the advantages of their experience, were often in
> imminent danger, when obliged to follow their example.[4]

Now the worst was past. On June 28th they reached Lady Franklin
Rock and, at the site of modern Yale, were safely out of the canyon.
It would be navigable water the rest of the way to the Pacific.

But now the character of the Indians changed. The Indians in the
lower Fraser Valley proved at best disagreeable, and at worst bent
on their destruction. Yet Fraser had to obtain canoes from them,
and by various expedients (generally trade combined with bluster
and the threat of his guns) he contrived to get at least the loan of
canoes. On July 2nd, just east of New Westminster, Fraser after
extended and difficult bargaining persuaded the local chief to go
with him in a large canoe to the mouth of the river. The agreement
was reached despite the declarations made by the local band that

4 *Ibid.*, p. 96.

the Cowichans at the mouth of the river were a murderous lot who would kill them all. Learning of the reputation of these Cowichans, Fraser's own men balked at going any farther, and even the brave Little Fellow refused to continue with them. Faced with this division in his own ranks Fraser acted decisively. "We paid no attention to their arguments, made them desist, and we embarked." As Fraser's men approached the Fraser delta they were followed by other canoes from the village they had just left, their occupants chanting a war song and making hostile signs. Opposite the site of New Westminster, an Indian directed them down the North Arm of the Fraser. Finally, with the Pacific in plain view, they came to the village at Musqueam. Landing, they were shown over one of the houses, but advised to leave before they were attacked.

About this time those that followed us from above arrived. Having spent one hour looking about this place we went to embark, [when] we found the tide had ebbed, and left our canoe on dry land. We had, therefore, to drag it out to the water some distance. The natives no doubt seeing our difficulty, assumed courage, and began to make their appearance from every direction, in their coats of mail, howling like so many wolves, and brandishing their war clubs.[5]

Once afloat, Fraser pushed on to another village near the tip of Point Grey. Then, in view of the mounting hostility of the natives, he reluctantly ordered the big canoe turned back up the river. His great journey had reached its end.

By now, of course, from their takings of the latitude, Fraser and his clerks knew they were far north of the mouth of the Columbia. Bitterly Fraser recorded:

The latitude is 49° nearly, while that of the entrance of the Columbia is 46°20'. This River, therefore, is not the Columbia. If I had been convinced of this fact where I left my canoes [north of Lillooet], I would certainly have returned from thence.[6]

The newly found river could not provide the eagerly sought route by which the interior posts could be supplied from the Pacific.

All the way back up the river as far as Yale, Fraser and his men

[5] *Ibid.*, p. 106.
[6] *Ibid.*, p. 109.

were harried by hostile Indians. At one point some of the men
mutinied and declared that they would have no more of this part of
the river but would travel by land until they rejoined it above Hell's
Gate. Fraser, Stuart and Quesnel remonstrated and reasoned with
the voyageurs. At last the men agreed to continue, everybody shaking
hands and swearing an oath: "I solemnly swear before Almighty
God that I shall sooner perish than forsake in distress any of our
crew during the present journey". Above Yale, they found the
Indians friendly as before and once again ready to assist them to
pass Hell's Gate. Indians from afar who had heard of the white men
were gathered to stare at them as the tattered little band doggedly
worked their way towards home. Rapids and portages continued to
test them to the breaking-point. They were grateful when the Indians
gave them some of their tough leather armour to make into shoes.
"We were much in want of this necessary article; continually
walking as we were among the worst of roads [trails], our feet were
covered with blisters, and some of the men were lame and in
perpetual torture." It was with enormous relief that they found their
own canoes and cached supplies safe where they had left them near
Leon Creek. During their absence, the Indians had faithfully kept
guard over them. On July 22nd, they met the old Atnah chief who
had been their guide. He and his brother were "so overjoyed to see
us that they annoyed us with caresses". Reluctantly, the Little Fellow
now took his leave of them. Near Soda Creek they bade farewell to
the old chief himself, repaying him for his many services with a gun
and ammunition.

Above the Soda Creek canyon, the Fraser gave them relatively
clear and open water; the horrors of the rapids and portages lay
almost entirely behind them. At noon on Saturday, August 6th, they
arrived back at the little post from which they had set out ten weeks
before. On hand to welcome them was Hugh Faries, the officer in
charge, and his two men. Fraser, had he known it, had written his
name across the map of British Columbia, for five years later David
Thompson, making the rough draft for his famous "Map for the
North West Company", affixed Fraser's name to the great river
which he had descended.

And what of Thompson's own explorations this year? On April

20th he left Kootenae House, travelled up Lake Windermere and Columbia Lake, crossed the narrow strip later named Canal Flats, and took canoe down the swift-flowing Kootenay River. After following it around its big southern loop into what is now the United States, he re-entered the Canada of today when he reached the marshland at the southern end of Kootenay Lake. Before him extended the broad expanse of Kootenay Lake's mountain-cradled waters. He had only to travel up them, turn down the lake's west arm, run the last twenty-five miles of the Kootenay River, and he would stand on the banks of the Columbia, at the site of modern Castlegar. From that point a plain easy descent of the wide Columbia would carry him to the Pacific. His major mission, left over from the previous year, would have been completed. But Thompson was not of the stuff of Mackenzie and Fraser. His furs, his wife, and his children would all be shortly heading east and he wanted to be with them. There may have been other reasons, but the fact remains that at this point David Thompson turned back.

On their homeward journey Thompson and his men did not have to work their way against the swift-flowing Kootenay River. From the Indians he had learned that a route via Moyie River and Moyie Lake would take him right across the top of the big bend of the Kootenay. On May 19th, having bought horses from the Indians and acquired a guide, he set out on this shortcut. The second day out their guide deserted them. At this point we may quote from the "Narrative" of his travels which Thompson compiled in his old age:

On the twenty second [of May] we waited with faint hopes for his return, when at ten AM I sent off two Men to the camp of the Kootenae and Lake Indians to procure another Guide, on their arrival, Ugly Head (so named from his hair curling) the Lake Indian Chief made a speech, in which he bitterly reproached them for want of a strong heart, and contrasting their cowardly conduct, with ours, who braved every hardship and danger to bring them Arms, Ammunition and all their other wants: calling upon them to find a man, or two, who would be well paid; but none answered the call: the dangers of the Mountains at this season were too great, and too well known to them, and I was not aware of this until it was too late; finding no answer given to his call on them, he said while I am alive, the White Men who come to us with goods, shall not perish in the Mountains for want of a Guide and a Hunter. Since your hearts are all weak, I will go with them; he kept his word, and on the evening of the twenty-fourth of May, he came with two men, and I thanked God, for the anxiety of my situation was great, and was now entirely relieved, for I knew the manly character of the Lake Indian Chief, and justly placed confidence in him.[7]

In fact, it took Ugly Head only a week to conduct Thompson and his party to the open range country of the upper Kootenay. Here they paused for a day or so to dry some of their three hundred pounds of furs. On June 3rd they were back at Canal Flats (or McGillivray's Carrying Place, to give it Thompson's name.) Three days later Thompson arrived at Kootenae House. The trip which he had just completed was an interesting one, and useful in its extension of geographical knowledge, but it must not be compared with Fraser's tremendous achievement.

When Thompson arrived at Kootenae House, he found it abandoned. Probably following a schedule previously laid down by Thompson, Finan McDonald, the clerk left in charge, had already started off for the prairies, taking with him Thompson's wife and children. Thompson needed only a couple of days to catch up with McDonald and then continued on up the Columbia and through Howse Pass.

Once across the Rockies, Thompson got his family and furs into a canoe and headed east. At a company post with the fascinating name of Boggy Hall, he dropped off his family. Then he pushed on with his voyageurs to Rainy Lake House, arriving there on August 2nd. Pausing only a couple of days to deliver his furs and pick up his trading goods for the next year, Thompson headed back west. By the beginning of October he was at Boggy Hall where he apparently picked up his family. By the end of the month he had again crossed the Rockies and on November 10th he arrived back at Kootenae House. He had cut things a bit fine in making his crossing through the Rockies as late as October, but had got through safely. One incident during this crossing gave him particular satisfaction. At the insistence of two of his fellow partners in the North West

---

[7] Richard Glover, ed., *David Thompson's Narrative 1784-1812*, Champlain Society 40 (Toronto, 1962) : 283-84.

Company, he had brought from Rainy River two kegs of alcohol which they regarded as very profitable for trade. Thompson, however, was determined that no intoxicating liquor should be traded in his territory and he took a suitable counter-measure:

... when we came to the defiles of the Mountains, I placed the two Kegs of Alcohol on a vicious horse; and by noon the Kegs were empty, and in pieces, the Horse rubbing his load against the Rocks to get rid of it; I wrote to my partners what I had done; and that I would do the same to every Keg of Alcohol, and for the next six years I had charge of the furr trade on the west side of the Mountains, no further attempt was made to introduce spirituous Liquors.[8]

We must regret that in 1808 Simon Fraser's great achievement had not been matched by anything comparable by David Thompson. But Thompson was hardly of the stuff of which leaders and heroes are made; and Fraser was.

[8] *Ibid.*, p. 287.

1809

Fraser returns to Canada — Thompson opens posts in the Flathead country.

Simon Fraser and David Thompson spent this year in very different fashion. In the spring Fraser journeyed to Fort William for the annual meeting of the North West Company's partners. Here he was granted a year's furlough and apparently travelled home to Canada.

For Thompson this was another active year in the West. Although the winter was mild in the Lake Windermere valley, he was able to get enough ice from the lake to make a "meat glacier" in which, between successive layers of ice, he stored away a large supply of thighs of the red deer and the antelope. June and July found him east of the Rockies delivering his furs and picking up more trade goods. In August he retraced his now familiar route by Howse Pass and the upper Columbia, but instead of resuming residence at Kootenae House he pushed on to the Kootenay River (McGillivray's River to give it Thompson's name), travelled down it to near Bonner's Ferry, and then cut over to Lake Pend d'Oreille where he established on September 10th Kullyspell [Kalispell] House. In November, further to the east on the Clark's Fork River, he founded another new post, Saleesh [Salish] House.

Thompson was opening up rich new fur trading country for his company, but he obviously was in no great hurry to find the much desired navigable route to the Pacific.

1810

*Stuart and Harmon at Stuart Lake — John Jacob Astor
founds the Pacific Fur Company — The* Tonquin *sails for
the Columbia.*

After Fraser returned to Canada, the superintendency of the North
West Company's recent establishments in New Caledonia passed to
that John Stuart who had accompanied Fraser on his great journey
to the Pacific. Stuart's fame has been so eclipsed by Fraser's that it
is only fitting to recall the great tribute Stuart would receive in 1829
from Governor Simpson of the Hudson's Bay Company when the
latter spoke of:

> ... Chief Factor John Stewart [*sic*], who may be considered the
> Father or founder of New Caledonia; where for 20 years of his Life,
> he was doomed to all the misery and privation, which that inhospitable
> region could bring forth, and who with a degree of exertion, of which
> few men were capable, overcame difficulties, to which the business of
> no other part of the country was exposed ... leaving the District as a
> Monument of his unwearied industry and extraordinary perseverance,
> which will long reflect the highest credit on his name and character, as
> an Indian Trader.[1]

Simpson rarely indulged in such an encomium.

This year Stuart was assigned a new clerk, Daniel Williams
Harmon, who arrived at Stuart Lake in November. Harmon, a
Vermonter by birth, was a serious and conscientious man and, moreover, an observant man who kept a most valuable journal for the
eight and a half years he was to spend in New Caledonia. Publishing
a revised version of his journal in 1820, he added a section on the
Indians west of the Rockies. Here we find a remarkable account of
the awe and superstition with which the Carrier Indians regarded

---

[1] E. E. Rich, ed., *Simpson's 1828 Journey to the Columbia*, Hudson's Bay
Record Society [hereafter referred to as HBRS] 10 (London, 1947):25-26.

the white men during these first years in which they were becoming acquainted with them. They believed that the newcomers were of miraculous origin, not begotten by men and women in the downright way of creation but set on the earth by either the sun or the moon. They credited the white men with omniscience, knowledge of all things past and of all things yet to come. The white man's books fascinated the Carriers. They decided that if a white man would only look in a book he could cure a sick person, no matter how great a distance the patient might be from him. As for that fascinating engine, the white man's watch, "they now firmly believe that a watch is the heart of the sun, because it is ever in motion, as they say, like that great body of light."[2]

One of the matters which must have engaged the conversation of Stuart, Quesnel and Harmon at Stuart Lake was when they would be able to supply New Caledonia from a depot at the mouth of the Columbia, using the route which their colleague David Thompson was supposed to be finding for them in the south. But Thompson, had they known it, had got involved in difficulties and delays and would not make his crucial journey to the mouth of the Columbia this year.

Meanwhile the North West Company was not alone in inheriting Sir Alexander Mackenzie's vision of a fur trade conducted on a transcontinental basis — a scheme which required a western depot at the mouth of the Columbia both receiving supplies and exporting furs, while the great river itself provided the highway to the interior. One man who fully perceived the scope and advantages of Mackenzie's "Columbian enterprise" was John Jacob Astor, an imaginative, energetic and ruthless German immigrant who, through domination of the fur trade in the United States, had become enormously wealthy. By 1810 Astor was ready to enter the fur trade on the Pacific Coast, and to establish a base at the mouth of the Columbia from which to penetrate inland.

Previous dealings with the Montreal fur traders had made Astor very much aware of the capabilities of the Scots who directed the affairs of the North West Company. They would almost certainly

2 Daniel Williams Harmon, *Sixteen Years in the Indian Country*, ed. W. Kaye Lamb (Toronto, 1957), p. 252.

be competing with him on the Pacific slope. Accordingly, while setting up his Pacific Fur Company this year, Astor proposed that the Nor'Westers come into the venture as partners, holding one-third of the shares. Negotiations followed but the Nor'Westers, who already had posts west of the Rockies and were steadily moving towards the Pacific, saw no reason for allowing Astor the major role in a combined venture, and were not eager to participate. Instead, they apparently sent instructions to David Thompson to hasten to the mouth of the Columbia and have the Union Jack flying there when Astor's people arrived.

Proceeding without the participation of the North West Company but badly needing the experience which it possessed, Astor obtained as partners[3] four ex-Nor'Westers who were at odds with the Company — Alexander McKay, Donald McKenzie, Duncan McDougall and David Stuart. Astor also acquired five American partners. As employees, he engaged a considerable number of French-Canadian clerks and voyageurs. Paradoxically, the American-owned Pacific Fur Company chiefly employed British subjects.

Plans for the Pacific Fur Company were well advanced by the summer of 1810. The "buoyant and aspiring mind" of Astor had worked out an admirable scheme for his new venture. An overland party led by Wilson P. Hunt, an American partner, would proceed from Lachine in Quebec, via the Mississippi and Missouri, and over the mountains to the Columbia. Simultaneously a maritime party with a cargo of trading goods would sail around Cape Horn to rendezvous with the overlanders at the mouth of the river. Should either party be overtaken by disaster, the surviving one could still establish that all-important post where the Columbia meets the ocean.

On September 6th the maritime party sailed from New York aboard the *Tonquin*. This was a vessel of some three hundred tons, mounting twelve cannon, and commanded by Captain Jonathan

---

[3] Astor, who put up the entire capital, held fifty of the shares. The other "partners", who contributed their services but invested no money, were given four shares each, except Hunt, who as Astor's personal representative in the field was granted five. Alexander Ross, *Adventures of the First Settlers on the Oregon or Columbia River*, ed. R. G. Thwaites (Cleveland, 1904), pp. 38-39.

Thorn, on leave from the U.S. Navy. The voyage of the *Tonquin* proved to be a nightmare. Although Captain Thorn was an expert seaman he was also a martinet, like most sea captains of the period; but ruthlessness in him was tinged with paranoia. In December, when the *Tonquin* put in at the Falkland Islands to get fresh water, eight or nine of her passengers went ashore to stretch their legs. When they failed to return promptly after the firing of a signal gun Captain Thorn, in a fury, hoisted sail and put to sea. Desperately the abandoned men scrambled into their little boat and vainly attempted to catch up with the ship. Finally the *Tonquin* turned around and picked them up, but only because young Robert Stuart, whose uncle was one of those left behind, had drawn a pair of pistols and told Captain Thorn either to turn back or have his brains blown out.

The incident hardly augured well for what would happen when the *Tonquin* reached the Pacific North-west in the coming year.

1811

The Americans found Astoria — The Tonquin *is captured by Indians and has a spectacular end — David Thompson belatedly reaches the mouth of the Columbia.*

Before resuming the saga of the *Tonquin*, let us mention briefly the New Year's celebrations which ushered in 1811 at the North West Company's establishment on Stuart Lake in New Caledonia. Daniel Harmon, who was stationed there, has left us in his journal an amusing account of how the Indians responded to the spectacle of drunken whites:

January 1, Tuesday. This being the first Day of the year our People have past it as is customary for them — Drinking & fighting. Some of the principal Indians of the place desired us to allow them to remain at the Fort to see our People drink, but as soon as they began to be intoxicated and quarrel among themselves, the Natives were apprehensive that something unpleasant might befall them also, therefore they hid themselves under beds & elsewhere, and said they thought the White People had become mad.[1]

But now let us return to that unhappy vessel, the *Tonquin*, which we left off the Falkland Islands. On March 22nd, with its crew seething with hatred of its captain, the ship arrived off the mouth of the Columbia. The weather was stormy, and frequent squalls whipped up great waves off the bar at the river mouth. Nevertheless Captain Thorn, bent on getting his ship into the river without delay, ordered his first mate to take five men with him in one of the ship's boats and find the *Tonquin* a passage past the bar. Two of the Company's partners vainly begged the captain to wait offshore until the sea abated. According to one of the Company's clerks, the first

[1] Harmon, *Sixteen Years in the Indian Country*, p. 136.

mate himself protested and was told by Thorn, "Mr. Fox, if you are afraid of water, you should have remained at Boston."[2] Without a further word Fox pushed off. Almost immediately, caught in the tremendous combers, he lost all control over the tiny boat. No trace of it or its occupants was ever found. Several days later Thorn sent out a second boat on the same mission. This managed to find a passage through which the *Tonquin* came to a safe anchorage within the entrance of the river. However, the little boat that had piloted her was swamped and three men were lost, including Aikin the third mate.

Coming ashore, the Astorians should have found a British establishment presided over by David Thompson, and the Union Jack proudly flying. They found nothing of the sort, and set about building their own post: "On the 18th [of May], as soon as the foundation was completed, the establishment was named Astoria, in honour of Astor, the projector of the enterprise."[3]

At the beginning of June the *Tonquin* left on a fur trading cruise to the north. Since her second mate, unable to endure Thorn's tyranny any longer, had transferred to shore duty, her captain took her north without a single ship's officer left to assist him. As supercargo he had Alexander McKay, chosen by his fellow partners to superintend the actual trading with the Indians. This was the same McKay who had accompanied Mackenzie years before during his epic journey to the Pacific.

Several months after the sailing of the *Tonquin* the Astorians began to hear reports from the Indians that she had been attacked and her crew massacred. Much later, details were received from an Indian, the sole survivor, who had shipped aboard her at Gray's Harbour as an interpreter. According to him, Captain Thorn had anchored the *Tonquin* in Clayoquot Sound and commenced trading. During the bartering the captain lost his temper in an argument concerning price, and contemptuously rubbed one of the furs in the face of an important chief. He with his people immediately left the ship. McKay, ashore at the time, learned on his return of the incident

---

[2] Ross, *First Settlers*, p. 76.

[3] *Ibid.*, pp. 97-98.

from the Indian interpreter and apparently urged Thorn to lose no time in putting to sea.

The next morning the Indians, appearing very friendly, came aboard carrying bundles of furs for trade. Something about them alarmed the interpreter who went to McKay who once more urged the captain to put to sea. This time Thorn was persuaded. The seamen were busy hoisting sail and raising the anchor when the Indians, pulling daggers and clubs out of concealment under their furs, began the slaughter. Only three or four of the *Tonquin*'s people managed to get into the cabin at the ship's stern and hold off the Indians by musketfire. They knew, however, they could not hope to recapture the ship and instead opened the stern windows and got down into the small boat which, as was the usual practice, was towed behind her. Cutting loose, they made off at top speed for the open sea. Seeing the last of the defenders flee, the Indians, intent on plunder, swarmed all over the *Tonquin*. They were unaware that, before leaving, the last survivors had lit a slow fuse leading to her powder magazine. Suddenly there was a tremendous explosion as the ship blew up. Arms, legs, bodies, heads flew in every direction. About two hundred Indians were killed by the blast. The three or four men off the *Tonquin* did not manage to make it to Astoria. They too were murdered by Indians somewhere along the way.[4]

Significantly there were two different reactions among the early historians when they learned the story of the *Tonquin*'s end. One was expressed many years later by one of the clerks, Alexander Ross:

How precarious is the life of an Indian trader, if we take into consideration the habits of the country and the spirit of the people he has to live among — a people who feel no remorse in using the instruments

[4] There survives only one really contemporary version of the Indian's account of the end of the *Tonquin*. This is to be found in the manuscript diary kept at Astoria by one of the clerks, Alfred Seton, and discovered only in 1945. The foregoing account of the *Tonquin*'s end is based upon Seton (W. R. Kime, "Alfred Seton's Journal: A Source for Irving's *Tonquin* Disaster Account", *Oregon Historical Quarterly* [hereafter referred to as *OHQ*] 71 (1970):314-15. Three of Seton's fellow clerks later published books in which they included versions of the Indian's account (Franchère in 1820, Cox in 1831 and Ross in 1849). Judge Howay was certainly right in regarding Franchère's account as the most reliable of the three. See Howay, "The Loss of the *Tonquin*", *WHQ* 13 (1922):83-92.

of death — a people who delight in perfidy! Perfidy is the system of savages, treachery and cunning the instruments of their power, and cruelty and bloodshed the policy of their country.[5]

His fellow clerk, Gabriel Franchère, indulged in no such rhetoric but put the blame on Captain G. W. Ayres of Boston. Some time before, Ayres, needing hunters for a sealing expedition off the coast of California, had put into Clayoquot Sound with his ship the *Mercury*, and recruited ten or twelve of the local Indians, promising to return them safely home at the end of the seal-hunting. Instead, at the end of the hunt he had left his Clayoquots to perish on a deserted island off the California coast. The Indians had finally managed to get ashore and started working their way north, but they were all in the end either murdered or enslaved by other Indians. Word of Captain Ayres' betrayal had reached Clayoquot and his victims' fellow tribesmen were hungry for revenge upon any whites, even before Thorn's affront to their chief.

A somewhat curious episode followed the gunpowder explosion at Clayoquot Sound. The survivors were aware that word of their devastating losses, especially of their young warriors, must become known to their inveterate enemies, the Indians of Barkley Sound. These, realizing how reduced in strength the Clayoquots were, would surely descend upon them, bent on their extermination.

But the Clayoquots had recourse to a novel stratagem — They got all their women to don men's clothing and do up their hair as the men of the tribe and upon the appearance of strangers they regularly walked or sat about as the warriors of the tribe are wont to do. By this they appeared to the few Barclay S[d] Indians, who were sent ahead to examine the situation, as being too strong and numerous ... and the idea of extermination was given up.[6]

Six weeks after the departure of the *Tonquin* there was a new arrival at Astoria. At long last, hopelessly behind schedule, David Thompson arrived at the mouth of the Columbia to find the Stars and Stripes flying where he was supposed to have planted the Union Jack.

[5] Ross, *First Settlers*, p. 173.
[6] Letter of Father Brabant, 15 May 1896, MS in PABC, File E-D-B72.4.

We must turn back now to consider the recent movements of David Thompson. On June 28th in the previous year, he had stopped over at New White Earth House where Alexander Henry, the officer in charge, noted, "Mr. Thompson embarked with his family for Montreal".[7] He was already two years overdue for his rotation leave and no doubt was looking forward to spending his year off with his family in a more civilized part of the world. This was not to be. On July 18th, when the Nor'Westers concluded their annual meeting at Fort William, their "Arrangements" for the coming year included a clause assigning Thompson to the Columbia. Professor Richard Glover seems to be on firm ground when he concludes that at this meeting the partners had decided to entrust to Thompson the responsibility of getting to the mouth of the Columbia and establishing a post there ahead of the Astorians.[8] The news of his mission was probably waiting for Thompson when he arrived at Rainy Lake House on July 22nd. At this point his journey to Montreal came to an end. He turned around and with four canoes, twenty-four men and three tons of trade goods headed west on his new assignment.

On this trip Thompson followed the somewhat unusual procedure of not travelling with the canoe brigade placed under his charge. Instead, he rode overland with William Henry and two or three Indians who had the task of hunting for game and delivering the meat at three-day intervals to the canoes as they moved upstream. On September 15th, drawing near to the Rockies, Thompson made the last of these contacts with his brigade. Four or five days later, after waiting in vain for the brigade to appear, he became alarmed. The brigade had, in fact, encountered the Piegan chief Black Bear who had told them that his people did not wish them to go through to the Columbia and that, if they proceeded further, they would meet with other Piegans determined to force them to turn back. (By supplying guns, ammunition and iron for arrowheads to the Indians beyond the Rockies, the Nor'Westers had incurred the wrath of the Piegans who had hitherto had little trouble terrorizing the trans-

[7] Thompson, *Narrative*, ed. Glover, p. xlix.
[8] For the evidence that Thompson had been given this assignment, see *Ibid.*, pp. l-lii.

montane Kootenays.) The brigade halted at the point where Black
Bear had met them and for two days awaited their leader. But
Thompson did not appear. Dispirited, his men went downstream to
an abandoned post belonging to the North West Company and
waited there for eleven more days.

On October 5th another officer of the Company, Alexander
Henry, found the men at the old post and took charge of them and
their valuable cargoes. The Piegans who had earlier blocked their
way had now moved off and nothing prevented them continuing
their journey except the mysterious disappearance of their leader.
Alexander Henry was vainly combing the country in search of
Thompson when his cousin William Henry, Thompson's hunting
companion, turned up at the post with the amazing news that David
Thompson was in hiding far up in the north. Thompson knew from
experience the ferocity of the Piegans and the other tribes of the
Blackfoot confederacy. He knew too that he had incurred their
special enmity earlier when three of his men, using their guns, had
helped the "Saleesh" Indians to defeat the Piegans in battle. Now,
having learned from scouts that the Piegans meant to stop his party,
Thompson had panicked and fled. Visiting Thompson in his hiding
place, Alexander Henry found that, despite his assurances that the
Howse Pass route over the mountains was again open, Thompson
simply would not risk using it.[9] Instead, when his brigade finally
rejoined him, he led them up north to the Athabasca River and
here, by its headwater, he discovered the Athabasca Pass. This pass
would provide the route by which, during the next four decades,
most travellers from the East would make their entry into British
Columbia.

Travelling over this newly discovered route, Thompson in mid-
January of 1811 reached the junction of the Canoe River and the
Columbia, the famous Boat Encampment of subsequent fur trade
annals. Precious time had been lost by Thompson's Piegan panic

---

[9] It is significant that there is a gap in Thompson's own diaries (upon which
he based his *Narrative*) for the period from his return from Rainy Lake until
after his flight from the Piegans. It has been suggested that Thompson himself destroyed the missing Book 23, realizing how much it would tell against
him. (See Glover, ed., pp. lx-lxi.)

and his subsequent long swing north, but he still had two months in which to get to the mouth of the Columbia ahead of the Americans. The river was open and he could have gone down it, but he made a winter camp instead. On April 6th Thompson was ready to embark for the Pacific in a boat he had made of cedar planks. But now he was paying the price of weak leadership. Only three of his men were ready to make the journey into unknown country with him. Giving way to the mutineers, Thompson decided to recruit more men in the country where he was already established. Turning upstream instead of down, he was soon once more on his old familiar route by Windermere and Columbia Lakes, the Kootenay River and Lake Pend d'Oreille. It was not until June that he left Salish House, crossed by way of Spokane House to the Kettle Falls, and then started down the Columbia arriving, as we have noted, months after the landing of the Astorians.

Various explanations have been advanced for Thompson's delays in reaching the Pacific. Probably we shall never know the full truth of much which happened. The unravelling of the Piegan episode we owe to Professor Glover's careful work using the diary of Alexander Henry rather than Thompson's own evasive, misleading, and downright dishonest account of what happened. It has been suggested that Thompson put off his arrival at Astoria because he believed that his own company was in partnership with the Pacific Fur Company, but no evidence supports this thesis.[10] Whatever the reason, Thompson got there late.

For a lively account of Thompson's arrival at Astoria, we are indebted to a sardonic eye-witness, Alexander Ross:

On the 15th of July, we were rather surprised at the unexpected arrival of a north-west proprietor at Astoria, and still more so at the

---

[10] True, when Thompson arrived at Astoria he did show a document relating to the North West Company becoming a partner in the venture, but this was merely a letter from the wintering partners saying that if the Astorians had successfully founded their post, and if Astor was still prepared to sell a one-third interest, and if his price was not in excess of £10,000, they were prepared to have the North West Company buy in, if William McGillivray, the dominant partner in Montreal, felt the course justified. (See Dorothy Bridgwater, "John Jacob Astor Relative to His Settlement on Columbia River", *Yale University Library Gazette* 24 (1949):53-54.)

free and cordial reception given to an opponent. Mr. Thompson, northwest-like, came dashing down the Columbia in a light canoe, manned with eight Iroquois and an interpreter, chiefly men from the vicinity of Montreal. M'Dougall [Duncan McDougall in charge at Astoria] received him like a brother. . . . [11]

The Astorians had been outfitting a party, headed by David Stuart, to go up the Columbia and begin founding the intended network of interior trading posts. A few days after Thompson's arrival, this party started off and Thompson accompanied them. However, on July 31st, Thompson somewhat unexpectedly took his leave of Stuart and his people.

The latter learned the reason for Thompson's somewhat precipi-tant departure when they reached the junction of the Columbia River and the Snake a fortnight later. Here, flying above the Indian encampment was a Union Jack and a written declaration, left by Thompson, that the country to the north was British territory and closed to the Astorians who were free, however, to trade up the Snake River which would lead them south. The Indians informed Stuart that Koo-Koo-Sint [Thompson] had given them various gifts and in return they were to see that the Astorians did not proceed any farther up the Columbia. Ingenuously they added that, of course, if Stuart were to give them gifts outweighing those of Koo-Koo-Sint, he would obviously be the greater chief and they would have to let him go wherever he pleased. Stuart took the hint and continued up the Columbia unmolested.

And what of Koo-Koo-Sint *alias* David Thompson? Having hoisted his Union Jack and left his declaration at the junction of the Columbia and Snake Rivers, he had headed up the Snake some considerable distance, then took to the land and rode over to Spokane House. From here he went back to the Columbia, reaching it at Ilth-koy-ope [Kettle Falls] where he had earlier started his descent of the river to Astoria. From Kettle Falls on August 28th he wrote a letter to his fellow Nor'Westers in New Caledonia to let them know of his successful though belated breakthrough to the Pacific. Handed to an Indian, the letter gradually found its way

[11] Ross, *First Settlers*, p. 101.

northwards until, the following April, it was opened by Daniel Harmon at Stuart Lake.[12]

After getting off this letter to his northern colleagues and building a canoe, Thompson began to ascend the Columbia. On September 4th he passed the site of the future city of Trail. The next day he passed the mouth of the Kootenay River, that point which he could so easily have reached in 1808. Still ascending the Columbia, he followed it into the Arrow Lakes, becoming the first white man ever to travel on their tranquil waters. Northward he went, into the winding course of the upper Columbia. On September 11th he passed the site of the future city of Revelstoke. Then came the grim work of battling upstream through the perilous canyons and rapids. Finally, on September 18th, he reached the hut which he had built at Boat Encampment.

Awaiting at Boat Encampment for fresh trading supplies to reach him via the Athabasca Pass, Thompson could reflect as he looked upon the passing waters of the Columbia that, at one time or other during the five years which lay behind him, he had travelled every inch of that great river's course from its source in Columbia Lake to its mouth on the Pacific. It was a great achievement and none of his frailties or failures could rob him of it.

In the end, insufficient supplies arrived over the Athabasca Pass and Thompson himself had to cross the Rockies to bring in more. Resupplied, he descended the Columbia to Kettle Falls, then turned east to his favourite hunting ground, the country between Salish House, Spokane House and Lake Pend d'Oreille.

Let us return now to the activities of the Astorians and specifically to David Stuart, whom we left travelling up the Columbia despite Thompson's attempts with his Union Jack, written notice and payments to the Indians to halt him at the confluence of the Snake.

---

[12] Harmon, *Sixteen Years in the Indian Country*, pp. 220-21. This type of Indian post was not unusual. The letter would be given to one Indian, who would carry it as far as suited him and then sell it to another Indian, who would carry it another stretch of the journey before selling it at a profit to yet another Indian, and so on and on until the letter reached its recipient, who would pay off the Indian who had brought it the final stretch. Harmon notes that the letter could easily have reached him at the end of one month instead of eight, interesting evidence that the Indians felt no urgency about getting the mail to its destination.

At the beginning of September David Stuart reached the junction of the Okanagan River and the Columbia. Here, in a treeless semi-desert, he founded what was to become known as Fort Okanagan. In a small cabin, built chiefly of driftwood and measuring only sixteen feet by twenty, Stuart left Alexander Ross to trade with the local Indians. Before heading north up the Okanagan River with the rest of the party, Stuart told Ross that he could expect him back about the beginning of October. October passed, so did November, and December, and still no sign or word of Stuart. Abandoned in his little shanty, with only his small Spanish dog Weasel for company, young Ross endured as best he could:

Only picture to yourself, gentle reader, how I must have felt, alone in this unhallowed wilderness, without friend or white man within hundreds of miles of me, and surrounded by savages who had never seen a white man before. Every day seemed a week, every night a month. I pined, I languished, my head turned gray, and in a brief space ten years were added to my age.[13]

[13] Ross, *First Settlers*, pp. 154-55.

1812

The Astorians trade at Kamloops — The Nor'Westers set up a rival establishment.

We left Alexander Ross, the young Pacific Fur Company clerk, in terrible loneliness in his shanty waiting and waiting and waiting for the return of his chief, David Stuart. January passed, and so did February, and still no sign or word of Stuart. Then on March 22nd, the barking of Weasel alerted Ross to the approach of some men. They were Stuart and his three subordinates. After welcoming them with enormous relief, Ross was able to report that his 188 days cut off in the wilderness had proved highly profitable for the Company. From the Indians he had obtained 1550 beaver skins as well as other pelts, worth an estimated £2,250 on the Canton market. In return he had given trade goods worth £35.

Of Stuart's journey north we know very little. Following up the winding Okanagan River, he crossed at Osoyoos Lake into what would one day be part of Canada. Continuing north along the river, he passed under the tremendous rock face of McIntyre Bluff and came to Vaseux Lake, alive with waterfowl. Then once more he travelled up the Okanagan River. At times he must have encountered bands of Okanagan Indians. Presumably, like Ross later, he found them "by no means ferocious or cruel, either in looks, habits or dispositions; but . . . , on the contrary, rather an easy, mild, and agreeable people."[1] Perhaps when he came to Okanagan Falls, the headquarters of the tribe, he found flapping in the breeze the insignia of their chief:

. . . a white wolf-skin, fantastically painted with rude figures of different colours — the head and tail decorated with higua [dentalium shells],

[1] Ross, *First Settlers*, p. 278.

150

bears' claws, and the teeth of different animals — suspended from a pole, in a conspicuous place near the chief's lodge.[2]

Onward Stuart pressed until he saw, extending towards the horizon, the blue water of the great Okanagan Lake, cradled amid its arid hills. Onward still Stuart and his men continued, deeper and deeper into a land which no white man had ever seen before, until they reached what Stuart called the "head waters" of the Okanagan. Here they left the dry country and, crossing over a low range of wooded mountains, hardly more than hills, descended into the valley of the South Thompson River, gliding peacefully with never a waterfall or even a rapid. It seems certain that he travelled down this tranquil river to its junction with the North Thompson, where the city of Kamloops now sprawls on hillside and valley floor. Next Stuart "commenced travelling for some time amongst a powerful nation called the She Whaps". Perhaps he became, during these travels, the first white man to see the gentle Wordsworthian beauty of Shuswap Lake. We shall never know how many of those wonderful fishing lakes around Kamloops, dotted now with summer cottages, were visited by Stuart, always watching for the gnawed stumps left by beaver, and their dams and lodges, as he tried to assess the value of this country for a fur trading company. So much time did he spend in these explorations that the snow was in the mountains when he and his men were ready to return:

. . . after waiting for fine weather the snows got so deep that we considered it hopeless to attempt getting back, and, therefore, passed our time with the She-Whaps and other tribes in that quarter. The Indians were numerous and well disposed, and the country throughout abounds in beavers and all other kinds of fur; and I have made arrangements to establish a trading post there the ensuing winter.[3]

Back at Okanagan, David Stuart paused for a while, then headed down to Astoria with the furs which he and Ross had acquired. He left Ross a couple of men at the post to give him help and company.

At Astoria, Stuart found that members of Astor's overland party had been straggling in during January and February after tremen-

[2] *Ibid.*, p. 277.

[3] *Ibid.*, p. 159.

dous hardships along the way. Then, in mid-May there was rejoicing at Astoria with the arrival of the first of the supply ships that Astor intended to send out annually. The depot on the Columbia was now fully manned and well supplied. Astor's project was clearly a success, and that American presence so eagerly anticipated by President Jefferson had been effectively established in the Pacific North-west.

While Stuart remained busy at Astoria, Ross set out from Fort Okanagan on a follow-up visit to the northern territory which had so favourably impressed his chief. Ten days of travelling in mid-May brought Ross to:

> ... a place called by the Indians Cumcloups, near the entrance of the north branch [of the Thompson River]. From this station I sent messages to the different tribes around, who soon assembled, bringing with them their furs. Here we stayed for ten days. The number of Indians collected on the occasion could not have been less than 2,000. Not expecting to see so many, I had taken but a small quantity of goods with me; nevertheless, we loaded all our horses — so anxious were they to trade, and so fond of tobacco, that one morning before breakfast I obtained one hundred and ten beavers for leaf-tobacco, at the rate of five leaves per skin; and at last, when I had but one yard of white cotton remaining, one of the chiefs gave me twenty prime beaver skins for it.[4]

Ready to start for home, Ross found he had a special problem to handle. Boullard, one of his two subordinates, had fallen in love with a native woman and, lacking the means to purchase her from her father, demanded that Ross supply the price. A horsewhipping having brought the amorous voyageur to his senses, the journey back was begun, and the party reached the post known as Okanagan (near Brewster, Washington) in mid-July.

Mid-August saw David Stuart pausing at Okanagan, en route with men and supplies to found a new post at Kamloops. Putting Ross in formal command at Okanagan, Stuart pressed swiftly on. This year Ross had the chastened Boullard and one other man to keep him company at Okanagan, but clearly the isolation this second winter depressed him to the point where he resolved to visit associates

---

[4] *Ibid.*, p. 199.

at other establishments. First there was a visit to Mr. Clarke at the Spokane post. Hardly back from Spokane, Ross decided to spend New Year's with Stuart up at Kamloops. Ten days of rapid travel brought him to Stuart's establishment but, to his surprise, he found not one but two trading posts there. The North West Company had been jealously watching the inroads of the American company and, as a result, in November a Nor'Wester, La Rocque, appeared on the scene and built a trading post right beside Stuart's. Those same "mild and insinuating manners" which helped Stuart to get on so well with the Indians were equally effective with La Rocque, and the rival traders co-existed in an atmosphere of personal friendship and cooperation. As Stuart mildly observed, he and La Rocque probably conducted their respective businesses at least as profitably as friends as they would have as enemies.

La Rocque was not the only Nor'Wester extending his company's range this year. In January, Daniel Harmon and James McDougall arrived at Babine Lake where they were hospitably received, but found the local Indians getting European trade goods from the coast.

Our chronicle for this year would not be complete without one other item. Late in April David Thompson, returning from the area ranging from eastern Washington to western Montana which he had opened for the North West Company's trade, arrived once more at Kettle Falls by the Columbia. Just as in the previous year, he travelled via the Columbia up through British Columbia to Boat Encampment, and continued over the Athabasca Pass, this time taking his final leave of our history.

No photograph of Thompson survives, no artist's portrait in oil, not even a hurried charcoal sketch to tell us what this strange enigmatic man looked like. All that we have to fall back upon is a verbal portrait left by the naturalist Bigsby, who met him in Montreal in 1817 and described him thus:

A singular-looking person of about fifty. He was plainly dressed, quiet, and observant. His figure was short and compact, and his black hair was worn long all around, and cut square, as if by one stroke of the shears, just above the eyebrows. His complexion was of the gardener's ruddy brown, while the expression of deeply furrowed features was

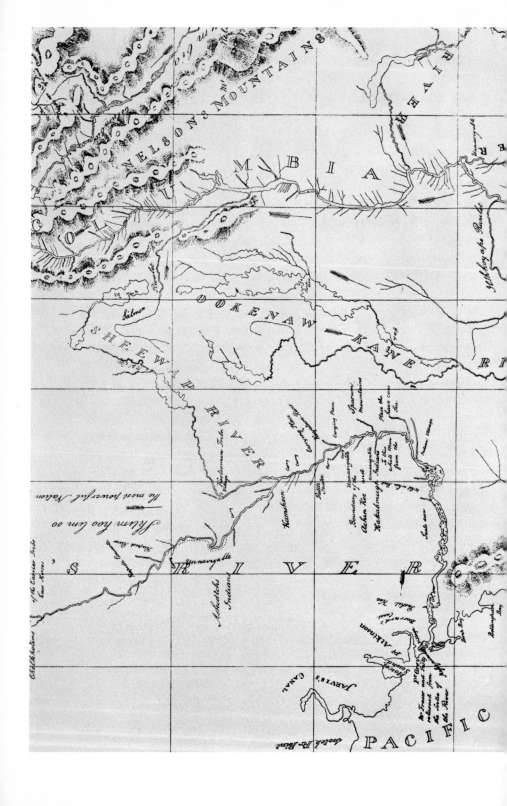

friendly and intelligent, but his cut, short nose gave him an odd look. His speech betrayed the Welshman.[5]

A description of the outer man is one thing, but much more important is an assessment of the inner man. And here history has rendered a mingled verdict. Thompson has had his champions[6] but they have been outweighed by his critics.[7] Consider Professor Morton's final indictment of the man:

> By failing to make the main object of the Columbian enterprise the main object of his activities, by turning away from the direct route by the Kootenay and the Columbia, by spending his summers taking out the furs instead of pressing on towards the sea, by establishing forts in the midst of, and arming, the enemies of the Piegans, David Thompson fixed the predisposing conditions of his failure. When the crisis was on, by not facing the Piegans and bargaining for an unmolested passage across the mountains, but changing the route to the unfrequented Athabaska pass, he failed to assert the right of Great Britain to the mouth of the Columbia by right of settlement before the arrival of the Americans. The Columbian enterprise entrusted to his hands went awry.[8]

But more must be said than this. Certain factors extenuate and explain, even if they cannot excuse, his major failure. David Thompson was a man of forty, an old age in the fur trade, when the Americans beat him to the mouth of the Columbia. Advancing years may have brought a weakening of the will and a slackening of the energies. Certainly he was never a leader of men, being essentially a "loner" except for his deep emotional dependence upon his wife and children. Deeply flawed, he could at times be self-righteous, petty and jealous. He was wily, and often less than honest. Generally he

---

[5] J. B. Tyrrell, "David Thompson, A Great Geographer", *The Geographical Journal* 37 (1911):58.

[6] e.g. Victor G. Hopwood, ed., *David Thompson: Travels in Western North America, 1784-1812* (Toronto, 1971); and H. D. Smiley, "The Dalliance of David Thompson", *The Beaver* (Winter 1972), pp. 40-47.

[7] Chief among these is A. S. Morton (who is quoted below), and Richard Glover, whose extensive introduction to his definitive edition of Thompson's *Narrative* has been particularly helpful to us in reaching our own position in what has become one of the most controversial areas in British Columbia history.

[8] "The North West Company's Columbian Enterprise and David Thompson", *CHR* 17 (1936):288.

could cope with a sudden danger, but there was a Hamlet streak in him that made him prone to indecision and delay. He was, however, the best topographer and surveyor in the employ of any of the fur trading companies, being known universally among his associates as "The Astronomer". And he has earned a place inferior only to that of Vancouver, Mackenzie and Fraser among the explorers of British Columbia.

1813

The Astorians sell out to the Nor'Westers — H.M.S. Racoon's absurd blunder.

Having celebrated New Year's with David Stuart at Kamloops in the old Scottish fashion, Alexander Ross set out for his own post. But now, in a country virtually unknown to white men, he gave way to curiosity and decided to do some exploring along the way. Instead of taking the now familiar Thompson-Okanagan route, Ross struck out in a more westerly direction towards present-day Merritt. The decision was not a fortunate one. Ross and his companion became lost in the deep snow in the mountains and the frozen crust on the snow cruelly cut the legs of their horses. Not a blade of grass could be found anywhere. At one point it took them five days to travel five miles and they were haunted by the fear that their horses, unfed for days, would give out completely. Fortunately, just in the nick of time, they discovered "a low and pleasant valley" where kindly Indians provided sustenance for both them and their horses. Then, following the Similkameen River to its junction with the Okanagan, they had a clear run home.

Meanwhile back at Astoria great excitement and no little anxiety had prevailed when, on January 15th, one of the partners had returned in great haste from Spokane House. Here a North West Company party had informed him that the previous June the United States government had declared war against Great Britain. The War of 1812 was now being fought. Urgent consultations at once took place. The situation of the Pacific Fur Company's wintering partners, clerks and voyageurs was a curious one. Almost all of them were former Nor'Westers who, though they had entered into the service of an American company, had remained British subjects. On the one hand, as liege subjects to the British Crown they were bound to serve their sovereign and give no aid to his enemies. On the other hand, they were bound either by contract or indenture to advance the interests of the American Astor. Events resolved their dilemma for this spring their anticipated supply ship did not arrive. They concluded, logically enough, that a British naval blockade was making it impossible for Astor to get any ships through to them. Under these circumstances they decided to abandon Astoria and the whole project of the Pacific Fur Company. Plans were laid to accumulate large supplies of dried food and a sufficiency of horses in preparation for a hazardous trek overland to St. Louis. After extended debate, the spring of 1814 was set for the commencement of this ordeal.

Such was the situation when in October of this year about seventy Nor'Westers in a squadron of ten canoes arrived at Astoria to take over the establishment. One of the leaders of the newcomers was John Stuart, the North West Company's officer in command of New Caledonia whom we last met at his headquarters at Stuart Lake. He had left that post in May and, travelling via Fort Kamloops and Fort Okanagan, had opened that tremendously important route which for decades would link New Caledonia with the Columbia River.

John Stuart and his associates had no artillery and, in fact, had no intention of storming the little fort. Its capture could be attended to by one or other of two ships en route to the Columbia. One was their own supply vessel the *Isaac Todd*, which they expected would be heavily armed and supplied with letters of marque; the other was a British warship. Camping beside the American fort, the Nor'Westers began their wait for the ships. Unfortunately they were low on provisions and had to buy food from the Astorians. At some point an important proposal was made: that the Astorians, many of them old friends and associates of the Nor'Westers, should sell them not just food but everything — their fort, their inland posts, their stock of trade goods, and the furs which they had accumulated over the months. Bargaining began, but it did not proceed quickly or easily. According to one account, the Astorians, to force completion of the deal before the arrival of an armed British vessel, cut off all food and threatened to use their few small cannon on the Nor'Westers unless the agreement was signed. At any event, on October 16th the deed of sale was signed. Down came the Stars and Stripes and up went the Union Jack. There was no longer an American settlement on the Pacific Coast.

A number of the erstwhile Astorians joined or rejoined the North West Company. Those who did not were assured of their maintenance until they could accompany a party of Nor'Westers back overland to the East. The North West Company undertook to pay each man any arrears in wages due to him from the now defunct Pacific Fur Company. Among those who rejoined the North West Company was Duncan McDougall, who had been in command at Astoria. Nineteenth-century American historians were to heap abuse upon him as a traitor who had betrayed Astor. Actually it is hard to see how he could have done much better by him. From the North West Company he secured for Astor bills of exchange, payable in Canada, for the sum of $80,500.[1]

The deal, from the American point of view, was consummated none too soon. At the end of November H.M.S. *Racoon*, 26 guns, entered the Columbia. To make sure of her despatch, the North West Company had made the Admiralty in London believe that a major American base existed at the mouth of the Columbia. Coming ashore, Captain W. Black, R.N., could hardly believe his eyes. Had he come all this distance to take over a few paltry log buildings surrounded by a palisade? "What, is this the fort I have heard so much of? Great God, I could batter it down with a four-pounder in two hours!"[2]

Despite the disappointment of himself and his men who had visions of prize money to be won by capturing Astoria, Captain Black proved "a gentleman of courteous and affable manners". His affability may have owed something to a partiality for Madeira wine. Tipsiness, or a passion for ceremonies, or that blind following of orders so common in the armies and navies of the world, may account for an absurd ritual carried out at Astoria on December 12th, just before H.M.S. *Racoon* put to sea. Astoria might be British

[1] Ross, *First Settlers*, p. 244.

[2] Gabriel Franchère, *Journal of a Voyage on the North West Coast of North America during the Years 1811, 1812, 1813 and 1814*, ed. W. Kaye Lamb, Champlain Society 45 (Toronto, 1969), p. 134.

already due to purchase by a Canadian company, but Captain Black
was going to seize it for Britain anyways. Coming ashore with a
lieutenant of marines, four marines and four bluejackets, Black was
feasted by the Nor'Westers. Franchère's journal continues:

After dinner, having distributed firearms to the servants of the Company, we mounted a platform where a flagpole had been erected. There
the Captain took a British flag that he had brought for the purpose and
raised in [it?] to the top of the staff; taking a bottle of Madeira, he
smashed it against the pole, proclaiming in a loud voice that he took
possession of the establishment and the country in the name of His
Britannic Majesty and named it Fort George.[3]

Setting out to sea, Captain Black prepared a coded despatch[4]
informing his superiors that his mission had been accomplished. The
ceremonial taking possession of Fort George had been a silly little
charade, but in the years which were to follow it would have very
grave consequences for Britain.

[3] *Ibid.*, p. 133.
[4] PRO, Adm. 1/1554/1698.

1814

Jane Barnes, barmaid, first white woman on the Columbia —
New Caledonia supplied from the Pacific.

At his remote and isolated post on Stuart Lake Daniel Harmon, temporarily in command of New Caledonia, had a welcome visitor this February. It was Donald McLennan, despatched from Astoria by Harmon's absent chief, John Stuart, with joyful news of the North West Company's acquisition of all the posts and property of Astor's Pacific Fur Company.

In February W. P. Hunt, one of Astor's American partners, arrived at the mouth of the Columbia in a ship, the *Pedler*. Sailing on April 2nd, he took with him the few Americans who had served at Astoria. Two days later most of the Nor'Westers, leaving a party to carry on the fur trade of the newly named Fort George, started for the remote colony of Canada. With them they took all of their erstwhile Astorian compatriots who wished to return to their Canadian homes. Ninety men, in ten canoes, commenced the long ascent of the Columbia en route to the Athabasca Pass.

Two weeks after the overland brigade had left, the spirits of the little group manning Fort George were raised by the long-delayed arrival of the North West Company's supply ship *Isaac Todd*. Along with her cargo of trade goods she brought something considerably more interesting — a white woman.

Miss Jane Barnes had been a lively barmaid at an hotel in Portsmouth, at which Mr. Mac[Tavish] had stopped preparatory to his embarkation. This gentleman, being rather of an amorous temperament, proposed the trip to Miss Jane, who, "nothing loth", threw herself on his protection, regardless of consequences, and after encountering the perils of a long sea voyage, found herself an object of interest to the residents at the fort, and the greatest curiosity that ever gratified the wondering eyes of the blubber-loving aboriginals of the north-west coast of America. The Indians daily thronged in numbers to our fort for the mere purpose of gazing on, and admiring the fair beauty, every article of whose dress was examined with the most minute scrutiny.[1]

Smitten by the charms of Miss Jane Barnes, the "Prince of Wales", as the heir of the local Chinook chief was jokingly known, proposed marriage to her. Alas, even though she was promised a hundred sea otter skins for her relatives, and precedence over all the other wives of the Prince of Wales, Jane declined his offer, and returned to England on the *Isaac Todd*.

October 18th was a historic day up at Stuart Lake in New Caledonia. Then it was that an astounded Daniel Harmon, at the post later to be known as Fort St. James, saw two canoes approaching laden with trading goods from the *Isaac Todd*. For the first time New Caledonia was receiving supplies from the Pacific Coast instead of the incredibly long and difficult overland route from Canada. The North West Company had finally completed its "Columbian Enterprise" with the arrival of that shipment. However, not until the Hudson's Bay Company took over some years later would the Columbia supply system be firmly established.

December 24th saw British and American commissioners at Ghent signing a treaty ending the War of 1812. Its main provision required each side to restore any territory which it had seized during the war. In those days of incredibly slow communications, the American negotiators knew nothing about the end of Astor's settlement on the Columbia. They were satisfied, however, that if Astoria had fallen to the British this clause would secure its return.

[1] Cox, *Columbia River*, pp. 156-57.

1815

A letter from John Stuart.

With trade on the lower Columbia now totally in its control, the North West Company proceeded to branch out in New Caledonia. The previous year it had established Fort Fraser on Fraser Lake, named in honour of Simon Fraser who had had a temporary base there in 1806. On April 25th John Stuart, back in New Caledonia, wrote a letter to his young Irish friend, Ross Cox, serving in the Columbia Department. In this letter Stuart had interesting things to say about the Indians and the beaver trade in what is now north-central British Columbia:

The Carriers are naturally of an open and hospitable disposition; but very violent, and subject to sudden gusts of passion, in which much blood is often shed. However, those quarrels are soon made up, and as soon forgotten.

They seldom, even in the most favourable seasons, kill many beaver in winter, the depth of the snow being, as they allege, too great. The utmost we can therefore do is to collect the produce of their summer hunt; which, as we have to go in different and distant directions, is a work of much labour, and takes up a great portion of our men's time. We have no cause to complain of last year's trade; and to finish my letter like a true North-Wester, I have great pleasure in acquainting you that our returns are about 95 packs. . . . [1]

Since the standard ninety-pound pack or bale generally contained about sixty beaver pelts, Stuart had obtained for the Company some 6000 beaver pelts, a valuable harvest indeed.

[1] Cox, *Columbia River*, p. 218.

1816

Ross Cox at Fort Okanagan.

Not every young man who sought his fortune in the fur trade was cut out for the work. Ebullient and loquacious, Ross Cox had his misgivings about the life even while he was still able to enjoy the company of other clerks. Christmas 1815 had found a group of them:

... striving to warm ourselves under the tarpaulin porch, half blinded by the puffs of smoke sent in by cold easterly gusts. . . . our thoughts wandered towards home, and the happy faces surrounding the quiet and domestic hearth: the contrast was too strong for our philosophy, and we were almost tempted to call down inverted benedictions on the unfortunate beaver, and those who first invented beaver hats, beaver bonnets, and beaver cloaks![1]

This year the young Irishman was placed in charge of a post of his own. He became, in his own grandiloquent term, "commandant" at Okanagan. To keep his men and himself busy, he rebuilt his post on a much larger scale, surrounding it for the first time with palisades strengthened by bastions. Nevertheless his spirits wilted at finding himself "without a colleague or a companion". (The officers of the fur trading companies, even if only junior clerks, did not mingle socially with their French-Canadian, Kanaka[2] or Indian canoemen or labourers.) Convivial by nature, Cox grew more and more unhappy in his isolation:

The summer of 1816 did not tend to diminish my growing aversion to the Indian country. Horse-racing, deer-hunting, and grouse-shooting were pleasant pastimes enough, but the want of companionable society rendered every amusement "stale, flat, and unprofitable." . . . Bad French and worse Indian began to usurp the place of English, and I

[1] Cox, *Columbia River*, pp. 223-24.
[2] The standard word then used for Hawaiian Islanders.

found my conversation gradually becoming a barbarous compound of various dialects.[3]

Receipt of letters from home finally brought on a crisis. Writing to the Company's partners, Cox begged for, and received, release from their service. A couple of years later he was back in the warm world of Dublin's pubs, telling tall tales of his doings in the Wild West.

[3] Cox, *Columbia River*, p. 247.

1817

Disaster at Dalles des Morts — Murder and cannibalism.

The life of the maritime fur traders, exposed to dangers of shipwreck or Indian attack, was a hard one, but it was nothing like as hard as that of the fur traders who travelled the inland routes in frail birchbark canoes, clumsy dugouts, or the larger "Columbia River boats". Let the inland voyageurs once lose their boats, and with them their muskets, ammunition and small supply of provisions, and their position immediately became desperate. The events of this year provide a truly tragic example of what could happen.

At the end of May the two canoes and twenty-three persons making up the North West Company's eastbound party this year, after a long and difficult ascent to the Big Bend of the Columbia, rendezvoused at Boat Encampment. Here they would leave their canoes and begin the arduous trip by foot through the Rocky Mountains. Looking over the party, the leaders, Duncan McDougall and Angus Bethune, decided that some of the men simply were not up to the arduous ordeal of crossing the Athabasca Pass. They resolved accordingly that these men (six voyageurs and an English tailor named Holmes) should turn back with one of the canoes and, running downstream, make for the North West Company's establishment of Spokane House.[1]

Mustering what energies they had, the seven men started down the Columbia. North of the present city of Revelstoke they came to the rocky narrows long known as "Les Dalles des Morts", and now named Death Rapids. As these were much too dangerous to navigate, the men went ashore and, with a line to the stern of the canoe, eased it down the rapids and with long poles pushed it into the stream whenever it veered towards the rocky shore. All went well until the

---

[1] Cox, *Columbia River*, pp. 278-79.

rope snapped. Grasped by the tremendous current, the canoe was smashed to pieces on the rocks below. Ordinarily, when descending such difficult stretches, the men would have unloaded their equipment and provisions, backpacked them the length of the rapids, and put them back in their canoe after it had safely made the passage. Unfortunately, in their weakened condition, the men had tried to save themselves that exertion. Consequently, when they lost their canoe they lost all their provisions and also, apparently, their firearms.

Hopeless though the prospect was, the only thing the men could do was to make their way on foot down the river in the thin hope of meeting friendly Indians. Unfortunately the river was in flood with the spring runoff, and they had no convenient bars to walk along. The men had to fight their way through the forest verge with all its deadfalls and tangled undergrowth. Moreover, the season was still too early for the ripening of berries which might have given them sustenance. On the third day one of the voyageurs, Maçon, died. His starving comrades cut up his body for food and struggled on, making only a few miles each day. Next to die was Holmes, the Englishman, who similarly became food for the others. A third man, a fourth, and a fifth all met, in turn, the same fate. Finally two survivors, La Pierre and Dubois, arrived at the head of Upper Arrow Lake. Here for two days they vainly sought for Indians. According to La Pierre, on their second night on the lakeshore Dubois' conduct made him suspicious. That night he only feigned sleep and so was able to grapple with Dubois when the latter struck for his neck with a clasp knife. The struggle ended with La Pierre, in self-defence, cutting Dubois' throat.

A few days later two Indians found La Pierre and carried him to Kettle Falls, from where he was conducted to Spokane House and told his story. Subsequently other Indians reported that, close to the remains of Dubois, they had found the remains of two white men marked by evidences of murder. Under the Canada Jurisdiction Act of 1803 crimes committed in the Indian Country could be tried in Lower Canada. The North West Company accordingly sent La Pierre east for trial, along with an Indian who was prepared to give testimony. The court however found the evidence insufficient and La Pierre was acquitted of the charge of murder.

This same year an attempt was made to find some route from Kamloops to the Athabasca Pass, one which would bypass the very dangerous stretches of the upper Columbia, and at the same time open up new fur country. This venture was entrusted to Alexander Ross, in charge of the North West Company's post at Kamloops. With only four men, though later joined by a guide, he went up the North Thompson, crossed to East Barriere Lake, travelled up the upper Adams River, cut across the mountains, and arrived at Canoe River some distance north of Boat Encampment. He estimated that the actual distance he had travelled was not unduly long. But there were other considerations besides distance:

From all I saw or could learn, however, in reference to the country generally little can be said in its favour. No road [trail] for the purpose of land transportation appeared to me practicable. . . . [2]

[2] Alexander Ross, *The Fur Hunters of the Far West* (Norman, Okla., 1967), p. 107.

1818

A legal quibble restores Astoria to the Americans — Anglo-American co-dominion over the Pacific North-west.

The Treaty of Ghent of 1814 had provided that Britain and the United States should each restore to the other the territory seized during the War of 1812. But what of Astoria which had been purchased from an American company by a British company and then, after it was already British, been pompously "seized" for Britain by the captain of H.M.S. *Racoon?* The Americans clamoured for its "restoration". After all, it had been "seized", had it not? The British, with all their interests in a burgeoning world-wide empire, were not really very concerned about what flag flew over an obscure little trading post on the far side of North America. Regrettably, Britain gave way. In October of this year H.M.S. *Blossom* arrived off Fort George, formerly Astoria, with British and American commissioners on board. There was an exchange of documents. The American flag was hoisted above the fort and saluted by the *Blossom's* guns. The best comment on the proceedings has been supplied not by a British but an American historian who has contemptuously remarked: " . . . the restoration of Astoria, as a post, had been secured — a private fur company's post, claimed after its sale, by the American government, as a national possession."[1]

The North West Company went on with its business at Fort George as usual after this silly and petty incident. Only it was to prove not so petty. In the strange, subtle, legalistic, treacherous world of diplomacy such ceremonies can be made to count for much, and Britain had needlessly strengthened the hand of the United States for a showdown still many years in the future.

Perhaps the British attached so little importance to the hoisting

[1] Katharine B. Judson, "The British Side of the Restoration of Fort Astoria", *OHQ* 20 (1919):327.

once more of the American flag at Astoria because they saw it as insignificant in the context of a bigger issue, that of sovereignty over the entire Pacific North-west. The British position was that she held clear title to everything between Spanish California to the south and Russian Alaska to the north. Her position rested upon the discoveries and claims made by Drake, Cook and Vancouver, upon the Nootka Convention, upon Mackenzie's crossing to the Pacific in 1793, upon the fact that a British naval officer had been the first to ascend the Columbia for some eighty-five miles from its mouth, and upon the fact that every white settlement in the entire area was that of a British trading company. Despite all this James Monroe, the American Secretary of State, in his instructions to his country's plenipotentiaries at Ghent, had laid it down that they must not believe that the British had "any claim whatever to territory on the Pacific Ocean".[2] Apparently he believed that his own country did have such a claim on the basis of Gray's rediscovery of the mouth of the Columbia, the Lewis and Clark expedition of 1805-1806, and the defunct Astorian venture. In August of this year, to augment the very weak American case, U.S.S. *Ontario* entered the Columbia and claimed the land on both sides of the river for the United States, blandly ignoring the fact that five years earlier this same territory had been claimed for Britain by H.M.S. *Racoon*, and that in 1792 Broughton had claimed for the same country the entire lower Columbia.

At this point neither Britain nor the United States was prepared to concede sovereignty to the other, the Americans making up for the weakness of their case by an aggressiveness of language which amazed the British. The consequence was the third article of a convention signed by the two powers on October 20th of this year:

ARTICLE III

It is agreed, that any country that may be claimed by either party on the northwest coast of America, westward of the Stony [Rocky] Mountains, shall, together with its harbours, bays, and creeks, and the navigation of all rivers within the same, be free and open, for the term of ten years from the date of the signature of the present convention,

---

[2] Frederick Merk, *The Oregon Question: Essays in Anglo-American Diplomacy and Politics* (Cambridge, Mass., 1967), p. 7.

to the vessels, citizens, and subjects of the two Powers: It being well understood, that this agreement is not to be construed to the prejudice of any claim, which either of the two high contracting parties may have to any part of the said country, nor shall it be taken to affect the claims of any other Power or State to any part of the said country; the only object of the high contracting parties, in that respect, being to prevent disputes and differences amongst themselves.[3]

The period of co-occupation had begun. It would last until 1846.

---

[3] *Treaties, Conventions, International Acts, Protocols and Agreements between the United States and Other Powers 1776-1909* (Washington, D.C., 1910) I: 632.

1819

Daniel Harmon makes a moral choice — The Hudson's Bay Company enters New Caledonia.

More than once in these annals mention has been made of Daniel Harmon, for eight years John Stuart's second-in-command in New Caledonia. The product of a pious Congregationalist family in Vermont, young Harmon had turned a little wild, and sought profit and adventure in the Indian Country with the North West Company. He had acquired, like most of his associates, a "fur trade wife", half Cree and half French-Canadian. This woman had accompanied him to New Caledonia in 1810, and had continued to bear him children there. Now, in 1819, Harmon was leaving the Indian Country for good and he had to decide what to do about her.

The normal thing for a Nor'Wester in his situation was simply to turn over his woman, with a dowry, to some other man in the service; and take unto himself a white wife when he rejoined civilization. But Harmon, during a period of total isolation at the fort while his men were off at Pinchi Lake picking berries, had undergone religious conversion. For Harmon, with both a Christian conscience and a very real attachment to his woman, the "easy" solution proved anything but an easy one. And yet how could he introduce his tawny mate into New England society as Mrs. Harmon? He grappled with his problem. Finally he reached his decision, which he entered into his journal on February 28th of this year, just before his departure for the East:

Having lived with this woman as my wife, though we were never formally contracted to each other, during life, and having children by her, I consider that I am under a moral obligation not to dissolve the connexion, if she is willing to continue it. The union which has been formed between us, in the providence of God, has not only been cemented by a long and mutual performance of kind offices, but, also, by a more sacred consideration. Ever since my own mind was turned effectually to the subject of religion, I have taken pains to instruct her in the great doctrines and duties of christianity. My exertions have not been in vain. Through the merciful agency of the Holy Spirit, I trust that she has become a partaker with me, in the consolations and hopes of the gospel.[1]

When Harmon arrived home in Vermont later this year, his woman, now properly and legally Mrs. Harmon, accompanied him, and there their children were duly baptized according to the rites of the Congregational Church.

Thus far in our chronicling we have noted that the fur trade west of the Rockies was, apart from the brief Astorian venture, entirely in the hands of the North West Company. This year, however, the Hudson's Bay Company sought to tap the lucrative New Caledonia trade. In February, John Clarke, commanding the Hudson's Bay Company's St. Mary's post on the Peace River, reported on negotiations with a group of Iroquois hunters who had previously worked with the North West Company. This season they would bring their New Caledonia furs to the Hudson's Bay Company. Moreover, while hunting in New Caledonia, they would induce the natives to give a friendly reception to the Hudson's Bay Company traders soon to appear in their territories. Unfortunately Clarke's plans went all awry. When the Iroquois returned from New Caledonia they failed to find any Hudson's Bay Company man awaiting them at the appointed rendezvous. On December 11th, Colin Robertson sadly reported:

Mr. Giasson arrived from towards the source of the Smoky River; this Gentleman missed the Free Iroquois, as they crossed the Mountain at the Peace River Portage; where they remained several days for us, and despairing of our arrival, they gave their Furs to the N.W.Co., say twenty four packs!! of pure Beaver.[2]

---

[1] Harmon, *Sixteen Years in the Indian Country*, p. 194.

[2] E. E. Rich, ed., *Colin Robertson's Correspondence Book, September 1817 to September 1822*, HBRS 2 (London, 1939):214. "Free Iroquois" were those not in the employ of either of the companies. The intrusion of the Iroquois into their hunting areas was bitterly resented by the tribes native to New Caledonia. Two years earlier the Carriers had murdered one of these interlopers, along with his wife and children.

1820

Fur trade rivalry in New Caledonia — The founding there of Fort George.

This year the Hudson's Bay Company made a second, more success-ful attempt to enter the New Caledonia trade. About the end of April Ignace Giasson, a clerk in the Company's employ, accompanied a party of Iroquois when they crossed into New Caledonia and penetrated to "the Forks of Fraser's River". In October he returned after a successful expedition. Letters by the Nor'Westers reveal an alarmed awareness this year of the incursions planned by the Hudson's Bay Company. Promptly they took some counter-steps of their own. At the confluence of the Fraser River and the Nechako (where Simon Fraser had had his advance base) the North West Company this year established a permanent post, Fort George, forerunner of the modern city of Prince George.

On March 12th of this year, Sir Alexander Mackenzie died in Scotland where he had retired to live the life of a laird. The young girl whom he had married lived until 1860.

1821

The wars between the North West Company and the Hudson's Bay Company — The companies amalgamate — A precarious banquet at York Factory.

This year the North West Company added another fort to its New Caledonia establishment. Built on the Fraser River, close to the most southerly point reached by Sir Alexander Mackenzie twenty-eight years earlier, this post was fittingly named Fort Alexandria. The founding of this fort was one of the last acts of the North West Company, for this year it ceased to exist following a merger with the Hudson's Bay Company.

The Hudson's Bay Company has so far received scant mention in our chronicle since Columbia and New Caledonia were the preserve of the North West Company. For many years a somewhat somnolent and ill-directed Hudson's Bay Company had been content to minimize competition and conflict with the highly aggressive Nor'Westers. This policy began to change after 1809 when the Earl of Selkirk and his associates secured control of the historic company. It is perhaps indicative of some quickening of the pulse that in June 1810 the Hudson's Bay Company sent its first trading party west of the Rockies. Led by Joseph Howse, it crossed the Howse Pass (actually discovered by Thompson a few years earlier) and headed southwards, until it established a temporary post close to today's Kalispell, Montana. In the summer of 1811 Howse and his men were back at Fort Edmonton with a good harvest of furs, but the venture was deemed too hazardous to repeat. Moreover, the Company was still anxious to avoid confrontation with the Nor'Westers. This situation was to change in a few years when the Company's London directors decided to adopt a much more aggressive policy urged upon them by Colin Robertson.

Colin Robertson was a one-time Nor'Wester who had turned

against his former associates. In a memorandum, submitted to the Hudson's Bay Company in 1810, he had outlined a policy which he was convinced would give the London company supremacy over the Montreal one. The essence of Robertson's plan was to defeat the North West Company by hiring some of the latter's own men, and utilizing the Nor'Westers' own techniques and practices. Thus the English company should no longer count solely upon its Orkneymen with their unwieldy boats but hire French-Canadian voyageurs with their swift canoes. Experienced traders, lured away from the North West Company, should be employed in an invasion of the Nor'Westers' Athabasca district. The prices which the North West Company offered the Indians for their furs should be bettered. And if the Nor'Westers resorted to their bullying tactics of the past, they should encounter matching toughness. Finally in 1814, following the failure of Colvile's "New Scheme", the directors of the Hudson's Bay Company were ready to accept in large measure Robertson's program. A comprehensive agreement was signed, and in September of this year Robertson arrived at Quebec from Liverpool. Skilfully, artfully, secretly he began engaging various dissatisfied Nor'Westers. On 17 May 1815 Colin Robertson left Montreal for the West with sixteen large canoes loaded with trade goods. War between the companies had begun. The unsuccessful attempt of the Hudson's Bay Company in 1819 to enter the New Caledonia trade must be seen as a minor episode in that war.

The Nor'Westers were quick to respond to the threat that now confronted them. When the Hudson's Bay Company offered the Indians higher prices, the North West Company offered still higher ones. Likewise the Nor'Wester partners raised the wages of their voyageurs and swiftly promoted to partnership good clerks who might defect. As the struggle grew more bitter Indian allies were recruited. Soon attacks were launched against each other's forts. There were duels and ambushes. Rival establishments burned in the winter nights. The struggle mounted in intensity, and in the process both companies headed towards bankruptcy.

After Lord Selkirk died in 1820, cool-headed men from both sides met and negotiated. There could be only one real solution — amalgamation of the companies. The bargaining was hard and

6. Sir Alexander Mackenzie
from the portrait by Sir Thomas Lawrence
in the National Gallery of Canada

17. Difficulties such as Confronted Early Explorers

Simon Fraser

19 Fort Astoria 1813

complicated but finally, on March 26th of this year, an agreement
of union was signed in London. On July 10th those proud "Lords
of the North West", the wintering partners of the North West
Company, assembled for the last time in their great hall at Fort
William and gave consent to the terms worked out in London. The
new company would keep the name and the charter of the Hudson's
Bay Company, but it would contain, with suitable rank, most of the
old Nor'Westers.

To mark the beginning of the new era, Governor Simpson of the
reconstituted Hudson's Bay Company held a great feast at York
Factory, bringing together the erstwhile rivals. A fascinating account
of that meeting has been left us by John Tod, a young clerk shortly
to be transferred west of the Rockies where he would spend the rest
of his long life.

I would endeavour to recall your memory to the summer immediately
succeeding the Junction of the two Companies — When that formidable
band of Nor.West partners first landed on the bleak banks of York
Factory. A bold energetic race of breached Highlanders from the North,
the heroes of the opposition who had fought & bled manfully in that
long contest now ended, they had undoubtedly been defeated in the
struggle, & their very name as a body in the commercial world now
entirely defunct, yet they were by no means apparently, humbled, or in
the least subdued in spirit, but stalked about the buildings of the old
dilapidated Fort, with the same haughty air & independant step, as if
they had merely met, as they were wont to do in more successful times
at their favourite Depot, Fort William.

At length the bell summoned us to dinner, when forthwith in walked
the heterogenious mass of human beings, but in perfect silence, & with
the most solemn gravity. As the whole group stood on the floor of that
gigantic mess hall, evidently for a moment uncertain as to how they
would seat themselves, I eyed them with close attention from a remote
corner of the room . . . the Nor.Westers in one compact body kept
together, & evidently had no inclination at first to mix up with their
old rivals in trade. But that crafty fox Sir George Simpson coming
hastily to the rescue with his usual tact & dexterity on such occasions,
succeeded though partially somewhat in dispelling that reserve in which
both parties had hitherto continued to envelope themselves, it was to
say the least of it, a critical moment, requiring reconciliation and union
of two irritable & powerful bodies of men . . . . accordingly it
soon became evident that his stratagems in bows and smiles alone would

eventually succeed in producing the desired effect on the exterior appearance of his haughty guests. Their previously stiffened features began to relax a little, they gradually but slowly mingled up together, & a few of the better disposed, throwing themselves unreservedly in the midst of the opposite party, actually shook each other by the hand. Then & not till then were they politely bec[k]oned to their appointed places at the mess table. Burns has remarked that "the best laid schemes of mice & men whiles gang agee[*sic*]", and so it happened to a certain extent here, for as soon as all had been well seated it was quickly perceived that in the occupation of chairs & benches, there had occurred, no doubt unintentionally, one or two awkward mistakes, which it had evidently been the Governor's intention from the first to prevent by every possible means. For instance, he whom they called "blind McDonald", all of a sudden found himself directly in front of his mortal foe of Swan River, the vivacious Chief Factor Kennedy. . . . [They] had hacked & slashed at each other with naked swords only a few months before their present unintentional meeting. One of them still bore the marks of a cut on his face, the other, it was said, on some less conspicuous part of his body. I shall never forget the look of scorn & utter defiance with which they regarded each other the moment their eyes met. The Highlander's nostrils actually seemed to expand, he snorted, squirted & spat, not on the table but between his legs, & was as restless in his chair as if he had been seated on a hillock of Ants. . . . . . . Simon McGilliavary . . . seeing the state of affairs near my quarter, sent a request couched in the most gracious terms to McDonald, to be allowed to take wine with him, which by the bye, had to be repeated more than once before the latter could be induced to remove the glare of his fierce eye from the person of his adversary. . . . Immediately on the right of McGilliavary sat that flexible character McIntosh, his ever shifting countenance & restless black eye might seem that nature had designed him the harbinger of plots, treasons, & stratagems, I allude to the same, who, some years before in Peace R[iver] tried hard to poison poor little Yale, but could not succeed, so invulnerable had the integuments of the latter's stomach become by long acquaintance with the rough fare of that inhospitable step-mother — New Caledonia. . . .[1]

Others who caught Tod's eye were Clark and McIntosh who had sought to settle things "by a round of pistol shots, which they actually & deliberately discharged at each over the bright blaze of a winter night's campfire separated only by the burning element". Another old hand, McVicar, was "coolly asked to take wine with his

[1] PAC *MS*, MG19 A, vol. 38, ff.1r-4r. (Tod's chronology is often inaccurate.)

old jailer, who had only a few months before kept him a prisoner for twenty four hours in a dark cellar, inhaling the fumes of brimstone & phosphorus". With guests such as these the host, Simpson, needed all the arts of tact, cajolery, firmness and will. Fortunately he possessed them in such measure that he remained head, in North America, of the newly amalgamated company until his death thirty-nine years later.

After 1821 the British red ensign with the initials HBC on the fly replaced the old flag of the North West Company at all the forts in the North-west. For many years the history of British Columbia was to be the history of the Hudson's Bay Company there. So important was the Company's role that we must now drop, for a space, our year by year chronicle of events, and supply our readers with an extended account of how the Hudson's Bay Company (henceforth to be called simply the HBC) operated during the coming decades.

The Hudson's Bay Company

Origins of the HBC — Union with the North West Company — Gentlemen and engagés — Thrift — "The Communication" — Brigades and expresses — Trade goods — "The Opposition" — Forts and outposts — Life in an HBC fort — The maritime department — Hardships in New Caledonia and Columbia — Prostitutes and fur trade wives — The HBC and the Indians.

As indelibly as upon any bale of beaver pelts, the letters "HBC" are printed across the early history of British Columbia. Settlers in the late nineteenth century, in half-blasphemous tribute to the early arrival of the Hudson's Bay Company, maintained that its initials stood for "Here Before Christ". In fact, as every Canadian schoolboy ought to know, it was established on 2 May 1670 by Charles II, under the title of "The Governor and Company of Adventurers of England Trading into Hudson's Bay". To the officers and men who subsequently went about its business it was simply "The Concern" — "I need not observe how necessary it is for the Interest of the Concern that these Horses come down. . . . ", wrote Chief Factor McLoughlin to Chief Trader Black in 1829.[1]

The new HBC which in 1821 arose out of the merger of the old HBC and North West Company retained many features of the original company. Its headquarters were still in London, where its Governor and Committee not only attended to the sale of its furs, but kept a close eye on all its operations in North America. When Peter Skene Ogden strayed into country east of the Rockies and south of the 49th parallel, a region which Britain had already

---

[1] B. B. Barker, ed., *Letters of Dr. John McLoughlin Written at Fort Vancouver 1829-1832* (Portland, 1948), p. 1.

recognized as American, he was sharply reminded from London that the Company forbade its officers to trade in American territory. At the head of affairs in the New World was the Governor-in-Chief of Rupert's Land, holding sway from the Pacific to Hudson Bay.[2] Annually he convened a Council of the chief officers of the Concern at Norway House, York Factory, or Fort Garry, to plan operations, assign responsibilities, and make any necessary transfers of officers.

One notable alteration had been made where the Company's officers were concerned. Before the union they had been salaried employees, even though paid bonuses for outstanding work. Now, like the officers of the old North West Company, they were made shareholders participating in the distribution of the profits made by their company. The basis of this distribution was carefully spelt out in a Deed Poll drawn up at the amalgamation,[3] and promulgated in revised form in 1834. Sixty per cent of each year's profits went to the Company's shareholders in Britain. The remaining forty per cent was divided into eighty-five shares. Each of the Company's Chief Traders was assigned one of these latter shares; each Chief Factor was assigned two. On the average, one of these eighty-five shares paid a little less than £400 annually,[4] in those days a very substantial sum. Most of the Chief Factors were affluent men when they retired, and most of the Chief Traders ended up financially comfortable. Retirement, by the way, was available on generous terms for any commissioned officer after he had spent four years above the rank of clerk. During his first year of retirement he was allowed to retain his share or shares. For the next six years he was permitted to hold one-half

---

[2] Following the union of 1821 there were for a while three governors: Simpson (Northern Department), Williams (Southern Department) and Pelly (Assiniboia). By 1826, however, Simpson was the sole governor and was being addressed by his subordinates as "Governor in Chief, Hudson's Bay Company Territory". Not until 1839 did the Governor and Committee in London give Simpson the title "Governor-in-Chief of Rupert Land".

[3] The original Deed Poll of 1821 is printed in HBRS 2:327-44.

[4] For a "Statement of the annual dividend per 1/85 share" for the years 1821-1871, see PABC:A-B-15-1. No dividend was paid for 1821 when the reorganized company was being brought into existence. In 1822 one of these shares reserved for the officers paid £203, in 1823 £342. In 1827 and 1828 such a share paid £560. The peak year was 1855 when, for special reasons, a share paid £872, only to sink to £339 the following year.

of his interest in the Company's profits. Then the whole was used to make possible the promotion of some clerk, or to advance a Chief Trader to the rank of Chief Factor.

The organization of the HBC was in every respect strictly hierarchical. Those whose labours sustained it were divided into two main divisions, each with its own rank structure — the gentlemen and the engagés. Lowest of the engagés (or hired men) were the trappers enlisted to catch beaver in areas where Indians did not trap on the scale desired by the Company. Above them were the labourers who worked chiefly in the depots and on the farms. Next came the voyageurs who paddled the Company's canoes along the waterways linking its forts. There was rank among the voyageurs. Lowest paid (£17 per annum) were the "middlemen". Better paid were the "boutes", at either end of a canoe. A bowsman got £20, and the steersman at the stern, on whose skill everything ultimately depended, received £22.[5] In New Caledonia and Columbia the canoemen were paid slightly higher wages because of the increased hardships. The guides who led parties across country were paid a little more. A good interpreter was an indispensable man and was paid anywhere up to £25. Much the same wage was received by any skilled artificer such as a blacksmith. Top man among the engagés was the "postmaster", occasionally to be found in charge of one of the Company's smaller outposts, or keeping accounts at one of the forts. A postmaster was paid up to £40, but he was not a "gentleman" and could not look for further promotion.

A gentleman commenced his career with the Company as an apprenticed clerk. Generally a Scot who had signed his indentures in London and then been shipped out to Hudson Bay, an apprenticed clerk was of comparatively little value to the Company while learning the business. Accordingly, he started off at a salary of about £20 per annum. Eight years later, as a "finished" clerk qualified to command a post or be an accountant, he earned £100 a year. After he had served from ten to fifteen years as a clerk, a man was eligible

[5] The preceding figures are taken from the "Standing Rules and Regulations" promulgated in 1834. A copy of this important document is preserved, along with the Deed Poll for this year, in the Bissett Papers in the McGill University Library.

for promotion to commissioned rank as a Chief Trader. Great was the jubilation when the long-dreamt-of "parchment" arrived from London, and a clerk at last entered the lucrative world of the commissioned officers.

The Company had in its service about 150 clerks. Some of them would never receive promotion and in time either quit the service in disgust or remain, objects of pathetic commisseration, clerks of thirty or forty years' service. The number of Chief Traders fluctuated, but generally there were only between twenty-five and thirty of them. Normally a Chief Trader was in charge of a fort and whatever outposts it had in its surrounding region. A number of these forts constituted a district, which was headed by a Chief Factor. There were between sixteen and twenty-five Chief Factors. West of the Rockies there were two districts. The more northerly was New Caledonia, headed by a Chief Factor stationed at Fort St. James. The more southerly was Columbia, headed by another Chief Factor stationed at Fort Vancouver, about eighty-five miles upriver from the mouth of the Columbia.

From 1825 to 1845 the Chief Factor at Fort Vancouver was Dr. John McLoughlin who, besides administering his own district, exercised a measure of authority over New Caledonia and enjoyed the title of "Principal resident Superintendent of the Honourable Hudson Bay Company's affairs on the west side of the Continent".[6] The character of Dr. McLoughlin will gradually emerge from the chronicle of the years of his power, but a few words may be said at this point. The Americans, because of McLoughlin's innumerable kindnesses to early colonists from the United States, have long since entered him into their pantheon of national heroes as the "Father of Oregon". Most of the officers who served under him in the HBC spoke of him with warmth, affection and admiration. After his death Dr. W. F. Tolmie, a veteran in the service, paid notable tribute to "The late great and good Dr. John McLoughlin . . . the head and front, the life and soul, the guide and chief director [of the HBC's

---

[6] So referred to by Governor Simpson in his letter of 20 March 1829 to the Governor of the Russian American Company. Barker, *McLoughlin Letters*, p. 17.

activities on the Pacific slope]".[7] On the other hand, not all of the HBC men who had served under McLoughlin admired him, and we shall have occasion to note serious flaws in him.

McLoughlin's immediate superior was Governor George Simpson (who in 1841 became Sir George Simpson), the redoubtable "Little Emperor" of the fur trade. From his home at Lachine, Simpson made constant field trips seeing at first hand how the work of the Company was proceeding in its various districts. The speed at which Simpson travelled became a legend. Never was a moment needlessly lost or wasted. Journeying by canoe, he often dictated letters to a secretary while his own picked crew of Iroquois, labouring at the paddles, carried him onward at an amazing clip. Upon occasion Simpson, instead of halting for a mid-day meal, would have a second canoe grapple alongside his own and one crew paddled while the other ate. Hastening across the prairies on a visit to the Columbia District in 1841, Simpson was reputed to have worn out up to two hundred horses, leaving them as food for the wolves. Discipline was the key to the success of the HBC, and personal discipline marked Simpson as much as any of his officers. He began each day with a plunge into the cold water of whatever lake or stream he had camped beside. Governor from 1821 until his death in 1860, Simpson never let up on the regime he had set for himself. On one of his last trips, he had with him a new recruit, Henry Moberly. Waking early one morning, Moberly found the old man, naked, about to enter the cold water. Shame drove the young man into taking the cold plunge with him. One indulgence Simpson allowed himself. He always had an eye for a pretty girl, and when in the Indian Country he did not lack for women. He had begotten children by more than one half-breed or Indian girl before he brought back a bride from England.

The policy of making shareholders of the Company's commissioned officers had notable results, not only in galvanizing the energies of these gentlemen, but in making them extraordinarily thrifty in conducting the business of the Concern. Every penny saved

---

[7] W. F. Tolmie, *The Journals of William Fraser Tolmie: Physician and Fur Trader* (Vancouver, 1963), p. 399. [Hereafter referred to as Tolmie, *Journals*.]

meant an increase in the profits to be distributed among them, and consequently exhortations to keep down expenses constantly recur. James Douglas solemnly spoke of "the sin of extravagance" when rebuking Peter Skene Ogden.[8] The smaller the number of clerks and men employed, the smaller the bill for wages and food, and again the more money for each Chief Factor and Chief Trader, as well as the shareholders in Britain. The result was that in each district the establishment maintained was absolutely minimal. The annual reports from the forts are full of pleas for additional staff, particularly additional clerks. During the summer when fur trading was slack and many of the Company's men were off manning the brigades which took out the furs, a few forts were closed down entirely. In others a clerk and two or three men were all who remained. In 1827 only one Chief Factor, one Chief Trader, and nine clerks were assigned to the vast New Caledonia district. Apparently they had less than fifty engagés to assist them. Later generations were to marvel at how the HBC with so few men had survived amid the thousands and thousands of Indians, often tumultuous and savage. The answer lay in the character of the HBC's carefully selected officers, their firm discipline, and the respect and confidence which they won from the Indians.

The vital link which joined the HBC's Pacific forts with the Company's eastern headquarters was "The Communication". This was the term applied to the chain of waterways and portages which linked Fort Vancouver on the Columbia River with York Factory on Hudson Bay. Along the route stood a whole series of forts — Fort Colvile, Jasper House, Fort Assiniboine, Fort Edmonton, Fort Pitt, Carlton House, Norway House and Oxford House. Along the Communication travelled the two annual expresses. The first was the eastbound spring express which set out with the accountant from Fort Vancouver bearing his accounts and those of the other posts for the past year, along with McLoughlin's despatches to Governor Simpson. Travelling with the express canoes were any officers going on furlough, retiring, or taking up new assignments east of the mountains. With them also went engagés who had served the term

---

[8] Hudson's Bay Company Archives [hereafter referred to as HBCA] B.226/b/3.

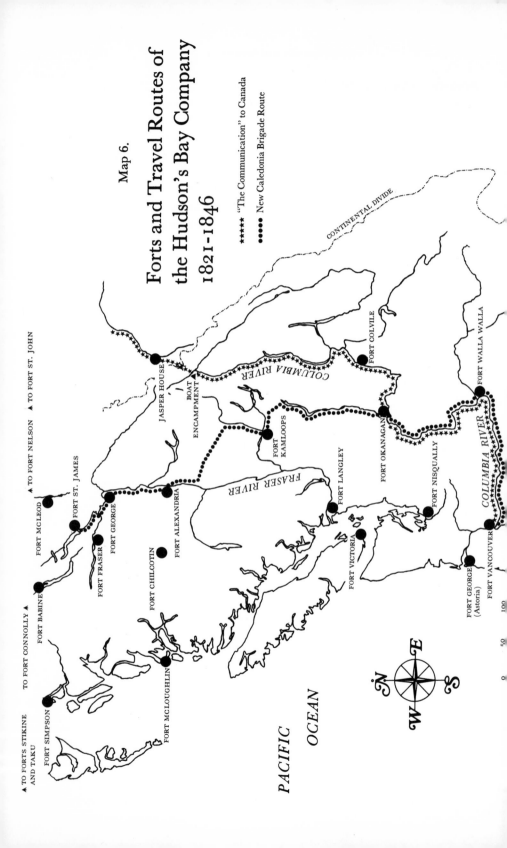

Map 6.

Forts and Travel Routes of
the Hudson's Bay Company
1821–1846

★★★★★ "The Communication" to Canada
●●●●● New Caledonia Brigade Route

of their contracts and had decided not to re-enlist. Sometimes the latter would be accompanied by their Indian wives and half-breed children, en route to a new home in the Red River Colony. At Norway House the express would split up, some went no further, others pushed on to York Factory to catch a ship for England, and still others headed towards the Ottawa valley and Montreal. A few months later the fall express carried the accountant back to Fort Vancouver, his records approved and audited. With him travelled various officers newly appointed to western forts, and parties of engagés similarly sent out to Dr. McLoughlin's domain. The fall express also brought despatches, newspapers and mail. Its arrival at Fort Vancouver was one of the major events of the year.

Another principal event was the arrival of the brigades from the Interior. Almost as soon as the ice was out of the lakes and rivers, the canoes began putting out from McLeod Lake, Fort Kilmaurs (Babine Lake), and the rest of the New Caledonia posts, with their rich burdens of baled furs (the furs from a single post were worth £10,000 in a good year).[9] Joining together like rivulets into a stream, they constituted the New Caledonia brigade. Southward the canoes travelled, down the Fraser River, until they reached Fort Alexandria. Here several hundred horses were waiting. The bales were taken out of the canoes and loaded on the horses, each with a ninety-pound bale on either side. Then began the long overland journey to Fort Kamloops (otherwise known as Thompson River Post or, very seldom, Fort Shuswap). The Kamloops contingent having joined the brigade, it headed along the shore of the South Thompson River, turned south at Monte Creek, crossed the height of land beyond and descended into the Okanagan valley. Here the brigade trail led south, close by the shores of Lake Okanagan and the Okanagan River. Finally Fort Okanagan was reached. Here a junction would be made with the Fort Colvile brigade which brought with it all the furs the year had yielded Fort Walla Walla (also known as Fort Nez Percé), Fort Colvile, Flathead House, Kootenay House and other outposts. Horses were now left behind as the brigade started down the Columbia in the "Columbia River boats",

---

[9] John Tod, *History of New Caledonia and the Northwest Coast*, PAC, MG 29, B35, Vol. 8:14 (Bancroft transcript).

sturdy, clinker-built craft each capable of carrying forty-five of the heavy bales of furs. Some days later there was a great exchanging of huzzahs and firing off of salutes as the brigade, striking a faster pace, came around the bend and up to the wharf at Fort Vancouver.

A month or so earlier the supply ship, or ships, had arrived from England. Their cargoes of trade goods were stored in the warehouses. Each post's "outfit" was made up in ninety-pound "pieces" in readiness for the coming year,[10] and each piece was plainly marked. The mark indicating that the parcel belonged to the Thompson River (Kamloops) outfit for 1863 was

'63
HB
R̵

Ashore came the brigade's cargo of furs, and into the emptied boats went the trade goods that would be their return cargo. No time was wasted on the turnaround — after all, four months were needed for the round trip from Fort St. James to Fort Vancouver. The brigade which arrived at Fort Vancouver on 11 June 1830 departed on June 29th. The furs received from the brigades were loaded into the Company's now empty supply ships and were soon en route to the London market.

The brigade route down the Okanagan to the Columbia and then downstream to Fort Vancouver was abandoned in 1849 when the HBC found it could no longer for various reasons transport its goods through what had become American territory. For the next twelve or so years a new route was followed. This took the brigade from Fort Kamloops to Tulameen, then the horses crossed the Cascade Mountains by a route north of the present Hope-Princeton Highway, coming out on the Coquihalla River and following it to Fort Hope. Here the brigade was met by boats, sent up from Fort Langley, which had brought up the outfits to be taken to the Interior forts for the coming year.

---

[10] If only one ship were used, its loss would deprive the forts of a year's supply of the essential trade goods. For this reason the stock for any year was generally sent out in several vessels so that at least part would arrive safely. As a further safeguard, whenever possible the supplies at Fort Vancouver were kept a whole year ahead of need and only in case of dire emergency were stocks touched ahead of schedule.

Another route must be noted, that (via the Nechako and upper Fraser rivers and Yellowhead Pass) by which the New Caledonia forts had access to "The Communication" at Jasper House. In the 1820s this route was used to bring in the dressed leather (as much as six or eight hundred large skins a year) required by the HBC posts in New Caledonia. This leather was used for robes and cords, and for the moccasins which constantly needed replacement in that rocky wilderness. Apart from what the HBC needed for its own use, some of this leather was traded with the Indians, who lacked a sufficient supply of their own. Because of the early association of this route with the leather shipments, the Yellowhead Pass was originally called the Leather Pass. (After 1830, leather was brought in over the Peace River-McLeod Lake route.)

In its trading with the Indians, the HBC made it a point of honour that its goods should always be of the first quality. Even where the Indians were more taken with colour and show than durability, the Company sternly resisted the temptation to deal in shoddy goods:

Our blue and scarlet blankets take with the Indians more on account of their softness and bright colours than of their quality otherwise, which however should not fall below the present standard.[11]

The excellence of Hudson Bay blankets became proverbial. G. W. Ebberts, a freeman trapper who sold his furs to both the HBC and the American Fur Company, declared that the HBC blankets were twice as good as those of its competitors. As for the scarlet cloth which the women used to make their leggings, the HBC cloth was far superior: " . . . this scarlet would last ten or twelve years, and the other would just go to pieces".[12]

In ordering its trade goods, the HBC kept a careful eye on the tastes and preferences of the Indians. Noting the great value which the coastal Indians placed on "coppers" (large plaques of the native metal cherished for prestige purposes), the HBC had facsimiles of these manufactured in England and sent out to the Coast. The Indians refused to have anything to do with these however —

[11] John Work to T. Fraser, London, 23 June 1860. HBCA, B.226/b/20.

[12] PAC, MG29, B35, Vol. 1:3 (Bancroft transcript).

perhaps because they lacked the aura of tradition and descent surrounding the coppers owned by their own chiefs. A similar disappointment attended the importation of ivory imitations of dentalia, the long thin cylindrical seashells which served as currency over the whole area between California and the Mackenzie River. Only the real dentalia would do.

A particular problem confronting the Company concerned alcohol. Aware of the devastation that liquor was working upon the native peoples, the HBC was opposed in principle to using it in trade. The Standing Rules and Regulations of 1834 stipulate:

> That none of that article, either for trade, sales, or gratuitous indulgence to servants, or allowance to officers, be imported into English River, Athabasca or McKenzie's River Districts.

The only reason why the HBC reluctantly traded liquor in the Pacific North-west was to counter the Company's "opposition" [competition]. Their American competitors persistently used liquor as a chief inducement when trading with the Indians. After the HBC and the Russian American Company, by a sustained and determined campaign of underselling, had driven the American trading ships out of business, they eliminated liquor from their own traffic with the natives. Earlier the HBC had cut off all traffic in alcohol in those districts in which it had no competitors. Thus in 1837 Governor Simpson was able to report to London: " ... in no part of the countries through which the Hudson's Bay Company's operations extend are spirituous or intoxicating liquors of any description sold to Indians, or used as a medium of barter or trade."[13]

The rates at which the HBC bartered its goods varied according to the degree of "opposition" encountered, either directly from the Americans or from intermediary tribes which dealt in goods which they had obtained from American trading ships. Thus in 1831, when the HBC men were satisfied that they had effectively driven the Americans out of the trade on the southern coast, the price for a 2½ point blanket was suddenly raised from one beaver pelt to two. Nostalgically the HBC men recalled the time when such a blanket

---

13 Frederick Merk, *Fur Trade and Empire: George Simpson's Journal 1824-25* (Cambridge, Mass., 1968), p. 334.

had sold for five beaver pelts. John Tod, a veteran trader, in his retirement recalled the following tariff for the Company's trade goods:

> Gun — 20 skins
> Coat — 6 skins
> One foot of twisted tobacco — 1 skin
> 1 gallon kettle — 1 skin
> Half size axe — 1 skin
> Large axe — 2 skins
> 2 gills of gunpowder — 1 skin
> 1 pound of shot — 1 skin[14]

While fur trading was by far the main concern of the HBC, it certainly was not its only interest. The Pacific North-west was a land of tremendous trees and incredible salmon runs. Almost inevitably the Company entered into an export trade in these commodities, sending them chiefly to Hawaii, California and Mexico. In 1848 Fort Langley put up 2000 barrels of salted salmon; in 1851 the Company sold 1700 barrels of Fort Langley salmon in Hawaii. As the Company's farms grew and prospered, agricultural produce was shipped to Alaska. Strenuous and not unsuccessful efforts were made to find markets for the coal discovered on Vancouver Island. Almost anything which might make a few pounds was considered as an article for export: cranberries (worth $30.00 a barrel in California), whale oil, porpoise skins, shingles, and even ice — a contract being made with some American entrepreneurs for the shipment of ice to San Francisco, Honolulu, and Hong Kong!

In the Interior, the HBC conducted its trading almost entirely at its forts and their outposts. On the coast, trade was carried on both from the Company's trading vessels and at forts.

The term "fort" was occasionally a misnomer, the fort being simply a sturdy log building, more deserving the older appellation of "house". Most of the Company's forts, however, were defended by palisades. The standard height for the palisade which ran around a fort was eighteen feet, with each post buried six feet deep in the earth. Sometimes the work must have been carelessly done. In 1833

---

[14] Tod, *History of New Caledonia*, pp. 47-48.

a sudden squall blew over the palisade at the front of Fort Nisqually. Dr. W. F. Tolmie tells us of the immediate consequence:

This unexpected catastrophe for a moment silenced the clamor [of the Indians who were complaining about Tolmie's exclusion of all but a few at a time from the fort] but it broke out again with redoubled fury & I trembled for the result, but was soon relieved from my apprehensions by hearing a loud guffaw proceeding from the brazen throats of the burly savages outside, who hesitated at first to cross the trench, but soon were crowding about the door of the shop.[15]

Running around the inside of the palisades, about four feet from their top, was a gallery from which riflemen could direct their fire against any attackers. Projecting at diagonally opposite corners of the palisaded enclosure stood two solidly built bastions or block-houses, fitted with cannon and gunports. From each bastion fire could be directed obliquely along two of the four sides of the palisades. On one side of the fort stood the main gate, a ponderous affair, its two halves studded with heavy iron nails. Posterns set within these halves were commonly used for entrance and exit from the fort. Only on special occasions were the great gates flung wide open. On the opposite side of the fort was a smaller rear gate.

The layout of the buildings within the fort was fairly well standardized. Typical is that of Fort Simpson, preserved for us in the ground plan drawn by P. N. Compton.[16] Facing the main gate, on the far side of the open square, was the Great House. This was generally a two-storied building containing at one end the quarters of the commanding officer and his family, and at the other the quarters of the junior officers and the officers' mess.

One of the daughters of Chief Trader John Work has left a vivid description of the quarters the family occupied when her father was in command at Fort Simpson. The walls of their large living room consisted of smooth boards lacking either paint or wallpaper, but hung with stuffed specimens of every kind of local bird from hummingbird to eagle — Mrs. Work being an expert taxidermist. On the floor was a huge cedar bark rug of natural colour with large

---

[15] Tolmie, *Journals*, p. 243.
[16] PAC, MG29, B35, Vol. 4:5 (Bancroft transcript).

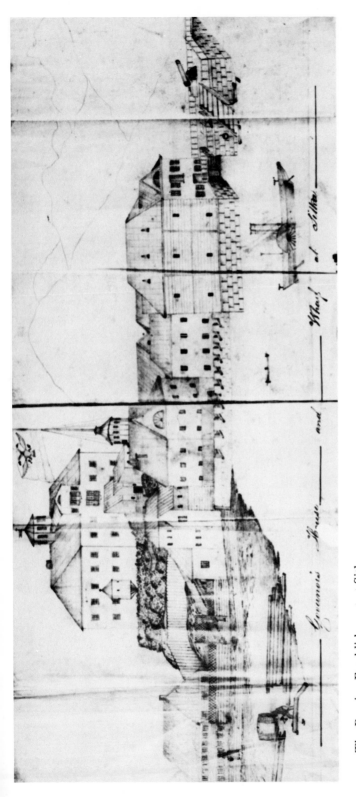

20.   The Russian Establishment at Sitka

21. Sir George Simpson

22. Dr. John McLoughlin

23. Peter Skene Ogden

24. Dr. W. F. Tolmie

25. S.S. *Beaver*

26. Capt. W. H. McNeill

27. Fort Simpson

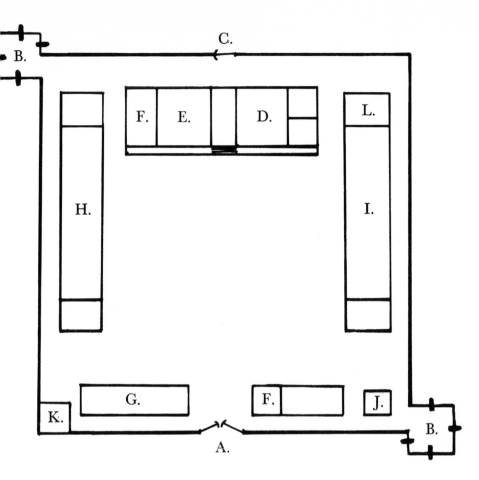

A. Front Entrance	G. Trade Shop
B. Bastions	H. Warehouse
C. Back Entrance	I. Men's Houses
D. Commanding Officer's Quarters	J. Blacksmith's Shop
	K. Carpenter's Shop
E. Mess Room	L. Kitchen
F. Officers' Quarters	

Diagram 7.

Plan of Fort Simpson

(based on an original sketch by P. N. Compton, who was at one time
stationed there. Overall dimension: 200 feet square.)

black checks, made in a single piece by the neighbouring Tsimpseans. At one end of the room was the desk where Chief Trader Work kept his private papers, at the other end was the table where Mrs. Work and the children, along with the families of the one or two other officers, had their meals. The furniture was all homemade of maple, an upholstered sofa being the major item. Mr. Work was fond of reading and a great many books, a number of them religious, were on the shelves. Brightly burnished copper lamps, fed with seal oil, cast a mellow light. Opening off the living room were the bedrooms. The parents' bed was draped with chintz but, ready for emergency, a pair of loaded pistols hung on the wall. Mrs. Work, even though a half-Indian "fur trade wife", was accorded all the status pertaining to a Chief Trader's wife. She and her girls never went into the kitchen where a Frenchman, Cantal, and his Indian assistants prepared their meals. Mr. Work of course dined with his assistants in the officers' mess.[17]

To the left of the Great House, extending along a second side of the central square, was the fort's warehouse. To the right of the Great House, along the third side of the square, stood the houses in which the engagés lived, and the kitchen where individually they cooked their meals. On the fourth side of the square, flanking the main gate, were the workshops of the blacksmith and the carpenter, some additional living quarters and the trade shop, where the actual bartering was carried on. This latter was a tedious process since the Indians generally drew out the bartering, skin by skin.

Entry to the trade shop was very carefully controlled, normally only two or three natives being admitted at a time. At Fort Rupert, where the Indians were considered particularly dangerous, an alley between long substantial fences permitted them to approach the fort gate only in single file. Once an Indian was admitted within the gate at Fort Rupert he was flanked by two trading huts into which he might enter, but a second strong gate set between these prevented him from continuing on into the fort courtyard.

Each fort had its bell, which in some cases was lodged in a belfrey

[17] This information is contained in a letter written by Anne Huggins, a granddaughter, who took down the information from her mother's dictation. See Oregon Historical Society Library, MS.1089.

set atop lofty posts in a corner of the fort's central square. Generally under the table in the Chief Trader's room there was a trap door secured with a heavy padlock. When this was opened, one descended into the depths of an excavated strongroom. If there was any liquor kept at the fort it would be found here, along with other items which needed special protection.

The occupants of an HBC fort on the Pacific slope in the first half of the nineteenth century formed a very heterogeneous group — the Chief Trader and his one or two clerks were generally Scots but occasionally included an Englishman or even a French-Canadian. The sixteen or so men who served under them were a mixture of French-Canadians, half-breeds, Indians, Orkneymen and Kanakas. The Orkneymen were an inheritance from the old HBC of the days before the amalgamation. Their taciturn, stoic self-sufficiency fitted them well for the lonely life in the Indian Country, where they proved particularly useful in handling boats. The Kanakas, as the natives of the Sandwich Islands (or Hawaii) were called, had been first brought to the Pacific North-west on the early trading ships. Their fidelity, courage and industry made them valued employees, and the Company found them generally much more reliable and adept than the Indians who could be hired on the spot. Local Indians were employed very sparingly, chiefly as interpreters or guides. The largest group in the forts was made up of the "Canadians", as the French-Canadian engagés were known. Cheerful, volatile and strong, they really were the mainstay of the Company's labouring force. They, along with Iroquois Indians also brought in from the East, provided the HBC with its famed canoemen or "voyageurs". Within the forts one heard a weird mixture of English, French, Hawaiian, and the Chinook Indian jargon (a *lingua franca* used by the tribes up and down the coast). Veteran officers retiring from the service after years in remote forts found it hard to adapt themselves to speaking straight English once again.

The life led by this polyglot work force began each day about 6 a.m., or even 5 a.m. in the summers, when they were called to duty and the fort gates were unlocked. After the men had worked for a few hours the fort bell announced, at 8 a.m., that it was time to breakfast. An hour later they were back at their labours. At 12 o'clock the bell rang again for their midday meal. An hour later they were back at work — cleaning and pressing furs into bales, chopping firewood, bringing up seaweed and spreading it as fertilizer for the gardens, digging potatoes, and attending to all the other chores. At 4 p.m. the men came in to cook their suppers, then went back to work for a final hour if the light permitted. It was a standing rule that all Indians must be out of the fort by 7 p.m. and the gates locked at 9 p.m. The officers ended their day's work at 6 p.m. when the Chief Trader and his clerk or clerks repaired to their little mess hall for dinner. The officers' mess in the average fort was not luxurious. The tablecloth on which the cook set the iron dishes consisted merely of a piece of packing canvas. Things were different of course in the depot at Fort Vancouver. When the Chief Factor, his officers and guests, sat down to their meal there, the table sparkled with cut glass brought out from England.

At 9 p.m. when the fort gates were carefully locked, the keys were handed over to the officer commanding the fort. In areas where the Indians were turbulent, especially on the Coast, through the night a watchman patrolled the galleries of the fort, at intervals ringing a bell and calling out "All's Well". Indians lurking in the vicinity were kept aware of the constant vigilance.

On Saturdays and Sundays the routine varied. Traditionally the men were issued their week's rations on Saturday (each cooked for himself) and allowed the afternoon to attend to their own work, making and mending. Sundays were scrupulously kept as days of rest. Honouring the Sabbath, the fort that day flew its flag. In obedience to a standing regulation of the Company, the commanding officer read divine service, using the Church of England's Book of Common Prayer. Everyone resident in the fort was required to attend. Indians might be present if they so desired. Young Dr. Tolmie at Fort Vancouver was struck by the impropriety of Chief Factor McLoughlin's reading of the service being punctuated by the noises of the horses in the fort courtyard, brought there for the young officers who would be off on a day's hunting once the service was concluded.

Not all of the Company's trade was carried on at its forts and their outposts. There were the vessels which made up its maritime department. These served two purposes: the first was to move up and down the coast, trading with the Indians; the other was to transport supplies, men and fur between Fort Vancouver and the other coastal forts. Dr. McLoughlin assigned the duties for the various craft at his disposal. Thus in 1831 he planned to use the two small schooners, the *Vancouver* and the *Cadboro*, for trading purposes. Their first duty was to shadow any American trading ship having the temerity to invade the coast which the HBC now regarded as its own. Wherever they found Americans starting to trade, the HBC schooners were to meet their prices and endeavour to draw the Indians away from them. When the American interlopers were defeated by such tactics, the two schooners set out on specific trading cruises of their own. Should a visit be contemplated to a tribe with a bad reputation, the *Vancouver* and the *Cadboro* would enter the area in consort, each ready to assist the other in case of attack. If a tribe had a reasonable record of peaceable behaviour, a single schooner would be sent to its village, but generally it would keep its boarding nets up to prevent attack, and the trading would be conducted through the portholes. Besides the two schooners, McLoughlin had in 1831 a large vessel, the brig *Dryad*. This he intended to use for transportation between Fort Simpson, Fort Langley and Fort Vancouver. When she was not needed on these runs, he would send her with lumber and salmon to the developing markets in California and Hawaii.

Life at Fort Vancouver, with its establishment of over a hundred men, its comings and goings of ships, brigades, expresses, visitors and missionaries, was paradisiac compared with the life in the other forts in Columbia and New Caledonia, with their terrible isolation and loneliness. Men dreaded assignment to the forts in New Caledonia. John Tod, who served there for many years, likened a posting to New Caledonia to banishment to the penal colony in Australia's Botany Bay. There is no lack of other testimony to the extreme hardship of life in New Caledonia. Chief Factor John Stuart, the officer commanding the District, when he submitted in 1823 his Summary Report of New Caledonia wrote:

... so hard is the labour that when added to the bad living, scarcely any thing but dried salmon of the worst quality, seldom any man, even the most robust, without destroying his constitution, can remain in New Caledonia more than two or three years.[18]

The Company itself recognized the special hardships of life in New Caledonia. The Standing Rules and Regulations of 1834 provide that its canoemen in "New Caledonia, Millbank, Nass & Stikine" should be paid £2 more per annum than those posted to the Columbia.

Not that life in the Columbia Department was an easy one. The mortality rate was horrendous. In 1830 twenty-six men lost their lives, mostly by drowning, rather more than one-tenth of the total establishment. In a personal letter from Fort Langley in January 1832, Archibald McDonald wrote:

> Man's life now in the Columbia is become mere lottery — your friend Joseph Moreau & 2 or 3 others were drowned at the Cascades [of the Columbia River] last summer — a couple of men also perished below Alexandria in Frazer's river, & ten to one there will be some loss in the Snake Country — this with the natural deaths make the scene melancholy enough.[19]

Part of the trouble with life in the early days in Columbia and New Caledonia was, as Stuart indicated, the appalling diet. When fresh venison, fish or game were available, they were of course eagerly consumed, but for most of the year they simply were not to be had. The officers were usually supplied with flour, rice, beans, bacon, tea and sugar (along with their Madeira wine and brandy), but at times these ran out and they had to join the engagés in simple meals of dried salmon and cold water. For the latter and their families at Fort Kamloops in 1827 the ration was: for a man three dried salmon, for a woman two dried salmon, and for a child one dried salmon.[20] According to Dr. McLoughlin, the ration at Fort Vancouver much of the time was one quart of Indian corn and two ounces of grease a day.[21] At times in some of the inland forts,

[18] HBCA, B.188/e/1, f. 3.
[19] PAC, John McLeod Papers, p. 291.
[20] HBCA, B.97/e, f. 2v.
[21] *Letters*, ed. Barker, p. 219.

especially in New Caledonia, supplies failed. If their dried salmon gave out, the occupants of a fort simply starved.

There were feasts as well as famine. Once in a long while, to mark some special occasion, the men would be given a "regale" such as that Dr. Tolmie reported at Fort Nisqually upon the arrival of the *Cadboro* in mid-September 1833:

The men have also received a "regale" of pork, potatoes, molasses & rum & are at present loudly chaunting their voyaging songs round the camp fire — poor fellows, they are very deserving of the treat, having fared poorly all the summer both as to food & shelter while they wrought constantly at heavy work without a murmur of discontent.[22]

A traditional occasion for a regale was when an express or a brigade had completed its first day outward bound on a long journey. Often a regale degenerated into a general drunken rout, as did festive occasions at the outlying forts.

For many officers, educated men stuck away in the snows for months in their tiny forts hundreds of miles from the nearest of their kind, the isolation and the loneliness were perhaps the worst features of HBC life. Mail was a great consolation, but it came through only once or twice a year, and only after enormously protracted travel. On 8 December 1833 Dr. Tolmie received letters written by his father and brother in Scotland the previous February 12th. Despite such long delays, HBC officers, hungry for letters, maintained their correspondence with assiduity. A notable recipient for their letters was Edward Ermatinger, a businessman and politician in St. Thomas in Upper Canada, who after a few years of service in the Columbia district had decided that the life was not for him and had returned east in 1827. Chief among Ermatinger's fur trade correspondents was quaint, quirky and humorous John Tod, whom Governor Simpson had banished to New Caledonia after learning that Tod had spoken out against Tom Taylor, Simpson's personal servant and the brother of one of his women. Tod's letters, extending from 1826 to 1874, now preserved in the Ermatinger Papers in the Public Archives of Canada, are an invaluable source for anyone working on the

[22] Tolmie, *Journals*, p. 236.

early history of British Columbia. We shall quote from them frequently in the course of this chronicle.

Newspapers and books were invaluable for the lonely men in the outposts. The HBC, aware of this fact, made a point of sending out files of *The Times* from England to the Pacific Coast. Books were read and reread. When John Tod arrived at McLeod Lake with only three books (his Bible, his Burns, and one other), he was overjoyed to find that Dease, his predecessor, had left a number of books behind him. Dr. Tolmie at Fort McLoughlin bought from one of the HBC skippers Robertson's historical works in six volumes, along with several other items.

But even Robertson's history in six volumes is a poor substitute for an intimate human relationship. And so the HBC officers and men turned to the ultimate consolation — women. There were of course native prostitutes:

"As usual, some women arrived in the evening for the purpose of hiring themselves to the people for the night." The men traded their tobacco and even their buttons for these creatures, until it was estimated that only two dozen buttons were left in camp.[23]

At Fort Vancouver a chief's wife known as "the Princess of Wales" had a whole string of prostitutes available for the fort. Such women could sell sexual release, but most of the men wanted something more, a genuine human relationship. And so there came into being the "fur trade marriages" or "blanket marriages", contracted by the men with Indian women, and by the officers usually with chiefs' daughters or half-breed girls. There were no priests to solemnize such marriages, so upon occasion the HBC performed its own marriages — the officer in charge of the post issued a certificate signed by the bride, groom, the witnesses and himself, then recorded the marriage both in the fort journal and in his annual report to Governor Simpson and the Council. Dr. McLoughlin performed such a marriage at Fort Vancouver in June 1840, joining together Archibald McKinlay and Sarah Julia Ogden. But such ceremonies were rare and usually occurred only when an officer of the Company

[23] H. D. Dee, "An Irishman in the Fur Trade: The Life and Journals of John Work", *BCHQ* 7 (1943):237-38.

was concerned to protect one of his own daughters when she took a man. No ceremony of any kind marked most of these "blanket marriages".

Many of these "fur trade marriages" were transitory affairs lasting only a year or so, and ending either with the transfer of the "husband" or the flight of the "wife". Often the men treated these liaisons lightly, indulging in crude humour about their "pieces of brown buff". A letter of Francis Ermatinger's is worth quoting here:

> However to counterbalance the misery of Darned[?] Dried Salmon with which we are obliged to sustain a miserable existence, we have the pleasure of fine horses, and can obtain a wife at every port, for a moderate charge, we come to. In this last sort of traffic, our friend Work, being fortunate enough to live upon a more juicy substance than myself, outdoes us all. Just before I left Spokan [sic] last fall he purchased a fine young Milcher, which with the fees to the relatives requisite cost him about £10-10- and took her on with him to the Flathead post, where he managed, to his own account, to shuffle the time away pretty agreeable. . . . [24]

But John Work, in his youth a holy terror among the squaws, was to settle down. He formed a lasting relationship with Susette Legace, a girl of mixed blood, who bore him a large family. In 1849 he and his Susette finally had an official Church of England wedding at Fort Victoria. In 1837 the Anglican chaplain at Fort Vancouver had sanctified the union which had existed for some ten years between James Douglas and Amelia Connolly, the half-breed daughter of Chief Factor Connolly. Years later, as Lady Douglas, Amelia was to be the first lady in the crown colonies of Vancouver Island and British Columbia.

Hardly ever did an HBC man try to bring in a white wife. The hardships of life in the remote trading posts were more than a woman from a civilized society could be expected to bear. John Tod tried the experiment, only to have his English bride go insane after experiencing life in an HBC post on the eastern side of the continent.

Crucial decisions had to be made when various of the Company's officers, upon retirement, decided to settle in Canada or Britain. It was impossible even to think of introducing an Indian wife into

[24] Letter of 14 March 1826, MS in Huntington Library.

polite society in Edinburgh or London. Retired HBC officers who had settled around St. Thomas, in what is now Ontario, were very upset when they learned that their former colleague Thomas Dears was actually proposing to bring out his Indian wife to live among them. The more or less universal practice for a man returning to civilization was to slough off his Indian wife and half-breed children, paying some other man, often an Indian, to take them over. The payment was euphemistically termed a "dowry".

The HBC did what it could to look after the interests of these native women. The concluding article in the Standing Rules and Regulations (1834) reads:

> That all officers and Servants of the Company having women or children, and wishing to leave the same in the country on their retirement therefrom, be required to make such provision for their future maintenance, more particularly for that of the children, as circumstances may reasonably warrant, and the means of the individual permit. . . .

The children were a real problem. Not surprisingly, in the absence of contraceptives, HBC officers prized a sterile "kloochman" [woman] above rubies. Unfortunately Indian women with an unblemished record of sterility in previous matches sometimes managed to become pregnant in the potent embrace of an HBC officer. And with the coming of children there were ties that grew as the father felt increasing affection both for his little boys and girls and for their mother. Where family ties grew permanent, plans for retirement to Canada or Scotland were scrapped, and a farm was bought in the Willamette Valley or near Victoria instead. The Company, concerned and paternalistic to the last, took note of the children of these marriages. In its "Regulations for Promoting Moral and Religious Improvement" it required:

> As a preparative to education, that the mother and children be always addressed and habituated to converse in the vernacular dialect (whether English or French) of the Father, and that he be encouraged to devote part of his leisure hours to teach the children their A.B.C., Catechism, together with such further elementary instruction as time and circumstances may permit.[25]

[25] These supplementary regulations were printed at the end of the "Standing Rules and Regulations of 1834" as a sort of addendum.

Some fathers sent their children to Fort Garry for schooling with the Métis there. (Métis, a French word for those of mixed Indian and French-Canadian descent, was rarely used west of the Rockies.)

Actually, the HBC was of two minds about these unions which their servants contracted with Indian women. In many ways the women were useful to the Company, especially on trapping expeditions such as Ogden repeatedly led into the Snake River country:

> ... an Indian wife on such an expedition was a distinct asset. She more than paid her way, for she sewed and gummed the canoes, when canoes were used; she made snowshoes and helped make traps; she skinned the catch and prepared the furs; when in the buffalo country she prepared the pemmican and did her share generally of the heavy work of travel. The expedition had to have her, and she had to have her children, so the lodges went along.[26]

At the forts also, the work of these Indian wives was useful to the Company. Moreover, these marriages cemented alliances with the tribes from which the women came. The Indian wives provided an invaluable channel for information concerning the moods, intentions and grievances of the natives. Living with them, the HBC men were able to gain insight into the psychology, beliefs and values of the Indians. Often, in the next generation, the children of these matches proved hardy, intelligent and devoted servants to the Company.

On the other hand, there were undoubtedly disadvantages also. Sometimes the Indian women would take lovers from their own race and then there could be real trouble. At other times, an Indian brave would become furious at finding that a white man had taken his woman. One HBC officer observed that nine-tenths of the murders of whites by Indians were due to trouble over women. At Fort Kamloops, when Francis Ermatinger found his "wife" had a Shuswap lover, he got Lolo the fort interpreter to hunt down the brown Lothario and cut the tips off his ears — the traditional Indian punishment. Chief Factor McLoughlin was not happy about the incident, which could have aroused dangerous hostility among the Indians, but he agreed that white prestige required that some such punishment be inflicted. Another worry for the Company was the

[26] D. A. McGregor, " 'Old Whitehead' — Peter Skene Ogden", *BCHQ* 17 (1953): 177.

expense incurred in feeding these native wives and their proliferating children. To reduce this expense, attempts were made at times to make the keeping of women a privilege limited to the Company's officers, but such a measure was hardly realistic and never long enforced.

Let us pass from consideration of the HBC's dealings with Indian wives to the Company's relationship generally with its customers, the Indians who brought their furs to its forts and ships. Throughout its history the Company insisted that the Indians must be treated with understanding, justice and fairness. The Standing Rules and Regulations of 1834 are very specific on this point. One of its articles reads:

That the Indians be treated with kindness and indulgence, and mild and conciliatory means resorted to in order to encourage industry, repress vice, and inculcate morality; that the use of spirituous liquors be gradually discontinued in the few Districts in which it is yet indispensable, and that the Indians be liberally supplied with requisite necessaries, particularly with articles of ammunition, whether they have the means of paying for it or not; and that no Gentleman in charge of Districts or Posts be at liberty to alter or vary the standard or usual mode of trade with Indians, except by special permission of Council.

Almost without exception the officers of the HBC lived up to the spirit of these regulations. Chief Factor Finlayson was later to recall: "A Hudson Bay officer would receive no thanks for cheating an Indian. The Policy of the Company was Honesty. . . ."[27] The Governor and Committee in London reminded Dr. McLoughlin, "While we derive benefit from the natives, it must never be forgotten that it is our sacred duty to confer benefit on them. . . ."[28]

There was of course the occasional man who got a bad reputation among his fellow officers for rough treatment of the Indians. Such a man was a clerk named McLean who was used as a sort of "enforcer" to hunt down Indians who had murdered officers or other servants of the Company. More enlightened officers deplored his tactics:

---

[27] *The History of Vancouver Island & the Northwest Coast*, PAC, MG29, B35, Vol. 6:66 (Bancroft transcript).

[28] E. E. Rich, ed., *The Letters of John McLoughlin from Fort Vancouver to the Governor and Committee, Second Series, 1839-44*, HBRS 6 (London, 1943):309.

He was used to making raids upon Indians. He would dash upon a band of savages, & in case a murderer was not found, he would take their horses, break their canoes, & commit such like deprecations.[29]

McLean's tactics violated an important Company policy that, though individual murderers were to be ruthlessly hunted down (an essential safeguard for its small groups of men living among thousands of sometimes savage tribesmen and hundreds of miles from the nearest succour), such punishment should never be extended to the tribe as a whole. Pressures might, of course, be applied to tribes to make them turn in, either dead or alive, the murderers of HBC men, but no punishment was to be inflicted upon a tribe because of the guilt of two or three of its members.

Inevitably there was the occasional officer who failed to measure up to the standards set by the Company. One such was Chief Trader Alexander Fisher, described by Governor Simpson as "trifling thoughtless superficial lying", who for some years was in charge of Fort Alexandria. Here he incurred the wrath of Chief Trader Black by trying to use the Indians' awe for the ceremonies of the Catholic Church to frighten them into bringing him their furs. In a letter of October 1832 from Fort Kamloops Black, who was concerned to have the Indians come to his post, wrote:

Lolo tells me of the many tricks wherewith you deceive the Indians, such as making holy water in wash basins, dressing up your cook to make him hold it, walking about the house with a whitewash brush in his hand with many mumblings and magical words, sprinkling the natives in said holy water, telling them that if they do not come to your place to dance and bring their furs with them this fall, they will be swallowed up like another Sodom into a fiery furnace or boiling caldron. . . . [30]

Contemptuously Black remarked that he could get furs from the Indians without "jugglery, tricks and profanations of God's holy rites and sacraments".

As far as the constant wars among the tribes were concerned, the Company consistently pursued a policy of strict neutrality. It did try

[29] *History of New Caledonia*, p. 10.

[30] A. G. Morice, *History of the Northern Interior of British Columbia* (Toronto, 1904), p. 151.

to reduce warfare among the Indians, however, by occasionally remonstrating or serving as a conciliator. When it was obvious that a tribe was preparing to attack one of its neighbours, the local HBC trader was apt to find pretexts for cutting back on the supply of guns and ammunition. The motive was not entirely humanitarian. The more Indians that were killed in these petty wars, the fewer there were left to trap furs for the Company. The HBC preferred to see the Indians on the trapline rather than on the warpath.

Similarly, the HBC did not try to intervene in the customs of the Indians, repugnant though they might be. One Indian practice which caused particular revulsion among the HBC officers was the status killing of slaves. When two bands met, a chief who was eager to demonstrate how rich he was in slaves would have one of them killed on the spot. To maintain comparable status the other chief would then have one of his slaves similarly slain. On a single occasion ten or so slaves might thus be summarily put to death to demonstrate the greatness of their masters. The HBC helped to bring an end to this practice by refusing to recognize any slave-killer as a chief. Sometimes the Company would purchase freedom for a slave. The motive for such redemptions was not always philanthropic. Chief Factor Finlayson recorded in his reminiscences:

Presents would be made to chiefs to liberate their slaves.... These slaves were dangerous, for if one of them was told by his master to shoot a white man, for instance, he was bound to do it, or himself be shot, and so we considered ourselves unsafe until the slaves were all liberated.[31]

There was for some years a curious anomaly where slavery was concerned. While the Company was firmly opposed to the whole institution among the Indians, it turned a blind eye when one of its own people bought a slave for his own use. After a shocked Anglican clergyman at Fort Vancouver wrote to London about this practice, peremptory orders came back that, under no circumstances, were officers or employees of the Company to have slaves as personal servants. One evil consequence of this practice lingered on: it gave

---

[31] Finlayson, *History of Vancouver Island*, p. 66.

some grounds for an American slander that the Company itself used Indian slave labour.

A particular ethical problem was posed for the Company when a sick Indian came to a fort for medical care. Unfortunately, Indian reasoning ran that if a medicine man failed to cure a patient he was responsible for his death, and must either be slain by the relatives of the deceased or compelled to compensate them with goods. The Indians carried over this reasoning when dealing with the white men. After an HBC officer had done his best, though to no avail, with his little stock of medicines, he was apt to find himself confronted by furious Indians demanding compensation out of the Company's trade goods. For this reason, HBC men generally refused to touch sick Indians, no matter how urgent the pleas. Here again there were exceptions. Chief Trader Manson, having in his service a "very useful Indian", consented to treat the man when he fell sick. After various remedies had been tried, the Indian still declared that he was possessed by the "skokum" or evil spirit which caused his disease. In desperation Manson fell back on Seidlitz powder. When the mixture turned effervescent and the Indian was told to drink it, he at first refused (thinking the water was boiling), but at last downed the concoction:

After a few minutes, as usual, up came a large quantity of the gas he had swallowed. "By jove," says Manson with ready wit, "there's the skokum at last." The Indian believed, was cured from that moment, and Manson and Seidlitz powders became a great magician.[32]

There was, however, one medical service which the HBC could safely offer the Indians and be sure of winning their gratitude in consequence. This was vaccinating them against the dreaded smallpox whose frequent epidemics wiped out whole bands of untreated Indians. We shall have occasion to note a very unusual side benefit gained by Chief Trader John Tod of Fort Kamloops from such vaccinating.

By and large, examining the record of the HBC, it is impossible not to be impressed by the fairness and equity, and at times the

---

[32] J. S. Helmcken, "Fort Rupert in 1850", Victoria *Daily Colonist* [hereafter referred to as *Colonist*] 1 Jan. 1890, p. 4.

kindness and understanding, with which the HBC dealt with the Indians. And the HBC men reaped their reward. Whereas the American trading ships by their outrageous tactics had filled the Indians with hatred for the "Boston men", every Indian knew that, though the Boston men were bad, the "King George men" were good. Visitors to British Columbia, right through to the latter part of the nineteenth century, were impressed by how consistently and relentlessly the Indians held by that distinction. No doubt the Royal Navy, the Royal Engineers and the early colonial administrators did a fair bit to support this article of faith, but it was the HBC to which the main credit must be given. Anachronistically the Indians still called the British and the Canadians "King George men" far into the reign of Queen Victoria. A principal reason why the nineteenth century passed without any wars between the Indians and the whites in the British territories was " . . . the nameless awe in which Indians held sacred the persons of those whom they knew to be King George's Tyhees [i.e. persons in authority]".[33] When the Americans launched their wars against the Indians in Washington Territory, no HBC man was ever attacked by the embattled Indians. In consequence, terrified American settlers presented themselves at the HBC posts seeking to purchase as safe disguises the capots which were, in effect, the uniform of the HBC engagés. No episode could bear more eloquent testimony to what the HBC had achieved by fairness and firmness.

[33] John B. Good, "British Columbia", PAC, MG29, B35, Vol. 6:24 (Bancroft transcript).

1822

What to do with the Columbia District? — Fort Kilmaurs founded on Babine Lake — The sparse Indian population in the Interior.

This year saw a crucial decision confronting the Governor and Committee of the HBC. The Columbia District, inherited from the North West Company, had not been administered with any vigour and its fur returns had been unimpressive. The question arose as to whether the HBC would not do best to abandon the Columbia region and concentrate on the richer fur country to the north. On 27 February 1822 the Governor and Committee wrote to Simpson:

> We understand that hitherto the trade of the Columbia has not been profitable, and from all that we have learnt on the subject we are not sanguine in our expectations of being able to make it so in future. But if by an improved arrangement the loss can be reduced to a small sum, it is worth a serious consideration, whether it may not be good policy to hold possession of that country, with the view of protecting the more valuable districts to the North of it; and we wish you to direct the attention of the Council to this subject and collect all the information which you can obtain from individuals acquainted with the country.[1]

Governor Simpson took heed of the message. As soon as he had the reorganized Company functioning satisfactorily closer to home, he would have to make a trip out to the West Coast, and take a good hard look at the Columbia country.

As for those "more valuable districts to the North" which constituted New Caledonia, this was a very bad year indeed. The Fraser River salmon run on which the forts depended almost entirely for their food failed. Even at Fraser Lake, where there had always been plenty of salmon, the Indians could barely keep alive during the season when they should have been catching and drying a prodigious

---

[1] Merk, *Fur Trade and Empire*, p. 175.

quantity of fish. The men at the HBC post there fared no better than their comrades at the other forts. However, one expedient was left. Babine Lake was part not of the Fraser River system but of the Skeena. Accordingly it offered an independent source of salmon even when the Fraser run failed. Largely because of the importance of the Skeena salmon, Chief Trader William Brown this year founded Fort Kilmaurs, commonly called Fort Babine, on the shores of Babine Lake. (Fort Kilmaurs took its name from Brown's birthplace in Ayrshire.) When the new post was completed Brown treated his men to liquor. They in their rejoicing fired off such a *feu de joie* that the Indians, terrified, fled into the woods. As far as fur trading was concerned, Fort Kilmaurs never reached real importance — perhaps because of a lack of beaver in the country, perhaps because of a lack of Indians to trap them (the Babine tribe only numbered some 700 men, women and children).

Too much should not be made of the scantiness of the population in the Babine Lake area. The Indian population of the Interior was always very sparse in comparison with that of the Coast. The report for the Fort Kamloops district this year estimates that its trading area, extending roughly from the present International Boundary to the upper reaches of the North Thompson River, and from the Fraser River on the west to the Monashee Range on the east, contained only about 1500 able-bodied men. Five years later Archibald McDonald estimated that there were about 3400 Indian men, women and children in the 30,000 square miles served by Fort Kamloops.[2]

This year the HBC sent west of the Rockies an eager young Irish clerk, John Wark or, as the Company entered his name and he accepted it, John Work. The enthusiasm with which he hunted out comely Indian women has already been noted. In time he would settle down, raise a large family and, as the Hon. John Work, be a member of the Legislative Council of Vancouver Island. We shall have frequent occasion to mention him.

The HBC Committee in London may have had thoughts of abandoning the Columbia country, but in Washington, D.C., there

[2] See HBCA, B.208/e, pp. 214-18; and B.97/e, p. 3.

were other ideas. The Americans had not forgotten that, although occupied and used by the HBC, Fort George (alias Astoria) had been recognized by the British as belonging to the U.S.A. This year a bill was "reported" to Congress for the establishment of an American colony in Oregon. No action was taken on it.

1823

Yale's men murdered at Fort George — Massacre at Fort St. John — The revenge of the HBC.

This was another bad year for New Caledonia. Spring floods destroyed the fort at McLeod Lake, and it had to be rebuilt. Worse befell little Fort George at the junction of the Fraser and Nechako Rivers. The officer in command here since 1821 had been James Murray Yale, small in stature but full of spirit or, as the Indians said, "a little man with a great heart". He had entered the service of the HBC as a clerk in 1815 but, partly because of what happened this year, he would not get his commission as a Chief Trader until 1844.

To while away the empty days at Fort George, Yale had taken unto himself an Indian woman. Off on an unauthorized journey to Stuart Lake, Yale left this woman with the two engagés to whom he had entrusted the fort. While Yale was absent two Fraser Lake Indians arrived. One of these was a former lover of Yale's woman who, apparently, once again extended her favours to him. The engagés, discovering the scandal, threatened to inform Yale upon his return. Frightened, the two Indians turned to desperate measures. When Yale finally got back to his fort he found the mutilated remains of his two men, slain in their sleep by the two Indians. The murder instrument had been one of their own axes. The murderers of course had decamped, and with them had gone Yale's woman. The young clerk was relieved of his command, and Fort George was temporarily abandoned. Governor Simpson in his 1824 report made a scathing comment on Yale having disregarded "particular instructions from Mr. Stuart not to absent himself therefrom [from his post] on any consideration. . . ."[1] For a while it looked as if Yale

<hr>

[1] R. H. Fleming, ed., *Minutes of the Council, Northern Department of Rupert Land 1821-31*, HBRS 3 (London, 1940), p. 107.

would be dismissed from the Company's service, but the next year the Council of the Northern Department meeting at Norway House decided not to discharge him, "no satisfactory evidence having been produced that such accident was attributable to him."[2]

Tragedy struck at Fort St. John in November. To the anger of the local Indians, the HBC had decided to abandon this post in favour of a new one at Rocky Mountain Portage, which would be more convenient for the expert Sekani hunters. As for the Fort St. John Indians, they would just have to reconcile themselves to going to Fort Dunvegan when they wanted to trade. But the local Indians were not to be reconciled to any such thing. Moreover, they may have already been incensed against the white men by a superstitious belief that the latter had "thrown some destructive medicine" on an Indian boy. Furthermore, Samuel Black had, apparently, got involved with one of their women. Such was the situation when Guy Hughes, in command of Fort St. John, found himself entirely alone there while his men were transporting supplies to the new fort. Realizing that they were dealing with a single, unaided HBC man, the Fort St. John Indians murdered him,[3] possibly while he was taking his customary daily walk along the banks of the Peace River, and then dragged his corpse into the fort. The following day a little group of the Company's engagés arrived unexpectedly. According to the tale as told to John McLean ten years later,[4] the voyageurs were paddling up to the bank, still singing their voyageur's song, when a burst of gunfire slew all four of them. Apparently they had been killed to gain time for the flight of Hughes' murderers.

The revenge of the HBC was unexpected and cruelly apposite. The Fort St. John Indians had committed these murders partly because they did not want their fort closed — very well, the Company would close not only Fort St. John but the Rocky Mountain Portage post and Fort Dunvegan as well. These closures could do the Company no harm: suspending fur trading for a few years would allow the territory to recuperate and yield the more richly

---

[2] *Loc. cit.*

[3] HBRS 3:104; and HBRS 10:9.

[4] *John McLean's Notes of a Twenty-Five Years' Service in the Hudson's Bay Territory,* ed. W. S. Wallace, Champlain Society 19 (Toronto, 1932), p. 142.

when the Indians would once more have a market for beaver pelts. But for the Indians the decision was disastrous. They had already grown dependent, for their hunting, upon the guns and ammunition available at these establishments. The closure, as Governor Simpson noted, "reduced the whole population of the upper parts of the River to the utmost distress". According to McLean, many Indians starved to death. In 1829, having taught the Indians the price of murdering HBC men, the Company decided to reopen Fort Dunvegan, but four years later McLean found Fort St. John still empty, the blood of Guy Hughes plainly visible on the floor.

Little of importance happened in the Columbia District this year. John McLeod, in command at Fort Kamloops, was able to report that the year's take there was up to 900 beaver skins, a fact which he generously attributed to the energy of his predecessor, Chief Trader James McMillan. He had disconcerting news of an imminent war among the Indians:

Since my arrival at Thompson's River the natives have hitherto conducted themselves very peaceably and would very likely continue so, if it had not been for the death of one of their principal Chiefs who was killed last November by the Fraser River Indians, which circumstance subsequently created great commotions amongst the Indians throughout the whole Department. There are now four different nations in confederacy against the murderers to revenge this Chief's death for which purpose no less than six hundred fighting men were expected to assemble at Kamloops this spring — I tried as much as I possibly could to disuad[e] them from going to war; but finding all my rhetoric only exciting their derision against myself I was obliged to desist.[5]

5 PAC, McLeod Papers, pp. 7-8.

1824

Governor Simpson's visit to the Columbia — He sends Chief Trader McMillan to reconnoitre the Fraser Valley — Samuel Black's expedition — He reaches the headwaters of the Finlay River and travels on to the Stikine.

As we have already noted, after the merger of 1821 the HBC's Governor and Committee in London had very serious doubts about retaining the unprofitable Columbia district. One thing was clear: the Company's resident governor in North America would have to journey out to the Pacific Coast and, on the spot, make a detailed study both of the existing situation and the prospects for future trade. Thus it was that on August 15th of this year Governor Simpson set out by canoe from York Factory on Hudson Bay for Fort George at the mouth of the Columbia River. With him, besides his crew of eight picked voyageurs, he had his personal servant and Chief Trader James McMillan, a veteran who years earlier had travelled west of the Rockies with David Thompson. On September 26th, approaching the Athabasca River, Simpson, who was intensely proud of the pace at which he travelled, had the pleasure of overtaking Dr. John McLoughlin, the burly giant who was en route to take over the command of the Columbia district. Gleefully, Simpson noted in his diary that McLoughlin had started from York Factory twenty days ahead of himself.

Simpson and McLoughlin had plenty to talk over as they travelled in company. For one thing there was that fundamental question as to whether the Company would do well to abandon the coastal trade and confine its activities to the east of the Cascade Mountains. Should their decision go against retreat, there remained other problems. Canning, the British Foreign Secretary, had made it plain to the Company that, to avoid friction with the Americans, he wanted them to stop using Fort George, alias Astoria, which though abandoned by the Americans was still legally theirs. Canning had made it clear that the HBC must establish a new depot on the north side of the Columbia River since any future boundary treaty would almost certainly give the Americans all the land south of the great river. But whereabouts, north of the Columbia, should that new depot be built? Even before leaving York Factory, Simpson (blissfully unaware that the Fraser River did not provide a navigable route to the Interior) had pretty much decided that this new depot should be established by the mouth of the Fraser, a good safe distance from any future area of American sovereignty. But was this really the best solution? Such were the questions debated by Simpson, McLoughlin and McMillan as their canoemen brought them closer and closer to the shining westward peaks.

On October 10th Simpson's party was at Jasper's House, ready to cross the Rockies. Even the somewhat prosaic Simpson was moved by the grandeur of the mountains as they toiled over the steep Athabasca Pass:

. . . the Mountains rise perpendicular to a prodigious height; the scenery Wild & Majestic beyond description; the track is in many places nearly impassable and it appears extraordinary how any human being should have stumbled on a pass through such a formidable barrier as we now are scaling and which nature seems to have placed here for the purpose of interditing all communication between the East and West sides of the Continent.[1]

At the summit of the pass Simpson, in honour of his Company's London board of management, gave the quaint name of "The Committee's Punchbowl" to a little lake whose outlets emptied on either side of the Continental Divide.

By October 19th the travellers were safely over the Rockies and bivouacing at Boat Encampment on the Columbia River. From here a week's swift journeying took them to the junction of the Columbia with the Spokane River. Now, for a day or so, Simpson left his party and rode sixty miles to Spokane House. Here, as he conducted his inspection, his suspicions about the Columbia management began to find confirmation. In his journal for October 27th he grimly noted:

[1] Merk, *Fur Trade and Empire*, p. 33.

... if my information is correct the Columbia Dep^{tmt} from the Day of its Origin to the present hour has been neglected, shamefully mismanaged and a scene of the most wasteful extravagance and the most unfortunate dissention. It is high time the system should be changed and I think there is an ample Field for reform and amendment.[2]

Rejoining his waiting boat at the Columbia, Simpson had at least one consolation. His companion during the past couple of days had been tough, rough, jolly Peter Skene Ogden, whom he had chanced to meet bringing up supplies from the ship *Vigilant*, newly arrived at Fort George from England. Talking with Ogden, he had found him ready and willing to take on the most arduous duty that the HBC could assign to any man, command of the annual Snake River trapping expeditions.

Knowing well that any year, with the end of the Anglo-American co-dominion, the lands south of the Columbia would become American territory, the HBC had introduced the Snake River expeditions with the avowed purpose of trapping these lands empty of beaver while they could still legally do so, and in the process discouraging American trapping parties from moving towards the HBC domain. Each year the Company sent a small raggle-taggle army of trappers, their women and children, more or less to live off the land while they roamed the vast wilderness extending between the Columbia district and the Spanish settlements around San Francisco Bay, and between the Pacific and the Rockies. Theirs was a hard dangerous existence, with threats posed both by hostile Indians and by wild American trappers from the Missouri, but they brought in a wealth of furs. Simpson could indeed congratulate himself that he had found a man of Ogden's fibre to take over the Snake River expeditions from the rather inadequate Alexander Ross.

Resuming his journey down the Columbia, Governor Simpson on November 1st reached Okanagan, the outpost (administered by Fort Kamloops) at the junction of the Okanagan River and the Columbia. Here he found a number of Fort Kamloops men ready to start for home with other supplies from the *Vigilant*. Simpson was already aware of the failure of Fort Kamloops to show any real profit on its furs. In his journal he now made an ominous memorandum

[2] *Ibid.*, p. 43.

about Fort Kamloops: " . . . if a very great amendment does not this year take place it ought in my opinion to be abandoned."

On November 4th the Governor was at Fort Walla Walla, often called Fort Nez Percé. Leaving this last of the Interior forts, Simpson and his party travelled down the lower Columbia, safely passing the dangerous whirlpools, reefs and rapids where it burst through the Cascade Mountains. Finally, on November 8th, Governor Simpson came ashore at Fort George. Proudly he noted in his journal that his crossing of the continent from Hudson Bay had taken only eighty-four days, twenty days less than the previous record.

Surveying the situation at Fort George, Governor Simpson could find hardly a thing which merited his approval. The fort itself impressed him as possessing "an air or appearance of Grandeur & consequence which does not become and is not at all suitable to an Indian Trading Post". Fort George's "grandeur" seemed a symbol of general extravagance and self-indulgence which shocked Simpson to the core of his thrifty Scottish soul. The Columbia men had not established any farms in the rich earth of the river valley. When Simpson demanded why no attempt had been made to raise food, some poor fool audaciously informed him that the Columbia men were fur traders, not farmers. That remark elicited a cutting retort: "Every pursuit tending to lighten the expense of the trade is a branch thereof." Scorning to turn into farmers, the fur traders on the Columbia had been living, in good measure, on flour and other provisions imported from California, from New England, and even from England itself. Angrily Simpson tried to bring home to the Columbians the unforgivable nature of their extravagance. At Spokane House, on his westward journey, when he first realized what was going on, he had contemptuously noted in his journal: " . . . all this time they may be said to have been eating Gold; such fare we cannot afford in the present times, it must therefore be discontinued. . . . "[3]

Simpson could hardly believe the lethargy and incompetence of those who had presided at Fort George since its purchase from the Americans in 1813. Here, with a base practically on salt water, not

[3] *Ibid.*, p. 47.

the slightest attempt had been made to acquire ships with which to compete with the American trading vessels. The latter, plying the coast, had been left unchallenged while they got not only the pelts of the coastal Indians but other skins, sent from the Interior, which should have been bartered at the New Caledonia forts. Moreover, no attempt had been made to open up the country to the north of Fort George — not at least since 1818 when an expedition sent to avenge the slaying of a trapper had botched its job and incurred the hatred of the Chehalis Indians. Led by Ogden, the avengers had stormed down upon a little village, taking the lives of thirteen inhabitants, chiefly of women and children. Since that calamitous event had turned the Chehalis Indians against them, none of the traders at Fort George had chosen to risk their lives by pushing northward into the country around Puget Sound, though this was precisely what McMillan had promised Simpson to do when he had earlier undertaken to make a reconnaissance of the Fraser Valley.

Ten days after their arrival at Fort George, Governor Simpson had McMillan on his way north. Leaving Fort George early on the afternoon of November 18th, Chief Trader McMillan had with him three clerks (Thomas McKay, François Annance and John Work) and thirty-six French-Canadians and Kanakas. Among these French-Canadians was a man, named Prevost, who had been one of Fraser's voyageurs in 1808 and so could recognize landmarks which would let McMillan know when he had indeed reached "Fraser's River". The strength of this party kept the Indians from attempting any attack upon it.

Travelling up the coast in three canoes by way of Willapa Bay and Grays Harbour, McMillan's men turned up the Chehalis River and the Black River, then portaged over to Puget Sound, coming out close to the site of modern Olympia. From here they paddled along the winding waterways of the Sound, ending at Semiahmoo Bay. Deciding that the nearby "Coweechin" river of which the Indians spoke must be the Fraser, they headed towards it. Because of rough water, however, they did not round Point Roberts and make for the mouth of the Fraser. Instead they went to the head of Semiahmoo Bay then (impeded by driftwood and thick growths of willow) worked their way up the little Nikomekl River and portaged over "a plain made soft & miry by the heavy rain".[4] The land, they noted, consisted of rich black mould, and they saw plenty of beaver. On December 16th they put their canoes into the little Salmon River and, after paddling about eight miles, reached the Fraser opposite McMillan Island, only a mile from where Fort Langley now stands. Annance noted in his journal:

Feeling inadequate to give a full description of the river, we only can say it is a noble and majestic stream: and the surrounding country marks thousands of beaver that exist therein and its environs.[5]

Next day they paddled up the Fraser to the vicinity of the modern town of Mission. December 18th was marked by the incessant rain so familiar to those who spend their lives in the Lower Mainland. However, amid the downpour, some trading was carried on with the local Indians.

The chief of this tribe is a fine tall good looking man, but his people are of low stature. Their elderly men have generally beards; all their heads are a little flattened. Their clothes consisted of blankets of their own manufacture, some white & some grey, with variegated bands of different colors mostly red & white. They wore mats to keep off the rain, & conical hats.[6]

After giving the Indians a letter to transmit to Fort Kamloops, McMillan decided against continuing upstream. At noon they started retracing their route. Travelling down the Fraser on the morrow they spotted a likely situation for a fort, and marked it by carving HB on some of the trees at the river's edge.

Making good time, they reached the mouth of the Fraser on December 20th, turned south, passed Point Roberts and camped for the night in Birch Bay. A few days' travel brought them back to the southern end of Puget Sound, and they were all safely back at Fort George by the end of the month. Simpson must have been pleased with their report. The Fraser was a noble river; it ran through country rich in beaver and elk; the land was fertile; the natives there were friendly; and a good site had been found for a fort.

[4] PAC, *Journal of John Work*, MG29, B35, Vol. 9:21 (Bancroft transcript).
[5] HBCA, B.76/a/1, f. 7d.
[6] *Journal of John Work*, p. 26.

There are four major explorers by land in the history of British Columbia — Sir Alexander Mackenzie, Simon Fraser, David Thompson and Samuel Black. Of these, the last is known hardly at all since his explorations in this year of 1824 were carried out in a country so mountainous, remote and barren that to this day it remains a vast wilderness, almost entirely devoid of roads and population. Samuel Black was the first to go into the fastnesses of central northern British Columbia, that country lying between Babine Lake and the Alaska Highway, the vast area comprising the Omineca and the Cassiar regions.

Since Black enters into our chronicle more than once, he merits some introduction. Born an illegitimate child in Scotland in 1780, he grew to be a great hulking giant of a man. In 1804 he became a clerk in the service of the North West Company, stationed in the Athabasca country. Here he was under instructions to demoralize the HBC men through constant harrying. In 1806 the harrassment of Black, "the most mischievous, malicious person I ever saw", drove poor Peter Fidler and his men from Nottingham House. In 1810 Black ganged up with Peter Skene Ogden to drive Fidler from the HBC post at Ile-à-la-Crosse, shooting at the flag and weather vane, chopping down the stockades, stealing the fishnets, and systematically keeping him and his men from obtaining food and firewood. The next year Black and his men burned down the fort at Ile-à-la-Crosse while Fidler and his men were absent. In 1817, after the HBC had rebuilt it, Black boldly seized this fort and, four days later, took another HBC post in the same area.

We noted earlier how, during this war, the HBC was strengthened by recruiting the ex-Nor'Wester, Colin Robertson. In 1818 while Robertson was at the HBC's Fort Wedderburn on Lake Athabasca conducting the funeral of one of his men killed in an accident, Black with a group of armed Nor'Westers burst into the fort and carried off Robertson as a prisoner. Fortunately Robertson soon contrived his escape. In September 1820 he was joined at Fort Wedderburn by a dapper young Scot, one George Simpson, sent out from London to learn the fur trade and prepare himself for greater things. It was not long before parties of Nor'Westers were ostentatiously marching past the gates of Fort Wedderburn brandishing swords and pistols. Only a mile and a half away stood the North West Company's own Fort Chipewyan. Soon Simpson discovered that the infamous Samuel Black was lurking here concocting "murderous plans" with "miscreants capable of the foulest crimes".[7] During the long winter Simpson must often have wondered when the villainous Black would launch a sudden attack on the fort, or stealthily set fire to it.

The opinion that Simpson formed of Black that winter was a lasting one. Twelve years later, entering his confidential assessment of the HBC's officers into his "Book of Characters", Simpson said of Black, "A perfectly honest man and his generosity might be considered indicative of a warmth of heart if he was not known to be a cold blooded fellow who could be guilty of any cruelty. . . . "[8] The verdict was less than just to Black, who certainly was a rough character but had only been excessively zealous in carrying out the avowed policy of his company. Little wonder, though, that most of the HBC officers feared and loathed Samuel Black. Thus when the union of the two companies was achieved in 1821, Samuel Black along with Peter Skene Ogden was specifically excluded from the new HBC. In the winter of 1822-23 the two men were in England putting their case before the Governor and Committee in London. The upshot was that they were accepted as clerks in the HBC service and the following year commissioned as Chief Traders.

Governor Simpson had supported the applications made by the two men. After letting them "sweat it out" during a year of suspense, he had decided that men of such resolute spirit, tremendous physical stamina, and great experience in the fur trade were too useful to be lost to the HBC. Probably more important were rumours that Black and Ogden, if they were unsuccessful in their appeal, intended to set up as independent fur traders competing with the HBC. Black at the dissolution of the old North West Company had been given by his associates a ring inscribed, "To the most Worthy of the Worthy

---

[7] Phrases used by Simpson in his letters. See R. M. Patterson's introduction to Samuel Black's *A Journal of a Voyage From Rocky Mountain Portage in Peace River To the Sources of Finlays Branch and North West Ward In Summer 1824*, ed. E. E. Rich, HBRS 18 (London, 1955) : xxxviii.

[8] *Ibid.*, p. xliii.

North-westers".[9] Any new trading company headed by Black and Ogden could quickly draw to it all the old Nor'Westers dissatisfied with service in the HBC. In that case, the great achievement of uniting the companies would be quickly undone, and the old anarchy and financial losses would once more return. Clearly it was safer for the HBC to have Black and Ogden within its membership than outside.

Simpson realized the impracticality of using the two men in positions where they would be in close association with old HBC officers. For each he designed a service where he would be off on his own. For Ogden, as we have seen, he had the command of the Snake River expeditions which travelled almost to the Gulf of Mexico. Black's immediate endeavours would be in another quarter. The Company was getting highly satisfactory fur returns from both New Caledonia and the Mackenzie River Department. But what of the immense territory which lay between? Upon arriving at York Factory from England, Samuel Black was informed that his first task in the service of the HBC would be to penetrate as far as he could into that area north of New Caledonia and learn what was there. On 13 May 1824 he set out from the Company's post at the Peace River Portage (near modern Hudson's Hope). With him he had one other officer, Donald Manson, six canoemen, a Chipewyan Indian who would serve as hunter and interpreter, and the latter's wife.

The first part of their journey, up the Peace and then up the Finlay River to its junction with the Ingenika, was along the route travelled by John Finlay in 1797. It was after they passed the Ingenika on May 26th that the party went right off the map. Already the journey had proved a hard one with men straining at pole and paddle to make headway against the swift torrent of the river. When on May 28th the little party was confronted by a chasm through which the river hurtled, two of Black's men, Bouché and Ossin, deserted. Heading to the Company's post at Ile-à-la-Crosse, they turned themselves in. After their trial at York Factory, they were sentenced to be exposed, handcuffed, for an entire day on

---

[9] PAC, "Recollections of George B. Roberts", MG29, B35, Vol. 2:8 (Bancroft transcript).

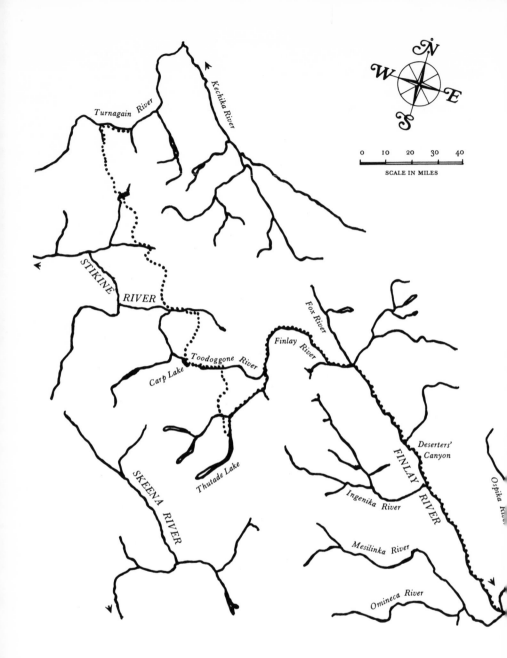

Map 8.

Explorations of Samuel Black 1824

the roof of the fort, to be imprisoned for a week during which they were allowed only bread and water, then to be assigned to different posts. This punishment was slight compared with what they would have endured had they remained loyal to Black.

After naming and passing Deserters' Canyon, Black's little party worked its way to the junction of the Finlay and the Fox Rivers. "The Old Slave", a Sekani who, with his wife and two children had joined the expedition as a guide and interpreter, was emphatic that they should continue along the Rocky Mountain Trench, following the Fox River, portaging to the Kechika, then travelling down it and the Liard to the Mackenzie. It was an attractive, tidy operation but Black would merely have skirted the unknown country which he was assigned to explore. Ignoring all protests, he ordered his men to stay with the Finlay, working their way through the terrible Long Canyon, equally fearsome Cascade Canyon and Reef Canyon and the other rocky defiles by which the Finlay forces its way through the Omineca Mountains. Black was unlucky in that the summer of 1824 was unusually wet and cold. Sometimes in the mornings the sides of the canoe would be found coated with ice. On June 14th, at the Fishing Lakes, they met a little band of Sekanis under old Chief Methodiates, who supplied a lot of useful information about the country. On June 23rd Black's party reached Thutade Lake, the source of the Finlay, cached their canoe and part of their supplies, and prepared to travel overland.

By this time Black's men had long grown bone-tired with "the River raging with great fury" and portage trails "scarcely imaginable". The change to travelling by land instead of water brought no lightening of hardships as the men staggered northwards under loads weighing 120 pounds. At Toodoggone Lake the party failed to find Chief Methodiates at the expected rendezvous. Pressing on through grass-covered mountains on which there were still large patches of snow, Black reached Carp Lake where he met not only Methodiates and his Sekanis but also members of a new tribe, the Thloadenni Indians, who had never met white men before. The Thloadennis entered the camp singing, decked out in their finest attire. Black for his part had his flag raised on a hurriedly erected flagpole. The Thloadenni "orator" was able to give Black a lot of topographical information but was discouraging in his report of what lay to the north, a terrible barren land empty of men and beaver. However, knowing that Indians, for reasons of their own, would often give false information to keep white men out of certain areas, Black resolved on pressing northward.

Late in July, on the bank of the Stikine River, La Prise, a Chipewyan Indian who had been with Black since the beginning deserted, taking with him his wife. Three days later Methodiates and his Sekanis took their leave more ceremoniously of Black. Onward the explorer continued his way, farther and farther north into "a scene of Tremendous Barreness passing description". On August 5th "The Old Slave" who had faithfully travelled with the party "between 3 and 400 Miles in these horrid mountains" slipped away in the night. Undeterred by these desertions, Black pushed on with his five remaining men, sometimes wading knee deep through the swamps in the valleys, at other times stumbling through snow on the sides of "terrific broken barren mountains". On August 16th, having crossed the divide between the Stikine (Pacific) and Liard (Arctic) basins, he reached an important new river.

The next day, amid pelting rain, Black faced the fact that he and his men were at the end of their tether and would have to turn back. He estimated that he was a little less than 100 miles (actually he was 125 miles) from the Liard River. To lighten the loads of his men so that they could get this far, he had periodically been caching food and supplies along the route, thus more or less committing himself to return that way. It would have been wonderful to build a canoe, paddle down this stream (which he now named the Turnagain River) to its junction with the Kechika, continue down the Kechika to the Liard, and then down the Liard to the Mackenzie and one of the HBC forts in that region — but such an enterprise was completely beyond Black's resources. Sadly he observed, "I wish I had wings to go & see", then he "fixed a Board on a Tree emblematical of our having been here in the service of the Honorable Hudsons Bay Company & for his Britanic Majesty"[10] and started back. On September 24th he and his men safely arrived at Fort Dunvegan on Peace River.

10 Black's *Journal*, pp. 173 & 175.

Black's journal of his great expedition has survived. It is a truly amazing document. Black clearly was determined to express himself in what he considered "literary English". Accordingly, he cannot say that he slept on late and awoke to find the sun shining on the lake; he must declare:

This morning involuntary indulged an hour longer than usual in morpheus chains, waking out of which the white resplendent orb of day was gloriously illuminating the blue azure sky & varigated Mountains reflecting his dancing beams in the silvery mirror of the Lake exhibited before our Torpid sences. . . . [11]

Black had been told that his expedition was intended to be scientific as well as commercial. Accordingly he filled page after page with pointless accounts of the shapes and colours of the rock formations he encountered, larding the whole with scientific terms which he admittedly did not comprehend:

. . . passed huge masses of petrifaction process which seems more or less to be an active agent in petrifying or endurating, concreting, cementing (for I do not understand the Terms used & have already apologized for prattling) the Rock & Stone in these mountains. . . . [12]

Living in a period before scientists had determined geological time and established the consequences of the ice ages, Black worried away at the problem of which geological formations were formed during the "Deluge" (Noah's flood) and which by subsequent inundations. Reading the pages of Black's turgid verbosity, one understands why Governor Simpson later wrote of Black that he was so prolix "that it is quite fatiging to attempt to follow him". Essential points did emerge from Black's report however: there were few beaver in the country which he had explored, and hardly any Indians to hunt them. Few fish were to be caught in its lakes. There could be no possible prospect of success for any HBC post established there. To this day the country has remained an empty wilderness. Only one man, Frank C. Swannell with his survey party in 1914, has ever followed Black by taking a canoe around the Big Bend of the Finlay River.

[11] *Ibid.*, p. 92.
[12] *Ibid.*, pp. 196-97.

1825

Governor Simpson's drastic changes in the Columbia district — He founds Fort Vancouver and Fort Colvile — The William and Ann *arrives with David Douglas — The HBC attempts to enter the maritime fur trade — The Alaskan boundary established — Origin of "The Panhandle" — The HBC proposes an Anglo-American boundary extending to the Pacific.*

We left Governor Simpson at the end of 1824 established at Fort George, digesting Chief Trader McMillan's report on his journey to the Fraser River. By mid-March, spring was sufficiently close for Simpson to begin his homeward journey. During his time at Fort George he had reached some very important decisions. First of all, he was now convinced that the HBC would be making a terrible mistake if it evacuated the Columbia. Quite apart from its great strategic value, the territory could be made to yield handsome profits (Simpson estimated at least £5000 yearly) once proper management took effect. There would have to be economies however. Simpson ruthlessly slashed the HBC personnel assigned to the Columbia from 151 men to 83. Another decision, entirely predictable, was to give a very high priority to raising staple crops. The Columbia would have to become self-sufficient where food was concerned. The importance which he attached to Company farms helped Simpson to select the site for the post which would replace Fort George — it would be some eighty-five miles up the Columbia at Lieut. Broughton's Bellevue Point, otherwise known as "Jolie Prairie". Here many acres of fertile open land could be put under cultivation without the felling of a single tree. Simpson was enthusiastic about this new establishment which he soon had under construction. He regarded it, however, as subsidiary to the great depot which he still intended to build at the mouth of the Fraser. (Increasingly disturbing reports about the difficulties of navigation upstream in the Fraser Canyon had not yet made Simpson aware that the HBC Pacific depot would have to be on the Columbia.) Another firm decision made by Simpson was to get the HBC actively engaged in the maritime fur trade. A beginning could be made this very spring by sending the supply ship from England, *William and Ann*, on a cruise upcoast while she was waiting for the brigades to bring down their furs from the Interior.

On March 16th Governor Simpson left Fort George en route back to the eastern part of the continent. Apparently he departed with some sadness, for he had formed an attachment to the Columbia district. In his journal he confided:

> I can scarcely account for the extraordinary interest I have taken in its affairs, the subject engrosses my attention almost to the exclusion of every other, in fact the business of this side [of the Rockies] has become my hobby. . . . [1]

Arriving at the new HBC establishment on Bellevue Point on March 18th he found its construction practically completed. On the 19th his last act before resuming his journey was formally to inaugurate the new post:

> At Sun rise mustered all the people to hoist the Flag Staff of the new Establishment and in presence of the Gentlemen, Servants, Chiefs & Indians I Baptised it by breaking a Bottle of Rum on the Flag Staff and repeating the following words in a loud voice, "In behalf of the Honble Hudsons Bay Coy I hereby name this Establishment *Fort Vancouver* God Save King George the 4th" with three cheers. Gave a couple of Drams to the people and Indians on the occasion. The object of naming it after that distinguished navigator is to identify our claim to the Soil and Trade with his discovery of the River and Coast on behalf of Gt Britain.[2]

Resuming his journey up the river, Simpson reached Fort Walla Walla on March 26th. Conversing there with Chief Trader J. W. Dease, Simpson presented him with ten bushels of seed potatoes and treated him to "a long lecture on the advantages to be derived from

---

[1] Merk, *Fur Trade and Empire*, pp. 122-23.
[2] *Ibid.*, p. 124.

attention to the Horticultural deptm^t of the Post". At Okanagan post, a few days later, Simpson reached his decision about Fort Kamloops. This post, he concluded, was too important a link on the brigade route to New Caledonia to be abandoned, even if its harvest of furs had proved disappointing. But there would definitely have to be a change of command with Archibald McDonald taking over from John McLeod, "who at best is nearly useless but (dogged as he is with a deranged Wife who even in her madness governs him) is now entirely so".

April 8th found Simpson conferring with a group of HBC officers at the confluence of the Spokane River and the Columbia. Now it was the fate of Spokane House, sixty miles to the east, that was in question. This time the decision was to close the post. Spokane House would be replaced by a new establishment close to where the Kettle River, with its great fishing site by the Kettle Falls, flowed into the Columbia. A week later Simpson had the pleasure of marking out the exact location of the new post:

> Lined out the Site of the Establish^t 150 feet Square on a bank facing and commanding a view of the [Columbia] River and I have taken the liberty of naming it Fort Colvile [after an HBC director] . . . likewise marked out the Garden and wrote Mr Birnie to Spokan House directing him to send a couple of Men across immediately to plant 5 or 6 Bushels of Potatoes. . . . [3]

On April 14th Governor Simpson left the site of Fort Colvile. A fortnight later he had crossed the Rockies and was at Jasper House on his way east.

Early in April, just a few weeks after Governor Simpson's departure, the expected supply ship from England, the *William and Ann*, crossed the bar of the Columbia. She carried a notable passenger, a hot-tempered, opinionated, enormously energetic young Scottish botanist named David Douglas. A protégé of the famous Dr. Hooker, Douglas had been despatched by the Horticultural Society to make a wide-ranging botanical survey of the Columbia region. The next two years would see him busy travelling around the country, intent on finding new species and new genera. The ship's doctor on the

[3] *Ibid.*, p. 139.

William and Ann was another ardent young botanist, also a former student of Hooker's, named John Scouler. Dr. Scouler in fact had taken the appointment on the *William and Ann* only because of the opportunity it would give him to devote his abundant spare time to botany.

Douglas and Scouler had become fast friends on the voyage out, but now they were to be separated. Simpson had left orders that once the *William and Ann* had discharged her cargo, she was to sail northwards up the coast and become the first HBC ship to participate in the maritime fur trade. Douglas would have liked to sail on this cruise with Scouler, whose duties as ship's doctor required that he go, but McLoughlin assured Douglas that the turbulent nature of the northern Indians would make it almost impossible for him to botanize in safety. Reluctantly Douglas remained behind and began working along the Columbia and its tributaries.

Dr. Scouler's journal preserves for us various details of the voyage of the *William and Ann*. Sailing to the west of Vancouver Island, she headed first for the Queen Charlotte Islands, then she made for the mainland, visiting Observatory Inlet and the area around the Nass River. Late July found the *William and Ann* once more off the Queen Charlottes, entering Skidegate harbour just as two American ships were sailing out. The Haidas, not surprisingly, made a notable impression on Scouler, eliciting considerable praise:

> The acuteness of the Queen Charlotte's Islanders has prompted them to adopt a great many customs of civilized life, & the cultivation of potatoes is very general among them, and had our time admitted of it we might have obtained any quantity of this usefull vegetable. This consideration alone, in my opinion, places them far above the natives of the Columbia in the scale of intelligence. . . . Poor Skittigass Tom [an interpreter] was the only Indian that ever expressed much anxiety to learn to read and write, & was very fond of obtaining a few ciphers. He made charts of Nass & Skittigass, which served to give a very good idea of the coast & of the different tribes settled along it.[4]

On her homeward voyage the *William and Ann* put in at Nootka, but this historic inlet proved a sad disappointment as far as trade

4 "Journal of a Voyage to N.W. America", *OHQ* 6 (1905) : 191.

was concerned. The local sources of furs had been pretty much exhausted and ships hardly ever put in there any more.

Nootka, which excited so much contention between the courts of Madrid & London, is now completely neglected by every civilised power, & the state of poverty in which they are at present affords little inducement to the visits of mercantile adventurers.[5]

After leaving Nootka, the *William and Ann* had one more mission to fulfill: to make the first European approach to the Fraser River from the sea. On August 8th she entered the Strait of Juan de Fuca. A week later, approaching her destination, she met the Lummi Indians, and her crew were entertained to find that these people took the captain's sextant to be a magical instrument which revealed to him the whereabouts of tribes with pelts to trade. Pushing northward, the *William and Ann* on August 23rd succeeded in finding the mouth of the Fraser.

Early in September the *William and Ann* was back on the Columbia, ready to sail for England. In the Company's eyes, her northern cruise had been pretty much of a failure. Captain Hanwell, afraid of losing his ship on the dangerous unknown shore, had generally spent so much of her time far out to sea that the clerk sent to barter with the Indians was able to obtain only a scant four hundred furs. At Skidegate a friendly American, Captain Kelly of the *Owhyhee*, had come aboard the *William and Ann* and, after pointing out that she was not properly fitted either for defence or trade, invited her captain to come over to his ship and see how she was set up. Captain Hanwell, who seems to have been profoundly uninterested in fur trading, declined the offer. One thing at least the HBC learned from the cruise of the *William and Ann*: the mouth of the Nass River was a great centre of trade for the Indians of the northern coast.

Following the return of the *William and Ann*, the two botanical friends Douglas and Scouler had a notable reunion. Douglas, recalling the occasion, wrote, "We sat and talked over our several journeys, unconscious of time, until the sun from behind the majestic

<hr/>

[5] *Ibid.*, pp. 194-95.

trees warned us that a new day had come."[6] A few weeks later the *William and Ann* was en route to England with Dr. Scouler, leaving poor Douglas the company only of hard-bitten HBC men who regarded with amusement and contempt a grown man who went around gathering flowers.

One major event of this year still awaits our attention — the creation of the "Alaskan Panhandle", that weird anomaly which today deprives British Columbia of half of its coastline. The Panhandle was the consequence of the Russian fur traders' steady movement southwards. Spain ineffectually had sought to halt that advance at the 60th parallel, but now Russian expeditions, reaching considerably farther south, were coming in contact with the advancing HBC. Clearly boundaries would have to be set for the competing British and Russian fur companies. Earlier the Russians had claimed sovereignty right down to the 51st parallel, but this unreasonable claim was now withdrawn and Russian sovereignty recognized over the land north of the 60th parallel of latitude and west of the 141st meridian. Moreover, to preserve for Russia the fur trade she had developed further to the south along the coast, she was granted also a strip of land as far south as 54°40′. This strip was to consist of the land lying within ten leagues (about thirty miles) from the nearest salt water. The treaty was regarded as a triumph for Britain in that she had deprived Russia of an enormous hinterland and confined her southward expansion to this narrow coastal belt. Moreover, the British had obtained from Russia the unimpeded use of all the rivers right down to the ocean. Nobody could have foreseen the problems that an Alaskan Panhandle would one day cause the province of British Columbia.

Consideration was being given this year to another boundary, the one which eventually would have to be drawn between Britain and the United States in the territory which the Americans called "Oregon". In London Governor Pelly of the HBC sent to the Hon. George Canning, Britain's Foreign Secretary, a comprehensive statement of the Company's views and position. In this he did not fail

---

[6] David Douglas, *Journal of David Douglas during his Travels in North America*, published under direction of Royal Horticultural Society (London, 1914), p. 60.

to point out that, apart from the ill-fated Astorian venture, the Americans had never had trading posts in the country, that no Americans had used their right under the Convention of 1818 to establish posts within the existing co-dominion, whereas his own company had thirteen permanent posts and various temporary stations all the way between the 45th and 60th parallels. In fact, wrote Pelly, "It does not appear that the Americans can establish any just claim to the Country on the Columbia or to the Northward of it." In conclusion, he recommended a line to be followed by the International Boundary west of the Rockies:

I have therefore to suggest that starting from Lat. 49° at the Rocky Mountains the line ought to be continued southward along the height of land [Continental Divide] to the place where Lewis and Clarke crossed the Mountains, said to be in Lat. 46°42', thence westerly along the Lewis River [Snake River] until it falls into the Columbia and thence to the sea, leaving the navigation of both these Rivers free to the subjects of both nations.[7]

The proposed boundary would have given Britain practically the whole of the present state of Washington, northern Idaho, and the north-western corner of Montana, an area within which there was not a single American settlement or trading post. On the other hand, it gave the United States all the fertile lands south of the Columbia, which were equally devoid of American settlement. It was an eminently fair and just proposal.

---

[7] Scottish Record Office, G.D. 45 3/319, f.1025. An almost identical wording is given in Merk, *Fur Trade and Empire*, p. 259.

1826

David Douglas discovers the Douglas fir — The brigades at Fort Vancouver — A reprimand for Chief Factor Connolly.

This was the year of David Douglas' greatest discovery. On March 24th he wrote excitedly to Dr. Hooker from the "Great Falls of the Columbia River":

> I rejoice to tell you of a new species of *Pinus*, the most princely of the genus, perhaps even the grandest specimen of vegetation. It attains the enormous height of from one hundred and seventy to two hundred and twenty feet, with a circumference of fifty feet, and cones from twelve to eighteen inches long. . . . The trunk grows remarkably straight and destitute of branches till near the top, where they form a perfect umbel; the wood of fine quality, yielding a large quantity of resin.[1]

Douglas had discovered the pine *Pseudotsuga menziesii*, commonly called after him the Douglas fir. Incidentally, he was not the only botanist working in that huge area which we call the Pacific Northwest. Another Scot, Thomas Drummond, having travelled overland from Hudson Bay, was botanizing among the headwaters of the Fraser River.

This year another of Governor Simpson's reforms was carried into effect. As we have seen, in 1814 the Nor'Westers sent up to New Caledonia supplies from a ship at the mouth of the Columbia. Apparently they lacked the energy to exploit this breakthrough. In the years that followed, other supply ships reached the Columbia River from Britain, but they were apparently used only to service the Columbia posts, with New Caledonia as in the past bringing in its supplies and sending out its furs by the long transcontinental route. To Simpson this was a bad mistake. In 1825 he put his views before the Council of the Northern Department which dutifully resolved:

---

[1] *Companion to Curtis's Botanical Magazine*, 2 (1836) : 106.

That William Connolly [at Fort St. James] be directed to take out the New Caledonia Returns to Fort Vancouver (Columbia River) next Spring, from whence he is to receive the ensuing Outfit for 1826.[2]

This year, the necessary arrangements having been completed on schedule, the New Caledonia forts did indeed, for the first time, send their furs to Fort Vancouver instead of over the Rockies. Francis Ermatinger, who travelled with the brigade on this maiden trip, found the experience a rather unhappy one. The "conductors" in charge of the operation jealously tried to outdo each other in setting a pace, and the same unfriendly spirit of competition animated the officers from the various forts. The consequence was that poor Ermatinger, "with the pigs and fowls in the worst boat of the Brigade", frequently arrived at camp after all the other gentlemen had been served their meal. Like his subordinate engagés, Ermatinger had either to prepare his own meal or go hungry to bed.

One significant event in New Caledonia this year was the founding of Fort Connolly on Bear Lake, north of the 56th parallel. By far the most remote of the New Caledonia posts, Fort Connolly was named by its builder, James Douglas, after his father-in-law, Chief Factor William Connolly, the officer commanding the New Caledonia district. Alas for Chief Factor Connolly, the honour done to him by his son-in-law was totally eclipsed by a reprimand he received this same year when the Company's Northern Council held its annual meeting at York Factory. The Council found Connolly and his assistant, Chief Trader Brown, alike blameworthy in not having put into the field a party of ten men designated to explore part of the Babine country. Accordingly the Council passed a resolution: "That both these Gentlemen receive the censure of Council for such mismanagement which has been productive of much loss, inconvenience and disappointment."[3] Plain speaking was the rule when Governor Simpson met with his Council.

When the autumn express from the East arrived at Fort Vancouver this year, it brought with it a kinsman of Governor Simpson, the elegant and fastidious Aemilius Simpson, a lieutenant in the

2 HBRS 3:106.
3 *Ibid.*, p. 146.

Royal Navy who had retired on half-pay some years earlier. The Governor had secured for him the command of the maritime department, whose trading ships, the Company hoped, would drive the American maritime traders out of business. Conscientious, competent and gentlemanly, Lieut. Simpson was to render notable service to the Company. Unfortunately these last few years of his life were not to prove happy ones. Most of the HBC officers regarded with suspicion this outsider who, they alleged, owed his position solely to his kinship with Governor Simpson.

1827

The founding of Fort Langley — A jaundiced report from Fort Alexandria — David Douglas crosses the Athabasca Pass.

This was a bumper year for the HBC. In 1821, the year of the union of the companies, there had been no profits. A year later a Chief Trader's share yielded him rather more than £203. Now, in 1827, the same share paid a little over £560. Governor Simpson's policy of stringent economy along with properly directed expansion was yielding dividends.

Despite the disappointing returns from the *William and Ann*'s pioneering trading voyage upcoast in 1825, the HBC was determined to take the maritime fur trade away from the Americans. This year two schooners were provided for the coastal trade. One was the newly-built *Cadboro*, of seventy-two tons burden, which arrived from England in company with the *William and Ann* and was promptly put under the command of Lieut. Aemilius Simpson. The other was the *Vancouver*, sixty tons, built at Fort Vancouver — but so inexpertly that her crew swore they could load six more barrels on one side of her mast than on the other. Actually these schooners were too small for the work for which they were intended. As Governor Simpson pointed out when calling for larger ships, many an Indian war canoe was longer than the *Cadboro* and rose higher out of the water, leaving the schooner terribly vulnerable if the forty or fifty Indians in the canoe should attempt to board her.[1] No attacks were made on the *Cadboro* this year, but in the autumn the Indians killed Edward Driver and wounded Peter Calder when the *Cadboro* landed a watering party on Vancouver Island.

As we noted earlier, one of the fixed notions that Governor Simpson entertained during his visit of 1824-25 was that the Fraser River

[1] HBRS 10:84

afforded access to the Interior and that therefore, safely removed from the Americans, the HBC's Pacific depot should be built near the mouth of that river instead of on the lower Columbia. This idea was promptly accepted by the Governor and Committee in London, who wrote to Simpson in February 1826:

We wish Frazers River to be established next season if possible, and that Mr. McMillan should be appointed to the charge of it, as his re-appearance among the natives may have a good effect. From the central situation of Frazers River we think it probable that it will be found to be the proper place for the principle [sic] depot.... [2]

This year, in compliance with the instructions from London, James McMillan, newly promoted to the rank of Chief Factor, set out to establish the new post on the Fraser. Once more he had with him three clerks: François Annance, who had been with him on the 1824 reconnaissance; Donald Manson, whom we last met with Samuel Black exploring northern British Columbia; and George Barnston, recently transferred from York Factory. On June 27th these four officers left Fort Vancouver with twelve French-Canadians, one French-Canadian half-breed, two Kanakas, two Iroquois, two other Indians, an Orkneyman and an Irishman — making a total party of twenty-five. Having travelled to Puget Sound by way of the Cowlitz River, they rendezvoused off Whidbey Island with the *Cadboro*, commanded by Aemilius Simpson.

Once the *Cadboro* arrived off the mouth of the Fraser, she required about five days to find a safe passage into the river. On July 24th, well into the river, the *Cadboro* reached the trees which had been marked with the HBC sign three years earlier. She then proceeded to where the Pitt River flows into the Fraser. A few days were spent in scouting along the river, but by the 29th a decision had been made to build in the area tentatively selected in 1824, where deep water permitted the *Cadboro* to come close inshore.

Next day the horses were slung ashore and the men started clearing a site. That night they all returned to sleep aboard the *Cadboro*, a precaution deemed necessary until more confidence could be placed in the friendly disposition of the Indians. (Several days earlier an

[2] Merk, *Fur Trade and Empire*, p. 267.

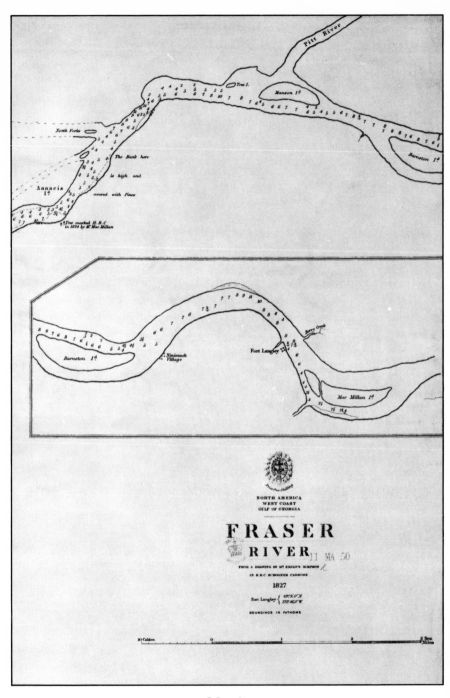

Map 9.
Aemilius Simpson's Chart of the Fraser River
at Fort Langley, 1827

Indian had warned that they would be annihilated if they attempted settlement.) Fortunately the Indians did not live up to this dire prognostication. The next day they came offering sturgeon in trade, and the following day forty or fifty Indians appeared with their chiefs, who made long harangues declaring friendship for the whites. The succeeding days saw the men continuing to clear land, cutting and squaring heavy timbers for the construction of the two bastions, making pickets for the stockade, and working in the sawpit. Amid these operations a forest fire came dangerously close to the building area. Bands of Indians drifted in to watch the activity and do a little trading — Skagits from the south and Musqueams from the Fraser's mouth. Occasional thefts by the Indians proved a continuing nuisance. With the raising of the palisades the working force could sleep ashore at night, though the three clerks stayed on guard through the hours of darkness, ready to raise the alarm in case of attack. On September 8th the defences of the new post were completed. That day George Barnston noted in his journal:

> The Picketing of the Fort was completed, and the gates hung. The Rectangle inside is 40 Yards by 45, and the two Bastions are 12 ft. square each, built of 8 inch Logs, and having a lower and upper flooring, the latter of which is to be occupied by our artillery. The *Tout ensemble* must make a formidable enough appearance in the eyes of the Indians. . . . [3]

Next came the erection of the buildings within the fort. A storehouse was completed on September 15th and trade goods were moved into it from the *Cadboro*, which sailed a few days later. Aemilius Simpson, her captain, had been occupying his time making the first hydrographic chart of the lower Fraser. After the *Cadboro*'s departure, the men pushed ahead with their second building:

> Our Wintering House gets on apace, and promises to make snug and comfortable quarters. It is 30 feet long by 15 in Breadth, and is divided into two apartments, each of which is provided with a fireplace and two windows.[4]

[3] HBCA, B.113/a/1.
[4] *Ibid.* (entry for Sept. 26th).

This was the season when the salmon were running and a succession of Indians passed the new fort en route to their traditional fishing sites upriver. Great war canoes, used as "luggage boats", were loaded with their possessions, and other canoes, yoked by planks lashed across them, served as rafts similarly laden. Hundreds of these Indians stopped at the fort, ready to trade. A somewhat unwelcome development came on October 11th when a party of eighty-six Cowichans passed upriver, bent on an attack upon the Chilliwacks. Eight days later they came back downstream:

The war Party of Cowitchins returned this afternoon from their expedition, in which they have managed to murder one man and a woman. The head of one of their victims was pendant at the Bow of the largest Canoe, presenting a spectacle as dismal and disgusting as can well be imagined, a spectacle the most shocking to humanity that this land of Barbarism can well produce. Several Women and children have been taken prisoners, who as a matter of course become Slaves, and the greater number of the Canoes are laden with dried and fresh provisions, Baskets, Mats, and other Furniture, the Spoils of the Camp of the unhappy creatures that were surprized.[5]

It turned out that their attack had been directed, not against the Chilliwacks, but a smaller tribe in the vicinity. A few days later a man from this tribe managed to ransom the captured women by handing over all that he possessed.

By November 26th the fort was complete in every respect. That day its flagpole was raised and the establishment was formally named "Fort Langley", after one of the London directors of the Company. To celebrate the completion of the project, the men were feasted at a regale.

In other ways than the founding of Fort Langley, the HBC was opening up new areas this year. Thus an expedition was sent into the Lillooet country west of the little town that now bears that name. Not much is known about this quest for new beaver country amid the rugged mountains stretching towards the ocean, but some slight evidence indicates that Francis Ermatinger, one of the Company's clerks, may have managed to find his way via Seton and Anderson

[5] *Ibid.*, (entry for Oct. 19th).

Lakes and the Pemberton valley to Harrison Lake, arriving at last where Harrison River empties into the Fraser.[6] The HBC's Standing Rules and Regulations required a detailed annual report from each of the Company's districts. One of the most interesting which survives in the HBC Archives is the Fort Alexandria report for 1827-28 (Outfit 1827),[7] submitted by Chief Trader Joseph McGillivray. Opening sections on the district's boundaries and means of transportation are followed by one headed "Nature of the Country — Soil & Vegetable Productions". In it McGillivray notes that his crops of vegetables and potatoes have both proved failures. Three of the local herbs, he notes, yield a strong decoction, highly esteemed in the treatment of venereal complaints. He further reports that coal is present in his district in great quantities. The next section, "Animals — Fur Bearing &c", contains an interesting comment on the little Indian dogs. These are "eagerly purchased by ourselves, the flesh constituting our Holiday meals for Christmas and New Years". A section on ornithology is followed by one on climate.

Next come passages of major interest for McGillivray's superiors. In these he lists the advantages and disadvantages of the post. Under "Advantages" he notes the usefulness of Fort Alexandria in getting the furs of the Atnah and Chilcotin Indians. Under "Disadvantages", McGillivray complains about the great amount of time expended in expeditions sent far afield to trade with remote Indian bands. He registers an indirect complaint against his associates at Fraser Lake, who are accepting skins which originate in his territory, thus swelling their own returns and unfairly diminishing his.

In Chief Trader McGillivray's section on "Means of Subsistence", we learn that the fort is almost entirely dependent upon the salmon, the Indians normally catching between 800 and 1000 daily between mid-July and October. This year the salmon run has failed, and he has had to bring in both salmon and potatoes from Fort Kamloops. This catastrophic failure of the salmon is mentioned in a letter written about this time by McGillivray's clerk, George McDougall: "Sheer

---

6 Malcolm McLeod, ed., *Peace River. A Canoe Voyage from Hudson's Bay to Pacific by the Late Sir George Simpson . . . in 1828: Journal of the late Chief Factor, Archibald McDonald . . . who accompanied him* (Ottawa, 1872), p. 38. See also HBRS 10:31-32n.

7 HBCA, B.5/e/1.

Starvation has caused the Death of a number of our Alexandria Indians since the Fall. . . . "[8] McGillivray's table of the year's consumption of food gives a fair idea of the diet at one of the New Caledonia forts:

8573	Dried Salmon	3	Horses
430	Large Fresh ditto	9	Dogs
1024	Small Fresh ditto	56	Kegs of Potatoes
154	Rabbits	100	Suckers
283	Berry Cakes	135	Pemmicans[9]
3	Beavers		

A section headed "Officers & Men their Conduct and Character" contains McGillivray's opinion of the six men with him in the fort. Anastias Campbell is "excessively nervous" but can speak the Carrier language. The conduct of Hyacinthe Desloge is "Generally Improper" and his character is "Naturally Bad". Etienne Gregoire is a steady man and good with the horses. George McDougall has an "unexceptional" character and is an efficient trader. Ambrose Massan is inclined to be troublesome. Eneas McDonell is a "Good Lad" and obedient.

Demographically interesting is the "General Abstract of the Indian Population". A detailed breakdown according to age and sex is followed by totals for the five tribes in the vast Fort Alexandria district:

Tluze Kuz	76
Naskotins	260
Talkotins	166
Atnay & Chin	510
Chilkotins	184
	1196[10]

A very lengthy section captioned "Characteristics, Morals &c" allows Chief Trader McGillivray to relieve his feelings about the Indians in his district. None of the other Indian nations with which

8 McDougall to John McLeod, 8 March 1828. PAC, McLeod Papers, pp. 218-20.
9 HBCA, B.5/e/1, pp. 15-16.
10 *Ibid.*, p. 25.

he has dealt can match the Carriers in "filth, nastiness and laziness". Excremental filth is to be found in their cabins. They never bathe, claiming that their all-enveloping dirt keeps them warm in winter and safe from the scorching sun in summer. They douse themselves with extra quantities of salmon oil on festive occasions and, when they approach the fireside, perfect faintness seizes one because of the stench. They like to wear European clothing, but in summer both men and women go totally naked. All the Indians are addicted to gambling. McGillivray tells how one Indian came to him in tears because, egged on by his friends, he had gambled away all the furs he had secured during three months of trapping.

Turning to the subject of the Indian women, McGillivray reports that the girls grow up completely promiscuous — "nor will they marry until Surfeited with a variety of men". The women frequently suffer miscarriages as a result of pressing their abdomens against digging sticks in their quest for roots. They also frequently commit suicide by hanging themselves from trees. Venereal disease carries off most of the men at an early age. McGillivray is scathing in his comments on the medicine men — ten to one they will kill a patient when they employ their practice of beating the afflicted part.

Obviously McGillivray was totally fed up with the Carriers. He inveighs against the ingratitude of those whom he has nursed back to health. He pours forth accounts of their inhumanity to each other — he cites the case of an Indian allowed to starve to death even though his relatives had plenty of salmon. His unfeeling kinsmen did not wait for his body to be cold before cremating it.

The year had seen the local Talkotins at war with the Chilcotins, and McGillivray spares nothing in reporting the atrocities:

> In the Battle of the 24th September 1827 — they killed some Chilkotins — raised the Scalps — mounted the dead bodies on Stumps — and exhibited them in this manner to the Atnahs — who were specially invited to witness these trophies of their valour — one would come with a Knife and cut at the Body — another with an Axe — a third would wing an Arrow — Women and Children followed the example — and all washing their faces and hands in the blood of their victims. . . . [11]

[11] *Ibid.*, p. 38.

Some Chilcotin prisoners had been taken by the Talkotins:

The War Dance began, and the unfortunate Prisoners were introduced in the middle of the Circle compelled to dance and join in the
Song — where at every turn the Scalps of their Fathers, Uncles and
Brothers were brushed across their faces — and with Savage fierceness
questioned whether it "Smelt good".[12]

Among the prisoners were two young children. The HBC men,
hoping to return them to their people, offered generous ransoms.
These were refused and the children murdered.

McGillivray may have loathed the Carriers but he entertained
quite different feelings about the Atnahs. The latter were cleanly in
their persons, their women chaste and modestly dressed, and some of
the men were industrious.

In his next section, "Narrative and Sketch of the Chilkotin
Country", McGillivray traces the course of the Talkotin-Chilcotin
war since its beginning in the winter of 1826 when four young
Talkotins were butchered while in the Chilcotin country. The
Talkotins had retaliated with a raid in which they killed twelve
Chilcotin men, women and children. The counterattack came on
September 24th of this year when eighty Chilcotin warriors appeared
at Fort Alexandria. Like so many tribes did when an HBC fort was
opened in their territory, the Talkotins had abandoned their earlier
villages and established a new one close to the white men's trading
post. Against this new village the invading Chilcotins for a while
launched their attacks and " . . . the bloody contest would have lasted
much longer and probably [have led] to the annihilation of the
Talkotins had not we given them assistance in Arms and Ammunition."[13] Having learnt that the HBC men were assisting their
enemies, the Chilcotins withdrew, threatening death to any white
man who should enter their territories. No wonder the founding of
Fort Chilcotin, scheduled for this year, was postponed.

McGillivray's report concludes with some miscellaneous observations. He notes that the use of the Columbia route had greatly
stimulated the New Caledonia trade. The war among the Indians

---

[12] *Ibid.*, p. 39.
[13] *Ibid.*, pp. 43-44.

has temporarily depressed local trade, but the year 1827-28 has brought to Fort Alexandria furs worth just over £1665. The Chief Trader recommends that the Talkotins be required to abandon the village that they have set up adjacent to Fort Alexandria — otherwise the Company will find itself involved in "incessant and dangerous broils". He urges that two gentlemen be always assigned to Fort Alexandria, one to command the fort when the other is off in the field "equipping and receiving the Hunts of the Indians". It simply is asking for trouble to leave the fort in the charge of an engagé — the Indians have no respect for the French-Canadians!

This Fort Alexandria report is much more detailed than those usually sent from the trading posts. McGillivray obviously took a real interest in drafting it and used much of its material in a letter to his friend Ross Cox who had retired from the Company's service.[14]

Retirements from the Company's Columbia and New Caledonia service were not infrequent. This year Douglas the botanist, starting his return journey to England, travelled overland with the annual spring express under the command of young Edward Ermatinger, who was leaving the Company's service. The route up the Columbia to Boat Encampment then over the Rockies by Athabasca Pass had by now become thoroughly familiar, but Douglas' account of crossing the pass when it was still deep in snow deserves quotation. Douglas himself travelled light. Although others carried his wardrobe and blanket, he personally carried his precious journals and specimens, a total weight of forty-three pounds. Douglas was lucky that his load was no greater, for the crossing was made on snowshoes and Douglas, who had never used them before, had a hard time of it. In his journal for April 30th he wrote:

The ravines or gullies unmeasurable, and towards noon becoming soft, sinking, ascending two steps and sometimes sliding back three, the snowshoes twisting and throwing the weary traveller down (and I speak as I feel) so feeble that lie I must among the snow, like a broken down waggon-horse entangled in his harnessing weltering to rescue myself.[15]

[14] Cox, *Columbia River*, pp. 367-83.
[15] Douglas, *Journal*, p. 258.

That day they made only nine miles. It says a lot for Douglas' stamina that, when they camped around mid-day on the morrow, he decided to climb one of the adjacent mountains:

... I set out alone on snowshoes to that on the left hand or west side, being to all appearance the highest. The labour of ascending the lower part, which is covered with pines, is great beyond description, sinking on many occasions to the middle. Half-way up vegetation ceases entirely, not so much as a vestige of moss or lichen on the stones. Here I found it less laborious as I walked on the hard crust. One-third from the summit it becomes a mountain of pure ice, sealed far over by Nature's hand as a momentous work of Nature's God. ... The ascent took me five hours; descending only one and a quarter. ... The sensation I felt is beyond what I can give utterance to. Nothing as far as the eye could perceive, but mountains such as I was on, and many higher, some rugged beyond any description, striking the mind with horror blended with a sense of the wondrous works of the Almighty. The aerial tints of the snow, the heavenly azure of the solid glaciers, the rainbow-like hues of their thin broken fragments, the huge mossy icicles hanging from the perpendicular rocks with the snow sliding from the steep southern rocks with amazing velocity, producing a crash and grumbling like the shock of an earthquake, the echo of which resounding in the valley for several minutes.[16]

Back at camp Douglas found his knees and ankles so painful he could hardly sleep that night. The party was on the trail by 4:15 next morning. An hour later they reached the little lake, right on the Continental Divide, which Simpson and McLoughlin a few years earlier had named "The Committee's Punchbowl". Quickly descending on the other side, they were into a temperature of 57° by afternoon.

*   *   *

Meeting in London on August 6th of this year, the representatives of Great Britain and the United States agreed that their co-dominion over the Pacific North-west should be continued indefinitely, with either country free to abrogate the arrangement at the expiration of twelve months' notice.

[16] *Ibid.*, pp. 258-59.

1828

Massacre of the Fort Langley express — Bungling avengers — Governor Simpson visits New Caledonia — He learns the hard way that the Fraser is not navigable — Jedediah Smith and the Umpqua Massacre — Young James Douglas' brush with death at Fort St. James.

This year began with tragedy. On January 3rd, when an HBC clerk, Alexander McKenzie, and four engagés were travelling along the Hood Canal bearing despatches from Fort Langley to Fort Vancouver, they were attacked by the Clallum Indians and all murdered. In July the Company took its revenge when Chief Trader A. R. McLeod led an expedition into the Clallum country. The achievements of this band of avengers are not among the more glorious in the annals of the HBC. For once the Company's men abandoned the HBC policy of punishing only guilty individuals and instead followed the American policy of wholesale reprisals against an entire tribe. Things seem to have got rather out of control. McLoughlin, reporting to London, mentioned as inconspicuously and ambiguously as possible a "report" that twenty-one Indians had been slain. Young Francis Ermatinger, a clerk who had been on the expedition, was in McLoughlin's bad books for years after the Chief Factor learned that Ermatinger had indiscreetly entered into his journal a detailed account of the proceedings. Fortunately for history, this journal has survived.

At dawn on July 1st, according to Ermatinger, members of the HBC party came unexpectedly upon two lodges, one of which they attacked:

The confusion was great and we were apprehensive that the men would kill each other by shooting in opposite directions. From the natives there was no danger, as those in the other lodge remained quiet. In vain did we call out to the men to spare the women; take care of your selves.

249

They continued on in the same order until they thought the whole of the inmates were killed. In fact, one half could not understand us when we did call. Two families, I believe, were killed, three men, two or three women, a boy and a girl. To this point I cannot speak positively as I saw none after they were down, but have the information from those who killed them. However, it was made a doubt whether the men were dead or not, as they were not seen after. . . . [1]

Having won this notable victory, McLeod's party went on to Port Townsend where they rendezvoused with the *Cadboro* and together journeyed to New Dungeness. Here McLeod and the skipper of the *Cadboro* squabbled over what was the best way to get the Indians in the local village to release a woman who had been captured while travelling with the Fort Langley party. Finally the local village was cannonaded. Once the inhabitants had fled from the *Cadboro*'s guns, a landing party went ashore, destroyed almost thirty canoes, searched the houses and burned them along with the Indians' stores of food and oil. During their search they found the "bedcloth" of the murdered McKenzie. The next day negotiations were carried on with the Indians. One of their number who had been seized by the HBC men was released in exchange for the "Helen of Troy" taken from the McKenzie party. Another Indian village was burned, and then McLeod started back for Fort Vancouver with his undisciplined little force. According to the Clallums, twenty-five of their tribe had been slain by the avengers, including two of McKenzie's murderers.

On July 12th, just three days before Chief Trader McLeod led his raggle-taggle little force home to Fort Vancouver, Governor Simpson left York Factory on Hudson Bay for the same destination. On this, his second visit to the Pacific, Simpson routed himself so that he could visit the New Caledonia forts and Fort Kamloops for the first time.

Travelling at his usual amazing speed along Sir Alexander Mackenzie's route up the Peace River and the Parsnip, the Governor with his travelling companions, Chief Trader Archibald McDonald and Dr. R. J. Hamlyn, arrived with their canoes and voyageurs at

---

[1] "Notes connected with Clallum Expedition fitted out under the command of Alex. McLeod, Esq., Chief Trader at Fort Vancouver on the 17th of June, 1828, by Frank Ermatinger, Clerk". Transcript in UBC Special Collections.

the Company's post on McLeod Lake on September 11th. It was a grim introduction to life in New Caledonia — John Tod and his two men stationed there were in a bad way. Subsequently Simpson was to report of Fort McLeod:

Its compliment of people, is a Clerk and two Men whom we found starving, having had nothing to eat for several Weeks but Berries, and whose countenances were so pale and emaciated that it was with difficulty I recognised them.[2]

Simpson's party left their canoes at McLeod Lake and started overland the hundred miles to Fort St. James on Stuart Lake. Simpson drove his men as mercilessly as his animals. The men were told that for this very long "portage" they would each have to backpack not the customary ninety pounds but one hundred. They were paired off, two by two, to aid each other with their burdens, and started along the hilly trail which had not been cleared during the past three years. At the end of the fourth day on the trail, Simpson's party entertained a little group of Carrier Indians with a tune on the bagpipes played by Colin Fraser, the Governor's own piper and personal servant. They also played some bugle calls, but what chiefly aroused the wonder of the Indians was a musical snuff-box, which they persuaded the Indians was controlled by the Governor's dog.

Late in the morning of September 17th, Simpson's party was approaching Fort St. James. Governor Simpson fully appreciated the value of ceremony; hence the display which accompanied his actual arrival. In his journal, Chief Trader McDonald has left us a notable description of the scene:

The day, as yet, being fine, the flag was put up; the piper in full Highland costume; and every arrangement was made to arrive at FORT ST. JAMES in the most imposing manner we could, for the sake of the Indians. Accordingly, when within about a thousand yards of the establishment, descending a gentle hill, a gun was fired, the bugle sounded, and soon after, the piper commenced the celebrated march of the clans — 'Si coma leum cogadh na shea,' (Peace: or War, if you will it otherwise).... The guide, with the British ensign, led the van, followed by the band; then the Governor, on horseback, supported by Doctor Hamlyn and myself on our chargers, two deep; twenty men,

2 HBRS 10:18.

with their burdens, next formed the line; then one loaded horse, and lastly Mr. McGillivray [with his wife and light infantry] closed the rear. During a brisk discharge of small arms and wall pieces from the Fort, Mr. Douglas . . . met us a short distance in advance, and in this order we made our *entrée* into the Capital of Western Caledonia.[3]

The "Mr. Douglas" who welcomed Governor Simpson to the fort was a young clerk, temporarily in charge during the absence of Chief Factor Connolly. In time he would become Sir James Douglas, Governor of the Crown Colonies of Vancouver Island and British Columbia. Two hours after Simpson entered the fort, by an amazing coincidence in timing, Connolly himself appeared, travelling a short distance in advance of the brigade with which he had been bringing up his year's supplies from Fort Vancouver.

After a week at Fort St. James to review with Connolly the state of affairs in New Caledonia and finding they revealed "excellent management", Simpson was once more on his way. Early on a misty morning his canoes slipped past the ruins of Fort George (abandoned since the murders there five years earlier). On September 27th the party reached Alexandria, where it split into two. While a clerk, James Murray Yale, with the expedition's two canoes and fourteen men started down the Fraser to its junction with the Thompson, Simpson, McDonald and Hamlyn, with a small party of horsemen, started overland by the Lac la Hache - Bridge Lake route to the North Thompson. Reaching that river near Little Fort, they found Lolo, the Fort Kamloops interpreter, waiting for them with a canoe. About dusk on October 4th Simpson arrived at Kamloops with his flag flying, his piper playing, and much exuberant firing of guns on both sides.

Simpson needed only a couple of days at Fort Kamloops, where he addressed the assembled Shuswap Indians and made gifts to two of their chiefs, Courtapolle and Tranquille. Then he started down the Thompson. Shooting the rapids in the Thompson Canyon proved a hair-raising experience. At one point the boat, partly swamped and out of control, barely escaped disaster in a whirlpool. But at length Simpson's drenched little group safely rejoined Yale

[3] *Peace River*, pp. 24-25.

and their main force at the junction of the Thompson and Fraser Rivers.

Ahead of Simpson lay a crucial experiment. He wanted to determine for himself whether or not the Fraser was navigable from this point southwards and so could serve as a trade route to link Fort Langley with the Interior. Two days later, when he reached Fort Langley, he had his answer:

Frazers River, can no longer be thought of as a practicable communication with the interior; it was never wholly passed by water before, and in all probability never will again: the banks do not admit of Portages being made, and in many places it would be impossible to use the line, on account of the height of the projecting Rocks which afford no footing; and altho we ran all the Rapids in safety, being perfectly light, and having three of the most skilful Bowsmen in the country, whose skill however was of little avail at times, I should consider the passage down, to be certain Death, in nine attempts out of Ten. I shall therefore no longer talk of it as a navigable stream. . . . [4]

Not for Fort Langley the distinction of being the HBC's principal depot on the Pacific! That proud destiny was to go to Fort Vancouver on the Columbia. Fort Langley, however, was to have a satisfactory career as a post of the second magnitude, especially when important exports of fish and lumber began to augment its harvest of pelts.

After a week at Fort Langley, Simpson headed out of the Fraser and south by water. Travelling down Puget Sound, he found dramatic evidence that the crude retaliatory expeditions of Ogden and McLeod had left the Indians of the Sound bitterly hostile:

. . . a telegraphic communication was made all along the coast that an Enemy was abroad, by Smoke during the Day, and large Fires at night on the different projecting head lands; but the Natives did not think proper to interfere with us, and by pushing on late and early the weather being favorable, we got to a Neck of Land between Pugets Sound and a Stream falling into the Columbia, on the 20th, where we Burnt our Boats to prevent their falling into the hands of the Indians; crossed the Cowliz Portage, (about 60 Miles) got Canoes from the

[4] HBRS 10:38-39.

Natives at the head of the Cowliz River, and reached Fort Vancouver on the night of 25th October.[5]

At Fort Vancouver Governor Simpson found that Dr. McLoughlin was giving asylum to four American trappers headed by Jedediah Smith. Simpson had neither liking nor respect for the "mountain men" of American frontier legend, those trappers who, making their approach by the headwaters of the Missouri, were providing the HBC with some competition south of the Columbia. He was to set forth his view of them in a caustic passage:

> ... the Trappers themselves are generally speaking, people of the worst character, run-aways from Jails, and outcasts from Society, who take all their bad qualities along with them: this "motley crew" acknowledge no master, will conform to no rules or regulations, and are never on their guard, so that they are frequently cut off and their camps plundered. When they fall in with Friendly Indians, their conduct is so indiscreet that they scarcely ever fail to make Enemies of them. . . . [6]

Even with views such as these, Simpson must have felt pity when he heard the story told by Jedediah Smith. In January of this year Smith had set out from San Francisco on a trapping expedition and by July had entered what is now southern Oregon. On the banks of the Umpqua River Smith and his eighteen men had made camp. Then, while Smith and two of his men were off on a reconnaissance to determine their future route northwards, the Indians had treacherously attacked his camp, killing all but one of the sixteen men who had remained there. Arthur Black, the sole survivor, had started working his way towards the Columbia. Late on the evening of August 8th, half-naked and emaciated, he had arrived at Fort Vancouver and hammered on the great gate for admission. Two days later Black had been joined by Smith and his two comrades who, returning to camp, had seen from their canoe sufficient evidence of the massacre and had lost no time in heading for the safety of the British fort.

It so happened that Smith and his few survivors had arrived just a little while before Chief Trader A. R. McLeod was due to start on

---

[5] *Ibid.*, p. 46.

[6] *Ibid.*, p. 64.

an HBC trapping expedition which would take him close to the scene of Smith's disaster. Dr. McLoughlin instructed McLeod to look into the whole affair. In December McLeod arrived back at Fort Vancouver, and from him Simpson and McLoughlin received a report on the Umpqua Massacre. What McLeod had to relate hardly reflected any credit on Smith and his crew. Since the HBC had been trading with the Umpqua Indians for several years and had won their confidence and friendship, McLeod had had little difficulty in making contact with them and receiving their account of what had happened. According to the Umpquas, they had received, in advance of Smith's coming, warnings from other tribes that bad white men were headed in their direction, white men who had killed Indians. This report had seemed partly verified when Smith's men had severely beaten an Umpqua whom they caught pilfering an axe (a trifling offence in Indian eyes). The incident that triggered the massacre had occurred, however, after Smith had left his camp. One of the Americans, a man named Rogers, had tried to force an Indian woman into his tent. When her brother had tried to protect her, Rogers knocked him down. At this point the Umpquas, kindled to fury and noting that the Americans (some sleeping and others eating) were maintaining no guard, suddenly attacked. Having heard the testimony of the Umpquas, McLeod decided that Smith's people were pretty much to blame for the whole affair. Accordingly, McLeod did not attempt reprisals but satisfied himself with recovering all he could of Smith's property, chiefly thirty-nine of his horses and about seven hundred of his beaver pelts, which he brought back to Fort Vancouver. Although these latter were in a "very damaged state", Simpson and McLoughlin agreed to purchase them from Smith so that he and his few remaining men would not be destitute when they left Fort Vancouver. They were also offered continued hospitality at Fort Vancouver until the coming spring when the Americans would be given free transportation to the Red River Colony with the eastbound HBC express,[7] an offer which was accepted.

Our chronicle for this year would not be complete without men-

[7] Governor Simpson to Jedediah Smith, Fort Vancouver, 26 Dec. 1828 in Merk, *Fur Trade and Empire*, pp. 302-306.

tion of a very dangerous adventure which befell young James Douglas, that clerk with a knighthood in his future, who welcomed Governor Simpson to Fort St. James. One night an Indian woman slipped up to the fort, and whispered through the palisades the news that one of the murderers of the Fort George men in 1823 was in the Indian camp. Gathering a force, Douglas entered the encampment and began a search. When he approached a pile of baggage behind which the murderer was hiding, the Indian shot an arrow which nearly struck Douglas. The men from the fort then moved in and killed the murderer on the spot.

Instantly the other Indians turned on Douglas, seized him, and held him prisoner. Carefully they explained that the dead murderer was not a member of their tribe, and that they would not have cared in the least if the HBC men had killed him somewhere other than in their camp. But, since he had been slain while with them, they would have to make their peace with his tribe. The only way they could do this would be by handing over guns, axes, tobacco, clothing, and other trade goods to the relatives of the dead man as compensation for their loss. The HBC, they said, must give them these items free.

Douglas realized that if he was to save his life, let alone regain his freedom, this demand must be met. He agreed therefore that the Indians should receive the trade goods. Recently Douglas had taken as his wife Amelia Connolly, daughter of Chief Factor Connolly, who commanded the fort. The Chief Factor was absent at this time and, according to one account, it was young Amelia who from the walls of the fort threw down the demanded goods until sufficient had been handed over and her husband was released.[8]

After this, Douglas would always be regarded with hostility by the local Indians. The next year, accordingly, his transfer to Fort Vancouver was arranged.

---

[8] A number of versions of this famous incident have come down to us. According to one, Douglas was saved from death only by the intervention of Chief Kwah. The foregoing account is based chiefly upon that of John Tod, *History of New Caledonia*. Tod was serving in New Caledonia at the time of the incident and certainly would have been well informed about it.

1829

The wreck of the William and Ann — *The first settler on the* Columbia — *John Tod's female companion* — *Fort Chilcotin and Fort Halkett are founded.*

One of the most dreaded navigational hazards on the entire Northwest Coast was the great bar at the mouth of the Columbia River. A long and melancholy list could be compiled of all those ships which, over the years, were to be lost either because they had misjudged the tides and currents or had failed to find the channel. On March 15th of this year Governor Simpson, who had wintered at Fort Vancouver and would leave for the East just ten days later, received shocking news which compelled him to add a lengthy postscript to the despatch which he had prepared for the Governor and Committee of the HBC in London. It was his regretful duty to inform them that on March 10th the *William and Ann*, the Company's supply ship from England, had been wrecked at the mouth of the Columbia, with the loss of her entire crew. Simpson made no attempt to minimize the problems created by this disaster. For one thing, it left Fort Vancouver with less than a month's supply of trading goods, just at a time when two American ships, the *Owhyhee* and the *Convoy*, had entered the Columbia, meaning to compete with the British there. (In the future the HBC would always keep a full year's supply of trade goods in reserve at Fort Vancouver!)

One of the reports that had most disturbed Simpson was that the captain and crew of the *William and Ann*, having taken to their boats, had safely got ashore only to be murdered by the Indians at Clatsop Point. No real evidence was ever found to substantiate this story. In mid-June, however, a friendly and trustworthy chief informed Dr. McLoughlin that the Clatsops had in their possession bales of goods off the *William and Ann*. Accordingly Chief Factor Connolly, supported by some fifty men, went to reclaim the Company's property. When the HBC men landed from their boats, the Clatsops opened fire. Ransacking their village before setting it on fire, Connolly's men found puncheons of rum which could only have come from the *William and Ann*. After the return of this expedition, Dr. McLoughlin informed London that in his opinion the crew had not been murdered.[1]

On May 8th the HBC's second supply ship, the *Ganymede*, safely crossed the Columbia bar. Even so she had a narrow escape when the Indians tried to lure her away from the main channel and into a bay where she would have come to grief.

Let us turn our attention from happenings by sea to happenings by land. Many of the HBC's engagés upon retirement moved to the Red River Colony, close to Fort Garry in what is now Manitoba, and took up farms. French-Canadians serving in the Columbia district could not fail but observe that here there was equally fertile land, in a more temperate climate and a more beautiful setting. Although the HBC was opposed to allowing colonists to take up land in its fur territories, Dr. McLoughlin this year for reasons of expediency allowed Etienne Lucier, a time-expired servant of the Company, to settle in the valley of the Willamette River, close to Fort Vancouver. Oregon had acquired its first white settler.

Let us turn from the salubrious Willamette Valley to the sterner climes of Fort Kamloops and the New Caledonia posts. This was a grim year, a starving time, at Kamloops, Francis Ermatinger writing from there on March 14th gives a report on the situation:

> The charge of Thompsons River devolves upon me, aided by Mr. Dears, and the misery we have had is unprecedented. The natives all round us, are actually in such a state of starvation, that it is impossible they can survive, some are already dead. . . . [2]

And what of John Tod, up at McLeod Lake, where Governor Simpson had found him practically starving the previous year? John Tod was enjoying at least the consolations of female company. Several years earlier, writing to Francis Ermatinger's brother back in

---

[1] McLoughlin to Governor and Committee, London, 5 August 1829. In E. E. Rich, ed., *McLoughlin's Fort Vancouver Letters, Series I, 1825-38*, HBRS 4 (London, 1941):73.

[2] PAC, McLeod Papers, 1:236.

Canada, he had confided that he had a female companion at McLeod Lake, one who "is possessed of an excellent ear for music & never fails to accompany me on the Flute with her voice when I take up the instruments".[3] Apparently Edward Ermatinger had made some subsequent enquiry about her, and Tod's reply, this year, tells us something both of his own character and of his appallingly lonely life in New Caledonia:

> You ask what is become of the girl who used to sing at McLeods Lake. I have a good mind to answer You as Mr. Boulton, our old messmate, would do but I have not his taste for smut unless it is wraped [sic] up in clean linen — Why then in plain language she still continues the only companion of my solitude — without her, or some other substitute, life, in such a wretched place as this [McLeod Lake], would be altogether insupportable.[4]

This year the HBC closed temporarily one of its remotest New Caledonia posts, Fort Kilmaurs on Babine Lake. Fort Kilmaurs, often known as Fort Babine, had been established six years earlier primarily to tap the Skeena salmon run during those years when fish were scarce on the Fraser, but it had been intended also to intercept furs being taken to American trading vessels on the coast. Apparently the post's fur returns had proved disappointing, and it was believed that it might prove more economical to send fishing parties up to Babine Lake than to maintain the fort there. After some time the fort was re-established and for a good many years it remained at least intermittently active. Around 1872 it was moved to the foot of Babine Lake. The settlement of Old Fort at the forks of the lake now marks the site of original Fort Kilmaurs.

If the HBC temporarily closed one fort in New Caledonia this year, it opened another. Back in 1823 the Council of the Northern Department had decided to establish a post in the Chilcotin country. For some years no action had been taken on this resolution because, as we have seen, the Chilcotins had turned against the Company after its people supported their enemies at Fort Alexandria. By 1829 things had become sufficiently quiet for Fort Chilcotin to be estab-

---

[3] PAC, Ermatinger Papers, Letter of 27 Feb. 1826.

[4] *Ibid.*, Letter of 14 Feb. 1829.

lished at the south end of Chilcotin Lake. It was a modest establishment, a mere outpost of Fort Alexandria. Obviously the HBC men
in New Caledonia were far from sanguine about its prospects of
success. Early in 1830 John Tod at McLeod Lake wrote to Edward
Ermatinger:

> That part of New Caledonia called Chill Cotten Country . . . was at
> long length settled last Fall: — Little is expected from it, and I believe
> it is only in consequence of an earnest request, repeatedly expressed by
> the Govr. & Council, that the Establishment has been formed there.[5]

Despite Tod's pessimistic remarks, Fort Chilcotin proved sufficiently
successful to survive for a number of years.

Another new fort opened this year was Fort Halkett, founded in
the extreme north of British Columbia where the Trout River flows
into the Liard. This, however, must not be numbered among the
New Caledonia forts since the HBC assigned to its Mackenzie
District all the area drained by these and other tributaries of the
Mackenzie River.

[5] *Ibid.*, Letter of 18 Feb. 1830.

1830

*"Columbia River Fever" — Death of most of the Indians —
Jedediah Smith's way of repaying those who saved him.*

Visiting the HBC's westernmost establishments in 1828-29, Governor
Simpson had found himself confronted with a major problem.
American trading ships, having over the years been the indirect
cause of the sea otter nearing extinction, were now seeking inland
furs from the Indians, and so coming into direct competition with
the HBC's western posts. Simpson's solution called both for increased
maritime trading by the Company and for the founding of a new
fort at the mouth of the Nass River, one which would intercept the
trade which was draining furs from western New Caledonia.

Before the new fort on the Nass was built there would, of course,
have to be a preliminary reconnaissance. This was entrusted to Lieut.
Aemilius Simpson who, on 8 July 1830, sailed from Fort Vancouver
with a little HBC squadron composed of the *Cadboro*, the *Eagle* and
the *Vancouver*. After frustrating delays, which entailed detaching
the *Vancouver* to supply Fort Langley, Lieut. Simpson on August
28th finally arrived at the mouth of the Nass and made a somewhat
hurried survey of the area. Back at Fort Vancouver in late September, he was able to confirm that the area was indeed rich in furs (in
three days he had obtained two hundred excellent beaver pelts) ;
that unfortunately the Americans were active in the area and had
driven up the price of skins; and, finally, that he had found a suitable
location for the projected fort.

It had been planned that once Simpson had completed his
exploratory cruise to the Nass and had reported satisfactorily upon
it, Peter Skene Ogden would leave immediately with men, building
essentials and trade goods needed to establish the new post. A totally
unexpected development, however, kept Ogden from going north
until the following year. During Lieut. Simpson's absence disaster

had struck in the Columbia — an appalling sudden visitation of an intermittent fever which wiped out three-quarters of the Indian population, and spread to the HBC's white servants as well. In mid-October Dr. McLoughlin reported to London, " . . . there are fifty-two of our People on the sick list. . . . this sickness obliged us to postpone our sending to Establish Nass. . . . "[1]

Just when the disease appeared to be waning, it broke out with renewed virulence. In a further report to London, late in November, McLoughlin wrote that he had had as many as seventy-five on the sick list, including both Ogden and Fort Vancouver's physician, Dr. Kennedy. Dr. McLoughlin had been attending to the sick himself, while trying to keep the fur trade functioning. Not least of his problems had been the number of infected Indians flocking to Fort Vancouver. These declared that they came hither because they knew that if they died at the fort the Company would give them burial.

It is impossible at this late date to diagnose the "Columbia River Fever", often called the "intermittent fever", which was to linger on for years. The most likely conjecture is that it was malaria brought from Mexico, possibly by the American ship *Owhyhee*, commanded by Captain John Dominis, which traded on the Columbia both this year as well as in 1829. Certainly the Indians held Dominis responsible, and not without apparent good reason. Dominis, knowing how the Indians dreaded the white man's diseases such as smallpox and syphilis, had apparently threatened the Indians with a new sickness if they would not let him have their furs. This threat and its terrible, even if coincidental, fulfilment increased Indian hatred for the rapacious "Boston men".

The "Boston men" meanwhile were keeping a jealous eye on the flourishing trade of the HBC within the area of Anglo-American co-dominion created in 1818. We noted earlier how in 1828 Jedediah Smith had found asylum in Fort Vancouver after most of his party had been massacred by the Umpqua Indians in southern Oregon. On October 29th of this year this same Jedediah Smith and his fellow partners in the fur trading firm of Smith, Jackson and

---

[1] Barker, ed., *McLoughlin Letters*, p. 140.

Sublette, wrote from St. Louis to John H. Eaton, the U.S. Secretary of War. They reported that Smith had been at Fort Vancouver from August 1828 until March 1829 and, drawing upon Smith's observations, they conveyed detailed information about Fort Vancouver, not omitting the fact that Smith had seen no cannon heavier than twelve-pounders. Blandly combining two lies in a single sentence, Smith and his associates said of the HBC men: "They do not trap north of latitude 49 degrees, but confine that business to the territory of the United States."[2] Maintaining the fiction that the Columbia was American, they asked that the Convention of 1818 be abrogated and the HBC be evicted from American territory.[3] The egregious trio ended by asking that their misrepresentations be passed on to President Jackson. If they were, he very properly ignored them.

[2] "Documents", *OHQ* 4 (1903) : 397.

[3] In 1828 the Umpqua Indians informed Chief Trader McLeod that when Smith came into their country he and his men declared themselves enemies of the British, and bragged that they would drive them out of the Columbia. (HBRS 10:61.) All of which makes a nice irony of the survivors' subsequent flight to the safety of the British fort.

1831

*Lieut. Aemilius Simpson founds Fort Simpson and dies —
Fort Langley prospers.*

In April Lieut. Aemilius Simpson sailed from the Columbia for the
Nass River with his brig the *Dryad*, and her consort the little
schooner *Vancouver*. With him he carried Peter Skene Ogden and
the men, materials and supplies needed for finally establishing the
first British settlement on the northern coast. On May 11th the little
expedition arrived at their destination and set about their task,
gratified to find that the local Indians, who had a very bad reputation, apparently welcomed their coming and created no problems for
them. Swiftly the buildings arose within their surrounding palisades.

Once the new fort was capable of its own defence, Simpson headed
off on a fur trading cruise. In mid-August, while the *Dryad* was
anchored in Skidegate Inlet, Lieut. Simpson was stricken by illness.
Heading back to the new fort on the Nass, he put himself under the
care of Dr. J. F. Kennedy, who became increasingly concerned by
the disease, apparently of the liver. On September 13th the patient
died. Cool, aloof, punctilious, very much the officer and the gentleman, Aemilius Simpson had served the HBC well. He was buried
outside the walls of the new fort which, in his honour, was now given
the name of Fort Simpson.

While Fort Simpson was coming into existence, Fort Langley far
to the south was prospering in a most satisfactory manner. Whereas
only 1400 beaver pelts had been obtained the preceding year, in
1831 the tally went up to 2500. Moreover, there were other sources
of profit. Charlton, the British consul who acted as the HBC agent
in Honolulu, had found that he could sell Fraser River salmon there
for ten dollars a barrel, and this year almost 300 barrels of salmon
were provided by Fort Langley. Nor was salmon the only article for
export from Fort Langley to Hawaii. Shingles from the fort sold on

Oahu at a highly satisfactory price. Moreover, plans were laid this year for starting a farm close to the fort, and Dr. McLoughlin promised to send ploughs and harrows to Chief Trader Archibald McDonald in the coming year. This farm was intended primarily to provide food for the fort itself, but there were good prospects that crops raised on the fertile lands of the Fraser Valley would, in time, swell the export trade of Fort Langley. Though fully aware of "the contempt entertained for everything out of the routine of Beaver at York Factory", Chief Trader McDonald exulted in the increasingly diversified trade of his post.

Only two things caused Dr. McLoughlin unhappiness this year as he presided over the HBC's prospering fortunes on the West Coast. First and most serious was a renewed outbreak of the Columbia River Fever, which this autumn raged with as much violence as in the previous year. The other was the arrival at Fort Vancouver of a second Chief Factor, Duncan Finlayson, to share in the governance of McLoughlin's empire. McLoughlin was due to go on furlough in 1833, and might at the end of his year's leave be assigned to some other part of the HBC's territory. It was only administrative good sense on the part of Governor Simpson to despatch a suitable successor to the Columbia a couple of years early. Serving for a while as McLoughlin's coadjutor, Finlayson could thoroughly learn the problems of the Columbia department before taking over command himself. Unfortunately, McLoughlin now regarded the Columbia as his own empire, and apparently was far from happy at the arrival on the scene of an heir-apparent. No difficulties of this sort arose in New Caledonia this year when Chief Factor Peter Warren Dease took over from Chief Factor William Connolly.

We may conclude by noting something that did not happen in 1831-32. It its issue of 5 July 1831 *The Missouri Republican* proudly noted that early in 1832 a thousand settlers would be setting forth from St. Louis for the Columbia under the auspices of the Boston-based American Society for the Settlement of Oregon. In its issue of November 8th the paper sadly noted that the scheme had been abandoned.

1832

American competitors vanquished — Capt. McNeill and the Llama — Character of Dr. John McLoughlin, the HBC's "Emperor of the West" — His secret American sympathies — Annance vainly seeks Canadian settlers — McLoughlin welcomes Wyeth's Americans.

For a third year fever ravaged the population of the lower Columbia. No whites died at Fort Vancouver, though some of the HBC men there suffered three or four bouts of the disease. The mortality among the Indians continued to be ghastly and yet somehow, despite the curse of the fever, business prospered for the HBC. Governor Simpson, reporting on the growing prosperity of the Columbia trade, paid generous tribute to the "great exertions, indefatigable labours and unremitting attention" of Dr. McLoughlin. Part of the improvement was due to the Company's success in overcoming the competition offered by the American trading ships. Chief Trader Archibald McDonald, writing from Fort Langley in January of this year, exulted that, having got rid of their American competitors, he and his men had been able to double the price for their trade goods. Indians would now have to pay not one but two beaver pelts to obtain a 2½-point Hudson's Bay blanket.[1] This prosperity did not extend to Fort Kamloops, which was now visibly in decline. James Douglas reported that he considered the fur supply in its area exhausted. Too much trapping had ended years of rich returns of beaver.

There was much activity upcoast at the new Fort Simpson on the Nass. Leaving there on September 14th, Donald Manson explored some distance up the Nass River before his return on September 20th. He seems to have been chiefly impressed by the dangers of its

---

[1] PAC, John McLeod Papers, p. 293.

currents and rocky precipitous banks. On October 19th he left on a second expedition, on which he became the first white explorer to venture up the Skeena. He penetrated only forty or fifty miles, and his report was not enthusiastic:

> ... not one solitary spot did I pass suitable for an establishment and with regard to its resources with the exception of salmon there is nothing to depend upon. . . . [2]

The achievements of the Company's trading vessels were less impressive than those of its forts. Much of the trouble lay with the ship's officers sent out from England — the London Committee seemed to have an uncanny knack for finding alcoholics to command the Company's ships bound for the North-west Coast. Even when sober, the commanders in the maritime department suffered from a woeful lack of knowledge both of the Indians and of the coast itself. One of the causes of the tension already beginning to grow between Governor Simpson and Dr. McLoughlin was that, while the Governor urged an ever-expanding use of trading vessels, McLoughlin, disillusioned by experience, felt that trade could be conducted more economically from a chain of forts along the coast. Typical of the inexperienced HBC skippers was Captain Kipling of the *Vancouver*. After the *Vancouver* suffered severe damage when caught in a gale, Chief Trader Ogden reported that if Kipling had possessed a reasonable knowledge of the coast he could have found a safe haven for his ship in any one of three harbours.

Despite his misgivings about trading vessels, McLoughlin this year sent Chief Factor Finlayson to Honolulu to purchase a ship to replace the *Vancouver* in the Company's coastal trade. Finlayson's mission was a notably successful one. Not only did he manage to buy at a remarkably low price an excellent American-built brig, the *Llama*,[3] but he was able to enlist in the Company's service the *Llama*'s skipper, W. H. McNeill, and his two mates. All three officers were thoroughly acquainted with the North-west Coast. When

---

[2] HBCA, B.201/a/2, f. 6v.

[3] Such is the correct spelling of the ship's name (*v.* Walbran, *B.C. Coast Names*, p. 298). Her name, however, usually appears as "Lama" in the records of the HBC.

Captain McNeill arrived at Fort George with the *Llama* on October 14th of this year, the HBC had, for the first time, a ship commanded by a man who really knew the coast. One unfortunate fact had to be faced. Captain McNeill was an American, and the Company had a consistent policy of employing only British subjects. Fortunately the Governor and Committee in London appreciated that McNeill's qualifications more than made up for his lack of British citizenship. They endorsed McLoughlin's action, and for many years Captain McNeill gave totally loyal and very valuable service to the HBC.

The misgivings with which the Governor and Committee of the HBC regarded the employment of Americans sprang in part from their continuing awareness that sooner or later there would have to be a showdown with the United States over national sovereignty in the Pacific North-west. Obviously the co-dominion of 1818 could not last many years longer. Already Americans were loudly proclaiming that everything between Mexico and Alaska belonged to the United States. The Company would need officers with total fidelity and vigilance if it was to maintain its position on the Pacific and hold the Columbia River line as the boundary between the United States and the British territory. Ironically, not Captain McNeill but Chief Factor McLoughlin would be responsible for undermining the British position on the Columbia.

A gigantic man physically, Dr. John McLoughlin was a giant also in his energy, his spirit and his determination, qualities to which we have seen Governor Simpson paying full and well-merited tribute. But there were other traits, considerably less admirable, in McLoughlin and these we find noted, along with his virtues, in a secret "Book of Servants' Characters" which Simpson compiled this year. Here, while characterizing McLoughlin as "a very busy bustling active man who can go through a great deal of business", and describing him as "very zealous in the discharge of his public duties and a man of strict honor and integrity", Simpson noted that the Chief Factor had no talent for getting on with his subordinates, that he set himself up as a righter of wrongs, and that he could be a most difficult colleague:

Very anxious to obtain a lead among his colleagues with whom he has not much influence owing to his ungovernable violent temper and

turbulent disposition, and would be a troublesome man to the Comp'y
if he had sufficient influence to form and tact to manage a party, in
short, would be a Radical in any Country under any Government and
under any circumstances. . . . Altogether a disagreeable man to do
business with as it is impossible to go with him in all things and a
difference of opinion almost amounts to a declaration of hostilities, yet
a good hearted man and a pleasant companion.[4]

John Tod who knew McLoughlin well came to regard him with the
utmost suspicion despite all the Chief Factor's profuse show of
benevolence. Writing to a friend in 1841, Tod said of McLoughlin:
"that man appears to me to have as great a share of duplicity as he
has of egotism". He filled out the portrait in another letter the
succeeding year:

> . . . that anomalous Mammoth McLoughlin . . . a character for whom
> I entertain the most deadly hatred — God forgive me — not from any
> unkindness I have received at his hands — far from it, but from a
> knowledge of his treatment of others — he of all men I know in this
> Country is the very last I should put any dependence in. . . . [5]

The duplicity of Dr. McLoughlin emerges in the manner in which
he connived to establish a strong American presence on the Columbia
River. The root of the trouble lay in that radicalism which had not
gone unnoted by Governor Simpson. That radicalism made him a
warm sympathizer with Papineau and Mackenzie after their rebellion
in 1837. His subordinate Dr. W. F. Tolmie, on furlough in Paris,
was interested to find McLoughlin's brother on friendly terms with
the banished Papineau.[6] In a private letter McLoughlin was to
characterize the constitution of the Canadian colonies as "despot-
ism".[7] It is doubtful if Simpson realized how close to treason Mc-
Loughlin's radicalism lay. If he had any suspicions he probably
persuaded himself that, as long as McLoughlin faithfully attended to
the Company's trade on the Columbia, his political opinions were
irrelevant.

---

4 Quoted by W. Kaye Lamb in his introduction to HBRS 4:c.
5 To Edward Ermatinger, March 1841 and 10 March 1842. PAC, Ermatinger
Papers, pp. 61 & 68.
6 Tolmie, *Journals*, p. 358.
7 To Edward Ermatinger, 27 Feb. 1841, PAC, Ermatinger Papers, p. 242.

And McLoughlin did faithfully look after the Company's trading interests, at least in the narrow and immediate sense. Whenever American competitors sought to encroach on the trade of the HBC, McLoughlin spared no effort to destroy their competition, and he won the plaudits of his employers by the manner in which he routed the Americans from the fur trade in the Pacific North-west. But even while he fought to exclude the Americans from the fur trade and so, he believed, justified his superiors' trust and maintained his own integrity, he consoled himself with thinking that he could do much to bring about future American political domination of the region. In fact, from a period prior to his arrival on the Pacific Coast, McLoughlin had given his political allegiance to the United States. In a letter in the *Oregon Statesman* of 8 June 1852 he made public profession of the secret which he had so long concealed from his employers:

I was born in Canada, and reared to manhood in the immediate vicinity of the United States. . . . The sympathies of my heart and the dictates of my understanding, more than thirty years ago, led me to look forward to a day when both my relations to others and the circumstances surrounding me would permit me to live under and enjoy the political blessings of a flag which, wherever it floats, whether over the land or the sea, is honored for the principles of justice lying at the foundation of the government it represents, and which shields from injury and dishonor all who claim its protection.

Complacently he looked back on his betrayal of that trust reposed in him when he was the man chiefly charged with the protection of British interests on the Columbia:

I early foresaw that the march of civilization and progress of peopling the American Territories, was westward and onward, and that but a few years would pass away before the whole valuable country between the Rocky Mountains and the Pacific, then used only as hunting and trapping grounds, and as the resting place of native tribes, must become the abode of another race — American. This could neither be successfully resisted, nor did I deem it politic or desirable to attempt it. In this spirit I prepared myself to encourage, hasten, and further what I thought would be not only attended with good, but inevitable.[8]

[8] This letter to the *Oregon Statesman* is reprinted in *OHQ* 8:294-99.

McLoughlin was right in seeing that colonization was inevitable. But it did not have to be American. Already in 1832 there was the first small colony in the Columbia. Others had followed the lead of Lucier and now a little settlement, made up entirely of retired French-Canadian servants of the HBC, occupied part of the lovely valley of the Willamette River. This year there was a project to bring in other settlers, not from the United States but from Canada. Significantly it was not Chief Factor John McLoughlin who advanced the scheme but one of the clerks at Fort Vancouver, the half-Indian Francis (or François) Annance. Petitioning Lord Aylmer, Governor-General of the Canadas, in a letter of 20 March 1832 Annance declared:

In all my travels from the Atlantic to the Pacific I have not seen a country so well adapted for a settlement than the Spot I have in view near the mouth of the Columbia. Therefore I humbly beg that Your Lordship would condescend to inform me and my colleague Mr John Tod of York Factory, whether we can get a grant from [the] Government to colonize that part of the country — There are [a] great many Canadians, who having retired from the service of the H Bay and other fur companies, are dispersed about that country, doing very little good to themselves or the Natives with whom they are often at variance. These men have often applied to me to assist and head them in settling themselves on the beautiful and luxurious plains between the Columbia and Fraser rivers. By beginning with these men accustomed to the country, in the course of three or four years several thousands can be admitted yearly.[9]

Poor Annance. It is unlikely his homely letter got past the Governor-General's secretary. If His Excellency ever saw it, he probably smiled. What a quaint idea to start an agricultural settlement out on the Pacific Coast! If there were any real arguments for such a colony, they would of course have reached him from the HBC's headquarters in London, and would be based on the advice of their man in command on the Columbia, Dr. John McLoughlin!

Dr. McLoughlin was able to aid American colonization this year. His opportunity came about in the following manner. In October there arrived at Fort Vancouver an utterly destitute little group of

9 PABC, E-A-An-7.

ten Americans headed by one Nathaniel Wyeth of Boston. They had come overland to meet a supply ship (which had in fact been lost in the South Pacific) and to commence an export trade in furs and smoked salmon. The dictates of humanity required that Dr. McLoughlin admit these men to his fort, and take care of them until they were in shape to travel. The interests of the HBC required that as soon as the Americans were fit again, and the season permitted, they should be given just enough supplies to get back to Missouri and be sent packing. Instead McLoughlin, after wining and dining Wyeth for months, permitted two of his Americans to remain as settlers in the Willamette. At the first arrival of Wyeth and his people the members of the French-Canadian Willamette settlement, anxious to protect the interests of their old employers, had refused to let the Americans have even a potato until told to do so by Chief Factor McLoughlin. Thus, it would have been utterly impossible for these two Americans to have become Willamette settlers had they not had the active cooperation of McLoughlin. The Union Jack might continue to wave over Fort Vancouver, but its commander could console himself that, through his assistance, Oregon had acquired its first American residents.

1833

Dr. Tolmie, fur trader, botanist and "enthusiast" — Forts McLoughlin and Nisqually — An Indian attack on Fort Mc-Loughlin — The Columbia Library.

When the supply ship *Ganymede* arrived at Fort Vancouver in May of this year she had among her passengers a very high-minded, very serious and very bright young Scot named William Fraser Tolmie, "an agreable and very clever Enthusiast".[1] Trained in medicine in Glasgow, though he had never taken his degree, "Dr." Tolmie had been engaged by the HBC on the recommendation of the formidable Dr. Hooker who, having had Tolmie as one of his students, hoped that he would be able to supply him with botanical specimens while serving as physician and fur trader in the Company's service. Coming ashore at Fort Vancouver early in May, Tolmie, aged only twenty-one, could hardly have imagined that the rest of his life would be largely spent in the North-west, right up until his death in Victoria in 1886, when he would leave behind him a son destined to become a premier of British Columbia.

Sandy hair framed young Dr. Tolmie's high forehead, and beneath his high-arched eyebrows two wide blue eyes took in all the strange scene that greeted him after his long months on shipboard. Into his voluminous diary he poured detailed accounts of all he saw and met:

The scene was now very animating — there were the Canadians mostly dressed in blue capots, glazed hats with a red military belt & having their coal black hair dangling in profusion about their shoulders — wild picturesque looking figures & their horses rougher & more shaggy than themselves.[2]

---

[1] So described by Lieut. Warre in his diary for 1845. *v.* PAC, MG24, F71, Vol. 2:1223.

[2] Tolmie, *Journals*, p. 171.

Tolmie had arrived when things had taken a decisive turn for the better in the Columbia district. This September twenty thousand beaver pelts were shipped from Fort Vancouver, setting something of a record. Back at York Factory it was noted that "The Columbia is now doing uncommonly well & making amends for the outlay of former days". Dr. McLoughlin's energetic policy of shadowing and underselling the American trading vessels was yielding its rewards. This year not a single one of the persistent Yankee ships appeared off the coast in "opposition" to the HBC. Finally, this was the lightest year for the Columbia Fever since that plague had first struck three years earlier.

Proof of the flourishing state of the Company this year is to be found in its founding of two new establishments, Fort McLoughlin on Milbanke Sound close to where Bella Bella now stands, and Fort Nisqually at the head of Puget Sound. These two posts served quite different purposes. Fort McLoughlin was a fur trading fort pure and simple, giving the Company a strategically placed base for obtaining the furs of the central coastal area between Fort Simpson on the Nass and Fort Langley on the Fraser. Fort Nisqually, on the other hand, was intended to be a depot where coastal ships could leave furs or pick up supplies without going around to Fort Vancouver and risking the Columbia River bar. (In 1830 a second HBC ship, the *Isabella*, had followed the *William and Ann* to destruction at the mouth of the Columbia.) Moreover, the flat lands around Nisqually could be made into rich farms for the Company's use.

Young Dr. Tolmie had hardly time to get introduced to Fort Vancouver before he found himself en route to Fort Nisqually. When he arrived there at the end of May the new post's warehouse was not yet completed, and the schooner *Vancouver* did not arrive until June 9th with the trade goods with which to stock it. Many men found Chief Trader Heron, in charge at Nisqually, a difficult man, but Tolmie with his bland good manners got along with him excellently, so much so that Heron allowed him time for a botanizing expedition on which Tolmie scaled one of the peaks of Mount Rainier. Diligently at Fort Nisqually Tolmie kept up his diary:

Wednesday, November 6: Occupied till dinner time in looking over numbers of the Edr. Evg. Post [Edinburgh Evening Post], Chamber's

Journal, Penny magazine & the Day — the two middle contained much useful information. Cannot justify to myself this infringing on the regular course of reading, to wit Guthrie's Geography &c but the day has not been lost as I have added a little to my stock of knowledge. . . . [3]

Dr. Tolmie seems to have been a little regretful when he left Fort Nisqually on December 12th, boarding the *Cadboro* for passage to Fort McLoughlin, where he was to serve under Donald Manson, the senior clerk who commanded the new establishment. Arriving at Fort McLoughlin after a miserable passage, Tolmie was shown around the post by Manson:

. . . accompanied Mr. Manson round the Fort — it is 150 [feet] in one direction & 140 in the opposite — the inequalities of the surface preventing its being an equilateral — the houses are built of strong & massive material & make those at Nusqually seem flimsy. . . . [4]

It was well that Fort McLoughlin was sturdily built, for the surrounding Indians were anything but friendly. A couple of months earlier one of the Company's servants at the fort, after being beaten by Manson for some misdemeanour, had deserted and sought out the local Indians. To secure his return Manson had taken hostage one of the local chiefs. The Indians in response had waited until some of Manson's men were outside the fort getting a fresh supply of water. Then, deeming the moment ripe, the Indians had launched an attack on the fort. This was successfully repelled, with one Indian being killed. As for the HBC men, one was captured by the attackers but the rest, one badly wounded, managed to get back inside the palisades. Hostilities had subsequently ended, with the HBC's hostage chief being exchanged for the Indians' white prisoner but Tolmie found the little garrison still very much on edge. Watches of four men and an officer were maintained throughout each night, the guards being carefully posted along the inner galleries which permitted a view out over the palisades.

Situated thus, where a walk beyond the confines of the fort might cost a man his life, Dr. Tolmie had little opportunity for botanizing. Conscientiously he devoted himself in his spare time to the regimen

[3] *Ibid.*, p. 248.
[4] *Ibid.*, p. 258.

of instructive and edifying reading he had laid out for himself — Dwight's *Sermons*, Adam Smith's *Wealth of Nations*, Paley's *Moral Philosophy*, Mackintosh's treatise on whooping cough and croup — with Scott's *Bride of Lammermoor* and Goldsmith's comedies for lighter fare. But Tolmie could see a problem. Where in the years which lay ahead could he find new books to supply his need? And so he got the idea of founding a circulating library. Let every officer of the HBC who so wished send in a subscription, and then the money and a list of desired books and periodicals could be sent to the Company's London office. Once the books arrived, they could be kept at Fort Vancouver and despatched upon request to each of the subscribers in his lonely outpost. Thus there came into being the Columbia Library, which flourished for the next decade.

The circulation of the Columbia Library did not extend to the remote forts in New Caledonia. For a glimpse of life in those God-forsaken posts we have a letter written this year by Thomas Dears, stationed at Fort Connolly on Bear Lake, up in the Omineca country. Writing to his friend Edward Ermatinger back in Upper Canada, he informs him of how his Indian "wife" has provided him with three children and a fourth is "on the stocks". He continues:

. . . my eldest is a very promising Girl and, I am told, handsome. She is now three years old and knows her alphabet backwards and forwards, and accompanies me with her voice when I play 'Life Let Us Cherish' upon a violin I have made, and it amuses sometimes. I am now in a most horrid melancholy place, the very bowels of elementary strife — not a living soul seen here but twice a year (to say Europeans). I get seldom or any news, and have nothing before my sight but eternal snows. In addition to this, there is a tribe to the S[outh] of us who we considerably dread. They are not inclined to trade their furs with us and I presume take them to the sea coast. At this very moment I have three in the fort and, as we cannot understand each other either by signs or otherwise, I cannot learn their object of coming here — I suspect to spy. But at any time, should they attempt violence, I shall fight hard to save my *Wig* [scalp] and, tho' I do not gain my £100 [annual salary] with the pen, I do it by risking my life. . . . [5]

Fort Connolly was not attacked, and in fact little of moment occurred in New Caledonia this year, though Chief Trader Simon

[5] PAC, Ermatinger Papers, p. 292.

McGillivray did do some useful exploring. Setting out with his men in June from Fort St. James, he travelled up to Babine Lake and then down the Babine River, which he soon found was not navigable at this season. Returning to the lake, he struck across country and so reached the junction of the Bulkley and Skeena Rivers at the site of present-day Hazelton. The names which he gave on his map[6] have all disappeared except for his "Roche Deboulez" which survives in today's Rocher Déboulé Range.

6 HBCA, D.4/126, f. 45.

1834

The Russians prevent Ogden from establishing Fort Stikine — The HBC establishes a new Fort Simpson and the Indians demolish the old — Tolmie's dilemma: to take an Indian woman or not — McLoughlin welcomes American missionaries — A Japanese junk — New Caledonia's profits.

Over the years, fur traders along the coast had made themselves fortunes out of sea otter pelts. The female sea otter, swimming on her back while cradling her pup on her breast, had always been an easy victim for the Indian hunters. But now the inevitable was happening and the sea otter was becoming extinct. This year only one sea otter pelt was offered in trade at Fort Nisqually. Fortunately for the HBC, tens of thousands of pelts of beaver and other fur-bearing animals were still obtainable within its vast Pacific empire, and the Company continued to prosper in Columbia and New Caledonia. Two new posts were founded this year, Fort Boisé in what is now Idaho, and an establishment at Honolulu. The Hawaiian post had, of course, little to do directly with the fur trade. It existed partly to market timber and salted fish from the Pacific North-west, and partly to deal in grain, hardware and naval supplies.

This year's plans called for the establishment of a fifth coastal post. The previous year Peter Skene Ogden had made a reconnaissance up to Alaska. Under the terms of the Convention of 1825, Russia had been given sovereignty over the Panhandle, but the British had received the right to sail up the rivers, through the narrow Russian coastal strip, to reach their own territories beyond. Thus it was that Ogden with the *Llama* had entered the mouth of the Stikine and found a good site for a fort upstream in British territory.

The Russians were angered when they learnt of the British plans since any HBC fort on the Stikine would intercept many furs which otherwise would come to the posts of the Russian American Company. Accordingly the Russians reacted decisively. When, on June 18th of this year, Ogden aboard the *Dryad* arrived at the mouth of the Stikine with men, materials and trading goods for the planned Fort Stikine, he found the Russians strongly established with their hurriedly erected Fort St. Dionysius, and a ship, the *Chichagoff*, carrying fourteen guns. A document was handed to the British, prohibiting them from trading in the area. An elderly Russian, repeating the essence of the letter, informed Ogden and his officers that, should they attempt to enter the Stikine, the fort would "buxom" them.[1] "Buxom" clearly meant "bombard". When Ogden pointed out that the Convention of 1825 gave him the right to enter the river, the Russians retorted that the Convention did not give him the right to be in Alaskan waters. They claimed, moreover, that each power was bound to keep away from the vicinity of a post already established by the other (e.g. St. Dionysius). While the *Dryad* rode at anchor off the mouth of the river, Ogden sent letters to the Russian governor at Sitka, appealing the ruling of the local commandant. On June 29th Ogden got a reply: there could be no passage for the British ship. Meanwhile the local Indians had made it plain that they too were against Ogden. The Stikines had a profitable business as middlemen, bringing furs from the tribes in the British interior to the Russian forts on the coast. They realized that, once Fort Stikine was established, many of the Interior Indians would trade there directly.

The Russians bitterly regretted that they had conceded so much in the Convention of 1825 and trusted that any hostilities would lead to a new treaty, which would give them more than the Panhandle along the southern Alaskan coast.[2] Probably they hoped that Ogden would try to force his way up the river. In this hope the Russians were disappointed. Rather than lose lives, Ogden withdrew. When he returned to Fort Vancouver he reported in full to Chief Factor McLoughlin who forwarded to the Governor and Committee in London a bill for expenses incurred in the aborted

---

[1] Tolmie, *Journals*, pp. 283-84.

[2] Hector Chevigny, *Russian America* (London, 1965), p. 190.

venture. This they submitted to the Russian authorities in St. Petersburg. Outrageously inflated though McLoughlin's bill was,[3] it proved very useful in the coming years when the HBC was negotiating a comprehensive agreement with the Russians.

Ogden did not return immediately to Fort Vancouver after the Stikine fiasco. Instead, he and the *Dryad* turned to another piece of business on the north coast. Fort Simpson, since its founding three years earlier at the mouth of the Nass, had proved to be most unfortunately situated "on a rocky point exposed to all the fury of the NE gales which, during winter rush down the Nass Estuary, hemmed in on both sides by lofty mountains; with tremendous velocity often driving the vessels from their anchorage".[4] After his departure from the Stikine, Ogden employed his men and supplies in moving Fort Simpson from the Nass to where Port Simpson now stands, some eighteen miles in a northerly direction from Prince Rupert. On July 21st work was commenced on clearing the new site and by the end of August, the new fort being completed, the old one was abandoned. As the hour for the whites' departure from the Nass approached, the local Indians became more and more threatening, wandering outside the palisades brandishing guns, boarding pikes and knives, while emitting "savage whoops and yells". Two hostage Indians were held aboard the *Dryad* until the last HBC man was safely on board. Twenty-five gallons of rum had been left behind but, to the amazement of the men on the *Dryad*, two Indian chiefs insisted on bringing the rum out to the ship and delivering it on board. Dr. Tolmie, who was present on this occasion, noted:

This act proved them to be possessed of more prudence & foresight than we would have given them credit for. Had the division been made amongst themselves bloodshed would in all likelihood have ensued. All night a constant hammering was kept up in the deserted fort & dawn revealed several gaps in the pickets made by those who were intent on procuring the iron spikes which attached the pickets to the bars.[5]

---

[3] W. K. Lamb, "McLoughlin's Statement of the Expenses Incurred in the 'Dryad' Incident of 1834", *BCHQ* 10 (1946):293.

[4] Tolmie to Dr. Hooker, 28 Oct. 1834. MS. in Library of the Royal Botanical Gardens, Kew, *North American Letters*, Vol. 72, No. 150.

[5] Tolmie, *Journals*, p. 291.

Next day, with the first light of dawn, the *Dryad* sailed for new Fort Simpson, where it arrived that evening. More than the name of Lieut. Aemilius Simpson had been transferred. His remains, disinterred, were carried to the new fort and given fresh burial there.

Her business at Fort Simpson attended to, the *Dryad* traded off the Queen Charlotte Islands. The Queen Charlottes had proved unpropitious to the HBC earlier this year when, on March 3rd, the Company's schooner *Vancouver* ran aground on the immense sand bar at Rose Spit. In fear of Indians who gathered on the scene, the crew got into the ship's boats and headed for Fort Simpson. Actually, had they but known, the next tide after their flight floated the *Vancouver* free, and the dreaded Indians had numbered only eight, though by lighting numerous fires in the night they had successfully tricked the *Vancouver*'s men into thinking that there were many more of them. Needless to say, after the crew had left and before the ship was destroyed by the sea, the Haidas took off her everything movable, not only her stock of trade goods but even her chains and cannons. The next year one of the tribe had the effrontery to offer one of the *Vancouver*'s teacups in trade at Fort Simpson.

The *Dryad* was luckier than the *Vancouver* in her Queen Charlotte cruise. In early November, having completed her business in the north, she headed south to the Columbia River. En route the ship put in at Fort McLoughlin where she returned Dr. Tolmie to his post. The months away on the Stikine expedition had proved a welcome break for Tolmie who was learning just how dull life in a fur trading post like Fort McLoughlin could be. Contemplating the happiness of his chief Donald Manson with his "fur trade wife" and his children, the young Scot's mind more than once turned to thoughts of obtaining an Indian "wife" for himself, but he stuck by the resolution which he had penned in his diary earlier this year:

... a wife is the only being to whom one could unreservedly pour out his soul, but one with whom could be enjoyed a sweet communion of mind is not to be met with in this country & it is only when I abandon the hope and wish of laying my bones in old Scotland that I will ever think of uniting myself in the most sacred of all ties with a female of this country.[6]

6 *Ibid.*, pp. 261-62.

Years later he would marry Jane Work, even though she was part Indian.

This year Chief Factor Duncan Finlayson left the Columbia on furlough, a complete reversal of men's expectations since he had been sent out to the Pacific, really, to take over during a furlough Dr. McLoughlin had been expected to take in 1833. But McLoughlin, deeply attached to his Columbian empire, was ready to pass up furloughs rather than see his dominion pass temporarily and possibly permanently under Finlayson's command. Tradition has it that a personal dislike of Finlayson contributed to McLoughlin's decision not to hand over to him, even for a single year. Tradition is reinforced by a personal letter in which McLoughlin permitted himself to vent his increasingly bitter feelings about his employers:

... in this Country you would be working for other[s] and people who Know Nothing of the Business — have the power of diciding [sic] on the Merits of your conduct — and who would place a Runt of a fellow that Knows Nothing — can do Nothing — as your Colleague — Merely because they want to reward — a Creature.[7]

It has been suggested that this "runt" was one of the Chief Traders with whom McLoughlin was having a quarrel, but Chief Factors did not generally dignify Chief Traders with the name of "colleague", and the passage almost certainly refers to Finlayson.

Stuck with the jealous and slightly megalomaniac McLoughlin, Finlayson was well advised to go on leave this year. At the end of his furlough he came back to the Columbia for another couple of years, but with McLoughlin still determined to remain there, Finlayson obviously had reached a dead end. He went on furlough a second time and then was appointed Governor of Assiniboia where, based at Fort Garry, he successfully held the line against American penetration. Finlayson was a really first-rate man: "Firm, cool, and decisive", to quote from Simpson's secret "Book of Servants' Characters". Had he assumed lasting command at Fort Vancouver in 1833 or 1834, it is just possible that the country north of the lower Columbia would be Canadian today. As things fell out, British interests there continued to be entrusted to the strongly pro-American McLoughlin.

7 McLoughlin to Edward Ermatinger, 1 Feb. 1835, PAC, Ermatinger Papers, p. 235.

In mid-October of this year the American entrepreneur Nathaniel Wyeth was once more at Fort Vancouver. Two years had passed since his earlier visit. During the interim he had returned to the United States with the amazing intelligence that the HBC's Chief Factor at Fort Vancouver (who normally would be expected to do everything in his power to discourage Americans from entering the Columbia) was in fact delighted to see them, to attend to their needs, to extend to them the hospitality of the fort, and in short to do all in his power to make them at home in the country, provided only they did not seek to compete with his Company in the fur trade. Heartened by these tidings, two American Methodist missionaries accompanied Wyeth's party on this second venture. One of them, Jason Lee, has left testimony to the warmth of Dr. McLoughlin's welcome:

Arrived at Fort Vancouver at 3 o'clock, found the governor and other gentlemen connected with the fort on shore awaiting our arrival, and conducted us to the fort and gave us food, which was very acceptable, as we had eaten our last for breakfast. We received every attention from these gentlemen. Our baggage was brought and put into a spacious room without consulting us and the room assigned for our use, and we had the pleasure of sleeping again within the walls of a house after a long and fatiguing journey, replete with mercies, deprivations, toil and prosperity. I have been much delighted today in viewing the improvements of the farm, etc. The dinner was as good and served in as good style as in any gentleman's house in the east. Fine musk-melons and water melons and apples were set before us which were, indeed, a luxury, after the dry living we have had for some time. After dinner took a turn in the garden and was astonished to find it in such a high state of cultivation. The orchard is young, but the quantity of fruit so great that many of the branches would break if they were not prevented by props. Dr. McLoughlin, the governor of the fort, seems pleased that the missions have come to the country and freely offers us any assistance that is in his power to render. It is his decided opinion that we should commence somewhere in this vicinity.[8]

Undoubtedly Dr. McLoughlin, nursing in his heart his fervent dream that some day all this goodly land would be American,[9] was

[8] "Jason Lee's Diary", *OHQ* 17 (1916) : 262.

[9] See under 1832.

delighted to see the American missionaries and to encourage them to establish themselves nearby.

There has always been some question as to why Lee and the succeeding missionaries came out to the Columbia. Did they come out of pure desire to christianize the Indians, or were their essential purposes political? In London the Governor and directors of the HBC never doubted that the missionaries had a powerful and dangerous political motive. Three years later the Governor and Committee were to write to James Douglas:

... we have all along forseen that the purport of their visit was not confined to those [religious] objects, but that the formation of a Colony of United States Citizens on the banks of the Columbia was the main or fundamental part of their plan, which, if successful, might be attended with material injury, not only to the Fur trade, but in a national point of view.[10]

In view of these suspicions, one may ask why the Company did not during the next year or so transfer McLoughlin to the Mackenzie River or some equally remote area where Americans never came, replacing him with a Chief Factor who could be counted upon zealously to guard the British interest and withhold that assistance which McLoughlin would provide in such abundance for Americans migrating to the Columbia. The answer probably is that the Company simply was not in a position to remove McLoughlin. All that could be actually charged against him was indiscretion, and to that charge McLoughlin could and did quickly reply that he was only showing decent kindness and benevolence, and that in any case he was expected to avoid making trouble with the Americans. Moreover, it would have seemed quite unjustifiable to remove McLoughlin when, as everybody knew, he had been signally successful in turning the Columbia from a district which lost money into one which contributed richly to the wealth of the HBC.

McLoughlin's position was even stronger than we have so far indicated. As the Company was keenly aware, McLoughlin, if he so decided, could retire from their service and, perhaps in association with Americans such as Wyeth, set up a company of his own in

10 HBRS 4:cxxiv.

competition with the HBC. With his special expertise and knowledge of the country, he would be a very formidable competitor. Mc-Loughlin, in fact, had already made a first move towards setting up in business for himself. In 1832 he had launched a scheme whereby he and some of the other HBC officers in Columbia, as a part-time venture for their private profit, would set up the "Oregon Beef and Tallow Company". This company would establish cattle ranches along the Columbia River and inaugurate an export trade, particularly in hides and tallow. The project, of course, was in flagrant violation of one of the fundamental rules of the HBC, that its servants must devote all their time and energies to the Company's own business. Not surprisingly the Company this year vetoed the proposal, emphatically stating that McLoughlin and his associates had no right to set up any enterprise of their own. At the same time, interestingly enough, Governor Simpson and the Council of the Northern Department advised London to pay McLoughlin a gratuity of £500, plus a retroactive increase of £150 per annum for the past four years, a proposal which, modified in London, was to bring McLoughlin a very substantial sum. John S. Galbraith is almost certainly right in saying that the motive for this special payment was not merely appreciation of McLoughlin's past services to the Company.[11] It is best viewed as balm for the wound inflicted by not permitting him his Oregon Beef and Tallow Company, balm which would keep him from quitting the Company and convince him that he would serve his own interests best by remaining with the HBC. The defection of McLoughlin with a group of the Columbia officers would have been a most serious blow to the HBC. Under these circumstances Governor Simpson in the coming years was hardly likely to make an issue of McLoughlin's fostering care for the Americans, however much he may have regretted it. In any event, the "Little Emperor" took no action against the "Emperor of the West" who continued to hand out aid and encouragement to Americans who, in the years ahead, would finally canonize McLoughlin as the "Father of Oregon".

One curious event of this year must not go unchronicled. Every so

[11] "The Early History of the Puget's Sound Agricultural Company, 1838-43", *OHQ* 55 (1954):237.

often over the centuries the Japan Current, or "Kuroshio", would bring to the shores of North America some Japanese junk which had been caught in a storm and rendered incapable of navigation. In 1876 C. W. Brooks in his *Japanese Wrecks Stranded and Picked Up Adrift in the North Pacific Ocean* listed no fewer than sixty incidents of this kind. One of the most interesting came to Dr. McLoughlin's attention in May of this year when some Indians handed him a letter "written in Chinese characters". It came, in fact, from the three survivors of the forty-man crew of a Japanese junk which, laden with crockery, had been carried ashore near Cape Flattery. To rescue the Japanese from the Indians, McLoughlin sent Captain McNeill with the *Llama* and that worthy, after taking three Indians as hostages, secured the release of the Japanese and brought them to Fort Vancouver. Having attended to their needs, McLoughlin was faced with the perplexing problem of what to do with them. Finally he decided to send them to England on one of the Company's ships. Writing to the Governor and Committee in London on November 18th of this year, McLoughlin declared:

I might have sent them to Woahoo [Oahu, Hawaii] and left them to find a passage to their own country the best way they could, but as I believe they are the first Japanese who have been in the power of the British Nation I thought the British Government would gladly avail itself of this opportunity to endeavour to open a communication with the Japanese Government and that by these men going to Great Britain they would have an opportunity of being instructed and convey to their countrymen a respectable idea of the grandeur and power of the British nation.[12]

McLoughlin, who according to his own subsequent statement was looking forward to the "political blessings" of living under the Stars and Stripes, must have hoped that London would be pleased by the British patriotism implicit in his last sentence. He was indeed, in John Tod's phrase, an "anomalous Mammoth".

Let us conclude our chronicle for this year with a look at how things were proceeding up in New Caledonia. In 1833 a new arrival had joined the Company's little corps of officers there. He was John McLean, a tall six-footer, rugged and limber. The route into New

[12] HBRS 4:128.

Caledonia was still the route of Mackenzie and Fraser — via the Peace River and its appalling Rocky Mountain Portage. McLean was aghast at the difficulty of that crossing, where eight days were required to cover just thirteen miles of abominable trail:

> ... leading sometimes through swamps and morasses, then ascending and descending steep hills, and for at least one-third of the distance so obstructed by fallen trees as to render it all but impassable. I consider the passage of this portage the most laborious duty the Company's servants have to perform in any part of the territory; and, as the voyageurs say, 'He that passes it with his share of a canoe's cargo may call himself a man.' "[13]

This year McLean learned why the Company persisted in maintaining, and even expanding, its posts in New Caledonia despite the terrible isolation and hardships. When Chief Factor Dease headed down to Fort Vancouver with his brigade this year, he took with him furs to the value of £11,000 (worth at the very least $250,000 in modern values). To secure these furs the HBC had incurred expenses in trade goods, wages and incidentals totalling £3,000, leaving a clear profit of £8,000 on the year's operations.[14]

Looking for even greater profits, the HBC was embarking upon a new series of explorations in the North. This summer Chief Trader John M. McLeod, one of the HBC's Mackenzie River district men, pushed up the Liard River and the Dease, discovered Dease Lake, and pushed beyond it to the Tuya River, a tributary of the Stikine. Gradually the geography of northern British Columbia was becoming known.

[13] *Twenty-Five Years' Service*, p. 143.
[14] *Ibid.*, p. 151.

1835

New Year's Day at Fort McLoughlin — Coal is found on Vancouver Island — More American missionaries on the Columbia — Character of Peter Skene Ogden.

New Year's Day was always a great occasion back in old Scotland, and the Scottish officers of the HBC saw to it that the day did not go unobserved in their little forts. Dr. Tolmie in his diary records the festivities of January 1st this year at Fort McLoughlin on Milbanke Sound:

Thursday, January 1, 1835: Busy trading all day. The men after breakfast visited us in the dining hall & after the compliments of the season received a couple of drams. In the evening they assembled in the same apartment & danced with great vivacity till 10, to vocal music. Manson & I danced several reels. The [French-] Canadians possess a natural ease of manner equally remote from the free and aisy of the Emerald Isle & the sheepishness so characteristic of Sawney [the Scot]. They sung several paddling songs. Our two Iroquois danced the war dance with great spirit of their tribe & the S. [Sandwich] Islanders sung Rule Britannia tolerably well. They all seemed to enjoy themselves highly.[1]

Undoubtedly the men had earned their festivities. They had laboured hard to complete the last of the buildings within the palisades, and had cleared the forest back for a hundred yards on all sides of the fort so as to permit a clear field of fire should the Indians attack. Ahead of them lay the hard work of preparing the black undrained peat so that a garden could be put in when spring came.

An important development came one day when the blacksmith at Fort McLoughlin was adding coals to his fire. One of a group of Indian onlookers asked where the Company obtained this coal. When the smith replied that it was brought from Wales in a ship

---

[1] Tolmie, *Journals*, p. 300.

which needed six months to carry it hither, the Indians were vastly amused. Why, they asked, did the HBC do things this way when they could get any amount of this soft black stone from Vancouver Island? The blacksmith passed on this interesting information to Dr. Tolmie, and Tolmie conveyed it to Dr. McLoughlin. Thus in due course the Company's new steamer, *Beaver*, put in at Beaver Harbour on northern Vancouver Island, where coal was indeed found to exist in considerable quantity.

Usually a dull routine marked Tolmie's days at Fort McLoughlin. His hopes of recreation in botanical research had proved illusory. In September he sadly wrote to Dr. Hooker:

Since October I have been stationed here in the capacity of Indian Trader, and regret to state that I have been entirely prevented from making any botanical collections — This place is situated in close vicinity to several populous villages & from these during spring and summer there is such an unceasing concourse of Indians to the Fort, as renders the presence of the trader always necessary.

While stationed here I have no hopes of doing anything in the way of Botany and at present see no prospect of removal, the glowing anticipations I formed regarding my pursuits in this country have been far from realised, instead of scaling the rugged mountains which guard the coast & penetrating its unexplored rivers I am confined from morning till night in the trading store, & even the exercise requisite for the preservation of Health, I take on the Fort Gallery.[2]

Tolmie also noted that, even should one have leisure to stroll beyond the fort, it was dangerous to do so. One man, venturing out alone, had been stripped of part of his attire by the Indians.

Dr. Tolmie was not the only person on the coast diligently keeping a diary this year. Chief Trader John Work, who had just been placed in charge of the Company's coasting trade, was a great keeper of journals. He gives a most thorough account of his experiences both at Fort Simpson and while accompanying Captain McNeill with the *Llama* on part of a trading voyage along the northern coast. American competitors were back on the coast this year and Work's diary becomes particularly interesting when he records how, in mid-May, he and McNeill arrived at the mouth of

[2] MS. in Kew Library, *North American Letters*, Vol. 72:157.

the Nass to find Captain Allan already there with the *Europa,* and trading blankets "far superior to ours both in size and quality."

Sunday, May 17. Still fine weather. The Indians assembled again in the morning as usual, and kept going between us and our opponents as usual. During the day we traded 94 Beaver, 5 Otters, 28 Bears, 21 Martens. We had more customers than our opponents owing to the superior quality of our Rum and Tobacco. Capt. Allan who must have been perfectly aware of our scale of trade, came aboard and enquired what we were giving, and on being told, got in a violent passion and declared that he would do his utmost to rise [*sic*] the price and make us pay as high as possible for all the furs we would trade on the coast this season, that he had plenty of goods to do so (& as our deck was full of Natives busy trading) without waiting to be spoke to went over the side and proclaimed to the Indians that he would give 4 gall. Rum & 8 heads of tobacco with one of his large blankets for a beaver. The Indians received this intimation with several loud hurrahs, and immediately ceased trading, and began to clear off to his vessel. It remained with us now either to lose the beaver or rise our price, the latter was preferred and we accordingly offered 5 gal. Mixed rum & 10 heads tobacco with a blanket per beaver, the result of which was that we secured, as we think, the best share of the day's trade.[3]

Back at Fort Vancouver at the end of October, Chief Trader Work found that a new arrival had taken up residence there during his absence. This was the Rev. Samuel Parker. The missionaries previously entertained by McLoughlin had been Methodists, but Parker had been sent out by the American Board of Foreign Missions which represented the Congregationalist, Presbyterian and Dutch Reformed churches. McLoughlin not only installed Parker in quarters at Fort Vancouver, but refused payment for the canoemen and supplies he provided so that Parker could make a reconnaissance around the lower Columbia seeking suitable sites for mission stations. Since McLoughlin was a man of complete probity in money matters, these expenses must have come not out of the coffers of the HBC but from Dr. McLoughlin's own pocket. By now word of McLoughlin's extraordinary kindness in receiving Parker and his Methodist predecessors was reaching Governor Simpson, who could not but be aware of possible political consequences. The next year he intimated

---

[3] H. D. Dee, ed., *The Journal of John Work: January to October 1835,* PABC Memoir 10 (Victoria, 1945), p. 42.

to McLoughlin that it would be as well if "the American Missionaries should with draw [sic] from our Establishments and provide quarters for themselves". In indignant response, McLoughlin wrote to London:

> The Reverend Mr. Parker a Presbyterian Minister Arrived here last fall and from the time of his Arrival to his Departure *took up* his Residence with us — But the Gentleman was Alone and Entirely Destitute and to have refused lodging and food to a Man of his character and functions at his time of life — above Sixty years of Age — Would have been Worse than churlish and would have Deservedly Exposed us to a merited Load of Obloquy.[4]

Dr. McLoughlin certainly had a point; but he was overlooking the fact that Parker and later Americans would not be coming out to Oregon destitute if they had not the comforting assurance that they would be looked after once they reached Fort Vancouver. Having returned to the United States, Parker in 1838 published his *Journal of an Exploring Tour Beyond the Rocky Mountains*. It would stimulate American immigration into Oregon in the early 1840s.

In New Caledonia the principal event this year was a change of command, with Chief Factor Peter Warren Dease leaving Fort St. James. To replace Dease, the Company chose the veteran Peter Skene Ogden, newly commissioned as a Chief Factor. Many years had passed since a fellow Nor'Wester, Ross Cox, had described him as "the humorous, honest, eccentric law-defying Peter Ogden, the terror of the Indians, and the delight of all gay fellows". Like his crony Samuel Black, after terrorizing the HBC during its war with the Nor'Westers, he had belatedly been commissioned as a Chief Trader in the reorganized company that emerged from the union of 1821. There had followed for Ogden the tremendous labours of his Snake River expeditions which took him to Utah, to San Francisco Bay, and almost to the Gulf of California. Year after year, amid incredible dangers, he had sought to trap the vast country bare of beaver before it could pass under American sovereignty. His failure to establish Fort Stikine in the face of Russian resistance had very properly been deemed by his superiors to show discretion rather than

[4] HBRS 4:175.

any lack of valour. Now a man of about forty, short in stature, heavy in build, beetling brows on a bull head set close on massive shoulders, Ogden retained his sense of humour unimpaired, being renowned as one of the best raconteurs in the Company's service. For Ogden residence at Fort St. James as the superintendent of New Caledonia was a welcome change after his years of arduous travel. In New Caledonia he could let down his roots. He would remain there for the next nine years.

One tragedy this year particularly depressed the morale of the little group of HBC men spread so thinly across the enormous territory of New Caledonia. Among the most popular of their number was George Linton, who was transferred this year from Fort George to Fort Chilcotin. He delayed moving to his new post as long as he could, hoping to obtain at Fort George much needed supplies of leather expected to be brought in over the Yellowhead or "Leather Pass". At last Linton felt that he could wait no longer since ice was already beginning to come down the Fraser. Accordingly, late this autumn he embarked in a canoe at Fort George, along with his wife and three children, his interpreter, and the latter's wife and child, and started on his trip down the Fraser then up the Chilcotin. None of them was ever seen again, but early on the day after their departure their dog appeared at the gates of Fort George.[5] The natural conclusion seemed to be that the party had come to grief while running downstream amid the floating ice. On the other hand, Indians with a bad reputation were known to be camped along the river, so there was always the lingering thought that they might all have been robbed then murdered.

5 McLean, *Twenty-Five Years' Service*, pp. 167-68.

1836

Arrival of the steamer Beaver — *Clerical gentlemen —*
Coming of the American spy, Slacum.

The grand event of this year was the arrival of a sturdy little
paddlewheel steamer, the *Beaver* — not the first steamboat in the
Pacific, as is sometimes claimed, but the first to ply the waters of the
Pacific North-west. Back in 1826, and again in 1827, Dr. Mc-
Loughlin had suggested that the HBC should acquire a steamer.
Clearly one would be ideal for threading the narrow waterways of
the coastal inlets, expeditiously moving from point to point while
adverse winds or calms left sailing ships, especially those of American
competitors, unable to move. Not until 1832 was the idea taken up
by Governor Simpson who then wrote to London:

> A steam Vessel would afford us incalculable advantages over the
> Americans, as we could look into every Creek and cove while they were
> confined to a harbour by head winds and calms, we could ascend every
> stream of any consequence upon the coast, we could visit our establish-
> ments at stated periods, in short a Steam Vessel would, in our opinion,
> bring the contest to a close very soon, by making us masters of the
> trade.[1]

Unexpectedly, Dr. McLoughlin who had initiated the scheme
now turned against it, urging that, though a steamer might be very
convenient, it would prove far too expensive. Since McLoughlin by
his own admission knew very little about the cost of a steam vessel,
the true reason for his opposition must be looked for elsewhere.
Almost certainly it grew out of a strong difference of opinion, growing into a quarrel, between Simpson and himself. Simpson, as we
have noted, believed that the maritime fur trade was best conducted
from ships; McLoughlin believed that forts could better play the

[1] Quoted by Dereck Pethick, *S.S. Beaver: The Ship that Saved the West*
(Vancouver, 1970), p. 13.

293

major role. For McLoughlin the *Beaver* came to symbolize the whole ships-over-forts policy, and consequently he always regarded her with odium.

Despite McLoughlin's firmly expressed opposition, the Governor and Committee in London approved in 1834 the steamboat project. On 2 May 1835 the ship was launched and given her name of *Beaver*, and on June 25th she took her trial cruise in the English Channel. The *Beaver* was a very sturdy little craft of 109 tons burden, built with a massive elm keel and timbers of English oak and African teak. Her two engines developed 35 horsepower each and turned her paddlewheels thirty times a minute when she was making her top speed of 9¾ miles per hour. These paddlewheels, set unusually far forward, measured 13 feet in diameter.[2] All her mechanical equipment had been ordered in duplicate to facilitate replacement after she had reached her remote destination on the far side of North America.

At the end of August the *Beaver*, her machinery dismantled and paddlewheels removed for the long journey, set sail rigged as a brigantine. For her consort on the long and risky voyage to North-west America she had the new supply ship *Columbia*. The two ships became separated in the Atlantic, but rejoined company off Chile. On March 19th the *Beaver* finally crossed the bar of the Columbia, being followed a day or so later by the *Columbia*. On April 10th the two ships anchored at Fort Vancouver. A jaundiced Dr. Mc-Loughlin set the fort's carpenters and the *Beaver*'s engineers to work fitting her out once more as a steamboat. On Tuesday, May 17th, steam was raised and, for the first time in the Pacific North-west, paddlewheels stirred the water as she made a little trip to take on a load of firewood. There followed several excursions along the river with ladies and gentlemen from the fort. On July 19th she left for her first trading cruise upcoast.

First port of call was Fort McLoughlin. The *Beaver* arrived here in rather battered condition, having had part of a paddlebox damaged by heavy seas. Moreover, she approached under sail having inconveniently run out of firewood the previous day. Fire-

---

2 W. K. Lamb, "The Advent of the 'Beaver' ", *BCHQ* 2 (1938) : 168.

wood constituted quite a problem, since the *Beaver*'s six axemen
needed two days to cut enough cordwood to keep her steaming for
one day. Obviously a system would have to be evolved whereby
cordwood would be stockpiled at various points along her routes.
The vessel's next stop was at Fort Simpson, where she arrived ahead
of an appalling epidemic of smallpox which this year wiped out a
third of the Indian population of the northern coast. From Fort
Simpson she continued up to Tongass to impress the Russians. Then
she started south on an extended trading cruise, putting in at this
Indian village and that as she headed towards Fort Nisqually on
Puget Sound. Never again was she to return to Fort Vancouver,
largely because of the risk involved in crossing the bar at the river
mouth.

One of the major benefits of acquiring the steamship was the
tremendous impression she made on the Indians. Psychologically she
was as effective a deterrent as a squadron of warships for hostile
Indians who might be entertaining notions of storming the HBC's
isolated little forts. At first the Indians were transfixed with fear
when they saw her, smoke billowing from her tall white smokestack,
churning up the channels and making a fine turmoil with her
paddles. One tribe (the Bella Bellas) resolved that they must have a
Beaver all of their own. Taking one of their largest dugouts, they
painted gunports on the sides, covered it over and made it resemble,
externally at least, the HBC's new steamer. Along its sides red
paddles dipped with a cyclical movement into the water, maintaining a steady three miles per hour. The only catch was that this
Beaver's paddles derived their motion from Indians concealed under
the canoe's top covering.[3]

More than one Beaver arrived at Fort Vancouver this year. The
other was the Reverend Mr. Herbert Beaver, newly appointed Anglican chaplain at the fort, who with his wife disembarked from the
Company's supply ship *Nereide* in September. The Rev. Mr. Beaver
was not the only clergyman to arrive at the fort this year. In the
wake of the Rev. Mr. Parker came more American missionaries —
Spalding, Whitman and Gray — to set up establishments at points

[3] John Dunn, *History of the Oregon Territory and British North American Fur
Trade* (London, 1844), pp. 271-72.

which Parker had selected. Moreover, the Roman Catholic ex-
servants of the HBC who had settled in the Willamette Valley were
not to remain much longer without spiritual direction. They had
commenced building a fine large house for the priest they expected
shortly to arrive from the Red River.

Peter Skene Ogden had some humourous remarks to pass on the
clerical gentlemen and assorted scientific persons who converged on
the Columbia this year:

Among the good many things their Honors from Fenchurch Street
[location of the HBC's London headquarters] sent us last summer was
a Clergyman and with him his wife, the Rev. Mr. Beaver, a very
appropriate name for the fur trade, also Mr. & Mrs. Coppendale (sp?)
to conduct the farming establishment; and by the Snake Country we
had an assortment of Am. Missionaries, the Rev. Mr. Spaulding &
Lady, two Mr. Lees and Mr. Shepherd — surely Clergymen enough
when the Indian Population is now so reduced. But this not all — there
are also five more Gent. as follows — 2 in quest of Flowers, 2 killing all
the Birds in the Columbia, and one in quest of rocks and stones. All
these bucks come with letters from the President of the U. States, and
you know it would not be good policy not to treat them politely. They
are a perfect nuisance.[4]

The year 1836 ended on an ominous note. In late December[5] one
William A. Slacum, who had chartered the brig *Loriot* in Honolulu,
arrived aboard her. Although his alleged purpose was to meet friends
who were travelling overland, Slacum was in fact an American naval
officer sent out as a spy. He spent a month ferreting out all the
information he could about the situation on the Columbia. Also, it
was important for him to meet with Jason Lee, the Wesleyan
missionary who headed the tiny American community in the Willamette Valley, and to get Lee's notable energies directed towards
securing American sovereignty in Oregon.

The newly arrived American settlers had found themselves much
handicapped by lack of cattle, and had wanted to bring in some

[4] Ogden to John McLeod, 25 Feb. 1837, PAC, McLeod Papers, p. 369.

[5] McLoughlin to Governor and Committee, 17 Jan. 1837 (HBRS 4:185).
Oddly enough, writing to Edward Ermatinger on 3 March 1837, he gave the
date of the *Loriot*'s entrance into the river as Jan. 2. (Ermatinger Papers,
p. 239.)

from California. This was an expensive venture, and Jason Lee's mission could only provide the quite inadequate sum of $400. Slacum, however, supplied a timely $500 (paid in his own name, though almost certainly out of U.S. government funds), and the ardently pro-American Dr. McLoughlin put up $900 more for the newly formed Oregon Cattle Company. When Slacum sailed on the *Loriot*, his non-existent friends from the East having failed to arrive, he gave free passage to California for the eleven men who were to purchase eight hundred head of cattle and drive them overland to the Willamette Valley.

Slacum could congratulate himself on having substantially aided these all-important first American settlers. Moreover, a key decision had been reached. As H. H. Bancroft, the American historian, subsequently noted: " . . . from the moment of the appearance of Slacum" the American missionaries' former acquiescence in the rule of the HBC turned to covert but determined opposition.[6] As for their leader's subsequent career Bancroft put things succinctly: "From this point we regard Jason Lee less as a missionary than as an American colonizer".[7] Lee was aided in his new career by the publication, during this year of 1836, of Washington Irving's *Astoria*, a highly popular work which made "Oregon" suddenly bulk large in the American consciousness.

---

6 H. H. Bancroft, *The History of Oregon* (San Francisco, 1886-88), I:141.

7 *Ibid.*, I:166. Actually Lee's political connections with the American government may have been forged in Washington in 1834, immediately prior to his first journey out to the Columbia. *v.* A. Atwood, *The Conquerors* (Boston, 1907), pp. 66-67.

1837

Slacum's report to Washington — Capt. McNeill looks for a base on southern Vancouver Island — Captain Belcher, R.N., at Nootka — Dr. McLoughlin avoids leaving Columbia.

Back in the United States this year, the spy Slacum submitted his report, a tissue of misrepresentations calculated to appeal to the anti-British prejudice rampant in the young republic. Whereas the Indian practice of slavery was a source of unhappiness to the HBC, Slacum affirmed, " . . . the policy of this company is calculated to perpetuate the institution of slavery, which now exists, and is encouraged, among all the Indian tribes west of the Rocky mountains". No word was given of how the HBC had exerted itself to regain for the American Jedediah Smith his goods seized by the Umpqua Indians; instead, the hostility of the Indians in southern Oregon was blamed on the HBC. After noting that the British company's parties had traded safely in this area, Slacum continued:

. . . every small American party (save one) that has passed through the same country has met defeat and death. The parties being much smaller than those of the Hudson Bay Company, the Indians attack them with success; and the Americans hesitate not to charge the subordinate agents of the Hudson Bay Company with instigating the Indians to attack all other parties.[1]

The Indian belief that the fever had been introduced into the Columbia by the American brig *Owhyhee* was dismissed as a malevolent invention of the HBC: "How easy was it for the Hudson Bay Company's agent to make the Indians believe this absurdity, for reasons, too, the most obvious!" Needless to say, no mention was made of the overflowing hospitality which McLoughlin, nursing his own dreams of coming American sovereignty, pressed on every

---

[1] "Slacum's Report on Oregon, 1836-37", *OHQ* 13 (1912) : 189.

citizen of the republic who showed up at Fort Vancouver. Slacum's "report" in fact was merely another piece of propaganda in the opening campaign for American annexation of the Columbia.

Concerned by the loss of supply ships on the Columbia River bar, and aware that American aggression might drive them some day from Fort Vancouver, the Governor and Committee of the HBC in London, and Governor Simpson in British North America, were concerned that a site be found on the northern shore of the Strait of Juan de Fuca where a new depot for the Pacific slope might be established. Thus it came about that this summer Captain McNeill with the *Beaver* steamed along the southern coast of Vancouver Island looking for a suitable site, one which had not only a well-protected harbour, but also adjacent plains where crops could be planted and livestock pastured. Finally Captain McNeill was successful and discovered at the south-eastern tip of Vancouver Island "an excellent harbour and a fine open country along the sea shore, apparently well adapted for both tillage and pasturage. . . . "[2] Here in the years to come would arise the city of Victoria, the capital of British Columbia.

This summer, for the first time since 1796, the Royal Navy visited Vancouver Island. On October 3rd the redoubtable and irascible Captain Edward Belcher, with H.M.S. *Sulphur* and H.M.S. *Starling*, put in at Nootka on their way south from Alaska. Out of curiosity Belcher got the Indians to show him the site of the Spanish settlement and found no trace of it remained:

Even on the spot where this fort stood, I searched for some vestige of mortar, of building stone, but now all was bare, rugged rock, overgrown with briars. They endeavoured to point out to me where the house stood; where the cross was erected; and where the potatoes grew; but every vestige had disappeared. . . . [3]

Since chieftainship descended in the matrilineal line, Belcher found the Maquinna who now ruled here was the son-in-law of Captain Vancouver's Maquinna. Belcher was very favourably

2 Fort Simpson Journal for 10 August 1837, quoted in Walbran, *B.C. Coast Names*, p. 392.

3 Belcher to Capt. Beaufort, Hydrographer of the Navy, MS. letter in the Office of the Hydrographer of the Navy, Taunton, Somerset.

impressed both by him and his young daughter, through whom the succession would continue:

> Her manner was very simple and winning; she had black expressive eyes; and her affection for her father, on whom she often clung, with her head reposing on his shoulder, was quite a novel sight amongst these people.[4]

Belcher feasted the chief and his family on rice, molasses and a diluted mixture of rum and sugar. He had a further treat in store for them:

> At dusk I landed, taking with me a magic-lanthorn and supply of fireworks. At the former they all exhibited the most unfeigned delight, to a degree quite outrageous; but at the ascent of the rockets, their impressions amounted to fear. I had several women grasping me by each hand, huddled in one group, and evidently trembling; and, by the light from the fire, I could perceive the tears rolling down the cheeks of Macquilla's wife and daughter, who fled to the bush the instant the fireworks were over; nor could they be persuaded to return, even to witness a second exhibition of the magic-lanthorn.[5]

On this cruise Belcher did not take his ships into the Columbia River so he did not meet Dr. McLoughlin who, in November, completed thirteen years of uninterrupted residence in the Pacific North-west. Earlier, as we have noted, he had passed up an expected furlough. Now the Governor and Committee in England were desirous of having him come to London for discussions about his department. This February they wrote to him making their wishes known, and arranging for him to travel to England on the supply ship *Sumatra*. But the "Emperor of the West" could not bring himself to hand over his empire to another and, pleading illness, remained at Fort Vancouver. The person who left this year was Chief Factor Finlayson, McLoughlin's coadjutor. He would never return.

This year the lengthening list of Columbia department forts was again increased when Dr. McLoughlin purchased from Nathaniel Wyeth the latter's Fort Hall, close to the junction of the Snake and Portneuf Rivers, a little north of today's Pocatello, Idaho.

---

[4] Edward Belcher, *Narrative of a Voyage Round the World Performed in H.M.S. Sulphur 1836-42* (London, 1843), I:109.

[5] *Ibid.*, I:110.

1838

Problems with the Rev. Mr. Herbert Beaver — McLoughlin leaves for London — James Douglas in charge — His suspicions about the American missionaries — Disaster overtakes British botanists north of Revelstoke — McBean awaits Chilcotins in his unfortified fort — Robert Campbell explores northern country — Meets Chief Shakes and is saved by a chieftainess.

Early this spring Chief Factor McLoughlin at long last left Fort Vancouver for England, but not before he had given a thrashing to the Rev. Mr. Herbert Beaver, Church of England chaplain at the fort. McLoughlin evidently had never had the slightest liking for a nominee of Simpson, or probably any other Anglican clergyman, taking up residence at Fort Vancouver. He himself was a Roman Catholic of sorts and received pious exhortations from his sister, a nun in Quebec, to see that the Roman Catholics serving under him were kept strong in the faith. He was, accordingly, more interested in having Roman Catholic priests come out to the Columbia. Thus it was that, although McLoughlin had been given ample advance notification that the Rev. Mr. & Mrs. Beaver were coming out and, months before their arrival, had received from the Company communion plate, Bibles, prayer books, registers and a church bell and pulpit, he took no action towards getting either a house built for them or a church erected in which the new chaplain could conduct his services. During his two years at Fort Vancouver the Rev. Mr. Beaver would have to conduct his services in the fort's mess hall.

Mr. Beaver, when he arrived, proved to be a small but opinionated person with a tremendous sense of his importance as a clergyman in the Established Church, responsible only to London, and charged with the spiritual and moral well-being of the inhabitants

of Fort Vancouver. His ego was comparable in size with McLoughlin's own and inevitably the two were soon at loggerheads. One issue
was religious education. Beaver expected to instruct the children in
the fort's school in the Christian religion as interpreted by the
Church of England. McLoughlin regarded them nearly all as
Catholics and was determined that Catholic children should not be
subject to Mr. Beaver's instruction. Pertinaciously Mr. Beaver examined the circumstances of each child and claimed that the schoolmaster had improperly listed as Catholics children, such as orphans,
who had no parents to declare that they should be brought up in the
Catholic faith. The upshot was that Dr. McLoughlin removed both
school and schoolmaster from Beaver's superintendency. At every
turn the new chaplain found himself blocked or rebuffed by Mc-
Loughlin, and only clandestinely did he manage to minister to some
of the fort's French-Canadians and baptize their infants. No doubt
Mr. Beaver contributed largely to his own difficulties by insisting on
special privileges, complaining about the rough furniture supplied
him by the fort and the lack of carpets on his floor, and generally
showing his distaste for the rather brutally rough life. Hearing that
one of the Company's trapping parties had hanged Indians for
stealing their horses, he considered the deed "murder", and he was
shocked to find the HBC officers buying slaves from the Indians and
using them for their own service — by writing to London he got the
practice stopped. Of little assistance to Beaver was "haughty Jane",
his wife, who made a great issue of the fact that the fort's cook
would not prepare her salmon in the way to which she was
accustomed.

Seeing how impossible his position was, Beaver, within two months
of his arrival, asked McLoughlin for passage home to England on
the Company's next ship. But now an unexpected development
occurred. Despite all his troubles with McLoughlin, Beaver, in
however narrow and bigoted a manner, had energetically striven to
do his best as a chaplain and a missionary, and found an unexpected
reward. Risking McLoughlin's wrath, thirty-four Protestants and
twenty-four Catholics signed a petition to Beaver asking him to
remain at his post. Great was Beaver's joy at finding that one of the
Catholic signatories was the carpenter David Dompier who, at

McLoughlin's urging, conducted public Catholic devotions.[1] Moved by this petition, Beaver made a brave decision — despite McLoughlin, he would remain at his post. The decision must have caused him great regret as the months passed by and difficulties steadily increased. He and McLoughlin, no longer speaking to each other, communicated only by letter. Finally even correspondence was broken off. Essential communication was carried on via Mrs. Beaver and Chief Trader James Douglas.

The main cause of Beaver's trouble was his anger and contempt directed against the HBC officers and men who had "fur trade wives". To him, these people were living in sin unless they had their unions sanctified by a marriage service conducted by himself. His heart rejoiced when he joined in the bonds of holy matrimony James Douglas and Amelia Connolly who had already been living as man and wife for over eight years. (Ultimately the courts in Quebec would rule these fur trade marriages were binding.) His anger flamed high when Dr. McLoughlin made no move to allow Beaver to hallow his union with Mrs. McLoughlin. The chaplain's fury was the more intense since each of the McLoughlins had participated in an earlier fur trade marriage with another partner. Filled with outraged righteousness, and employing his customarily reckless and exaggerated language, Beaver wrote to the Governor and Committee in London. Foul sexual sin, he informed them, was rampant in Fort Vancouver. Mrs. McLoughlin, who was universally respected for her goodness and kindness, he characterized as "a female of notoriously loose character" and "the kept Mistress of the highest personage in your service at this station".[2]

Several months after this outrageous letter was despatched to England, Dr. McLoughlin saw a copy of it for the first time. Later that same day, as the enormous McLoughlin was crossing the courtyard of the fort, he encountered the cocky little chaplain. For what happened we have an account from that unfortunate divine:

I was walking across the Fort-yard to speak to my wife, who was standing at the door of our house, when this monster in human form

---

[1] Herbert Beaver, "Experiences of a Chaplain at Fort Vancouver 1836-1838", ed. R. C. Clark, *OHQ* 39 (1938):26.

[2] HBRS 4:cxx.

... advanced towards us, apparently in a violent passion, and upon my making way for him to pass, he came behind me, kicked me several times, and struck me repeatedly with his fists on the back of the neck. Unable to cope with him, from the immense disparity of our relative size and strength, I could not prevent him from wrenching out of my hands a stout stick, with which I was walking, and with which he next inflicted several severe blows on my shoulders. He then seized me from behind, round my waist, and attempted to dash me on the ground, exclaiming, *"you scoundrel, I will have your life."* In the meantime the stick had fallen to the ground; my wife, on the impulse of the moment, picked it up; he took it, to use the epithet of an eye-witness, *"very viciously"* out of her hands, and again struck me with it severely; we were then separated by the intervention of other persons.[3]

A few days later McLoughlin was on his way, overland, for England. In November the Beavers took ship for the same destination, the clergyman intent on setting the law on his assailant. In this mission he failed, and was discharged from the service of the HBC.

It was on March 22nd that Dr. McLoughlin left Fort Vancouver to cross the mountains on the first stretch of his journey to England. At Lake Winnipeg he met John Tod. Conversing with him, Mc-Loughlin allowed himself to be carried away by his tumultuous republican passions, which surged forth when the conversation turned to the recent unsuccessful rebellion in Canada, sparked by Louis Joseph Papineau, who had fled to the United States and there sought American intervention. Tod subsequently mentioned this conversation in a letter to an old friend:

The Doctor, who has at length descended from his roost, I met in Lake Winnipeg — we breakfasted together, & talked incessantly all the while on the late events of Canada — he was strenuous in support of that arch rebel Peppeneau & his party. I took the liberty to say in a jocund way that it was fortunate for him, he had not been with me last winter [in Canada], otherwise, I should have most probably been now carrying an account of his trial. . . . [4]

James Douglas took over the command of the Columbia Department for the period of McLoughlin's leave. He had a busy and sometimes an anxious time. In May an unprecedented flood on the

---

[3] Beaver, "Experiences", p. 31.

[4] PAC, Ermatinger Papers, p. 51.

Columbia overflowed the banks and dikes around Fort Vancouver and destroyed with "stunning effect" eighty acres of newly-seeded land. The Company, incidentally, had decided to establish a new farm on the Cowlitz River. One of Douglas' tasks was to bring this new farm into being. Cattle and agricultural implements were sent north easily enough, but great difficulty was found in getting men to work the new lands. None of the Willamette Valley settlers could be persuaded to move from that pleasant locality.

Writing to London in October, Douglas reported on this growing Willamette colony, and gave its total strength as fifty-one persons. Of these twenty-three were French-Canadians, formerly employed by the HBC, whose loyalty could be relied upon, eighteen were "vagrant Americans", mostly from California, and ten were members of the Methodist mission. Taking the opportunity afforded by McLoughlin's absence, Douglas sent his own warning to London that these American missionaries so dear to the absent Chief Factor represented potential danger:

> ... the vagrant Americans respect power and integrity; but I fear that the Methodists nourish secret views, at variance with our interests. The Revd. Mr. Lee, their superintendent, returned this summer, by the overland route, to the United States, to make arrangements for importing goods. ... It is difficult to anticipate their real intentions, and perhaps unfair to question them; but I am naturally anxious about the designs of a body of men, who have the power of seriously injuring our business, and whose conduct may justify suspicion. . . .
>
> I am probably dwelling, too long on this subject, but I feel its importance, and a deep anxiety to expose the true nature of our position. . . . [5]

The implications of this letter are plain — that Dr. McLoughlin had concealed from the Governor and Committee "the true nature of our position" vis-a-vis the missionaries, that with the American government not yet recognizing the Columbia River as the international boundary, the growth of American settlement begun by the Methodists in the region was an ominous development.

In November of this year, about the time that the Rev. Mr. Beaver and his wife were leaving, Douglas welcomed at Fort

[5] HBRS 4:242-43.

Vancouver Father Blanchet and Father Demers. Despatched from Canada, they were the first Roman Catholic priests in the Pacific North-west since the Spaniards had departed from Nootka.

Along with his worries caused by floods and Americans, Douglas could find sources of satisfaction. The Company's trade was prospering and, in consequence of the routing of competitors, Douglas was able to suspend the sale of guns and ammunition south of Fort McLoughlin. (In this area the Indians did not have to have them to secure their livelihood, which came from the sea, but were too ready to use them in their wars against each other, and in threats to the whites.) Moreover, in May of this year, the British government renewed the HBC's licence of 1821 which gave the Company:

... the exclusive privilege of trading with the Indians in all such parts of North America to the northward and to the Westward of the lands and territories belonging to the United States of America as should not be part of any of Our provinces in North America.[6]

This year two young botanists set out on a long journey across the Atlantic and overland to the Columbia. Noble lords who wished to secure for their grounds and gardens the admired new conifers and other trees and shrubs reported by David Douglas, were finding it almost impossible to do so. Accordingly Joseph Paxton, the famous gardener of the Duke of Devonshire, set up a cooperative scheme (in association with Sir William Hooker, soon to become Director at Kew; Professor Lindley, a moving spirit in the Horticultural Society; and a number of private collectors) to despatch two agents to the Pacific North-west. For this assignment Paxton chose two of his best gardeners at Chatsworth. In April the two young men, Robert Wallace and Peter Banks, landed at New York and made for Montreal, where they joined an HBC party travelling overland to the Pacific.

During the journey across the plains romance developed, and at Fort Edmonton Wallace married Maria, an illegitimate daughter of Governor Simpson and Betsy Sinclair. Pressing on with the rest of the party, Wallace and his bride traversed the Rocky Mountains by the Athabasca Pass and safely arrived at Boat Encampment, where

[6] PABC, A-A-10-G 786 k.

they were to commence their journey down the river to Fort Vancouver. Unfortunately there were too many people for the available boats, so Chief Trader John Tod, the "conductor" of the party, took as many as he could down to the Arrow Lakes and then sent a boat back to bring down the remainder, including the young Wallaces. On October 22nd this final group climbed into their boat and started down the river. North of Revelstoke lie the ominous Death Rapids, then known as Dalles des Morts. These were safely passed, but just below them the party encountered some further rapids. Evening was coming on, and everybody was in a hurry so, in Tod's absence, the canoemen let the passengers omit the usual precaution of going ashore, walking down to the foot of the rapids, and re-embarking there.

Fathers Blanchet and Demers, who were with the main party waiting at the "Maison des lacs" at the head of the Arrow Lakes, have left us a vivid account of the consequences of the second party's rashness. As time passed and the priests and their companions saw no sign of the second party, they became increasingly worried. At length they saw in the distance "a half wrecked bateau":

It was indeed the one that had been sent. They did not hear at all the joyous song of arrival at stations. The men sadly grasped the oars, seemingly powerless to ply them. They approach; people rush to the shore; and grief spreads among the travelers. The bateau had been wrecked, and of the 26 persons it was carrying 12 had perished! Too heavily loaded and too encumbered it had first filled at the *dalles des morts*. They succeeded in emptying it, but the things it contained remained water-soaked. They shoved it into open water, and at the first impulse of the oars it filled again. At that critical instant they could still have reached land in the turmoil at the foot of the narrows; they were only a short distance from it. The men had attempted to stand up to cast themselves forward; the guide had succeeded in stopping them. Women and children were screaming; everyone was frozen with fear — suddenly Mr. Wallace stands up, removes his coat, puts his foot on the side of the bateau, and hurls himself into the water with his wife, shouting "courage, my friends!" The bateau loses its equilibrium, over-turns, and all are precipitated into the midst of the waves![7]

[7] *Notices & Voyages of the Famed Quebec Mission to the Pacific Northwest* (Portland, 1956), p. 8.

Such were the consequences of Wallace's desperate bid to get to the shore with his young wife.

News of the disaster reached Douglas at Fort Vancouver on November 7th, and that same day he wrote to London communicating the tragic news:

A Boat which Mr. Tod had sent back from the Upper Columbia Lake [Upper Arrow], left the Boat Encampment on the 22d October with the last of the party. In the evening of the same day, when running one of the Rapids below Dalles des Morts, the Boat unfortunately filled, and the following persons perished in attempting to gain the shore

| Mr. and Mrs. Wallace Mr. Banks | Botanists |

| Mr. Leblanc and his three children Keneth McDonald Fabien Vital J. Bte. Laliberté Two Children of André Chalifoux | in the Coys service |

in all twelve persons, who have travelled from their distant homes to find an untimely grave, beneath the raging waters of the Columbia.[8]

There was Indian trouble in New Caledonia this year. The storm centre was Fort Chilcotin where William McBean, the clerk in charge, entered in his journal a vivid account of difficulties with the turbulent Chilcotins and their chief:

Dec: Sunday 23. Snowing all day — Yesterday the Chief Allaw wished to come into my Room when I was busy writing to Mr. Fisher [McBean's superior at Fort Alexandria] and getting his men off — I desired Bte [Baptiste] to show him into the Mens Ho[use] telling him I did not wish to be disturbed particularly as he had no Furs to trade & only wished to pass away his time — He expected I would give him tobacco, however I was too busy to think of that, and if I had I would not have given [it] him as he was not deserving of it — He set off quit[e] displeased and this day an Indian was sent to me by his orders to apprize me that he has forbidden all the Indians to hunt and that he expected we would be off from his Lands immediately so that they might have the pleasure of burning the Fort — stating that the whites

8 HBRS 4:293.

did them no good — Could not smoke when they wished — that the
F[or]t at this time was always destitute of Trading goods — that we
rejected their bad Furs and sold at a high Tariff. I sent him word back
that there was no compulsion in the Trade — they were at liberty to
do as they pleased either hunt or not hunt — I was master of my Goods
— & they at liberty to do as they thought fit with their Furs — at the
same time I let him know that I despised his menaces and would not
quit my Fort until I received Instructions to that effect from a Chief
whose shoes he was not worthy to pick up.[9]

On Christmas Day word was received that the Indians planned an
imminent attack. Grimly McBean noted in his journal for that day:

... I am badly provided to receive them as my Fort is not fortified and
destitute of a single Bastion — nevertheless I shall endeavour to sell my
life as dear as I can. . . . [10]

The next day, while McBean was busy strengthening his palisades
and building a bastion, Chief Allaw appeared in a conciliatory
mood and asked if he was forbidden to visit the fort in the future.
He declared that, though other Indians had talked about attacking
the fort, he had never himself ever spoken of doing so. McBean
continued the work on his defences, confiding in his journal, "I
place no confidence in Allaw's justification — He is deceitful and
cunning". The crisis was over, however, and McBean did not have
to sacrifice his life in the service of the HBC.

An interesting chapter in the history of the exploration of northern
British Columbia dates from this year. Setting out from Fort Halkett
on the Liard River, Robert Campbell, a thirty year old clerk,
retraced Chief Trader McLeod's route of four years earlier, and in
July, after reaching Dease Lake, founded a trading establishment
there. Leaving the bulk of his party at Dease House, he pushed on
with his interpreter and "2 fine young Indians, Lapie & Kitza".
Passing McLeod's point of furthest penetration at Terror Bridge, "a
rude ricketty structure of pine poles spliced together with withes &
stretched high above a foaming torrent", they made friendly contact
with some Nahanni Indians who led them to an enormous Indian
encampment on the banks of the Stikine River. Here Indians from

[9] HBCA, B.37/a/1, f. 7.
[10] *Loc. cit.*

the whole area had converged for the salmon run and here Campbell met the great chief Shakes. Following his usual custom, Shakes had come to the rendezvous with boats filled with trading goods which he had obtained from the Russian fort at the mouth of the river. Shakes produced a bottle of whiskey and he and Campbell had a friendly drink together. Actually, Shakes was anything but pleased to find that he and the Russians would be having competition from the HBC. Campbell's life was in real danger, but what probably saved him was the friendship of the chieftainess of the Nahannis:

She commanded the respect not only of her own people, but of the tribes they had intercourse with. She was a fine looking woman rather above the middle height & about 35 years old. In her actions & personal appearance she was more like the Whites than the pure Indian race. She had a pleasing face lit up with fine intelligent eyes, which when she was excited flashed like fire. She was tidy & tasteful in her dress. To the kindness and influence of this Chieftainess, we owed much on more than one occasion; in fact in all probability we owed our lives to her more than once.[11]

Even so, in the face of mounting hostility from other Indians egged on by Shakes, Campbell found it politic to retreat to Dease House. While on the Stikine he had "hoisted the H.B.C. flag, & cut H.B.C. & date on a tree, thus taking possession of the country for the Company".

Back at Dease Lake, Campbell and his men spent a winter of incredible hardship. They had no provisions and had to live off the country. Fishnets were placed in the lake but few fish were caught. Hunters were sent out but the game which had been plentiful during the summer had disappeared. To increase their chance of survival, Campbell placed his men by twos or threes at various places along the lake, multiplying their chances of coming upon game. One grim day a single squirrel was all the food to feed nine men. Relief came briefly with a visit from their benefactress the Nahanni chieftainess, who gave the starving men "a sumptuous repast" of "excellent dried salmon & delicious caribou meat". Unfortunately she could not remain long and they were left once more to starve and to endure their other torment, the constant harrassment of "Russian Indians"

[11] Clifford Wilson, *Campbell of the Yukon* (Toronto, 1970), p. 28.

intent on driving them out of the country. Set on by Shakes, the Indians robbed them of their stores and utensils, and even some of their clothing. When the ghastly winter ended Campbell and his assistant, A. R. McLeod, gathered together their men at Dease House and prepared for the journey of six hundred miles to the nearest HBC fort. Their last act was to take the gut strings off their snowshoes and the parchment "windows" from their house and boil them down to a glue-like gruel which was their last meal before leaving Dease Lake on 8 May 1839.

1839

HBC leases the Panhandle from the Russians — And founds
the Puget's Sound Agricultural Company — The mounting
American threat to the Columbia — Return of Dr. Mc-
Loughlin — "The Catholic Ladder".

This year the HBC had the satisfaction of reaching a comprehensive
agreement with the Russian American Company. So remote were
the Russians in Alaska from supply bases in their own country that
they had had to obtain foodstuffs and other commodities from California and Hawaii. American captains coming to the Pacific North-
west to trade in furs would have found their ventures generally
unprofitable in the face of HBC competition had they not been able
to combine their fur trading with a profitable business in bringing to
Alaska the produce of more temperate climes. For years the HBC had
been unhappy about the situation. As early as 1829, when Aemilius
Simpson visited Sitka, he carried with him a letter from McLoughlin
offering to provide the Russians with these necessary supplies as part
of a cooperative undertaking which would drive the American fur
traders from the coast. The Russians had made no move to accept
this offer, and the two great monopolistic companies had, indeed,
become alienated by the *Dryad* Incident of 1834 when the Russians
had prevented the founding of Fort Stikine. But the *Dryad* Incident
itself led to negotiations which reached a final triumphant conclusion on February 6th of this year when Governor Simpson for the
HBC and Baron Wrangell for the Russian American Company
signed at Hamburg a most important and far-reaching agreement.[1]

Under the terms of the pact signed that day, the Russians leased
to the HBC, for ten years, the whole of the Alaskan Panhandle,
though not the offshore islands. The Russians agreed also to turn

[1] For the text of this agreement see E. H. Oliver, ed., *The Canadian North-
West, Its Early Development and Legislative Records* (Ottawa, 1915),
II:791-96.

over their own post on the Stikine River, which would now become the HBC's Fort Stikine. They agreed, moreover, to let the HBC found additional posts on the mainland as far north as Mount Fairweather. The Russians bound themselves not only to abstain from all fur trading within the leased area but also not to deal in furs originating within this territory. In return for the Russians' surrender of their fur trade on the mainland of southern Alaska, the HBC bound itself to pay an annual rental of "2000 seasoned Land Otter Skins" and to sell the Russians every year up to 2000 additional otter skins from west of the Rockies, and 3000 from east of the Rockies.

Under a very important article of the agreement, the HBC bound itself to supply the Russians annually with 160 cwt. of flour, 130 cwt. of dried peas, 130 cwt. of "Grits & hulled Pot Barley", 300 cwt. of salted beef, 160 cwt. of salted butter and 30 cwt. of pork hams. The prices to be paid for this food were carefully specified in the agreement. Moreover, the HBC agreed to ship to the Russians from Britain, at a fixed cost of £13 per ton, all those commodities of British manufacture that the Russians wished to order for their own Alaskan establishments. Finally, the HBC dropped all claims against the Russians for compensation for the *Dryad* Incident.

Great was the jubilation in the HBC's headquarters in London, on Fenchurch Street, when Simpson arrived with the Russian agreement. Clearly a whole new era was about to begin for the Company on the Pacific. Over the years its farms at Fort Vancouver, Fort Langley and Fort Nisqually had prospered. But even their abundance would be sorely taxed to fulfill the contract with the Russians. Some sort of special agricultural organization would have to be set up to supply Alaska and those other export markets which the Company hoped to open in the years which lay ahead. But a difficulty arose. The Company's lawyers pointed out that the HBC was set up as a fur trading company. They opined that the Company might well become vulnerable to lawsuits if any part of its capital were used in an agricultural enterprise. It might even risk loss of the charter which it had held since 1670.

A solution was soon found: let a new company be set up, but under conditions which would make it impossible for the new company ever to pass out of the control of the HBC! Thus there came into being the Puget's Sound Agricultural Company. Under the terms of a prospectus presented at the end of February of this year, this new company was capitalized at £200,000, the money to be raised through the sale of 2000 shares, with a down payment as low as 10%.[2] HBC shareholders in England showed little inclination to purchase in the new company, but almost without exception the HBC's Chief Factors, Chief Traders and clerks in North America bought the shares allocated for them, doing so not so much out of confidence in the new company's future as in response to pressure exerted from above. The Company's officers at the fur trading forts made no secret of their suspicion that the HBC was trying to finance its new venture at their expense.

The HBC lost no time transferring to the Puget's Sound Agricultural Company (PSAC) its large grazing areas at Fort Nisqually on Puget Sound. Under the direction of Chief Trader Tod, work was pushed ahead on a new farm for the PSAC where the trail to Nisqually on Puget Sound started from the Cowlitz River. Cattle were obtained from California and improved breeds of sheep — Leicester, Southdown and Cheviot — were shipped out from England. Plans were made to bring out English farmers with their families, experienced Scottish shepherds, and French-Canadians from the Red River Colony.

During recent years Governor Simpson and the HBC's headquarters in London had become increasingly aware of the threat of an American takeover of Oregon. Slacum's visit, the activities of propagandists for American colonization, and various other portents had not gone unheeded. A sense of crisis developed when Senator Linn of Missouri in 1838 got wide support in the U.S. Congress for a bill to annex Oregon, send out troops, and fortify the Columbia. Ultimately the bill failed to carry, but the HBC could see the shape of coming events. The Company's directors clearly realized that the only effective way of strengthening their claim to the country north of the Columbia (the south they regarded already as lost) was to open it to settlement and get a substantial British population established there as soon as possible. A major purpose, therefore, of the

[2] Leonard A. Wrinch, "The Formation of the Puget's Sound Agricultural Company", *WHQ* 24 (1933):4.

Puget's Sound Agricultural Company was to advance British colonization north of the Columbia. Of this purpose of the PSAC there
was never any doubt. George Roberts, an HBC man who had
arrived on the Columbia in 1831, recorded in his "Recollections":

I've no doubt there was a political object in starting this co. with an eye
to the future — that is they could urge they had farms fisheries &c all
over the count[r]y and [were] the vertual possessors. . . . [3]

Dr. W. F. Tolmie, who in 1843 became the superintendent of the
PSAC, later recalled:

The idea was that the British were to have the north side of the
Columbia River, and probably this was working up to that idea. The
Puget Sound Company was founded for the furtherance of this idea —
occupation.[4]

The American historian John S. Galbraith has very properly interpreted the whole venture as an attempt "to checkmate the Americans by British colonization".

On October 17th Dr. McLoughlin arrived back at Fort Vancouver, bringing with him a newly recruited "principal shepherd"
for the PSAC. If the new venture was to succeed it would have to
have the fullest possible assistance from McLoughlin. To try to make
sure of his cooperation, the Governor and Committee had passed a
special resolution:

The great extent of the Columbia District together with its growing
importance arising from the recent arrangements entered into with the
Russ. American Fur Company the projected operations of the Pugets
Sound Agricultural Company and other commercial objects in con-
templation involving a greater degree of responsibility in the principal
Superintendence or management of that District than heretofore It is
resolved that the Chief Factor who shall be appointed to the principal
superintendence or management of that District shall in addition to the
emoluments arising from his Chief Factorship be allowed a Salary of
Five Hundred Pounds p. Annum. . . . [5]

McLoughlin would be getting about half as much again as the other
Chief Factors in the Company's employ.

[3] Roberts, "Recollections", p. 8.
[4] Tolmie, "History of Puget Sound & The Northwest Coast", PAC, MG29,
B35, Vol. 3:10-11. (Bancroft transcript.)
[5] W. K. Lamb, "Introduction", HBRS 6:xii.

Those who had no liking for McLoughlin with his short temper, vast ego and unreliable evasiveness, had said at the time of his departure for England in 1838 that Simpson, tired of his growing intractability, hoped to see him sternly spoken to by the Governor and Committee in London. If Simpson had indeed entertained any such hopes they soon evaporated. Dr. McLoughlin with his tremendous physical presence, his energy and self-assurance, and that charm which he could exercise so effectively, had made a great impression in London. John Tod, pausing amid his labours in setting up the Cowlitz farm, wrote to a friend:

> The Big Doctor has again returned to this quarter with new powers & fresh honors — their Honors at home having placed in him the most unbounded Confidence in all affairs Connected with the Columbia.[6]

McLoughlin stood, in fact, at the high point of his career. He would continue there for a year or two, but then his path would be downhill all the way.

Other developments were not lacking this year. The original Fort Langley, built in 1827, was replaced by new buildings on a better site. In October Chief Trader James Douglas, commanding the Columbia department during McLoughlin's absence, reported to London on this move:

> We have abandoned the old Langley establishment which was in a delapidated state, as well as inconvenient in some respects for the business, and removed all the effects, into a new fort built a few miles higher up on the banks of Fraser's River, the stockades of which, four block houses, and nearly all the necessary buildings are now erected. It is fully as convenient for the fur and Salmon trade, as the former site and, moreover, possesses the important and desirable advantage of being much nearer the farm.[7]

Douglas had interesting other news from the Fraser. The warlike Cowichan Indians appeared to be becoming farmers!:

> ... the Cowegins around Fort Langley, influenced by the Council and example of the Fort, are beginning to cultivate the soil, many of them having with great perseverance and industry cleared patches of forrest

[6] Tod to Edward Ermatinger, Feb. 1840, PAC, Ermatinger Papers.

[7] Letter of 14 Oct. 1839, HBRS 6:216.

land of sufficient extent to plant each 10 Bushels of Potatoes; the same spirit of enterprise extends, though less generally to the Gulf of Georgia and De Fuca's Straits. . . . [8]

Farther north the Indians were keeping to the bad old ways. When the steamer *Beaver* put into Bute Inlet this year to trade for the season's furs, not a single Indian came out to greet her. The entire population had been exterminated in a raid by the dreaded Yucultas from around Johnstone Strait. Farther north war flared between the Haidas and the Tsimpseans and "engrossed the energies of both parties" to the detriment of the fur trade.

Civilizing influences were however spreading. Important were the missionary endeavours of the Roman Catholic fathers who had so recently arrived from Red River. Of the two "Black Robes", as the Indians called them, Father Demers was a gifted linguist who quickly picked up the Indians' own languages and preached the gospel to them in their own tongues. Poor Father Blanchet lacked any such facility, and therefore directed his labours chiefly to the spiritual care of the HBC's French-Canadians. Upon occasion, however, Blanchet also had to work with the Indians and, out of the limitations imposed by his ignorance of their tongues, he made a notable invention — "The Catholic Ladder". This was a great vertical scroll, hung from a tree or pole. On it ascending horizontal bars and rows of dots marked off the centuries and years between the creation of Adam and Eve (at the foot of the chart) and the Mission to the Columbia (at the top). Along the line of ascent special symbols marked the building of the Tower of Babel, Solomon's Temple, the Coming of the Wise Men to Bethlehem, Calvary, and the spread of the Protestant Heresy. In a report to the Archbishop of Quebec, Father Blanchet told of how he preached at Fort Nisqually this year, using his newly-devised Catholic Ladder:

These poor natives showed themselves very eager to hear tell of the *Great Master*. Petit-vieux served as interpreter, and translated into their language, the Chinook jargon, of which I made use in instructing them. I explained to them the creation of the world, the fall of the first man, the promise of a Saviour, His birth and death, the love of Jesus Christ for the human race. All this explained with the help of pictures

[8] *Loc. cit.*

and of a historico-chronological chart sketched on paper, and suited to catch the eye of savages, seemed vividly to stimulate their attention.[9]

So impressed were the Indians by the Ladder that they were soon clamouring for copies of it to bear away with them. For the next half century the Catholic Ladder printed on linen would be part of the equipment of the Roman Catholic missionaries up and down the coast and far into the Interior. The effectiveness of the device was not lost on the American Protestant missionaries, usually so ineffective in dealing with the Indians. In a short time they were trying to make Methodists and Presbyterians out of the natives by employing a Protestant Ladder.

This was the year that A. C. Anderson, one of the HBC clerks in New Caledonia, made the first census of the Indian population there, district by district. Many years later Father Morice was to maintain that Anderson very badly underestimated the population. Anderson, however, was a highly intelligent person, and his figures merit consideration. They do give us some indication of just how sparse the Indian population of New Caledonia was.

	Men	Women	Children	Total
Fort McLeod	49	40	113	202
Fort St. James	62	79	147	288
Fort Fraser	98	87	100	285
Fort George	75	50	62	187
Fort Alexandria	292	233	232	747
Fort Chilcotin	224	132	244	600
Fort Connolly	28	30	87	137
Fort Babine	69	47	65	181
Grand Total				2627[10]

Twenty years earlier Daniel Harmon had placed the Indian population of New Caledonia at not more than five thousand.[11] In the interim the diseases brought by the white men had almost halved the population.

[9] *Famed Quebec Mission*, p. 40. A reproduction of the Catholic Ladder will be found facing p. 44 of this work.

[10] Morice, *History of Northern Interior of B.C.*, p. 191.

[11] *Sixteen Years in the Indian Country*, p. 282.

1840

Fort Langley burns — Fort Stikine established in Alaskan Panhandle — Fort Taku — Chief Factor Douglas — An international "neck-tie party" — McLoughlin frustrates French-Canadian colonization on the Columbia — Death of the great Chief Kwah.

On April 22nd of this year Chief Trader James Douglas left Fort Vancouver for Alaska to secure for the HBC its rights obtained under the agreement made with the Russians the previous year. En route overland to Fort Nisqually on Puget Sound, from where his party was to travel north on the *Beaver*, he received profoundly disturbing news:

> A few miles below the [Cowlitz] Farm we were joined by an express from Langley conveying the disastrous intelligence of the total destruction of that establishment by fire during the night of [April 11]. It broke out in the forge, consumed building after building with rapid and relentless fury unquelled by the efforts to arrest its course until the Fort lay a waste, reduced to a heap of smoking ruins, the trade Goods, a Bundle of Furs and seven barrels of salmon were alone rescued from the flames; houses, utensils, furniture, a large stock of salt provisions and all the seasoned barrel staves for the approaching fishery have fallen a sacrifice to the devouring element.[1]

The loss of the salted provisions was a shock for Douglas since he had counted upon them to feed his men while setting up a new post for the Company on the Taku River.

Late on the afternoon of April 30th, Douglas with the *Beaver* arrived at what had been Fort Langley. The next day he wrote in his diary:

Mr. Yale had already erected a stockade enclosing a space of 100 feet

[1] Herman A. Leader, ed., "Douglas Expeditions, 1840-41", *OHQ* 32 (1931): 5-6.

by 70 within which he resides with the persons and property of the establishment in perfect security. The work of destruction has been fully fearfully complete extending to every part of the premises of which a few blackened stumps alone remain. The natives committed a few petty thefts during the confusion and darkness of the night on which the fire occurred, but they offered no further molestation.[2]

To help Yale, Douglas remained a few days while his own men built a bastion to strengthen the defences, and squared timber for construction of the new buildings. Then the *Beaver* churned off on its northward journey.

A couple of days later she was at Cape Mudge where Douglas paused to trade with the Comox Indians, "numerous, saucy, and unreclaimed by the discipline or influence of the whites". On May 14th, Douglas reached the HBC's northern depot at Fort Simpson. May 20th found him off the mouth of the Stikine River but, when he went ashore to take over the fort under the terms of the 1839 agreement, the local Russian officer protested he had no authority to make the transfer. Going on to the Russian capital at Sitka, Douglas quickly got things straightened out, and on June 1st he formally raised the Union Jack over Fort St. Dionysius, which now became the HBC's Fort Stikine.

The Russians, who had maintained a considerable force at Fort St. Dionysius, were startled when Douglas left it in the care of just two clerks (McLoughlin's son-in-law William Glen Rae, and John McLoughlin Jr., the elder son of the Chief Factor) along with the usual small party of a dozen or so labourers — but such was the parsimony which allowed the HBC to make a profit where the Russians could find none.

Life at Fort Stikine proved far from attractive for its new occupants. Later McLoughlin's daughter was to recall:

... my husband and myself stayed in Stickeen a year in 1840. It was a miserable place, a Russian establishment. There were only flat rocks and no trees around close — within half a mile; just bare rocks. The Indians were very troublesome. They [the two clerks] never opened the gate to receive more than one Indian at a time to trade. The water was not close by the Fort there. We had a trough made with two

2 *Ibid.*, p. 14.

boards for half a mile to bring in water. When the Indians got drunk or in a bad humour they would destroy the trough so that we could not get water. It was a terrible place.[3]

While the Raes and young McLoughlin were enduring this life at Fort Stikine, James Douglas with the *Beaver* was farther north where the Taku River flows into Taku Inlet. A suitable site being found about ten miles south of the river's mouth, Douglas' men began building a new establishment there. By August 5th construction was complete, the flag raised and, with suitable ceremony, the new post given its official name of Fort Durham, after the Earl of Durham, Governor-General of the two eastern colonies which then constituted Canada. The name of Fort Durham never really took, however, and almost invariably the new establishment was referred to as Fort Taku. In charge of Fort Taku, Douglas left Dr. J. Kennedy, assisted by Roderick Finlayson.

Back in Fort Vancouver at the beginning of October, James Douglas found a glittering reward awaiting him: his commission as a Chief Factor in the service of the Hudson's Bay Company. To realize what that promotion meant for Douglas, we have the recollections of an old HBC hand about the glory which attended a Chief Factor:

This exalted functionary was lord paramount; his word was law; he was necessarily surrounded by a halo of dignity, and his person was sacred, so to speak. He was dressed every day in a suit of black or dark blue, white shirt, collars to his ears, frock coat, velvet stock, and straps to the bottom of his trousers. When he went out of doors he wore a black beaver hat worth forty shillings. When travelling in a canoe or boat he was lifted in or out of the craft by the crew; he still wore his beaver hat, but it was protected by an oiled silk cover, and over his black frock coat he wore a long cloak made of the Royal Stuart tartan, lined with scarlet or dark blue coating. The cloak had a soft Genoa velvet collar which was fastened across by mosaic gold clasps and chains. . . . Salutes were fired on his departure from the fort and on his return.[4]

[3] Mrs. Harvey, "Life of John McLoughlin", PAC, MG29, B35, Vol. 3:13 (Bancroft transcript).

[4] "Recollections of Joseph William McKay". See Walbran, *B.C. Coast Names*, p. 330.

Moreover, as a Chief Factor, Douglas would have his income doubled.

Back on the Columbia, Douglas learned that the American population had been substantially augmented by the arrival that spring of the ship *Lausanne*, bearing fifty-one additional men, women and children from the United States. What Douglas did not learn was that the passage of these new immigrants had been subsidized by the American government out of its Secret Service funds. (Only after the international boundary was established in 1846 was that secret let out.) [5]

This year there were disquieting rumours of imminent war between Britain and the United States, not concerning the western boundary but arising out of the "Aroostook War" between Maine and New Brunswick. Let war once break out and the notorious American "mountain men" might descend on Fort Vancouver. Filled with worry, John Tod wrote to his friend Edward Ermatinger back East:

In the Snake Country, there are a band of real tatterdimalions who, on the first intimation of hostilities, will undoubtedly pour down with the speed of blood hounds on Vancouver, which, from its defenceless state would not but fall an easy prey to their Rifles. [6]

A clash might be coming between the British and the Americans, but McLoughlin seized upon an episode this year to show the Indians that the whites of either nation stood united when attacked by the red man. Kenneth McKay, out to trade for salmon with the Indians, while sleeping in his tent was murdered by Whalaki, a slave from the west coast of Vancouver Island, and an accomplice from the Cape Flattery district. Dr. McLoughlin lost no time in despatching Dr. Tolmie with a punitive force. Whalaki was killed in an ambush, and his accomplice taken prison to Fort George (Astoria). Here an international "neck-tie party" was held, partly made up of Americans whom McLoughlin had recruited from the Willamette colony, and partly of HBC men. For a rope they used a deepsea sounding line obligingly lent by an American brig. Every-

[5] Bancroft, *History of Oregon*, I: 177.

[6] PAC, Ermatinger Papers, Letter of 1 March 1841.

body present took hold of the line and pulled as the unfortunate Indian rose off the ground.

This year the Hudson's Bay Company pushed ahead with its plan to promote British immigration to the Columbia to counterbalance the growing influx of Americans. The nearest source for British nationals was the Red River Colony adjacent to Fort Garry, so Chief Factor Finlayson, in command there, offered substantial inducements to get suitable persons to migrate to the Columbia. The HBC was prepared to put them on farms and allow them half of the profit. Moreover, the Company would build houses for immigrants, provide cattle, sheep and horses, and let them have necessary farming equipment without any advance payment. Each family would be allocated one hundred acres and, once the United States had agreed to the Columbia River boundary and a British government on the north side of the river could provide the necessary legal mechanism for the transfer of land, the new settlers would be given title to their holdings.

Although Simpson and Finlayson pushed through this policy established by the Governor and Committee in London, there was no cooperation on the West Coast. Knowing what we now do about McLoughlin's secret hope to see the country become American,[7] we need not be surprised to find that he actively sought to discourage this proposed British immigration. Writing to London in November of this year McLoughlin declared:

> I regret to see you intend to send 20 families to this place and I hope after the receipt of mine of March last you will have altered your intention as we have no Prairie Land on the Cowelitz [River] on which to place them and as to placing them on wood Land it would be worse than useless as our timber is so heavy. . . . [8]

The words were something less than honest. As we have seen, considerable clearing had already been done at Cowlitz portage, and other suitable agricultural land was readily available nearby. All that was needed was for McLoughlin to get work crews clearing

[7] See under 1832.

[8] HBRS 6:17.

land for the people who would be coming from what is now Manitoba.

One final event of this year must be chronicled. Sometime this spring there died at Fort St. James, aged about eighty-five, Kwah, paramount chief of the Carrier Indians. A great leader of his people, a man of unusual intelligence and character, Kwah while still a young man had assumed the chieftainship in consequence of his success in leading an avenging expedition against the Chilcotins. Sensing the approach of death, Kwah gave specific directions for his burial. His people were to bury him on the bank of Stuart River, just below where it leaves Stuart Lake. With him they were to bury his ceremonial rattle which he would use, when he saw the salmon coming upstream, to signal the happy news to his people.

1841

Chief Factor Black shot down at Fort Kamloops — Search for his murderer — Father Demers preaches at Fort Langley — McLoughlin welcomes Commodore Wilkes, U.S.N. — Sir George Simpson inspects the HBC's forts — Meets the Russians at Sitka — Sinclair brings settlers overland from Red River.

This year opened with the veteran Samuel Black in command of the HBC's Fort Kamloops. In the years since his epic exploration of northern British Columbia in 1824, he had been in charge of various interior posts of the Columbia Department and, in 1837, since he was to be in charge of all these inland posts during Dr. McLoughlin's furlough, he had been promoted to Chief Factor.

By 1841 Black was into his sixties, mellow, relaxed, living contentedly with his Indian wife and their children in his dilapidated fort at the junction of the North and South Thompson Rivers. In this same year Donald Manson wrote from Fort Kamloops:

... the Fort here [is] in a wretched state of defence, the house & store being completely rotten, and were it not for the number of Props, placed against them, they would have been down long ere now, the Fort Pickets and Bastions are even worse than this, and I am really astonished that any Gentleman would have allowed an Establishment to go to ruin in this manner, without doing something towards renewing it.[1]

Black's relations with the Indians were generally very good, but this year he had been having a little trouble with a chief whom the French-Canadians, because of his usually peaceful temperament, had named Tranquille. The trouble with Tranquille had been very

[1] Letter to Gov. Simpson, 6 Dec. 1841. HBRS 18:233.

minor. Another Indian, Capot Blanc, had bought a gun at the fort and had left it with Black, requesting him to trade it for him to get a horse. Then Tranquille had arrived and declared that Capot Blanc intended him to have the gun. Black, keeping his agreement with Capot Blanc, had refused to turn over the weapon. Angry, Tranquille had retired to a camp at Pavilion on the Fraser River and there he died. On his deathbed he said to his followers: "Go to Mr. Black, he has a good heart, and tell him I am sorry for what passed between us, and ask him to send men to have me buried according to the white man's custom." The message was carried to Fort Kamloops, and Black sent two of his men, Edouard and Fallerdeau, to see the late Tranquille buried in the dignity of a coffin.

At this point all should have ended well. Unfortunately a little while later a nephew of Tranquille, losing his temper in a quarrel with his mother, struck her and she retaliated with a retort that he was brave enough to strike an old woman, but not brave enough to revenge the death of his uncle. (Some Indians had attributed Tranquille's death to "bad medicine" used against him by Black.)[2] Stung to fury, the young man headed for the fort. Here Black received him hospitably and, since the day was cold, ordered a fire lit in the Indian Hall and invited him and two other young Indians to come in. The date was February 8th.

As the afternoon wore on, the other two Indians took their departure but Tranquille's nephew, maintaining it was too cold for him to return home, remained and announced that he intended to stay overnight at the fort. As dusk was falling, Chief Factor Black had occasion to pass through the Indian Hall on his way to his own quarters. Stepping through the doorway into the room where his wife and children were, Black was shot in the back by the Indian

---

[2] For accounts of the murder of Black and the pursuit of his slayer, see John Tod, *History of New Caledonia*; Chief Trader Archibald McDonald's letter to McLoughlin, 17 Feb. 1841, in HBRS 6:247-49; and Archibald McKinlay, *Narrative of a Chief Trader of the HBC*, PABC transcript E-E-M21, pp. 10-16.

Some accounts make the murderer the son of Tranquille, but in view of the importance of matrilineal descent among the Indians, Tod and Dr. Mc-Loughlin in a letter of this year are probably right in identifying him as a nephew. In the account which follows, all three above sources have been utilized.

and died instantly. Terrified by the sudden murder, the Company's engagés fled from the fort.

On March 2nd Chief Trader John Tod, in command at Fort Alexandria, learned of the murder. We have his report of the action he then took:

> We left for Kamloops, snow 3 feet deep. With Mr. Ogden [Chief Factor Peter Skene Ogden] who was in charge of N[ew] Caledonia I had not had time to communicate; & the case being a desperate one, started with 3 others — on horse back. We pushed on as rapidly as possible; about 250 miles, and we got there on the 3rd day! Near to the fort I told my men to keep behind & that I would go on alone. Reaching Kamloops I found the body of Mr. Black lying unburied. The laborers — French Canadians, had fled, some to Vancouver; some to Colvile & so on.
>
> I found his wife & family, and an Indian named St. Paul [also known as Lolo] in charge of the fort, awaiting some one to arrive. I buried the remains of Mr. Black; took an inventory of the goods in the fort & found everything all right; nothing had been meddled with.[3]

Tod had scarcely completed this business when an HBC clerk named McLean, despatched from Fort Colvile by Chief Trader Archibald McDonald, arrived on the scene. Countermanding McLean's instructions to abandon the fort and transfer the furs and trade goods to Fort Okanagan, Tod returned to his own post. After Tod's departure, McLean was joined by a punitive force of some twenty men, led by Archibald McKinlay and Francis Ermatinger, whom Dr. McLoughlin had despatched from Fort Vancouver. McLean, using the rough tactics which got him a very bad name, mercilessly harried the Indians in the Kamloops district but was totally unable to intimidate them into handing over the murderer. Finally McLean was taken off the case and John Tod put in charge. At this point we may return to Tod's narrative:

> Doctor McLoughlin sent a dispatch to me requesting that I should take charge of Kamloops with a force of only five men, and a young gentleman, a Mr. Cameron was to be my assistant — a native. I was to

---

[3] Tod, *History of New Caledonia*, pp. 7-8. In these reminiscences written in 1878, Tod says that he learned of the murder in February, but in a postscript dated March 2nd, hurriedly added to his letter of March 1st to Edward Ermatinger (PAC, Ermatinger Papers), Tod says he has just received the news.

make no attempt to catch the murderer until the fall, on the arrival of the large party from the other side of the mountains, — that I should then be sufficiently enforced to act.

I was determined to act upon my own responsibility; at once I returned all the horses taken from the Indians by McLean, & finding out the value of their property destroyed, paid the Indians for it — to their great amazement. This occupied 2 weeks; the Indians were unable to understand me. I called them together, made a speech, telling them that I would have the murderer, but would not harm one of them. That if they would only tell me where he was, they should have a reward. A few days later an Indian came to me at midnight & said he was ready to guide us to the place of concealment of the murderer. "Very well, says I, there's your reward". The Indian replied, "No, the Indians told me that I was to take nothing, but that I ought to give up the murderer.[4]

Tod swiftly despatched a party, conducted by this guide, to bring in the murderer. Unfortunately the first attempt to take the man failed, though one of his children was captured. A second attempt was more successful. Abandoned by the little band which had been protecting him, the wanted Indian, camping for the night near Cache Creek, was captured by an HBC force headed by Cameron and St. Paul [Lolo]. En route back to Fort Kamloops, when the posse was crossing a river (presumably the Thompson near Savona), the prisoner contrived to capsize their canoe and make his escape. Unfortunately for the murderer, when he staggered ashore he found himself confronted by the young chief Nicholas [or Nicola], who all along had supported the whites. Desperately the murderer begged for life, but Nicholas opened fire, hitting him in the hand. In a last vain bid for freedom, the murderer plunged back into the river. He was immediately finished off by the guns of Cameron and his party.

This year, for the first time, Christianity was preached to the Indians at Fort Langley. On a mission to announce "the divine name of Jesus" to new tribes north of the Columbia, Father Demers had arrived at Fort Langley around the beginning of September. He was ceremoniously received by James Murray Yale, the clerk in command, who broke out the fort's flag and fired a salute with the cannon. Outside the fort were crowded five or six hundred Indians,

---

[4] *Ibid.*, pp. 10-11.

nearly all of whom had heard praise of the "Black Robes", and some of whom had picked up a smattering of Christianity from converted tribes. With difficulty Father Demers worked his way through these ardent welcomers and entered the gate at Fort Langley.

Later in a letter to the Bishop of Juliopolis, in charge at Red River, Father Demers gave some details of his splendidly successful mission to the Cowichans and adjacent tribes:

> The assemblies were held a short distance from the fort in a low and level prairie. I was continually surrounded by fifteen to sixteen hundred natives of an age to understand my instructions, and all listened with an incredible attention and fervor. God blessed us altogether; for on the 3rd of September I baptized ninety-nine children, on the 4th I baptized fifty-six of them, and on the 5th I baptized 136 of them. On the 6th I was surrounded by a multitude which I can estimate, without exaggeration, at 3,000 persons, and I baptized seventy-one children. ... All these nations had forgotten their hatreds and their projects of vengeance to come and listen in common to the holy word.[5]

The Indians laid their weapons at the feet of Father Demers, then abandoned them altogether. Indians from more distant areas hastened to Fort Langley when they learned of the coming of the priest. New arrivals laid before him gifts of beaver skins and salmon then listened while, using the six-foot scroll of the Catholic Ladder, he told them of God's creation of the world, the coming of Christ, the Heaven that lies beyond Death, the seven "medicines" (sacraments of the Church) which open to all, white or brown, the way to salvation.

On September 3rd, Father Demers baptized 99 children. Each succeeding day brought new baptisms until by September 8th the good priest had christened no less than 758 children and was nursing an aching arm.

The ardor for the heavenly things did not abate one bit; the evening hours were not spent in useless conversations. Until eleven o'clock one heard the chant of canticles and, at intervals, the loud voice of a chief uttering edifying speeches to his people. They made the sign of the cross; they repeated what they had understood and retained of the

---

[5] *Famed Quebec Mission*, p. 105.

explanations of the historic ladder. In short, there was universal zeal, ardor, enthusiasm.[6]

The time had come for Father Demers to return to his base. Before he left he distributed, not for the first time, crosses and religious medals. He promised his converts that he would return and, his heart exultant, took his departure.

Meanwhile there had been significant events on the lower Columbia. Meeting on February 18th in the Willamette valley a group of settlers, chiefly American, elected a "legislative committee", and a judge who was to act in accordance with the laws of the State of New York. If nothing came of this move, it was not because of any hostility on the part of Dr. McLoughlin, who certainly did not wish to see the laws of Canada extended to his domain. Several weeks later he could not conceal his anti-British feelings when writing to Edward Ermatinger:

> ... what is the constitution of Canada — It is a Despotism in Disguise ... the time must come when even the House of Lords in Britain will be Elected — and if this had been the case you may Depend that she would never have spent such Vast treasures and shed such Oceans of Blood in Wars Worse than Useless.[7]

Presumably McLoughlin counted among the wars "worse than useless" those in which British forces had twice driven invading American armies out of Canada.

Inspired by this animus against the government whose representative he was,[8] Dr. McLoughlin was in no way saddened by the arrival this spring of an American naval squadron under the command of Commodore Charles Wilkes, U.S.N. First to arrive was the flagship U.S.S. *Vincennes* accompanied by U.S.S. *Porpoise* which, finding the weather bad off the Columbia, headed for the Strait of Juan de Fuca and on May 2nd came to anchor in Port Discovery on the

[6] *Ibid.*, p. 107.

[7] Letter of 27 Feb. 1841. PAC, Ermatinger Papers, pp. 242-43.

[8] McLoughlin was fully aware of his responsibilities here. In a letter of 20 Nov. 1845, he could speak of "my imperative duty as superintendent of the only British settlement in this part of the world, and through which alone the British Government retains any hold upon this Country. . . . " E. E. Rich, ed., *The Letters of John McLoughlin from Fort Vancouver to the Governor and Committee, Third Series, 1844-46*, HBRS 7 (London, 1944) : 144.

south shore of the Strait. Constituted as the "United States Exploring Expedition", Wilkes' squadron had, in the preceding three years, charted 1600 miles of Antarctica and done useful work among the islands of the Pacific. Now Wilkes commenced the "exploration" of Puget Sound. Various of his officers were sent to undertake the "exploration" of the Columbia River up to Fort Colvile and the region between Spokane and Yakima. While these "explorations" were being conducted in waters thoroughly charted by Vancouver and lands intimately known to the HBC, Commodore Wilkes received every possible cooperation from Dr. McLoughlin. To McLoughlin's very eager assistance he paid consequent tributes, admitting "my expressions are few in comparison with the numerous kindnesses we all received."[9]

Culminating these kindnesses was a grand banquet given for Wilkes and his officers at Fort Vancouver. Present was Governor Sir George Simpson, fresh from receiving the accolade at Buckingham Palace. The atmosphere at the dinner seems to have been a trifle strained, Wilkes sensing that Simpson regarded him with some suspicion.[10] Sir George had good grounds for doing so. Subsequently he wrote to London:

> Commodore Wilkes was by no means communicative on the object of these surveys and examinations; but I collected from a very intelligent and confidential member of the expedition, that it was the intention of Captain Wilkes to recommend strongly to his Government, to claim the whole of the territory on the shores of the Northern Pacific; from the Mexican northern boundary in Latitude 42° to the Russian southern boundary in Latitude 54°40'.[11]

Wilkes' surveys and examinations in the area were, in fact, simply reconnaissances in preparation for any war in which the U.S.A. might seek to enforce this outrageous claim.

Various considerations had brought Governor Simpson to the

---

[9] Charles Wilkes, *Narrative of the United States Exploring Expedition During the Years 1838, 1839, 1840, 1841, 1842* (Philadelphia, 1845), V:135.

[10] Bancroft, *Northwest Coast*, II:681.

[11] Glyndwr Williams, ed., *London Correspondence Inward from Sir George Simpson 1841-42*, HBRS 29 (London, 1973):145. Simpson's information was correct. In his report to Congress next year, Wilkes strongly argued for American annexation right up to Alaska.

Pacific Coast this year for the first time since 1828-29. He wanted to see for himself the workings of the pact which he had negotiated with the Russian American Company. He needed first-hand knowledge of the resources, operations and potential of the newly founded Puget's Sound Agricultural Company. He hoped to thresh out a growing number of differences of opinion between himself and McLoughlin. And, in any case, Simpson made a point of being active in the field, of personally visiting the Company's far-flung posts and of basing his policies upon his own direct knowledge.

Setting out from Fort Garry early in July Simpson, travelling at his usual fantastic speed, arrived at Fort Colvile on August 18th, having covered 1900 miles in 47 days of actual travel. On this trip he had decided against the customary northern route via Jasper's House, Athabasca Pass and Boat Encampment, then down the Columbia. Instead, boldly striking out in a more direct line, he entered the Rockies by way of the Bow River and was conducted by Peechee, his Indian guide, across the Continental Divide by way of Simpson Pass. From there he travelled by way of Red Rock or Sinclair Canyon to the headwaters of the Columbia, crossed to the Kootenay River at Canal Flats, left the Kootenay to follow the Moyie River cutoff, and then worked overland to Fort Colvile.

Allowing himself only a couple of days rest at Colvile, Simpson started down the Columbia on August 20th. Brief stops were made at Fort Okanagan, Fort Walla Walla and the American missionary station at "Whaspicum". Finally, on August 25th, Simpson arrived at Fort Vancouver.

A week sufficed for Sir George to attend to the business at Fort Vancouver, including sniffing out the real purpose of the two American warships anchored off the fort. Then he was on his way again, down the Columbia, then up the Cowlitz, en route to Fort Nisqually on Puget Sound. En route, Simpson could not help but note a sad change since his earlier visit:

When I descended the Cowlitz, in 1828, there was a large population along its banks; but since then the intermittent fever, which commenced its ravages in the following year, had left but few to mourn for those that fell. During the whole of our day's course, till we came upon a small camp in the evening, the shores were silent and solitary, the deserted villages forming melancholy monuments of the generation that had passed away.[12]

At Fort Nisqually, home base of the *Beaver*, Sir George found the little paddlewheeler ready to carry him upcoast for his rendezvous with the Russian governor of Alaska. Originally both Chief Factors McLoughlin and Douglas had been expected to make the trip with Simpson. Most regrettably in the light of later developments McLoughlin had begged off, and Douglas alone stood by Simpson's side as the smoke belched out of the tall smokestack, the paddles began to turn, and the long trip north began.

Steaming along the eastern coast of Vancouver Island, the *Beaver* put in at Port McNeill, both to satisfy its insatiable hunger for firewood and to trade with the Indians. Simpson has left us a colourful account of the proceedings:

Stationing himself at the steerage hatchway, Captain McNeill threw down each skin, as he examined it, with its price chalked on it — the equivalents being handed up from below by the two or three men that were in charge of the store. The natives, now that they no longer dare to employ force against the whites, still occasionally resort to fraud, practising every trick and devise to cheat their trader. One favourite artifice is to stretch the tails of land-otters into those of sea-otters. Again, when a skin is rejected as being deficient in size, or defective in quality, it is immediately, according to circumstances, enlarged, or coloured, or pressed to order, and is then submitted, as a virgin article, to the buyer's criticism by a different customer.

... our traffic continued till the following noon; and, meanwhile, such of our men as were not occupied in trading or watching had been cutting wood, which the Indians conveyed on board in their canoes. The furs, amounting in value to about five hundred pounds sterling, consisted of martens, racoons, beaver, bears, lynxes, and both kinds of otters; while the equivalents were blankets, tobacco, vermilion, files, knives, a small quantity of cloth, and only two guns, with a corresponding allowance of ammunition. Generally speaking, the natives were tiresome in their bargaining, and they were ever ready to suspend business for a moment in order to enjoy any passing joke. They appeared, however, to understand the precise length to which they

[12] Sir George Simpson, *Narrative of a Journey Round the World* (London, 1847), I:176. This account was prepared chiefly by Adam Thom, working from the very detailed field journals which Simpson had dictated to his secretaries.

might go in teasing Captain McNeill. They made sad work, by the by, of his name; for, whenever his head showed itself above the bulwarks, young and old, male and female, vociferated, from every canoe, Ma-ta-hell, Ma-ta-hell, Ma-ta-hell — a word which, with the comparative indistinctness of its first syllable, sounded very like a request on their part that their trader might go a great way beyond the engineer's furnace.[13]

While at Port McNeill, the observant Sir George did not fail to note that both the men and women were good physical specimens, with good features — " . . . indeed, the girls were exceedingly pretty". One of the reasons for the striking appearance of these Kwakiutls was that, as yet, they had escaped the ravages of smallpox. Knowing that their good luck could not possibly last much longer, Simpson and his subordinates begged the chiefs to allow them to vaccinate the children. When the chiefs, afraid of the unknown "medicine" of the whites refused, the HBC men did not persist in their offer. They knew that almost any subsequent disaster such as a failure in the salmon run, would almost certainly be blamed on them and their vaccinating.

From Port McNeill the *Beaver* steamed to Fort McLoughlin, close to the present village of Bella Bella. Here Sir George received a report from Charles Ross, the one-time classical scholar who was in charge of the post. Ross must have made a good impression on the Governor, for the next year he got his commission as a Chief Trader. At Fort McLoughlin Sir George first saw the labrets which so disfigured the lower lips of the northern Indian women. But things had changed since Vancouver's crews had recorded their disgust, and Simpson thankfully observed, "This hideous fashion, however, is now wearing out, having been found to be disagreeable to the whites, to whose opinions and feelings the native ladies pay the highest possible respect."[14]

Again the little steamer put to sea, her paddles clunking until two days later she arrived at Fort Simpson, the northern depot of the HBC. Here Chief Trader John Work was in command, banished thither half a dozen years before by a hostile McLoughlin, and

<hr/>

13 *Ibid.*, I : 188, 192-93.
14 *Ibid.*, I : 204-205.

destined to remain there another seven. Sir George was impressed by the cleverness and ingenuity of the local Indians: "They carve steamers, animals, &c. very neatly in stone, wood, and ivory, imitating, in short, every thing that they see, either in reality or in drawings. . . . "[15] One of the Indians was found to prepare very accurate charts of this part of the coast.

Two days later Simpson and the *Beaver* were off Fort Stikine, commanded by John McLoughlin, Jr. (son of the Chief Factor), assisted by a second clerk, Roderick Finlayson. At the more important establishment of Fort Simpson, Work's clerk had been found failing in health and would have to be taken out, leaving the Chief Trader no other officer to assist him. The parsimony of the HBC provided no excess clerks for such contingencies. To provide Work with the needed assistant, some less busy post would have to be reduced to a single officer. Looking at the good job young McLoughlin was doing at Fort Stikine, Simpson felt he could handle the situation without Finlayson's aid. Accordingly, Simpson decided to transfer Finlayson to Fort Simpson. That decision would lead to tragedy a few months later.

Once more the *Beaver* headed northward, this time to Fort Durham at Taku, the most recent of all the forts. Here a storm blew up and, for longer than he had planned, Sir George remained the guest of Dr. Kennedy, the clerk in command of the post. Finally Sir George was en route again, southward now, to Sitka or New Archangel, the capital of Russian America. Four days proved sufficient for Simpson to transact his business with Governor Etolin, four days which Simpson obviously enjoyed. The Governor's wife proved to be a charming and beautiful lady from Finland. French cuisine provided the dishes for the Governor's table. The rooms in his mansion were "handsomely decorated and richly furnished". Simpson, with an eye for beauty and style, was suitably impressed. Meeting together, the two governors agreed that after the end of 1843 both their companies would cease trading in liquor with the Indians.

Little need be said of Simpson's return voyage. Fort Stikine, Fort

15 *Ibid.*, I: 207.

Simpson and Fort McLoughlin were all revisited and, finally, the *Beaver* tied up safely at Fort Nisqually. Here Simpson's attention turned to matters agricultural. With satisfaction he noted not only the flourishing condition of the Puget's Sound Agricultural Company's Nisqually farm with its 4530 sheep and 1000 cattle, but also the amount of good land as yet unused in the area. Here the settlers from the Red River and Britain could be placed. To London he reported:

> Between the head of the Cowelitz River and the shores of Puget Sound, a distance of between 50 and 60 miles, there is a chain of plains ... some of which are well adapted, both for tillage and pasture farms, with a considerable quantity of plain country upon the shores of Puget Sound and Hoods Canal and upon the banks of the Chehalis and Black Rivers, very favourable for settlement. . . . [16]

McLoughlin's dire account of the unsuitability of the land, made probably in his attempt to head off immigration from Red River, was quite unfounded.

Back in Fort Vancouver by October 22nd, Simpson found that in his absence the first party of immigrants to be sent out from the Red River under HBC auspices had already arrived. Led by the stout-hearted, part-Indian James Sinclair, these settlers had departed from Fort Garry on June 3rd. Their progress had been slow as they drove their creaking carts across the prairie. En route they had been overtaken by Governor Simpson, who left at Fort Edmonton explicit directions for Sinclair to use the Athabasca Pass. Disregarding these orders, Sinclair when he left Fort Edmonton had decided to follow the Governor's own example and seek a more southerly way through the mountains. Their carts left behind and their belongings loaded on packhorses, the migrants followed Simpson's route up the Bow River and into the Rockies, though here their guide, Mackipictoon, found them a much superior way through the mountains, that known today as the Whiteman Pass. Pressing onward, they reached the Kootenay River and rejoined the route Simpson had followed a few weeks earlier. Like him, they passed through the frightening Red Rock gorge which today, as Sinclair Canyon, perpetuates the name

[16] Letter of 25 Nov. 1841, HBRS 29:75.

of their leader. After following Simpson's route across south-eastern British Columbia, they were warmly welcomed at Fort Colvile by Chief Trader Archibald McDonald. After a pause to recuperate and enjoy the abundant produce of Fort Colvile's farm, the party pushed on to Fort Vancouver. Here their reception was something less than enthusiastic: not for them the warmth with which Chief Factor McLoughlin welcomed American immigrants. These newcomers, whose allegiance, even if rather nominal, was to the British flag, were merely something Simpson had wished on him. McLoughlin, from the outset, " ... seemed to evade placing these people on the farms at Cowlitz and Nisqually in accordance with their contract with the company."[17] For weeks Sinclair and his people were kept hanging around Fort Vancouver, partly ignored, partly set to labours which were no part of their contract.

Sinclair was deeply annoyed that the fulfillment of the Red River people's contract had been temporarily sidetracked, for as the days wore on and nothing was done to place them on their promised land, the people grew increasingly restless and disgruntled, and Sinclair was in no position to help them further. He had also discovered that there were a number of American sympathizers within Fort Vancouver who had lost no time in making an issue of the Red River settlers' position, and were using every means to turn them to their cause.[18]

Things changed with the return of Governor Simpson. Late in November Sir George crisply reported to London:

On my return from the North West Coast, I found the emigrants from Red River safely arrived at Fort Vancouver, amounting in all to 116 souls. Of these, fourteen heads of families, amounting in all to 77 souls, principally English half-breeds, have been located at Nisqually. ... The remainder of the party, being seven families containing 38 souls, all Canadians [i.e. French-Canadians] and half breeds ... have been placed near the Cowelitz farm. ... [19]

But the damage had been done. When Simpson was off on his journey around the world McLoughlin, far from persuading these

[17] D. Geneva Lent, *West of the Mountains: James Sinclair and the Hudson's Bay Company* (Seattle, 1963), p. 156.

[18] *Ibid.*, p. 157.

[19] HBRS 29:76.

colonists to remain north of the Columbia, encouraged them to cross to the south bank and join the Willamette settlement, where they gradually absorbed the prevailing Americanism. The reports which these new colonists sent back to Red River certainly did not encourage others to follow them. Thus, although the HBC had looked for successive annual migrations from Red River,[20] this first expedition proved the last. McLoughlin's tactics had worked well. When the day came for fixing the international boundary, there would be no British colony of any consequence on the north bank of the Columbia to counterbalance the American colony on the south bank.

On November 25th Sir George Simpson, this time accompanied by McLoughlin, sailed from Fort Vancouver to complete his inspection of the posts under the latter's superintendency. Their first destination was San Francisco, where a few months earlier McLoughlin (on the advice of James Douglas and Alexander Simpson, who had both been there) had established an HBC post. A serious delay of three weeks kept their ship the *Cowlitz* at the mouth of the Columbia, awaiting suitable weather for the dangerous crossing of the bar. This experience was not wasted on Simpson. Remembering the Company's supply ships which had been lost on this same bar, he was strengthened in a belief that the Company's southern depot should be transferred to somewhere more safely and easily accessible to shipping than Fort Vancouver. Finally, on December 30th, Simpson and McLoughlin arrived at Yerba Buena, or San Francisco, to be welcomed by McLoughlin's son-in-law, William Glen Rae, in command of the new post there.

[20] Speaking of Red River in a letter from York Factory, George Gladman commented: "... there can be little doubt many of its present inhabitants will migrate annually to Columbia". Letter of 5 Aug. 1842, PAC, Ermatinger Papers, p. 280.

1842

Conflict between Simpson and McLoughlin — Young Mc-Loughlin's men kill him at Fort Stikine — Simpson's perfunctory investigation — Dr. McLoughlin cries for justice — Ominous American developments — The final burial of Chief Factor Black — Father Demers carries the gospel to New Caledonia.

January saw Governor Sir George Simpson and Chief Factor Dr. John McLoughlin travelling in California. Their interests ranged beyond the business being transacted at the Hudson's Bay Company's little post at Yerba Buena, or San Francisco, and they visited Sonoma, Monterey and Santa Barbara. The feeble and corrupt local government, lacking control and direction from Mexico City, could not long endure. The only question was whether California would pass under the Stars and Stripes or the Union Jack. A British California was a real possibility, since a scheme was afoot to have Mexico transfer California to Britain in payment of her very large debt to the latter country. Simpson hoped for a British California, but his keen sense of realities told him that an American California was much more likely. Still, he wanted to see around the country.

At the end of the month Simpson and McLoughlin, aboard the *Cowlitz*, sailed from Santa Barbara for the Sandwich Islands as Hawaii was still named. Several weeks later they arrived at Honolulu where George Pelly, a cousin of Sir John Pelly, Governor of the Hudson's Bay Company, managed the Company's local post. With his kinsman at the very top of the HBC hierarchy, Mr. Pelly was hardly likely to be given a bad report and deprived of his comfortable berth under the blue Hawaiian skies; still an examination had to be made of the Company's trade there. A month later, all business having been attended to, McLoughlin was ready to sail for Fort

Vancouver aboard the *Vancouver*, while Simpson remained a few more days to call upon the King of Hawaii at his palace at Lahaina on the Island of Maui. From Lahaina, the *Cowlitz* would take Simpson to Sitka whence a Russian vessel would carry him to Siberia for an overland journey to St. Petersburg.

Before McLoughlin and Simpson parted, a most important and serious piece of business had to be attended to. Simpson had now completed his inspection of the "Emperor of the West's" domain, and he was far from satisfied with what he had seen. On March 1st Sir George, to use his own word, "apprised"[1] McLoughlin of the reforms which he must institute.

Part of Simpson's greatness as an administrator lay in an elasticity of mind which kept him viewing things afresh in the light of new circumstances. One major change on the Pacific coast he had already discussed with McLoughlin and proposed to London in a letter from Fort Vancouver. Now, without waiting for confirmation from Governor Pelly and the Committee, he made it the basis of orders to McLoughlin. The Chief Factor's northern forts would have to go. Coastal forts had made sense in the days when the HBC's skippers were disastrously unfamiliar with the complexities of the coastline and when American trading ships might appear in any quarter. But now the Company had Captain McNeill, who knew the coast almost as well as the back of his hand; and the Russian agreement had helped to end all maritime competition. Fort Simpson was to be retained as the HBC's northern depot, but Fort McLoughlin, Fort Stikine and Fort Taku were all to be abandoned. The furs which they acquired could be obtained more cheaply by periodic visits by the steamship *Beaver*. Only one concession was made in Simpson's parting letter which formalized his instructions to McLoughlin:

... as it may be inexpedient to abandon at one and the same time the three posts, say Fort McLoughlin, Stikine and Tacow [Taku], that of Stikine may be continued during the year 1843, and the other two posts ... you will be pleased to abandon. ... [2]

An ironic smile must have played on Simpson's lips as, with polite

[1] HBRS 29:108. For the letter to McLoughlin, see HBRS 6:262-72.
[2] HBRS 6:263.

formality, he wrote that "pleased". He could not but know what a wrench it would be for McLoughlin to see these jewels taken from his diadem.

McLoughlin's designation of the *Beaver* as the replacement for the forts added to McLoughlin's hurt. Ever since she had arrived on the coast, the *Beaver* had been McLoughlin's *bête noire*, the symbol of interference by London and Simpson. Whenever he could lay her up, he had done so. At intervals he had urged she be permanently converted to sail. Several weeks earlier, knowing what Simpson had in mind, McLoughlin had mustered statistics to show that the Company's old sailing ship *Llama* had made more money annually for the HBC than her replacement the *Beaver*. But, just as Simpson was right about the forts, so was he right about the *Beaver*. He had travelled several thousand miles in her in all kinds of weather. He had seen for himself how she could put in at places and extricate herself from situations impossible for a sailing ship. He had seen the tremendous psychological effect she had on the Indians.

One argument that McLoughlin had advanced against the *Beaver* was that she lacked sufficient cargo space. But Sir George had an answer. During his journey to Alaska he had seen that the offshore islands afforded protection which made the coastal waterways of the North-west ideal for tugs and barges. The hundreds of tugs which today pull their tows along the British Columbia coast are the evidence of the prescience of Simpson's vision. But McLoughlin could see nothing in favour of any barge or "lighter". In this parting letter, Simpson firmly overruled all McLoughlin's protests:

> In order to render the *Beaver* Steamer more usefull than she has heretofore been in transport I have to beg that a decked Lighter, of about 150 tons, to be towed by her, be built in the course of the ensuing winter at Nisqually, after a plan & specification that will be forwarded by the *Prince Albert*. This lighter should be considered as part and parcel of the vessel, to accompany her everywhere. . . . [3]

Elsewhere in this letter of instructions, Simpson acted on his entirely justified conclusion that the losses and delays caused by the

---

[3] *Ibid.*, p. 264. In fact, through evasion and delay, McLoughlin managed at last to get this project shelved.

bar at the mouth of the Columbia (not to mention the long journey upriver to Fort Vancouver) required the transfer of the Company's southern depot to some more safely accessible spot. The southern shore of Vancouver Island appeared to Simpson the logical place. He already saw that Britain might not win the Columbia River as the Anglo-American boundary and, in that case, the 49th parallel might well become the border. What better way to secure at least a deflection of that boundary line southwards through the Strait of Juan de Fuca, and so to preserve Vancouver Island entire for Britain, than to have a major HBC post in existence on the north shore of the Strait of Juan de Fuca? Accordingly, Sir George instructed McLoughlin:

> ... I have pointed out the expediency of forming a depôt as early as possible at the Southern end of Vancouver's Island. . . . I have now to request the favor that you will take the necessary steps to have the Southern end of Vancouver's Island very particularly examined in the course of the ensuing Summer, in order that a proper place may be selected. . . . [4]

But Dr. McLoughlin, comfortable in his headquarters at Fort Vancouver, was not interested in moving the depot elsewhere. Not that McLoughlin was opposed to a new fort on Vancouver Island! But he wanted it built at the northern end where, with the other forts he had built, it would constitute the final link in a chain of roughly equidistant establishments extending from the Columbia River to the northern end of the Alaskan Panhandle. But Simpson had decided against any fort on northern Vancouver Island for the same reasons that he was abandoning Forts McLoughlin, Taku and Stikine.

There was one final twist of the knife. Simpson had decided that McLoughlin's son-in-law had made a poor job of running the San Francisco post. Coolly he ordered the post abandoned by the autumn of 1843.

Angered by Simpson's letter, McLoughlin retorted with one of his own written the same day. In it he unfairly and illogically argued that Simpson had not decided upon the closure of the northern forts

[4] *Ibid.*, p. 263.

in consequence of his tour of them, but had arrived from the East with the scheme preconceived:

It seems to me by your mentioning that the plan for a lighter is to come by the *Albert*, that it must have been determined, before you left London, that Ft. Durham [Taku], Stikine & Ft. McLoughlin were to be abandoned, and the business of these places carried on by the Steamer. . . . [5]

This aspersion on Simpson's good faith may have given some satisfaction to McLoughlin, but it helped him not at all and only added to the growing hostility between the two men.

As McLoughlin sailed back towards Fort Vancouver, anger must have swept his soul when he thought of how so much of what he had created was now being dismantled by Simpson. He probably did not feel any better when he recalled how in Honolulu Simpson, aware that McLoughlin's intransigent conservatism and growing incompetence threatened future trouble, had urged him to retire. To McLoughlin, Sir George had held out the inducement that he would be put "on the footing of the most favored Chief Factor who had up to that period retired from the service."[6]

In mid-April the *Cowlitz* arrived at Sitka with Simpson, and began to unload the goods which she had brought as part of the new agreement between the Russians and the HBC. When she was ready to sail with other supplies for Fort Taku and Fort Stikine, Governor Etolin kindly provided a Russian steamer to tow the *Cowlitz* to these two posts. Simpson, with time to spare, decided to use the opportunity to take a second look at these posts[7] which McLoughlin was so opposed to closing.

On April 25th the Russian steamer, with the *Cowlitz* in tow, arrived at Fort Stikine. Immediately it was apparent to Simpson's party that something was very seriously wrong at the fort. Both the British and Russian flags were flying at half-mast, and young McLoughlin, the officer in command, was not at the wharf to greet

[5] *Ibid.*, p. 275.

[6] Simpson to Governor Pelly. HBRS 7:lix.

[7] Perhaps in consequence of this second visit, Simpson extended the life of Fort McLoughlin and Fort Taku until 1843, and permitted Fort Stikine to survive. (*v.* HBRS 29:166n.)

them. Instead, a solitary man came out through the fort gate to meet the new arrivals as they came ashore. From this man and his skulking fellows Simpson got the news. On the night of April 20th-21st, Mr. John McLoughlin had been murdered — shot in the breast by one of his own men, whom the others indicated was probably Urbain Hereux.

Taking sworn depositions from Thomas McPherson, Philip Smith, Benone Fleury and George Heron, Simpson found that they agreed in their story: on the night of the murder McLoughlin, roaring drunk, had been terrorizing his men and his slaying had been an act of self-preservation. Simpson considered the account in the light of what he knew about the character of the murdered man.

Although young John McLoughlin's conduct of his post had appeared satisfactory to Simpson on his earlier visit in 1841, the young man previously had a decidedly poor record. After being brought up near Montreal by his great-uncle, the young man had been sent to Europe to study medicine under the supervision of his father's brother, a successful medical practitioner in France. Here he had won golden opinions; but some gross misconduct, the nature of which is now unknown, made his uncle refuse to have anything more to do with him, and he returned to Montreal in disgrace. Entrusted with money there, he showed such a prodigal thriftlessness that the great-uncle who had cared for him in boyhood washed his hands of him. Chief Factor McLoughlin, learning of his son's misbehaviour, turned against him but at length relented and offered him one last chance. Failing to use this final opportunity, the wild young man had plunged deeply into debt. Finally he joined an expedition being assembled by an eccentric unbalanced character, James Dickson, who styled himself "Liberator of the Indian Nation" and was recruiting part-Indian sons of HBC officers. When Sir George Simpson began manoeuvring to disrupt Dickson's scheme and prevent him from reaching the Red River, he secured the defection of young John McLoughlin by offering him a post as a clerk and surgeon in the Company's service. When McLoughlin accepted, Simpson sent him out to the Columbia to serve under his father's supervision. Entry into the HBC service seemingly had marked a turning-point. From that time until his death, the son had discharged his duties creditably. He had won a reputation as a competent fur trader, though admittedly a martinet in the handling of his men.

With this knowledge of the dead man's background, Simpson concluded that, in the loneliness of Stikine, young McLoughlin had reverted to the wildness of his earlier years. He accepted, without cross-examination, the sworn statements already mentioned. A cursory look around the fort persuaded Simpson that the furs had not been properly cared for and that the fort's books were in disorder. Two days after his arrival, Simpson wrote two letters to Chief Factor McLoughlin informing him of the murder of his elder son. The first, a personal one, has been lost; but the second, the surviving official communication, can only be described as inexcusably cruel. It reads in part:

From all I can collect, the whole conduct & management of Mr. McLoughlin were exceedingly bad, and his violence when under the influence of liquor, which was very frequently the case, amounting to insanity. . . . The occurrence having taken place within Russian Territory, no legal steps against the parties can be taken by me; but my belief is, that any Tribunal by which the case could be tried, would find a verdict of "Justifiable Homicide". . . . The business of the post seems to have been very badly conducted. . . . I consider it due to the people to say, that as a body, their conduct throughout has been fully better than could have been expected under such inhuman treatment as they were frequently exposed to. . . . The accots [accounts], I fear, are in a very irregular state. . . . [8]

Nowhere in this letter, official though it may have been, did Simpson extend a single word of sympathy on behalf of himself or the Company to the bereaved father. These letters were sent south on the *Cowlitz*, after Simpson had placed her mate Dodd in charge of the fort. He himself headed for Sitka on the Russian steamer.

Various factors help to explain the superficial nature of Simpson's investigation. It was, of course, a disgraceful thing to have an officer of the Company murdered by his own men, and the more quickly the incident could be glossed over the better. Since the Russian governor had been so good as to lend him the steamer, it would be

[8] HBRS 6:344-45.

hard to keep her at Stikine during a laboriously thorough examination. If Simpson could arrive at a verdict of his own of "justifiable homicide", he would not need to confront his host, Governor Etolin, with a very difficult decision about how to deal with a British subject charged with murder in a British fort located on land under lease from Russia. The outcome was that, though Hereux was handed over to the Russians at Sitka, he was not placed on trial for murder. Simpson and Etolin attended to some final business and then, on May 23rd, Sir George sailed for Siberia.

Simpson's decisions had been the convenient ones — but they had been profoundly wrong. Upon receipt of Simpson's letters, Dr. McLoughlin swung into action. The men stationed at Fort Stikine, he knew, were some of the worst in the Company's employ — hard cases deliberately banished to the far reaches of the north. Collusion and lies could be expected from them. McLoughlin ordered them transferred, under arrest, to other posts. And he instituted a thorough process of examination and cross-examination. Soon the statements made to Simpson were being refuted and retracted. The real breakthrough came on June 21st, aboard the *Cadboro*, when Kanaquassé, an Iroquois involved in the happenings at Fort Stikine, informed Chief Factor James Douglas that he wished to make a complete statement as to what had really happened.

The truth was very different from what Simpson had so readily accepted. With no officer to support him, young McLoughlin had found it desperately hard to keep on top of the situation at Fort Stikine. To preserve order, he forbad the men to bring Indian women into the fort, or to leave the premises themselves after nightfall. While he slept, however, the men had stolen trinkets from the fort stores and, slipping away from the fort, had purchased with them favours from the Indian women. When McLoughlin sought to prevent such depredations, the men began to plot against him. In the late autumn of 1841 Thomas McPherson, the shoddy semi-illiterate who was the nearest thing to a second-in-command at Fort Stikine, drew up a compact to murder McLoughlin. All but one of the men had signed that pledge. Aware of the plot, the unhappy victim had for months lived in fear of his life, but still intent on carrying out his duties. Despite the appalling strain and loneliness, he had not taken to drink. Confirming evidence was found to clear the dead man of the slanders used by his murderers. Dodd, after checking the fort's inventory against the books, found a total discrepancy of about £11, as small a one as Dr. McLoughlin had encountered in all his years of fur fort audits. His son's allowance of brandy and wine was found to have been scarcely touched in the months since Finlayson had left him. Indians, including the dead man's "wife", testified to Chief Trader Work that young Mc-Loughlin had not been drinking.

As the new evidence came in, McLoughlin despatched it to London, along with a succession of emotional and confused letters of his own. In these he did himself no good by declaring Simpson the murderer of his son in consequence of the Governor's transfer of young McLoughlin's fellow clerk Roderick Finlayson from Stikine to Fort Simpson. London was reluctant to discredit their principal officer by accepting McLoughlin's account instead of his. However, McLoughlin had the evidence and in the end London moved to set the record straight. On 27 September 1843, Governor Pelly and the Committee in London wrote to McLoughlin:

> After a careful perusal of the depositions which you forwarded to us, relative to the fatal occurrence at Stikine, we expressed our opinion on the subject to the Governor [Simpson] and Councils of the Northern and Southern Departments in the following terms. "Along with the Dispatches from Fort Vancouver, we have received copy of a considerable body of additional evidence respecting the atrocious crime committed last year at Fort Stikine. From this evidence it appears that the murder of Mr. John McLoughlin was the result of a preconcerted plot, and that there was no just foundation for the charges of drunkenness and of excessive severity in punishing the men under his command, which were brought against him after his death."[9]

It must have been gall and wormwood for Sir George Simpson to find his report thus discredited by his superiors, especially if their letter was read at the Council board before the assembled Chief Factors and Chief Traders. But Simpson had nothing to fear. On every other point in his war with McLoughlin he had London on his side. In December this year, after the Chief Factor had appealed to

[9] *Ibid.*, pp. 310-11.

London urgently and verbosely against the closing of the northern forts and the use of the steamer *Beaver*, and had brazenly declared that, in defiance of Simpson, he was going to maintain these posts, the Governor and Committee sent a chilling response:

> ... you will take the necessary steps for the abandonment of those posts as soon as convenient after receipt of this, if such has not previously been done: and we hope the *Beaver* will be kept so actively employed that no falling off in the trade will arise from the change.... [10]

The outrage at Fort Stikine had one fortunate consequence. Governor Simpson and Governor Etolin, conferring at Sitka immediately after the murder, decided to advance the date of their agreement to cut off all trade in liquor. The prohibition, coming into force simultaneously this autumn at all posts both British and Russian, and on all their trading vessels, left the Indians with no source for drink. Denied liquor, the Indians denied the white men their furs. For two months the fur trade came to a halt. Finally, to induce the HBC to break the new rule, the Indians at Fort Simpson brought all their best furs, sea otter, beaver and silver fox, and spread them out like a great blanket before the gates of the fort and offered to let the HBC traders have them for their own price, if only they would once more let them have liquor. The HBC men remained adamant. Then the Indians moved up to Sitka with their furs, only to find the Russians equally firm in holding by the new agreement. Finally the natives weakened, at first trading only for ammunition, but gradually returning to trading for blankets, beads, axes and all the rest of the Company's stock.

As a result of this compact between the companies, the Indians were protected from the ravages of alcohol until the influx of miners in 1858 made it impossible any longer to cut them off from intoxicants.

We have noted that one of the orders that Simpson left with McLoughlin required an examination of the southern coast of Vancouver Island to determine a fit site for a depot on the Strait of Juan de Fuca. Actually such a survey had already been made by Captain McNeill in the early summer of 1837. After examining

[10] *Ibid.*, p. 297.

Sooke, Esquimalt and Victoria harbours, McNeill had singled out the last for his most favourable comment. Now, for once obedient to Simpson's instructions, McLoughlin sent Chief Factor Douglas off on the *Cadboro* to make a second, more detailed examination. Critically Douglas examined Port Sy-yousung [Sooke], Whyring [Belcher Bay], Metcho-sin [Metchosin], Is-whoy-malth [Esquimalt], and Camosack or Camosun [Victoria]. Esquimalt did not attract him at all: "its appearance is strikingly unprepossessing, the outline of the country exhibiting a confused assemblage of rock and wood". Very different was his enthusiasm for Camosack where:

... there is a pleasant and convenient site for the establishment, within 50 yards of the anchorage, on the border of a large tract of clear land which extends eastward to Point Gonzalo [Gonzales] ... being the most picturesque and decidedly the most valuable part of the island that we had the good fortune to discover.[11]

Leaving Douglas elated over the site of that future Fort Victoria over which he would one day rule just as Dr. McLoughlin had ruled over Fort Vancouver, let us turn our attention to developments elsewhere. On August 9th of this year the Webster-Ashburton Treaty was signed, establishing the boundary that now exists between Canada and the United States in the area of New Brunswick and along the Great Lakes. It would have defined the international boundary also in the region which the British called Columbia and the Americans Oregon, had it not been for total deadlock here. The British insisted upon the Columbia River line. The Americans equally insistently rejected it.

This year Commodore Wilkes, whose visit in 1841 we noted earlier, submitted his report to the U.S. Secretary of the Navy. In it he urged military action to secure all the territory between California and Alaska. While paying tribute to the "kind and gentlemanly treatment" which the HBC had extended to his expedition, and acknowledging "They afforded every assistance that lay in their power, both in supplies and means of accomplishing our duties," Wilkes had no compunction about robbing them of their lands, and

---

[11] Douglas to McLoughlin, 12 July 1842. Printed as part of *Parliamentary Paper No. 619*, 10 August 1848, p. 6.

had only contempt for the forces with which the Company might defend itself:

> It is true that the servants of the company are bound to bear arms during their term of servitude, but they are without any sort of discipline, few in number, generally of the class of farmers, worn-out Canadians, some few Iroquois Indians, and other tribes from the Canadas, and ill adapted to bear arms. . . . [12]

Very properly he dismissed the Company's "forts" as insignificant:

> In the event of hostilities in this country, the posts, so called, of the Hudson Bay Co. are not to be considered of strength against any force but Indians; they are mere stockades. . . . [13]

Wilkes warned against settling for the 49th parallel:

> The boundary line on the 49° parallel would throw Frasers River without our territory, cut off and leave seven-eighths of the fine island of Vancouver in their possession. . . . [14]

Wilkes declared that the United States could best undertake the military annexation of the Pacific slope from a central base at Walla Walla.

If the American government was not yet quite ready to coerce Britain, by threat of war, into relinquishing the Columbia line, it was because that government, with Yankee shrewdness, realized that time was on their side since it would clearly bring increased American colonization along the Columbia. An estimate of population in the Willamette settlement in February of this year showed some 75-80 French-Canadians established there, as against 50 Americans. But this American element was very considerably strengthened in September by the arrival of the first real overland party of American immigrants, some 140 in number. Their leader, Dr. Elijah White, carried with him a commission (totally invalid under the terms of the 1818 Convention) signed by the American Secretary of War, appointing him Sub-agent of Indian Affairs west of the Rocky Mountains. Writing to London in October, Dr. McLoughlin reported that Dr. White:

[12] "Document: Report on the Territory of Oregon", *OHQ* 12 (1911):298.

[13] *Ibid.*, p. 297.

[14] *Ibid.*, p. 294.

... called a meeting of the Settlers to whom he shewed his Commission ... and told them the United States intended to take them under their protection, which information was received with pleasure by the American Citizens, but with great coolness by the Canadians. It was also reported that American Troops are to be here next year.... [15]

Lieut. Fremont of the U.S. Army was, in fact, busy this summer, surveying the pass leading from the River Platte to Oregon.

Dr. McLoughlin, in direct defiance of his instructions,[16] gave seed and equipment on credit to the newly arrived American settlers.

* * *

This year, at Fort Simpson, a certain Edward Allan conducted a school both for the children of the HBC men at the fort and any others who wished to attend. As the first teacher within the confines of the future province of British Columbia, he deserves to be better known.

* * *

Interesting developments occurred at Fort Kamloops this year. As noted earlier, Samuel Black had let the buildings become shockingly rundown and dilapidated. Taking stock of the situation, Chief Factor Ogden (in command of New Caledonia) and Chief Traders Manson and Tod decided to abandon the old fort and build a new one north-west of the confluence of the rivers there. Squared logs for construction of the new fort were rafted down the North Thompson. The construction was supervised by John Tod, who had recently assumed command of Fort Kamloops.

When the fur brigade from the northern posts reached Fort Kamloops this summer, the body of the murdered Chief Factor Black was exhumed from the grave where, wrapped in a horsehide and enclosed in a coffin of heavy plank, it had lain for over a year. Probably it was Chief Factor Ogden who had decided that the remains of his old friend should join those of other HBC men in the little cemetery at Fort Vancouver. Unfortunately, on the first day out from Fort Kamloops, a sad misadventure occurred. According

[15] HBRS 6:76.
[16] HBRS 29:xxxvi.

to one tradition a packhorse carrying the coffin stumbled and fell
into Monte Creek. According to another story, the coffin was being
gingerly passed along the single log bridging Monte Creek when one
of the Indian carriers slipped, and the Indian and coffin both ended
up in the stream. In any case, the corpse, having been thoroughly
soaked, obviously could not be transported on the long hot journey
south. A hole was dug under the roots of a great ponderosa pine, and
here the remains of Black found their final resting place on the land
which in time would be part of the Bostock Ranch. Not one out of a
hundred thousand British Columbians who today whiz along the
nearby Trans-Canada Highway realizes that in the land he sees to
the south lies the unmarked grave of one of British Columbia's major
explorers.

Leaving Chief Factor Black in his lonely grave, the brigade
pressed on to Fort Vancouver. On its return journey it brought with
it Father Demers who, because of the imminent arrival in Fort
Vancouver of two new missionary priests, Fathers Langlois and
Bolduc, could be spared for a mission to the Carrier nation.

The good father has left us a vivid picture of the discomforts as he
travelled the dusty trails of the Okanagan, the enormously long
packtrain constantly churning up the fine dust:

There is a feverish atmosphere, an oppressive sun, a choking dust, a hill
to climb, a ravine to cross. The first days, especially, one experiences
general discomfort and numerous inconveniences through the irksome
position when on horseback, having on the crupper one's church plate,
bed, household equipment, and even kitchen. Good luck indeed if some
untoward wind does not force us to breathe a thick dust which prevents
us from seeing two rods ahead of us. A low buzz of conversation is
heard with a monotony only broken when passing through a creek or a
river. Then we draw closer together, horses hesitate, men shout, get
angry, jostle each other, tumble; and often wrecks [spills] follow,
exciting general hilarity and reviving conversations for the rest of the
day.[17]

Camp was made early each afternoon. The supplies for the forts
were unloaded from the horses and stacked in orderly piles, and the
horses themselves were turned loose to pasture. In the morning,

[17] *Famed Quebec Mission*, p. 153.

hours were spent rounding up the horses, which could have wandered off for miles. More hours went into saddling the horses and carefully reloading the supplies — a bungled job could leave a horse with raw sores which would render him useless. Preparations as extensive as these meant that the brigade was not on the trail again until mid-morning and Father Demers discovered that the brigade was lucky to achieve four hours of travel each day. But these four hours were uninterrupted — the inconvenience of halting the long caravan was so great that it was a standing rule that once on the trail the packtrain did not halt until it ended its day's journey.

August 10th found Father Demers at Kamloops, where for two days he preached to a concourse of Indians who had heard of his coming. Twelve days later he was at Fort Alexandria, where for the first time he met the Carrier Indians, the particular object of his mission. He found them sunk in vice. Depressed, he wrote: "Suicide, murder and a thousand other disorders are the daily consequences of the relaxation of family laws and of the vices that secretly threaten the unfortunate nation." Unlike the Indians at Fort Kamloops and at Fort Langley the previous year, the Carriers regarded with apathy the coming of Father Demers. He sought to console himself:

> Doubtlessly God will cast merciful eyes upon this straying portion of His flock. They do not know, these poor natives, what mercy for them is the visit of a minister of God in their faraway forests. Alas! if I were another Augustine, a Remi, a Patrick. . . . [18]

Still, even though he was dealing with a people so primitive that they had no concept of a god of any kind, not even idols or fetishes of their own, Demers manfully set about his preaching.

Perhaps because of the negative response of the Fort Alexandria Carriers, Father Demers accepted an invitation to continue north with the New Caledonia brigade:

> Although Fort Alexandria was at the outset the end of my journey and mission, I believed that Divine Providence was calling me to still other more remote places, where I would very certainly meet numerous detachments of natives ready to receive the light of the gospel.[19]

[18] *Ibid.*, p. 156.
[19] *Ibid.*, p. 159.

On September 6th Father Demers was at Fort George (now Prince George) and ten days later he arrived at Fort St. James. Here, at the capital of New Caledonia, he celebrated high mass. Father Demers had only three days at Fort St. James before he had to leave with a party of voyageurs returning south. Five days journeying downstream brought them to Fort Alexandria.

Apparently the seed which Father Demers had sown during his earlier visit had begun to grow. He now found the Carriers friendly and cooperative. Under his direction they started building a church, the first to be erected in British Columbia if we except the Spanish chapel at Nootka. On December 4th the new building was sufficiently completed for Father Demers to celebrate mass in it. We have the most meagre description of this historic church: "A cross decorates one of its gables, and a fireplace placed at the other served to heat it during this rigorous season."[20]

During the construction of this church Father Demers found time to spend sixteen days with the Shuswap Indians at Williams Lake, where he stayed in the house of Chief William. When January came, he returned thither to find that the Shuswaps had built themselves a chapel measuring 41 feet by 19 feet. Unfortunately, working on their own, the Indians had overlooked an important architectural feature:

Their chapel was built, and a large fireplace permitted a fire to be made there. Unfortunately there were no windows, and I had to give several instructions [sermons] in the icy January air. Finally we succeeded in securing some skins [parchments] by way of panes and sashes, and there we were, comfortable, very comfortable. However, O vexatious disappointment, don't we see some miserable starved dogs begin to eat our windows? We had to set traps and catch several guilty ones to put a stop to the scandal.[21]

Of the success of his mission to Williams Lake Father Demers has left us amusing testimony:

An unusual throng crowded the chapel, to the extent that one day when I could not get there early enough, it was impossible for me to reach my place except by passing over the shoulders and heads of my

20 *Ibid.*, p. 161.
21 *Loc. cit.*

neophytes, without touching the ground from the entrance to the back of the chapel.[22]

Late in February, having an opportunity to travel with Chief Factor Ogden, Father Demers left for the south. A gifted linguist, he had acquired sufficient knowledge of the Carrier and Shuswap languages to translate various hymns and prayers for the Indians, "and left them able to pray, sing, and explain the Catholic *Ladder*."[23]

Arriving at Fort Vancouver on 13 April 1843, he found Father Blanchet kneeling as he recited his breviary. Happily the two embraced. On Easter Day Father Demers sang high mass and "rendered earnest acts of thanks to God for having preserved me from all accident on a journey presenting so many dangers."

[22] *Famed Quebec Mission*, p. 162.
[23] F. N. Blanchet, *Historical Sketches of the Catholic Church in Oregon and the Northwest* (Ferndale, 1910), p. 52.

1843

Founding of Fort Victoria — Americans pour into Oregon — Character of the American settlers — McLoughlin's dilemma — A bloody reckoning at Fort Babine.

This year's great event was the founding of Fort Victoria, the future capital city of British Columbia.

We have seen how in 1842 Simpson ended McLoughlin's dogged fight to keep Fort Vancouver the Pacific depot of the Hudson's Bay Company by giving unequivocal instructions to get a fort established on the southern shore of Vancouver Island. We have noted also that a suitable site had, in fact, been found by Captain McNeill back in the early summer of 1837, "an excellent harbour and a fine open country along the sea shore, apparently well adapted for both tillage and pasturage."[1] McLoughlin, predictably, had had no enthusiasm for McNeill's discovery and had done nothing about it. This, however, was the site which Chief Factor Douglas decided upon for Simpson's new depot after re-examining the southern end of Vancouver Island in the summer of 1842.

In a personal letter, written in February of this year, Douglas (normally so cool and cautious) threw restraint to the winds as he eulogized the country around the inlet which the Indians called Camosack or Camosun, where he was to build the new fort:

The place itself appears a perfect "Eden", in the midst of the dreary wilderness of the North west coast, and so different is its general aspect, from the wooded, rugged regions around, that one might be pardoned

---

[1] Fort Simpson journal for 10 Aug. 1837, quoted by Walbran, *B.C. Coast Names*, p. 392. For Douglas' letter to Governor Simpson about McNeill's examination of Victoria, Esquimalt and Sooke harbours, see W. K. Lamb, "The Founding of Fort Victoria", *BCHQ* 7 (1943):71-92. This article, written to mark the centenary of the founding of Victoria, is of the first importance for anyone interested in the history of the city.

for supposing it had dropped from the clouds into its present position. . . .

The grouth of indigenous vegetation is more luxuriant, than in any other place, I have seen in America, indicating a rich productive soil. Though the survey I made was rather laborious, not being so light and active of foot as in my younger days, I was nevertheless delighted in ranging over fields knee deep in clover, tall grasses and ferns reaching above our heads, at these unequivocal proofs of fertility. Not a musquitoe that plague of plagues did we feel, nor meet with molestation from the natives.[2]

On March 1st Douglas with fifteen men left Fort Vancouver to found Fort Victoria. Following the much-travelled Cowlitz route, he arrived at Fort Nisqually on Puget Sound where the *Beaver* was in readiness to sail for Camosun. Also at Fort Nisqually was Father Jean Baptiste Bolduc. Douglas invited Father Bolduc along so that the priest could conduct a mission among the Indians who would be the HBC's new neighbours.

Late on March 14th the *Beaver* reached her destination and the next day Douglas went ashore at Clover Point. Immediately he had a difficult question to answer — just which site on the twisting little harbour would prove best for the fort? In his diary he entered a notation:

I am at a loss where to place the Fort, as there are two positions possessing advantages of nearly equal importance, though of different kinds. No. 1 has a good view of the harbour, is upon clear ground, and only 50 yds. from the beach, on the other hand vessels drawing 14 feet cannot come within 130 feet of the shore, we will therefore either have to boat cargo off and on at a great destruction of boats, and considerable loss of time or be put to the expense of forming a jettie at a great amount of labour. No. 2 on the other hand will allow of vessels lying with their sides grazing the rocks, which form a natural wharf, whereon cargo may be conveniently landed from the ships yard, and in that respect would be exceedingly advantageous, but on the other hand, an intervening point intercepts the view so that the mouth of the Port cannot be seen from it. . . . I will think more on this subject before determining the point.[3]

---

[2] *The Hargrave Correspondence 1821-1843*, ed. G. P. Glazebrook, Champlain Society 24 (Toronto, 1938) : 420-21.

[3] PABC, A-B-40-D75.4A. This is Douglas' original field journal.

Further thought persuaded Douglas that Site No. 2 was the right one.

The next day Douglas set six of his men to digging a well, and another six to squaring building timbers. Addressing the Songhees Indians, he "informed them of our intention of building in this place which appeared to please them very much." The Indians in fact forthwith offered to cut stakes for the palisades that would be raised around the new establishment. In short order Douglas made a bargain with them, lending them axes and promising a 2½-point blanket for every 40 pickets meeting his specifications of 22 feet in length and a yard in diameter.

Just as Rome at its founding had its omen, so Victoria had its. On the evening of March 17th a luminous streak shone in the heavens from dusk until nine p.m., extending in an arc until the moon obscured it. On the next four nights the "Luminous column" again appeared.

Curiously enough, Father Bolduc in his account of the proceedings makes no mention of this augury which the pious priest might so well have construed as a sign of Divine Blessing. Bolduc, however, after the first few days when he had had some doubts about trusting himself among the Indians, was very busy indeed with his mind on other things:

The 18th being Saturday, I employed it for constructing a temporary altar for celebrating on land the Lord's day. M[onsieur] Douglass gave me several of his men to help me in that work. Long fir branches formed the sides; the awnings of the steamboat the covering.

On Sunday early in the morning, more than 1,200 natives from three large tribes, Kawitshins [Cowichans], Klalams [Clallums] and Tsamishes [Samishes], assembled around the modest temple. Our bourgeois [the Anglican Douglas] forgot nothing that could contribute to rendering the ceremony imposing. ... He was present in person at the mass, as well as several Canadians and two Catholic ladies. It was among this numerous gathering that, for the first time, our holy mysteries were celebrated on that ground, for so many years the theater of hell's abominations. May Heaven effect that the Blood of the Lamb without stain make fertile this land, and cause it to produce an abundant harvest![4]

4 *Famed Quebec Mission*, p. 194.

After celebrating Mass, Father Bolduc went to a nearby village where he baptized Indian children and had to shake hands with over six hundred of the natives. This he described as "a terrible ceremony", explaining, "The dirtiness of those people is truly disgusting, which engenders among them a great variety of skin diseases. To refuse one's hand is an insult." On March 24th Father Bolduc started south to Puget Sound by canoe, Douglas with the *Beaver* headed north somewhat later.

On June 3rd Douglas and the *Beaver* were back at Camosun. In the interim he had closed down Fort Taku and Fort McLoughlin and had brought back with him the forty or fifty men who had been stationed there. These were now set to work raising the stockade, bastions and buildings of Fort Victoria, and the trade goods from the other forts were brought ashore for use at this new establishment. On June 9th, satisfied that the work was well in hand, Chief Factor Douglas headed down to Puget Sound on the *Beaver*. Subsequently the schooner *Cadboro* arrived from the Columbia River with additional supplies and soon the *Beaver* was back again, this time with a load of horses and "wild Spanish cattle"[5] from the Puget's Sound Agricultural Company's farm at Nisqually.

For a while there was some uncertainty concerning the name of the new fort. At one time Fort Albert was a real possibility, but the Queen won out over her consort and Fort Victoria it became — or "Victola" as the Indians called it, having trouble with the white man's sounds. In charge of Fort Victoria was Chief Trader Charles Ross, with a clerk, Roderick Finlayson (he who had once served at Fort Stikine with the hapless elder son of McLoughlin) as his second-in-command. In November Douglas, at Fort Vancouver, proudly wrote to Sir George Simpson reporting the near completion of Fort Victoria. McLoughlin, apparently to minimize the significance of the new establishment, had told Douglas to build the fort only 210 feet to the side but Douglas, as his letter reveals, had deliberately ignored that petty injuction:

In planning the Fort, I had in view the probability of its being converted into a Depot for the coasting trade and consequently began

---

[5] Finlayson, *History of Vancouver Island*, p. 23.

on a respectable scale, as to size. It is in form a quadrangle of 330 x 300 feet intended to contain 8 buildings of 60 feet each. . . . On the 21st September when we last heard from Ross the Pickets and defences were finished, and two of the buildings completed so far as to be habitable, and they are engaged in hauling out the logs of a third building.[6]

Douglas added that there had not been a rainy day at Fort Victoria between June 10th and September 8th. The sunny summer might have been taken for another good omen had it not dried up the stream near the fort and sent the first Victorians hauling water one and a half miles from another source.

Despite the successful inauguration of Fort Victoria, this was a dark year for the British, as represented by the HBC, on the Columbia. When 1843 began there were some three hundred Americans, men, women and children, settled in the Willamette valley. In March, sixty-five of these settlers petitioned the U.S. Senate to annex the territory. In May a meeting of the American settlers at Champoeg elected a legislative committee and officers for Oregon, and decided that the laws of Iowa should generally apply. In this project the Americans had to proceed without the French-Canadian settlers, fifty of whom opposed the Americans while only two sided with them. In July the Americans held a meeting at which "Organic Laws and Articles" were adopted. The land law approved at this meeting was deliberately directed against the HBC. Since the new "government" had to depend upon voluntary contributions from a portion of the community for its financing, it cannot be regarded with any real respect even though Americans, writing the history of Oregon, have taken the view that "Champoeg" marks the beginning of its government. As Dr. W. Kaye Lamb has very properly remarked, "In truth, it was not in reality a government at all; it was simply a voluntary association of individuals, mostly Americans, in sympathy with the American point of view."[7] All the same, Champoeg was most certainly a portent, indicating the shape of things to come.

Bad as the Champoeg development was, worse was at hand. The

[6] Quoted by Lamb, "Founding of Fort Victoria", *BCHQ* 7:89.

[7] HBRS 7:xxviii.

Methodist missionaries, through their publications in the United States, had created a most roseate vision of Oregon as a land of milk and honey, a wonderful country clearly intended by God, and "manifest destiny", as part of the young republic. Consequently, 1843 became the year of the "Great Migration", with a succession of wagon trains following the Oregon Trail westwards. Most of the newcomers arrived in their Promised Land during the autumn. Numbering almost nine hundred, they reduced the original French-Canadian settlers to a tiny minority. Chief Trader Tod, up at Fort Kamloops, learning of the influx, observed that the Willamette settlement "will become pure Yankee".[8] At Fort Walla Walla right on the migration route, Archibald McKinlay noted, "Americans are getting as thick as Mosquettoes in this part of the world."[9]

What was the nature of these founding fathers of the State of Oregon? A romantic stereotype of American history, lovingly depicted on canvas and film, is that of the Heroic Pioneer. Indomitable in spirit he strides, rifle slung across his arm, at the head of the wagons. With him is his wife, her face intent and touchingly lined, but obviously of a spirit as valiant as her mate's. Behind them ride their young, fit heirs to carry on the heroic tradition and hasten the day when the banner of equality and freedom will fly in the Pacific wind. "From every mountainside let freedom ring."

The vision is noble and compelling, but it happens to be largely untrue. No doubt among the immigrants there were brave, decent, honest men, and women who were valiant and industrious helpmates. But Sir George Simpson knew what he was talking about when he declared that most of the Willamette settlers were "worthless and lawless characters of every description from the United States." A distinguished American geologist and traveller, Clarence King, years later, after describing an immigrant family en route to California, indulged in some comments which would have applied equally to many of the American Oregon pioneers. Analyzing the urge which drove families to the new frontier, King could not help but observe how often that impulse:

[8] Letter to James Hargrave, *Hargrave Correspondence*, p. 423.
[9] *Ibid.*, p. 426.

... degenerates into mere weak-minded restlessness, killing the power of growth, the ideal of home, the faculty of repose, it results in that race of perpetual emigrants who roam as dreary waifs over the West, losing possessions, love of life, love of God, slowly dragging from valley to valley till they fall by the wayside, happy if some chance stranger performs for them the last rites, — often less fortunate, as blanched bones and fluttering rags upon too many hillsides plainly tell.[10]

Certainly a fair number of the newcomers which converged on Oregon in 1843 were members of what King called "this dreary brotherhood".

Deep in the bloodstream of the emerging community was the spirit of violence and lawlessness so notable in American history. Soon newcomers from the United States were talking of running out of the country any white man who had an Indian wife. There was talk, too, of ridding the country of the Indians themselves. Some of the Indians sensed the threat that these "Boston men" posed to their very existence. Relevant are the recollections of Francis Pettygrove of Maine, himself one of the immigrants of 1843:

... a band of Klamath and Molalley Indians came to the place, crossed the Willamet River, and tried to get the Indians of the country to assist them to kill the whites of Oregon City. They feared the whites were going to overrun the country, and determined upon their extermination. The Indians would not assist these intruders, but immediately came over to Oregon City and informed the whites of what the hostile Indians wanted them to do. When the hostile Indians returned to Oregon City, Dr. Elijah White, special U.S. Agent with a posse of men attempted their arrest. In the conflict two whites were killed and an Indian Chief, which created great excitement thro'out the country. The Indians at the Dalles being a connection of their[s], threatened to come down into the valley and kill off all the American settlers, or Bostons as they called them; which difficulty was settled by the H.B.Co. They gave the Indians blankets to make peace, for tho' they were not responsible for the trouble they would have had the blame [from the Americans] for it and suffered the consequences if there had been war. . . . [11]

Warned by the HBC engagés that the "Bostons" would drive them from their hunting grounds, a group of Indians visited Dr.

---

[10] *Mountaineering in the Sierra Nevada* (London, 1872), p. 105.

[11] "Oregon in 1843", PAC, MG29, B35, Vol. II:5 (Bancroft transcript).

McLoughlin and asked him if the report was true. "What dog said so?"[12] replied McLoughlin. He must have known that the Indian hunting grounds were doomed. Even if he could tell himself that by using his counter-question he had not lied to the Indians, his evasion was shameful. The Indians, believing in the word of the HBC and taking McLoughlin to mean their lands were safe, did not attack.

And how did McLoughlin conduct himself towards these hundreds of newcomers from the United States? Although he was under direct instructions from London neither to encourage nor assist the American immigrants, he kept up his customary flow of benefits. Some of the newcomers were appreciative of "the Doctor's" aid. Daniel Waldo, a Virginian who came out to Oregon this year, was one of these and in later years gratefully recalled:

Dr. McLoughlin was a perfect gentleman; all the Hudson's Bay men were.

You will find very few such men as the old Doctor. I saw him trust an immense number of men there. He never asked them if they could ever pay or not. He gave them all the goods they wanted. We had his boats for 9 days. I wanted to pay him but he would not have a cent. I told him we had damaged his boats. He said they would "soon mend that, soon mend that". He was a magnificent old fellow; there are very few men better than he. We could hardly have lived if it had not been for the Hudson's Bay Co. They had plenty of goods and sold them very cheaply. They sold goods a heap cheaper than we had ever bought them for in the States.[13]

On the other hand, all too many of the new settlers, even while surviving through the credit which McLoughlin gave them at Fort Vancouver, talked darkly of the "tyranny" of the HBC and threatened to storm and loot the fort. In November McLoughlin had to write to London asking that British troops or warships be sent to protect the property of the HBC. This must have been an excruciating decision for McLoughlin. Obviously he was incapable of admitting that his long romantic idealization of the United States was unrealistic, and sought to persuade himself that the American threat was due only to a restless minority. In his letter calling for

[12] *Ibid.*, p. 6.
[13] "Critiques", PAC, MG29, B35, Vol. 2 (Bancroft transcript).

British arms he could not bring himself to speak baldly of the need for British bluejackets or British troops. What was needed, he said, was "a protection":

To avoid the evils, that may arise, from ... encroachments, and the collision of conflicting rights, I would beg to recommend, that a protection should be received from Government, and that we should be empowered to take such measures, as may appear to us, necessary for the Security of our property. . . . [14]

Even McLoughlin must have realized that events were refuting his oft-repeated argument that the way to avoid trouble with the Americans was to greet them warmly upon their arrival on the Columbia, to supply their needs, and to extend every possible hospitality.

This year tragedy struck in New Caledonia. Young William Morwick was the "postmaster" in charge of the little fort on Babine Lake. In January there was a petty quarrel over the price Morwick should pay an Indian, named Lèkwè, who had killed a caribou for him. This resulted in a fracas in which Lèkwè and Morwick's interpreter, Charles Toin, inflicted wounds upon each other. A false report that Lèkwè had been slain was carried to his son-in-law, named Grand-Visage. Hastening to the fort, Grand-Visage found a space in the palisades through which he could thrust and aim his rifle at Morwick's dwelling. It happened that the parallel parchment windows of this house had inset in them two small panes of glass. Grand-Visage saw his victim silhouetted between the glass and fired. Morwick fell dead.

Morwick was widely known and admired by his colleagues — Chief Factor Archibald McDonald considered him "one of the best men I ever saw in the country"[15] — and news of his murder caused shock and horror among the HBC men. Grimly Chief Factor Ogden despatched from Fort St. James an avenging party headed by one of his clerks, W. B. McBean, and accompanied by the dreaded "Waccan" (Jean Baptiste Boucher), a sort of master-of-arms who disciplined the Company's employees, handled the Indians when

[14] McLoughlin to Governor and Committee, 15 Nov. 1843, HBRS 6:141.
[15] *Hargrave Correspondence*, p. 425.

they got unruly, and upon occasion routed them out from their villages and got them hunting instead of going on with their interminable gambling.

When the avengers arrived at Babine Lake, they found that Grand-Visage and his friends, in preparation for their coming, had constructed a crudely built but effective fort of their own, one which the HBC men preferred not to storm. Instead, they sent word to Grand-Visage that if he would come out and negotiate, the matter could be settled without any shedding of blood. Grand-Visage hesitated to accept the offer but a Babine Indian, faithful to the HBC but trusted by his own people, assured him that he had nothing to fear. Out from his strong place stepped Grand-Visage, accompanied by his daughter carrying his gun. Two shots rang out, and he sank to the ground dead.[16] William Morwick had been avenged.

Morwick's death came at a time when the fur trade, generally speaking, had seen its best days. Chief Trader Tod, at Fort Kamloops, attributed the great fall-off of the trade to the cupidity of the former Nor'Westers who were now approaching retirement from the service of the HBC:

... the country being now in all quarters completely exhausted of fur bearing animals, which have been hunted up by the sordid cupidity of the old Nor.West partners, who have gleaned all that was worth looking after, are now fast retiring from the field.[17]

Tod was grossly exaggerating, and indulging a private antipathy. Still the situation was becoming serious.

[16] Morice, *History of Northern Interior of B.C.*, p. 209-13.
[17] PAC, Ermatinger Papers, Letter of 20 March 1843.

1844

The HBC moves to get rid of McLoughlin — The American-dominated provisional government of Oregon — American presidential campaign and the Oregon issue — Roderick Finlayson at Fort Victoria — A change of command in New Caledonia.

The time had come for the downfall of the proud Dr. John Mc-Loughlin. All things considered, it is amazing that the Hudson's Bay Company had tolerated for so long his insubordination and growing incompetence. Although he had been warned several years earlier that he must end his quarrel with Simpson and cooperate with his superior, he had failed to do so. He had been ordered to close the Company's San Francisco establishment but had persisted in keeping it open. He knew he was forbidden to extend credit, but had advanced £6,600 to the American immigrants.[1] His entire policy of aiding American settlement had set to naught the policy of the Company[2] and the interests of Britain. He "had been even less successful than usual in handling the shipping on the Coast; the affairs of the Puget's Sound Agricultural Company were in a far from flourishing state. . . . "[3] Even worse, the returns from his department's fur trade were steadily shrinking. Simpson figured that the Company was now actually losing money in the Columbia Department.[4] Meanwhile McLoughlin continued to be obsessed with the murder of his son, filling letters with verbose and angry discussions of that event while leaving the Governor and Committee in

[1] HBRS 7:lviii.
[2] Writing to Lord John Russell in May 1840, Sir John Pelly, Governor of the Company, had assured him that it was the policy of the HBC to discourage American colonization. *v.* HBRS 29:xxxv.
[3] Lamb, "Introduction", HBRS 6:lviii.
[4] *v.* HBRS 7:lvi-lvii.

London without information which they badly needed in framing their trading policies. Little wonder that on March 4th of this year Archibald Barclay, Secretary of the HBC, wrote to Sir George Simpson, " . . . nothing will now do but McLoughlin's removal".[5]

The Company was singularly gentle as it moved to get rid of McLoughlin. There would be no forced retirement, but his powers were to be reduced sufficiently to deprive him of control over the Company's business on the Pacific Coast. London hoped, and the hope was soon borne out, that McLoughlin himself would choose to resign rather than endure the humiliating loss of status. It was on November 30th of this year that the process of clipping "The White Eagle's" wings began: Barclay wrote to McLoughlin that the Governor and Committee had not found the advantages anticipated when they had put the whole of the area west of the Rockies under McLoughlin's direction. As of the end of May in the coming year, he would no longer be receiving the special salary of £500 allowed him as "general superintendent". He was further informed that the Company intended dividing his empire into two or more districts[6] — a scheme subsequently dropped in favour of setting up a board of management on which Douglas and Ogden would sit as McLoughlin's equals. Of these developments McLoughlin learned nothing until letters from London reached him late in the spring of the following year.

Meanwhile McLoughlin presided over an increasingly difficult situation in the Columbia. The influx of American settlers continued, with 1400 new arrivals from the United States moving in this year. Many of them, ardently believing absurd propagandistic slanders about the HBC circulating in the U.S., were impatient to drive the Company out of the country. In June a committee recommended to the "provisional government" that the:

. . . Militia of Oregan shall be arranged into one Regiment two battalions & Companies, it shall consist of Invantry [sic] district Companies, light Invantry, riflemen, artillery men, and dragoons as mounted riflemen. . . . [7]

[5] *Ibid.*, lvii.
[6] *Loc. cit.*
[7] HBRS 7:227.

With this sort of project being mooted, McLoughlin was relieved on July 15th to find H.M.S. *Modeste*, a sloop carrying 18 guns, come to anchor opposite Fort Vancouver. Her appearance was a cooling reminder to the more bellicose among the American Oregonians that, if there were to be a war, they would be speedily attended to by the Royal Navy which vastly outnumbered the naval forces of the United States.

During the *Modeste*'s visit, Chief Factor James Douglas took her commanding officer on a tour which included the Willamette settlement, increasingly known as Oregon City. Douglas was rather disappointed in Commander Baillie, especially when he introduced him to the non-American minority:

> The Canadians without displaying much enthusiasm, nevertheless, gave Her Majesty's Officers a warm reception; but Baillie did not attempt to play the envoy, or awaken feelings of loyalty and attachment to their country's cause, by one single expression of sympathy or interest about them, which might, by a little tact have been done, without any infringement of orders. While the American Party are pouring petition after petition into the hands of their government and keeping their national feelings alive, by a system of ceaseless agitation, we are doing nothing; British feeling is dying away so much, that Englishmen, in the Wallamatte, are either afraid or ashamed to own their country.[8]

The "ceaseless agitation" which Douglas mentions was in fact only an extension of the agitation about Oregon going on back in the U.S.A. This was the year for a presidential election. The Democrats, supporting Polk, fought that election on a platform of "Re-Occupation of Oregon, and Re-Annexation of Texas". A bemused outsider might wonder how the Americans could "re-occupy" a territory they had never occupied, but it was an article of faith among the more fervent Americans that the years between 1811 and 1813, when Astor's abortive American Fur Company had had its few forts in the North-west, constituted an "occupation" which made everything between California and the Russian boundary at 54°40′ latitude north the possession of the United States, despite the co-dominion negotiated with Britain. In the American presidential election this year, extremists who were ready to fight for "the whole

[8] Douglas to Simpson, 5 March 1845. HBRS 7: 181.

28.   Crossing Athabasca Pass

29.   Boat Encampment

30. Fort Victoria, 1846

31. Haida Woman Wearing a Labret

32. Flathead Woman, Cowlitz River
(with artificially deformed skull)

33.   Lieut. Warre's Dancing Partner, Fort Victoria, 1845

34. Return of a War Party, Fort Victoria

35. Indian Battle on the Strait of Juan de Fuca

of Oregon", helped to secure the election of Polk, the Democratic candidate.

American patriotic passion having subsided somewhat in the Columbia, H.M.S. *Modeste* stayed only three weeks at Fort Vancouver before she sailed downstream to the mouth of the Columbia River where U.S.S. *Peacock* had been lost on the bar a few years earlier. The *Modeste* herself struck hard several times in her first attempt to cross the bar, but her luck held and, after making repairs, she safely got out on her second try, sailing in the wake of the HBC's *Cowlitz*. A few days later H.M.S. *Modeste* was at Victoria, taking on supplies before heading north to Fort Simpson.

The *Modeste* arrived at Fort Victoria only a month or so after the death of Chief Trader Charles Ross, the officer commanding there. He had been in indifferent health, though his end (possibly through appendicitis) appears to have been sudden and unexpected. On Ross' death, the command of Fort Victoria passed to his clerk Roderick Finlayson. Finlayson may, upon occasion, have had a bit of a weakness for the bottle; but by and large he was an outstanding officer. Several years later Douglas praised him highly when writing to Governor Simpson:

Roderick Finlayson has managed the affairs of Fort Victoria, remarkably well, since his accession to the charge of the Post, and I assure you it will not be an easy matter to find a better man for the place. He is not a man of display, but there is a degree of energy, perseverance, method and sound judgment in all his arrangements. . . . [9]

Finlayson had indeed earned Douglas' praise. Very soon after taking command, he had defended Fort Victoria with courage and ingenuity against an attack by the Cowichan Indians. Since we have his own account of that stirring episode, we cannot do better than repeat it:

I was not long in charge, when the Indians killed some of our best working oxen & horses left feeding on the surrounding grounds — I then sent a message to the chiefs demanding the delivery of the perpetrator of this unprovoked deed, or payment to be made for the animals killed which they declined doing — I then suspended trade or any

[9] HBRS 6:389.

dealing with them until this matter was settled — Whereupon they sent
word to some of the neighboring tribes — to come to their assistance, as
they intended to attack the Fort. In the meantime I kept all hands at
their arms set watches night & day, to prevent surprise — After a
couple of days [of] negotiations when a large number assembled, they
opened fire upon the Fort riddling the stockade & roofs of the House
with their musket balls, it was with the greatest difficulty I could
prevail on our men not then to return the Fire, but wait for my orders.
After the firing of about half an hour was carried on, I spoke to the
principal chief informing him that I was fully prepared to carry on the
battle, but did not like to kill any of them without first explaining to
them that they were wrong, and giving them another chance of making
restitution — A Parley ensued among them during which I sent our
Indian Interpreter out to speak to them — telling him to make it
appear that he escaped without orders, and to point out to them the
Lodge I was determined to fire on, and for all its inmates to clear out
— This they did at the suggestion of the Interpreter, who upon making
a sign to me, as agreed upon, that the Lodge was clear — came towards
the stockade and was admitted into the Fort by a back gate — seeing
there was no sign of their coming to terms, I pointed one of our nine
pounder carronades loaded with grape shot, on the Lodge, which was
a large one, built of cedar boards, fired, and the effect of which was
that it was completely demolished, and splinters of the cedar boards
flying in fragments in the air — After this there was an immense
howling among them, from which I supposed a number were killed,
but my plan, I was happy to find, had the desired effect. I was aware
that these Indians never saw the effect [of] grape shot fired from
cannon — After the excitement of the effects of the shot was over — a
deputation of the Chiefs called out [to] the Interpreter that they
wanted a parley with the White Chief — I then arranged with them,
that if two of them came in within the stockade, to make arrangements
with me, I would send out two of our men as hostages, to which they
agreed — I then fully explained to them, that I had it in my power to
destroy all their houses, and kill many of them, but that I did not like
to do so, and that it was fortunate for them that none of our men was
shot —- that I was determined to have the offende[rs] punished, or
payment made for the animals they killed — They preferred the latter,
and before that day closed furs to the full amount were delivered at the
gate — After which we smok[ed] the pipe of peace, with a promise on
their part, that our animals would not in future be molested — so we
parted good friends, trade was resumed as formerly & after this no
more of our animals were ki[lled].[10].

[10] Finlayson, *History of Vancouver Island*, pp. 23-25.

The Indians had, in fact, been so impressed by the discharge of the cannon that they begged for a repeat performance. Glad to oblige, Finlayson loaded a cannon, but this time with a cannon ball instead of grapeshot, and fired it at a canoe in the harbour. The Indians were amazed to see the cannon ball not only pass through the sides of the canoe but bound across the water beyond and finally disappear into the forest on the far side of the inlet.

Finlayson's problems with the local Indians were not quite at an end. One day some Whidbey Island Indians arrived at the fort to trade. As they were heading back to their canoes, near Beacon Hill, the local Indians, who had a feud with them, set upon the visitors and robbed them of all they had acquired in exchange for their furs. When the distressed Whidbey Islanders came back to the fort, Finlayson admitted them and gave them protection. Summoning the chief responsible for the attack, Finlayson made it very clear to him that the HBC insisted that *all* Indians must be free to come and trade unmolested. He secured restitution of the stolen property, and then sent the Whidbey Island Indians home, convoyed by a canoe containing four HBC men. From this point on, Indians from the southern shore of the Strait of Juan de Fuca and from northern Puget Sound traded with confidence at Fort Victoria.

Peace now firmly established, Finlayson was able to start his men clearing the forest adjacent to the fort. Farms and pastures were laid out, not only to sustain Fort Victoria but to meet the heavy continuing demands of the Russian contract.

This year there was a change of command in New Caledonia, with the veteran Peter Skene Ogden handing over to Donald Manson. For the guidance of his successor Ogden wrote some "Notes on Western Caledonia".[11] If we did not have plenty of testimony of Ogden's irrepressible high spirits, humour and poise, we might from reading these comments get an entirely misleading picture of a most unhappy man. The Carrier Indians Ogden dismisses as "a brutish, ignorant, superstitious beggarly sett of beings". Nor is he any more charitable about his own men, characterizing those who have recently arrived from Canada as "the refuse of

---

[11] "Peter Skene Ogden's Notes on Western Caledonia", *BCHQ* I (1937):45-56.

brothels and Gaols". He concedes, however, that the veteran voyageurs who have been longer in New Caledonia, although "represented as [a] most worthless dishonest disolute sett of beings", are
"by no means as bad as represented". Since Fort Chilcotin is taking
in less than 100 beaver pelts a year, he suggests that Manson
consider closing down that establishment.

This year Chief Factor Archibald McDonald made an important
discovery on Kootenay Lake during one of his trips afield from his
base at Fort Colvile. On a hillside on the east side of the lake he
discovered a mineral, its ore lying "in loose lumps among the
earth". Gathering specimens, he sent them down to Fort Vancouver,
whose crude facilities were able to produce fine lead out of the ore.
McDonald, in fact, had made one of the greatest mineral discoveries
in the history of British Columbia. For years thereafter hunters and
trappers would head to that hillside to mould bullets out of the rich
unrefined ore. Here, in time, would be the Bluebell Mine, legendary
in its riches. Not until 1972, after successive fortunes had been made,
would the ore body be finally exhausted and the mining cease.

The significance of this discovery was not lost on McDonald.
Looking across the lake, he sensed the great mineral wealth that one
day would be found there. Writing to Douglas he noted:

The west shore . . . presents one of the most splendid views in nature to
the eye of the ecologist — every strata bold, clear & distinct, & I am
much mistaken or they are indications of a very rich mineral country.[12]

Ending his letter, McDonald wrote half sportively:

By the light of a blazing fire which warmed myself & my two naked
companions for the night, I cut my initials in a large tree alongside of
us to commemorate my own dear name . . . I do not know but I may
yet claim the Kootenais treasure as *my own*. . . .

[12] HBCA, A.11/70, f.86d. Part of this letter is printed in HBRS 7:62.

1845

Anti-British feelings of the American settlers — Encroachments upon HBC property — The HBC joins the provisional government — President Polk's belligerent inaugural address — H.M.S. America and H.M.S. Modeste on the coast — British army officers, Warre and Vavasour, come overland to reconnoitre.

Things went from bad to worse for the HBC (and hence for Britain) this year in the lower Columbia. American immigrants continued to pour in, nearly three thousand arriving this year. Many of the new "Oregonians" came with bitter prejudices already instilled in them against the HBC. Some carried with them copies of speeches made by Senators Linn and Benton of Missouri, and by Senator Buchanan of Pennsylvania, containing the outrageous slander that the British, through the HBC and the Indians, had murdered five hundred American citizens in the Pacific North-west.

Even McLoughlin, who so long and so ardently had championed American immigration, was appalled by this bitter and totally unjustifiable hostility:

... though every American knows these Reports against us to be false, yet there are many among them, who it seems cannot overcome these feelings of national hostility. One of them speaking a few days ago to a person on whose veracity we can depend, observed, "It is true these are good folks and treat me kindly, but somehow or other I cannot like them, and moreover do not like those who like them." Another who left this [country] to go to the States, observed that the only regret he had in leaving the Country, was that he did not burn [Fort] Vancouver, as he had left the States with that intention.[1]

[1] Letter of 19 July 1845, McLoughlin to Governor and Committee, London, HBRS 7:87.

373

McLoughlin, however, could not really face the fact that all along he had nurtured a romantic unrealistic view of American virtue, and elsewhere in this same letter he sought to dismiss American hatred as a mere "antipathy" held by several individuals. McLoughlin's coadjutor, Chief Factor James Douglas, saw things more clearly. He minced no words when writing to Governor Simpson about these immigrants:

> The Doctor [McLoughlin] has communicated the wicked and absurd plan, started by a few Americans here, with the view of expelling the half breeds and other population not of American origin from this country. These sentiments are not confined to the few concerned in that plot; many would join heart and hand were they not restrained by prudential considerations.
>
> No people can be more prejudiced and national than the Americans in this country, a fact so evident to my mind, that I am more suspicious of their designs, than of the wild natives of the forest.[2]

McLoughlin and Douglas received an intimation of the problems ahead for the Company when, on February 15th of this year, a rough character named Henry Williamson with two or three other Americans moved on to the HBC's land close beside Fort Vancouver, erected a shanty and nailed on a nearby tree a notice of possession. McLoughlin ordered the tree chopped down and the shed demolished. About a month later Williamson arrived on the scene once more, this time with a land surveyor to lay out building lots on a square mile of HBC land. In the ensuing confrontation the giant, whiteheaded Chief Factor, anger flashing in his blue eyes, spelt out for the American the "nature and grounds of the Hudson's Bay Company's rights in this Country", after which the truculent Williamson gave up his project.[3]

Though the HBC did have "rights" in the Columbia, the Company could appeal to no local government to defend these rights against characters such as Williamson. Fortunately the more reasonable and respectable Americans now secured a rephrasing of the

---

[2] *Ibid.*, p. 190.

[3] For McLoughlin's detailed report on the Williamson case made to the nearest British official, Her Majesty's Consul-General at Honolulu, see HBRS 7:259-69.

oath of admission which made it possible for British subjects to preserve their allegiance to the Crown while participating in the "provisional government", and so obtaining some measures of security from it. Moreover, to secure participation by the HBC, the "provisional government" was prepared to give the name "Vancouver district" to the land on the north shore of the Columbia, and to abandon a plan to divide it into counties named after Lewis and Clark. Hence, on August 15th on behalf of the HBC, McLoughlin and Douglas signed the deed of association. In a confidential letter to London, McLoughlin set forth reasons for this unusual step. Chief among them was:

The critical position of our affairs, the danger to which the large property of the Company in this country was exposed in the midst of a hostile population living without restraint of laws. . . . [4]

The days of McLoughlin's rule were beginning to run out. Meeting at Red River in June this year, the Council of the Northern Department of the HBC had named a Board of Management, consisting of Douglas, Ogden and McLoughlin to take over west of the Rockies. In November, making his final report to London as superintendent for this vast area, McLoughlin could not restrain his anger against those Americans who had abused his hospitality and betrayed his faith. Bitterly he denounced:

. . . the designs of many desperate and reckless characters, men acknowledging no law and feeling not the restraints of conscience, the outcasts of society, who have sought a refuge in the wilds of Oregon. With their natural turpitude of disposition embittered by national hostility, such men would not shrink from the commission of any crime; they were determined at all risks to intrude upon the Company's land claim, and they made no secret of their plans if ejected by force. If not supported by their countrymen, they were to seek an easy revenge by firing our premises, destroying our barns, or such like deeds of cowardly villainy.[5]

If events on the Pacific Coast gave the HBC grounds for disquiet, it could find no consolation in developments in the East. On March 4th James A. Polk, elected on a platform which called for an Ameri-

[4] HBRS 7:98.
[5] HBRS 7:101.

can takeover of the Pacific North-west, was sworn in as President of the United States of America. In his inaugural address he solemnly declared that the American claim to the disputed lands was "clear and unquestionable".

Alarmed at the uncompromising position taken by the new American administration, Sir George Simpson asked that four British warships be despatched to the mouth of the Columbia in order to seize and fortify Cape Disappointment and thus secure command of the entrance to the river. He declared that in the event of war the HBC could raise a force "of about Two Thousand men, half-breeds and Indians" to serve in the hostilities, but efficient officers should be supplied by Britain to "command and discipline these people".[6]

Polk's address did not go unheeded in another direction. In May, Rear-Admiral Sir George Seymour, Commander-in-Chief of the Royal Navy in the Pacific, saw newspapers informing him "that the President of the United States asserted Rights over Oregon which Her Majesty's government would not suffer. . . . " Writing to the Admiralty from his flagship at Callao, Seymour noted that he had already extensively discussed with Commander Baillie of H.M.S. *Modeste* the threat facing the HBC's officers and:

. . . it does not appear to me likely that they will be able to maintain their ground in the Columbia by force of arms without military assistance from England, although the influence of the Hudson's Bay Company with the Indians may prevent further encroachment to the northward.[7]

He regretted that the French-Canadian colonists had become integrated with the Americans on the south bank of the river. They would have been far more capable of mutual dependence and defence if they had been settled on the north shore.

In this letter Admiral Seymour noted also that a few months earlier he had instructed Captain the Hon. John Gordon, in the course of a cruise with H.M.S. *America* (50 guns and about 500 officers and men) to enter the Strait of Juan de Fuca, communicate

[6] B.M., *Add. Ms. 40,563*, f.394.

[7] For Admiral Seymour's letter, see PRO, Adm. 1/5550, Y158.

with the officer commanding Fort Victoria and, by way of Fort Nisqually on Puget Sound and the Cowlitz portage, to make contact with Fort Vancouver. (Unfortunately it was not feasible for a ship of the size of H.M.S. *America* to cross the Columbia bar and proceed directly to Fort Vancouver.) In late August H.M.S. *America* arrived in the Strait of Juan de Fuca and took up station at Captain Vancouver's old Port Discovery. On September 8th two of her officers, Captain Parke of the Royal Marines and Lieut. Peel, R.N. (a son of the British prime minister) arrived at Fort Vancouver to consult with Dr. McLoughlin. En route they had passed the first American homestead on Puget Sound.

Dr. McLoughlin, caught between his old emotional attachment to the U.S. and his recent bitter experiences with the more vehement Americans, was sadly perturbed to find the young officers gaily contemplating the drubbing they would give the Yankees in any war. One of the HBC clerks later recalled the scene:

> I came late to dine & Parke was telling the Doctor [McLoughlin] the means they would employ; no stone to be unturned well Doctor, if they persist in bringing this on, we will hit them harder than we would other people, I can still hear the Doctors saying in astonishment — "Oh Capt. Parke! Capt. Park!"[8]

While Peel and Parke were off on their mission, the captain of the *America* decided to have a little sport deer-shooting and salmon-fishing on Vancouver Island. Roderick Finlayson later recalled that occasion with amusement:

> Capt. Gordon crossed with me to Victoria in a launch where he remained some time. We had some fine horses for the use of the Captain & his officers & we paid them every attention. We went out on one occasion to Cedar Hill [Mount Douglas]. . . . The country looked beautiful, carpeted as it was with beautiful wild flowers. Capt. Gordon was a great deer stalker. We met a band of deer & had a chase after them on horseback. The deer ran for a thicket into which the horses with their riders could not penetrate and of course no deer were had. The Captain felt much disappointed & was anything but happy. I said to him that I was very sorry we had missed the deer etc, and also remarked how beautiful the country looked. He said in reply — "Fin-

---

[8] Roberts, "Recollections", p. 5.

layson I would not give the most barren hills in the Highlands of Scotland for all I see around me."[9]

The Captain's ill humour was not improved when he learned that many of the salmon in this part of the world had to be taken with a net since they would not rise to the fly. "Capt. Gordon felt greatly dissatisfied because he could not have the use of a rod and fly."

When Peel and Parke returned to their ship, accompanied by Chief Factor Douglas, they brought with them a letter from a confused McLoughlin who was now minimizing his difficulties with the Americans in the Willamette valley:

... the inhabitants are, generally speaking, peaceable and orderly, and ... though national feelings run somewhat strong at times, no overt acts of violence have been committed. . . . [10]

The two young officers had made a personal inspection of the Willamette colony, and Lieut. Peel's report on it makes interesting reading:

Every year an increasing number of Emigrants come into the Country from the United States; they are almost all from the Western Provinces, and chiefly from the Missouri. Some are induced to come over from not finding a market for their produce in that Country; others come merely from speculation and a restless disposition, and some either to recover or get rid of their debts, or to escape justice. In general, they arrive with a very hostile feeling against Great Britain, and particularly against the Hudson's Bay Company! but in course of a twelvemonth, from seeing their dependence on the Comp^y as a Market, and how much they are indebted to them, for the peaceful conduct of the Indians, their opinions greatly change.[11]

---

[9] Finlayson, *History of Vancouver Island*, p. 40.

[10] PRO, Adm. 1/5564. (Imperfect transcripts of this and other relevant documents will be found in L. M. Scott, "Report of Lieutenant Peel on Oregon in 1845-46", *OHQ* 29 (1928):51-76. Scott does not indicate where he found this text, other than they were copied in London by Joseph Schafer.)

It is perhaps indicative of McLoughlin's harrassed and confused state that during this year, although at times he speaks out strongly against the Americans, at other times he minimizes or completely ignores the unpleasant aspects of their conduct. Writing to Edward Ermatinger on 4 March 1845, in a letter expressing a hope that Francis Ermatinger will decide to retire in Oregon rather than Canada, McLoughlin blandly affirms "now there are about four thousand Inhabitants on the Willamette who are peaceable and orderly." (Ermatinger Papers.)

[11] PRO, Adm. 1/5564.

Lieut. Peel also noted that the American settlers were entirely destitute when they arrived, and were sustained by the HBC which, on credit, outfitted them with their necessary supplies. (The HBC also bought all the grain the settlers wished to sell.) Captain Gordon, making his own report to the Admiralty, commented on:

... the Hudsons Bay C⁰ˢ People, who seem to have treated them [the immigrants] in the most liberal manner, and I should fear greatly induced the flow of Emigration, the Emigrants being assured of getting all manner of supplies at their arrival.[12]

On October 1st H.M.S. *America* sailed from the Strait of Juan de Fuca, arriving at Honolulu three weeks later. There, finding an American ship about to sail for Mazatlan, Captain Gordon decided to send Lieut. Peel by her on the first stretch of a hurried journey to England so that the British government might receive the latest information about the Columbia situation. On 13 February 1846 Lieut. Peel delivered his letters in London. The most urgent message which he conveyed from Captain Gordon was that, if the international boundary were to follow the 49th parallel, it must do so only up to salt water and then be deflected through the Strait of Juan de Fuca. On no account should the boundary cut off the southern extremity of Vancouver Island.

A week after H.M.S. *America* left the Strait of Juan de Fuca she was replaced there by H.M.S. *Modeste*. By a fortunate chance Commander Baillie here met Chief Factor Douglas. After his earlier narrow escape on the bar of the Columbia, Baillie was anxious not to risk his ship there a second time. He put to Douglas, in writing, the question: "Whether you consider the entrance of the *Modeste* into the Columbia River essential for the protection of British interests in that quarter?" Douglas in his written reply certified that both in his opinion and that of McLoughlin the presence of the *Modeste* was "essentially necessary".[13] Accordingly, the *Modeste* entered the Columbia and remained there until the international boundary was established by treaty in the following year.

One little anecdote remains from that period. The settlers were

[12] *Loc. cit.*

[13] HBRS 7:304.

invited on board the British warship to see a play put on by the ship's company. It began with a preliminary little speech:

> I heard *Modeste*'s our ship
> And Modeste men are we!
> One word more and up shall rise the scene.
> Ladies and gentlemen all, "God Save the Queen."

As the audience rose to their feet and uncovered, it was seen that one sturdy American patriot had not removed his slouch hat. In the quiet before the national anthem, a bluejacket was heard plaintively appealing to one of the officers, "Please, sir, may I pitch that chap overboard?"[14]

If the Royal Navy was present this year, so also was the British Army in the persons of Lieut. Henry James Warre, of the 14th Regiment, A.D.C. to Lieut.-General Sir Richard Downes Jackson, Commander-in-Chief, British North America; and Lieut. Mervin Vavasour of the Royal Engineers. In view of the likelihood of war to prevent the Americans from taking over on the Pacific, Britain obviously needed a reconnaissance by professional soldiers. Better men could hardly have been found. Warre was not only an acute observer, but an amateur artist whose many sketches and water-colours made on this journey attest to his skill. Vavasour was an expert cartographer. Their instructions directed them:

> ... to acquire a knowledge of the character & resources of the country situated between the Sault de Ste. Mary and the shores of the Pacific, and of the practicability of forming stations therein and conveying troops thither, with a view, should it hereafter become necessary, to the occupation thereof for Military operations. ... [15]

Setting out from Montreal on May 5th, in company with Governor Simpson, the two young officers travelled to Fort Garry where Simpson handed them over to Peter Skene Ogden. Ogden was about to leave with an express party with which Warre and Vavasour would travel to the Pacific. In a letter to Ogden, Governor Simpson requested that:

[14] Roberts, "Recollections", p. 33.
[15] HBRS 7:96.

... the objects of Messrs. Warre and Vavasour's journey be not disclosed, but that, it be given out that, they are known to us only as private travellers for the pleasure of field sports and scientific pursuits.[16]

Setting out from Fort Garry on June 16th, Warre and Vavasour and the rest of Ogden's party reached Fort Colvile on the Columbia on August 12th. They had come through the Rockies by a pass leading from the Bow River. The journey must have been a rough one indeed for, whereas they had left Fort Edmonton with sixty horses, they had only twenty-seven when they reached Fort Colvile. Warre's diary, preserved in the Public Archives of Canada, gives us some account of what they had been through, especially along a burned-over stretch leading towards Sinclair Canyon:

> The trees had fallen in every direction and the black burnt stumps covered us with ashes. . . . the rocks made fearful havoc with the horses' feet, more than one being left to his fate. . . . We had to jump our horses over the immense trees. . . . I never saw such surefooted animals.[17]

From Colvile the two officers travelled down the Columbia River. En route they studied Fort Walla Walla with particular interest. "This vicinity", Warre noted, "I consider the most important point of all the inland Posts of the Columbia." Thoughtfully he added, " . . . it is by this route that troops would be sent by the U. States, should it ever be necessary to forward them to the Oregon Territory."[18]

On August 28th Lieuts. Warre and Vavasour finally reached Fort Vancouver. Viewing it with a professional eye, Warre curtly noted, "The Fort is badly situated as regards defence — being commanded by a ridge. . . . " Naturally, Warre and Vavasour were very interested in the relationship between the HBC and the American settlers. They, like Captain Gordon of H.M.S. *America*, put the responsibility for the dangerous American presence squarely on the shoulders of Dr. McLoughlin and those under his direction:

> ... whatever may have been the Orders or the motives of the Gentlemen in charge of the Hudsons Bay Company's posts, their policy has

---

[16] *Loc. cit.*

[17] Warre, *Columbia Diary 1845,* Vol. 1 : 1050-51.

[18] *Ibid.*, pp. 1099-100.

tended to the introduction of the American Settlers into the Country. We are convinced that without their assistance, not thirty families would ever have been in the settlement.[19]

After a few days to recuperate, the two were off to inspect the American colony called Oregon City and here, at the Falls of the Willamette, they had the totally unexpected pleasure of meeting Peel and Parke. Learning that H.M.S. *America* was at anchor in the Strait of Juan de Fuca, they resolved at once to accompany them thither. In his diary Warre vividly communicates his joy at finding himself once more among his own kind:

At about 8 o C we came in sight of Protection Island in front of, and giving protection (in all weathers) to the magnificent harbour & anchorage called "Port Discovery". H.M. Ship America was at anchor about 5 miles up the bay, and looked civilized & beautiful in the midst of this wild scenery. Canoes filled with still wilder looking Savages surrounded the ship offering vegetables & fish for barter.

At 10 o C a m we reached the Ship. We were introduced by Peel to all the officers by whom we were most kindly and hospitably received. Capt. Gordon was away, up the harbour on a shooting and botanising excursion. . . .

Capt. Gordon returned at mid day and very fully confirmed the invitation we would remain on board as long as the Vessel remained in the Harbor & consider ourselves quite at home.

The delight at meeting with our own Country men and brother Officers in this wild and distant land, the recognitions that soon followed of my being the brother of "Jack Warre" well known to many of the officers — whose shipmates he had been, and the kindness with which we were treated soon removed all strangeness and can only be thoroughly appreciated after a six or 8 months tour with strangers deprived of all the ordinary comforts of civilized life.

Capt. Gordon kindly insisted upon our dining with him on the two following days, but we lived in the gun room and had our Cots slung on the Main Deck.

We amused ourselves in fishing & observing the Indians, who constantly surrounded the Ship, bartering Potatoes, Venison and their baskets & fish with the Sailors and Marines for their old clothes etc. Several Indians were allowed to come on board and were shown over the ship. The turning lathe attracted great attention. Guns were fired during the day to show the ricochet of the shot along the water. All this amused us and astonished the natives.

[19] HBRS 7:286.

On the 26th the ship got under weigh & stood out of Port Discovery into the Straits of Juan de Fuca — The savages seemed more amused with the sailors running up the rigging, than all the other sights. It was obliged to anchor, after having made about 6 mi[les]. The wind failed & the tide was setting too strong up the Straits to enable the ship to make progress.

Early on Saturday the 27 September we took leave of our new acquaintances and embarking in the barge kindly lent us by Captain Gordon we set sail for Fort Victoria on Vancouvers Island 25 miles distant.[20]

Guests of Roderick Finlayson, the two military gentlemen set about getting the information they needed about the military preparedness of Fort Victoria. They were glad to note that the fort's six warehouses and two dwelling houses were musketproof. They noted also that three hundred men could be lodged in the storehouses. However, they were disappointed to find that the fort had no powder magazine, and that its water supply was "very indifferent outside the Fort, liable to drought during summer". (Wells sunk in the fort had failed to strike water.) About the best they could say of Fort Victoria from a military point of view was that it was "capable of making a good defence against an irregular or Indian force."[21] Conscientiously going into details, Warre and Vavasour recorded that, at the time of their visit, Fort Victoria had 35 men,[22] no sheep, 1 pig, 7 horses, 23 "meat cattle", and that the land under cultivation totalled 120 acres. Their time in Victoria was not devoted entirely to such laborious research. On October 6th they were guests at a dance. Warre's sketch of the Indian lady who was his partner is one of the most delightful of his many sketches. It shows well the artificially deformed "sugarloaf skull" which the Indians deemed beautiful and secured by tightly binding the heads of their infants.

Disappointing news awaited Warre and Vavasour upon their return to Fort Vancouver. A principal purpose of their journey had been to examine the approaches to the mouth of the Columbia

---

[20] Warre, *Columbia Diary*, pp. 1133-34.

[21] "Report of Lieuts. Warre & Vavasour", PRO, F.O. 5/457, p. 122(b).

[22] It should be noted, however, that in a table of "Establishments of the Honble Hudsons Bay Company in the North West" (F.O. 5/457, f.86), Warre and Vavasour credit Fort Victoria with only 20 men.

and determine where guns would have to be placed to control entry into the river. Sir George Simpson had earlier seen that Cape Disappointment was the key site, and had instructed Ogden "to take possession of that headland on behalf of the Hudson's Bay Company, ostensibly with a view of forming a trading post and 'Pilot's Lookout' thereon."[23] By using Ogden as a front, Simpson hoped to assure British possession of Cape Disappointment without tipping off the Americans to the strategic implications. But Warre discovered that, though Ogden had "purchased" the Cape, the seller had turned out to be a man without legal title to it. The two Americans who had registered their title with the provisional government were demanding payment for themselves. Through the winter negotiations dragged on, until an increasingly restive Ogden finally bought the Cape from the two Americans for a thousand dollars and surveyor's fees.[24] The deep secret about the real reason for the presence of Warre and Vavasour, and the real purpose of the purchase of Cape Disappointment, obviously had leaked out. Father Demers, in a letter of 30 March 1846 noted:

MM. Warre and Vavassour two English engineers, have succeeded in procuring, in the name of their government, the very terrain on Cape Disappointment which protects the entrance of our river.[25]

Only a few days before this letter was written, Warre and Vavasour had started back to Canada, travelling by way of Athabasca Pass. On 20 July 1846 they were back in Montreal. With them they had brought copious notes and sketches, and meticulously drawn plans of key strategic points and settlements. To the officer commanding the Royal Engineers in Canada, Vavasour submitted a report based on the premise that it would be impracticable to bring British troops overland from Canada. Instead they would have to travel by sea, land at Fort Nisqually on Puget Sound (close to modern Olympia), and then proceed overland to the aid of Fort Vancouver. Meticulously he noted what garrison artillery would be needed at Cape Disappointment and other key positions.

[23] "Documents: Secret Mission of Warre and Vavasour", *WHQ* 3 (1912) : 139.
[24] *WHQ* 3 (1912) : 143.
[25] *Famed Quebec Mission*, p. 236.

36. John Work   37. Mrs. John Work

38. John Tod   39. Mrs. John Tod

40.   Fort Rupert

41. Indian Village Adjacent to Fort Rupert

42. Bishop Demers   43. James Sinclair

44. Fur Press

Among the documents drawn up by Warre and Vavasour[26] is a statistical table setting forth the establishment maintained by the HBC, both in its forts in New Caledonia and Columbia and on its ships. These figures show that the HBC had a total of 643 employees west of the Rockies. On its farms it had 3005 acres under cultivation, and livestock totalling 8848 sheep, 1906 pigs, 1716 horses and 4430 cattle. Accompanying this is a census of the native population, tribe by tribe, west of the Rockies, in the area north of latitude 42°. The totals given are:

Males	33,956
Females	35,182
Children	1,584 under 12 years
Slaves	5,146

75,868 — From Census taken in 1839, 40 & 41

11,080 — Estimated Numbers belonging to Tribes not included in the above Census

Total	86,948

As the year of 1845 approached its end, everyone sensed that settlement of the boundary question could not be delayed much longer. Father Bolduc put forcefully the need to delineate the areas of national sovereignty:

As for our civil affairs, they are going from bad to worse. The population is growing from day to day by the emigration from the United States, yet, however, no government at all; for one must not call by that name the convention of settlers who have agreed to make laws, which everybody violates without ceremony without there being any authority to prevent it.[27]

The year ended on an ominous note. In the 1820s American immigrants had begun to settle in that portion of Mexico known as Texas. In 1836 these Americans rebelled against the Mexican

26 PRO, F.O. 5/457, ff.86-88.
27 *Famed Quebec Mission*, p. 243.

government and, after defeating the forces sent against them, declared Texas an independent republic. Mexico steadfastly refused to concede the independence of Texas and looked forward to re-establishing her authority in the area. Now, in December of 1845, the United States proceeded to annex the territory. "The Annexation of Texas" attended to, the next item on President Polk's agenda was "The Re-occupation of Oregon".

1846

*John Tod's vaccination trick saves Fort Kamloops men —
Anderson explores the Harrison-Lillooet and Coquihalla
routes seeking a new brigade trail — "Fifty-four Forty or
Fight" — The Royal Navy prepares for hostilities — War
averted.*

On March 20th, while on furlough, Dr. John McLoughlin reached
for his pen and wrote to Governor Sir George Simpson: "... it is
not my Intention to Resume Active Duty in the Service of the
Hudson Bay Company".[1] Thus ended McLoughlin's curiously
mottled career as an officer of the HBC. In the beginning he had
been a devoted and obedient servant of the Company, efficiently and
profitably rehabilitating the great Columbia Department; in the end
he had become sullen and irreconcilable, deliberately ignoring the
orders of his superiors, and even sabotaging their policies. All the
time he had served in the Columbia, his had been the responsibility
for protecting British interests; yet because of his constant and covert
pro-Americanism, and in particular his assistance to American
immigration, no man had done greater damage to those interests.
Looking back over the long and somewhat ambiguous career of Dr.
John McLoughlin, we may say his taints and virtues equally
weighed. He was, in John Tod's memorable phrase, an "ambivalent
mammoth".

A sad irony marks McLoughlin's final years. In May 1849, at the
earliest possible moment after the American takeover of Oregon and
Washington, he achieved his ambition of becoming an American
citizen. But the crude and entirely unjustifiable American prejudice
against the HBC now attached itself to McLoughlin. James Thur-
ston, who had arrived from the eastern United States in 1847, used

[1] HBRS 7:157.

the Oregon Land Donation Law of 1850 to deprive McLoughlin of legal title to his holdings at Willamette Falls. Fortunately no act of physical dispossession was attempted. An extremely bitter and disillusioned man, McLoughlin died in 1857. Five years later, in belated and partial compensation, the Oregon Legislative Assembly permitted McLoughlin's legatees, upon payment of one thousand dollars, to receive title to this land.

John Tod was now in command of the Company's Thompson River Post, as Kamloops was officially known. This summer as usual he sent off his men to obtain dried Fraser River salmon from the Indians at Pavilion, remaining in the fort alone with his family and a half-breed boy. Two days after the salmon party left there was a knocking at the fort gate. Looking through the half-opened door, Tod saw Lolo, or "St. Paul", the fort's Indian interpreter. Lolo had grim news: en route with the salmon party, he had been warned by another Indian to turn back since an ambush was being prepared for the annihilation of the men from the fort. By Tod's own admission this news put him "in an awful state of mind" but, by the next morning, he had thought things through and made his decision. Mounting a fine white mare and taking the half-breed boy as his only companion, Tod rode forth to deal with the situation.

Catching up with his salmon party, he found them entirely unaware of any danger, Lolo not having told them of the peril ahead. Riding in advance of his men, Tod saw a large band of Indians on the banks of the Fraser. Observing that they were wearing war paint, flourishing guns and knives, and had not a single woman or child in their company, Tod realized that Lolo's warning, which he had begun to disbelieve, was completely true. Returning to his little party of half a dozen French-Canadian engagés, Tod placed them in hiding in bushes, from whose concealment they could watch the proceedings. They were told that if they saw him fall, they were to retreat to Kamloops.

Riding alone, John Tod headed towards the war party of some 1500 Indians, "charging & prancing towards them on my fine white mare with main [sic] & tail flowing in the wind". Startled, the Indians demanded of Tod why he came. Tod was ready with his answer — had they not heard that the smallpox had broken out at

Walla Walla and was spreading throughout the country? Mention of the dreaded smallpox demoralized the war party; especially when Tod, gesturing towards where some 10,000 salmon were drying on racks, observed that if he had not come to vaccinate the Indians they would soon all be as dead as those salmon.

Before starting to vaccinate, Tod waited until the Indian women came out from hiding and started to trade the dried salmon. Meanwhile, to gain time for this bartering, he ordered the warriors to fell a large tree, on which he then sat himself. Finally, the Indian warriors having washed their right arms, Tod set to work with a will: "I had in my vest pocket three smallpox scabs; I commenced to cut & vaccinate; those who were more noted rascals than others I laid into with a vengeance."[2] After all his vaccine had been used up, he gave his lancet to the Indians and told them that once their vaccination scabs had formed they were to draw off fresh pus from them and complete the process among the hundreds still unvaccinated. Then Tod followed his men back to Kamloops, confident that sore arms, if not gratitude, would keep the Indians from resuming their hostile intentions.

Tod's nearest neighbour was Alexander C. Anderson, in command of the HBC post at Alexandria. Very much aware that, if the international boundary were extended along the 49th parallel to the Pacific, the HBC would probably lose its brigade route down to Fort Vancouver, Anderson the previous year had volunteered to seek a new route for the fur brigades, one which would bring them out at Fort Langley without ever dipping south of the 49th parallel.

Now in May of this year Anderson with six picked men set out on this hazardous venture. After leaving Kamloops, he travelled west along the Thompson River a while, then struck overland past Cache Creek to "The Fountain" on Fraser River. Travelling on foot, Anderson's men followed the Fraser down to Lillooet and then, using what must have been a route well known to the Indians, they travelled, sometimes by foot and sometimes by canoe, along the Seton and Anderson Lakes route which led to Harrison Lake by way

---

[2] For Tod's own detailed account of the famous episode, see his *History of New Caledonia*, pp. 56-63.

of Lillooet Lake and River. From Harrison Lake it was an easy
journey to Fort Langley. Here Anderson told Chief Trader Yale that
the route he had just travelled, with its alternation of long lakes and
overland stretches, was simply not feasible for brigade travel.

The logical next move was to seek a brigade route east of the
Fraser, traversing the Cascade Mountains. Setting out from Fort
Langley, Anderson and his little band first took canoe up the Fraser
and the Coquihalla Rivers. Then, turning their faces east, they
confronted the towering peaks of the Cascades and, in a territory
where no Indian trails could guide them, sought to thread a way
through the mountains. Later Anderson commented laconically that
they made their way "hap-hazard".[3] They did, however, manage to
find a route which finally took them over the summit of the Cascades
and down to the headwaters of the Similkameen. Unfortunately the
route had climbed so high into the snows of the mountains as to
make it almost totally impossible for the fur brigades to follow.
Anderson decided that he must look for a better way the next year.

One of the guests whom Anderson had upon occasion put up at
Fort Alexandria was a timid little Jesuit missionary named Father
Nobili. Making himself overcome handicaps of physique and temperament, Nobili strove manfully to carry out the duties entrusted to
him by Bishop Blanchet. This year he not only became the first
missionary to penetrate to the shores of Babine Lake, but on his
return established the first mission on Okanagan Lake at a place
known to us only as "the Taillis d'épinettes".[4] This mission survived
for only three years. The real evangelizing of the Okanagan lay
much further in the future.

By and large, 1846 was a year spent in the shadow of war.
President Polk had won his election on a platform which called for
an American takeover of Oregon, and now the more rabid of his
supporters were raising a clamour for seizure of all that lay between
California and Alaska. "Fifty-four Forty or Fight!" became the war
cry. The slogan was daubed on the walls of barns and houses, either

---

[3] A. C. Anderson, *History of the Northwest Coast*, UBC transcript, p. 50. (For
Anderson's journal of these explorations, see HBCA, B.97/a/1846.)

[4] Anderson, *History of N.W. Coast*, p. 134.

in its original form or as "P.P.P.P." (standing for a heavily whimsical "Phifty-Phour Phorty or Phight").[5]

As the belligerence of the Americans became ever more evident, the British prepared for hostilities. British regulars — the Sixth Regiment of Foot along with Royal Engineers and some artillery — arrived at Fort Garry. On the West Coast, of course, the fighting would have to be done by the Royal Navy. For many months H.M.S. *Modeste*, a sloop of 18 guns, had been at anchor in the Columbia, giving a measure of defence to Fort Vancouver. Now Rear-Admiral Sir George F. Seymour, Commander-in-Chief, Pacific, aware of the American naval forces being assembled in his area, moved quickly to reinforce the British position in the North-west. First to arrive was the frigate H.M.S. *Fisgard* (42 guns), Captain Duntze, in April. Too large to cross the Columbia River bar and ascend that river, the *Fisgard* took up station at Fort Nisqually at the southern end of Puget Sound. From here she could rush a relief column, if need be, to aid Fort Vancouver. June saw the arrival of three more British men-of-war: H.M.S. *Herald* (a barque of 26 guns), H.M.S. *Pandora* (a brig of 6 guns), and H.M.S. *Cormorant* (a sidewheel steamer bearing 6 guns). Accompanying the squadron was a supply ship, the *Rosalind*. The force should have been augmented by H.M.S. *America* (50 guns) which had been in these waters the previous year, but her arrogant captain had taken her back to England without either the knowledge or consent of his admiral. Her absence could have made the difference between victory or defeat for the Royal Navy had the Oregon dispute ended in war. Not surprisingly, Captain Gordon was later court-martialled for desertion of his station, but was let off surprisingly leniently.

Even without H.M.S. *America*, the little British naval force displayed high morale while awaiting war with the Yankees. Roderick Finlayson, commanding Fort Victoria, noted that the men of the Royal Navy declared they could take the whole of the Columbia country in twenty-four hours. Meanwhile there was plenty of

---

[5] It has long been a mistaken notion that this was a campaign cry during Polk's presidential election campaign in 1844. Such, however, was not the case. See Edwin A. Miles, " 'Fifty-four Forty or Fight' — An American Political Legend", *The Mississippi Valley Historical Review* 44 (1957):291-309.

surveying and charting for them to do. The British warships, in fact, upon arrival in these waters found little to guide them other than Captain Vancouver's maps and *Voyage*, and some notes left by H.M.S. *America*. The tide rips, the rocky ledges, the summer fogs, all posed difficulties and dangers. Not least of their problems was that of finding Fort Victoria, which lacked any notable landmark towards which one could set a ship's course. The captain of H.M.S. *Cormorant*, in his Remark Book, offered the following solution to the problem:

> Ships entering these Straits for the eastward, unless sailing very fast are allways visited by Natives in canoes several talk English slightly, but all know the name of the officer in charge of Fort Victoria, and I believe asking for Mr Finlaison is the quickest way to find Victoria.[6]

So much for navigational aids in those days before the *B.C. Pilot*!

When the Royal Navy found its way to Fort Victoria, it was delighted by what it saw. Midshipman Chimmo of H.M.S. *Herald* rhapsodized in his diary:

> ... in passing through the wood of Vancouver [Island] and the smaller islands, we could not but be struck at the lofty and magnificent cedar, pine, oak, and cypress trees, and the blossoms of yellow laburnum scenting the air; every slope and undulation was a lawn and natural garden, studded with wild plum, gooseberry, currant, strawberry, and wild onion.[7]

In another account of the voyage of the *Herald* we read of the scenery around Fort Victoria:

> It is a natural park; noble oaks and ferns are seen in greatest luxuriance, thickets of the hazel and the willow, shrubberies of the poplar and the alder, are dotted about. One could hardly believe that this was not the work of art. . . . [8]

---

[6] Royal Navy, Office of the Hydrographer of the Navy, (Taunton, Somerset), "Remark Book of H.M.S. Cormorant, 1846", p. 4.

[7] *Euryalus: Tales of the Sea* (London, 1860), p. 172.

[8] B. Seemann, *Narrative of the Voyage of H.M.S. Herald During the Years 1845-51* (London, 1853), I:102. This portion of the book, dealing with events prior to Seemann joining the *Herald*, is generally credited to Midshipman Bedford Pim.

This writer, possibly Midshipman Pim, went on to record that already there were about 160 acres under cultivation, and that plans were being made to double the size of the fort. This same author provides us with an interesting account of the Songhees village across from Fort Victoria:

> On the opposite side of the harbour is a large native village; the distance across is only 400 yards, and canoes keep up a constant communication between it and the fort. . . . The houses are dirty in the extreme, and the odour with which they are infested almost forbids close examination; but they are built with solidity, the climate rendering it necessary to guard against the cold, — and arranged with some degree of order in streets or lanes with passages running up between them.[9]

Similarly, Midshipman Chimmo was an interested observer of the local Indians. He noted that one never saw a deformed youngster, since the Indians always put deformed babies to death. Spotting that a number of the Indians had a joint or two missing from their fingers, Chimmo discovered that deliberate amputation of the missing joints had been part of the ritual mourning for a close relative.

Dealing with the Indians, the bluejackets and their officers began to learn a bit of the Chinook jargon:

> Their vociferations are ludicrous in the extreme: "Jack you patlach me shirt," "Makook salmon," "Clooosh salmon," "Waâke jacket." are specimens of them. 'Patlach' is give; 'makook,' buy; 'clooosh,' very good; and 'waâke,' very bad. If something very old and bad is offered, they turn it over with scorn, pronouncing it 'peeshaaak,' a term of contempt and reproach, for which they seem to have a great aversion if applied to themselves. . . . They sometimes ask for 'muk-a-muk,' something to eat, and oftener for 't-chuckk,' something to drink. 'Pill-pill,' or vermilion paint, and 'pullale,' or gunpowder, are also in request.[10]

In the autumn the warships all sailed away except the little paddlewheeler H.M.S. *Cormorant*. The *Fisgard* took with her a young "flathead" boy (one with the deliberately deformed sugarloaf skull admired by the coastal Indians). During his journey to England he learned English and some Spanish, giving the lie to the

[9] Seemann, I: 105.

[10] *Ibid.*, I: 108.

misconception that head-binding caused idiocy. Before his premature death he had become a general favourite:

> . . . his disposition was such as to endear him to every person on board, and before his death he had made much progress in reading and writing.[11]

The *Cormorant* lingered on after the other warships to investigate for the Navy the coal deposits near Port McNeill. Accordingly, in mid-September, she left Victoria for the north. On September 23rd, passing through Johnstone Strait, she navigated some very difficult water to which she gave the name of "Sir George Seymour's Narrows". Late on September 24th she arrived at Port McNeill:

> An abundance of coal was discovered, some pits were dug, and a coal formation found to exist. The steamer obtained sixty tons from the Indians, who brought it off in their canoes; blankets, tobacco, &c. being bartered for it, thus costing the government 4s. 6d. per ton. It appeared that they gathered it from the surface of the soil. Some of it was afterwards consumed by the *Cormorant*, and pronounced to be of a very fair quality.[12]

This final mission completed, H.M.S. *Cormorant* lingered only a few weeks longer before sailing for the British naval base at Callao in Peru.

The reason why the British warships departed this autumn was the news that there would be no war with the U.S.A. Over the years succeeding British governments had maintained that, though the Americans had valid claims to lands south of the Columbia, they had no just claim to any territory north of that great river. But at last the British had surrendered to the Americans all the land north of the lower Columbia, as far as the 49th parallel. On 15 June 1846, under the terms of the Treaty of Washington, the Americans, without any shadow of right or justice but solely by the threat of war, obtained a great part of the future State of Washington and deprived the future province of British Columbia of some fifty thousand square miles of territory.

---

[11] Anon., "Recollections of Six Months in Puget Sound", *Nautical Magazine* 21 (1852):318.

[12] *Ibid.*, p. 315.

The Loss of Southern Columbia

The Treaty of Washington establishes the international boundary — The American and British claims reviewed — The U.S.A. without rights to any land north of the lower Columbia — A pacifist British Foreign Secretary surrenders the "Triangle" — The U.S.A. attacks Mexico — Lament for a lost kingdom.

The surrender of the land north of the Columbia really meant very little for Great Britain, which could easily spare so small a corner from what was already the world's vastest empire. But for Canada, a kingdom yet unborn, that treaty had serious consequences.

Had right and justice prevailed in 1846, Canada would today have not one but two provinces on the Pacific, with a total population more than double that of British Columbia. The consequences would have been profound. That chronic imbalance of population between East and West which permits the provinces of Ontario and Quebec to dominate the Canadian political and economic scene would have been substantially corrected, and Canada today would not be a country with such a chronic list to the east.

Contemplating so great a loss, one inevitably asks how it came about. One speculates: "Could it have been avoided?" One wonders: "Who was responsible?" One demands: "Who must share in the blame?" Let us conclude this volume with trying to find answers.

The British case rested upon three declarations of sovereignty: that by Drake over New Albion in 1579; that by Vancouver in 1792 to all the territory lying between latitude north 39°20' and the entrance to the Strait of Juan de Fuca; and that by Broughton, later in the same year, to the basin of the lower Columbia. A fourth declaration of sovereignty, overlooked by the British, had been made by David Thompson in 1811 when he had hoisted the Union

Jack at the junction of the Snake and Columbia rivers and posted a notice claiming for Britain all the country to the north.

Declarations of sovereignty count for less than exploration and settlement. Britain's advocates distinguished between "vague discovery" as represented by Drake, and "accurate discovery" as represented by Vancouver. In both the British had clear priority over the Americans, and they enjoyed this priority not only on the coast but in the interior of this vast domain. The first explorer to cross it overland had been Sir Alexander Mackenzie in 1793. As for exploration along the Columbia River itself, the first white man to explore the first eighty-five miles upstream from the mouth of the Columbia was Lieut. Broughton, R.N., in 1792, who had gone through the ceremony of taking possession for Britain at the farthest point of his penetration. The Columbia River from its junction with the Snake to its source had been first explored by David Thompson. Fur traders in the service of British companies had, in fact, done by far the greater part of the exploration of the area.

Strongest of all territorial claims is that which rests upon actual occupation and settlement. Here again the British had the stronger case. They had been first to establish posts west of the Rockies (e.g. McLeod Lake in 1805). They had developed and extended their trade so that by 1846 they had a chain of posts, centering on their great depot at Fort Vancouver, extending from Fort Umpqua in southern Oregon to Fort Connolly in northern New Caledonia. Moreover, thousands of acres were under cultivation on farms operated by the Hudson's Bay Company's affiliate, the Puget's Sound Agricultural Company.

By comparison, the American case was almost pathetically weak. Since only Congress could proclaim sovereignty, the United States had no such declarations as had been made by the British. As far as exploration was concerned, the Americans rested their case on the fact that, although the Spaniard Hezeta had discovered the Columbia River in 1775,[1] and Captain Vancouver passing that way on 23 April 1793 had not failed to notice "very light river-coloured water" and adduce the presence of "some very considerable river or

---

[1] Hezeta had named the river "Rio de San Roque". See Cook, *Flood Tide of Empire*, p. 78.

rivers", the American Captain Robert Gray the following month became the first white man actually to enter the river, giving it the name of his ship, the *Columbia*. Where interior exploration was concerned, the Americans made much of the second overland crossing to the Pacific, that of Lewis and Clark who reached the Pacific in 1805, twelve years after Mackenzie. During their journey Lewis and Clark had become the first white men to travel the two hundred miles of the Columbia upstream from the point reached by Broughton in 1792.

Where settlement was concerned, the Americans had to pin everything on the founding of Astoria in 1811. This claim should have meant little, since the Astorians had sold out to the North West Company in 1813. However, the absurd action of the captain of H.M.S. *Racoon* in formally taking possession of the post recently purchased by a British company had given the Americans a legalistic argument for the restitution of Astoria under the terms of the Treaty of Ghent. Britain had shortsightedly acquiesced, and the Americans had formally and briefly raised the Stars and Stripes once more over the post. But the years had passed without the Americans reestablishing Astoria and this abandonment had, in fact, negated any future American claims based on settlement as represented by Astoria. The really valid American claim, based on settlement, came in the early 1840s with the influx of settlers into the Willamette valley — and this settlement was in territory south of the Columbia River, which Britain had been prepared to concede all along.

Realizing how very weak their claims were, the Americans had sought to bolster them. Hence in 1819, when the United States signed the Adams-Onis Treaty with Spain, it included a clause by which Spain transferred to the U.S. all its rights north of the 42nd parallel. But Spain, having long before withdrawn from Nootka and Neah Bay, and her shipping for decades having been absent from the North Pacific, no longer had any "rights or claims" in the area. Nevertheless, there was to be much American trumpeting of how the U.S. had inherited the Spanish claims.

Two other elements must be noted in connection with the contending American and British claims. A very important consideration in such disputes is the principle of "contiguity", that (other things being equal) the country whose territory lies closest to a disputed area has the best claim to it. Since both Britain and the United States recognized each other's territories as extending up to the Rocky Mountains, there was nothing really to be made of this, though a remarkable number of red herrings were dragged in under the title of "contiguity". One other consideration was the interest of the indigenous population. The Indians of course detested the Americans, and consistently preferred to deal with "King George Men" rather than with "Boston Men".[2] The Americans treated this argument with the contempt that they felt it deserved.

Now that the cases of the two claimants have been reviewed, we may consider somewhat briefly the course of boundary negotiations between the signing of the Treaty of Ghent in 1814 and that of the Treaty of Washington.

When in 1814 President Monroe briefed the delegates he was sending to Ghent to end the War of 1812, he gave them explicit instructions that they were not to agree to anything less than the 49th parallel:

On no pretext can the British Government set up a claim to territory south of the northern boundary of the United States. It is not believed that they have any claim whatever to territory on the Pacific ocean. You will, however, be careful, should a definition of boundary be attempted, not to countenance, in any manner, or in any quarter, a pretension in the British Government to territory south of that line.[3]

The Americans, under a misapprehension that the Treaty of Utrecht had established the 49th parallel as the dividing line between the British territories and "Louisiana", regarded this as their northern boundary. In 1818 they did manage to persuade the British to acknowledge it as the international boundary as far as the Rocky Mountains. They very much wanted it to become the border all the way to the Pacific, but the British did not see why, though an arbitrary line of latitude might have to serve as the boundary across the great plains where natural landmarks were lacking, it should be

---

[2] This argument of the preference of the Indian population was brought up by Adam Thom, Recorder of Rupert's Land, in *The Claims to the Oregon Territory Considered* (London, 1844), pp. 41-42.

[3] Quoted by Merk, *Oregon Question*, p. 7.

continued into the Pacific North-west where mountain ranges and rivers provided natural boundaries. Nor did the British see why they should surrender the lower Columbia basin, in which their traders were active, to a country which did not have a single citizen dwelling therein.

After 1814 the Americans never relinquished their claim to the 49th parallel, even while accepting the temporary expedient of co-dominion with Britain over the disputed territory. The one time when the Americans did seem on the verge of settling for something less was in 1818 when an American representative in London offered to give England the lands draining into Puget Sound in return for the Columbia basin south of the 49th parallel. The offer was rejected by the British, who still could see no reason for abandoning the Columbia basin to the Americans. They were prepared, however, to share it, and offered the Americans the territory to the south of the lower Columbia. When the Americans refused this, co-dominion was reluctantly accepted as the only alternative to war.

By 1845 the Americans were ready to force the British to accept a boundary that would give the United States everything at least as far north as the 49th parallel, and conceivably all the way to the Alaskan boundary at 54°40′. In his inaugural address the new Democratic president, James Polk, after speaking of the American annexation of Texas, continued:

Nor will it become in a less degree my duty to assert and maintain by all constitutional means the right of the United States to that portion of our territory which lies beyond the Rocky Mountains. Our title to the country of the Oregon is "clear and unquestionable" [a quotation from his party's election platform] and already are our people preparing to perfect that title by occupying it with their wives and children. . . . To us belongs the duty of protecting them adequately wherever they may be upon our soil.[4]

When the text of Polk's inaugural address reached Britain, there was a thoroughly understandable counter-explosion. Sir Robert Peel in the House of Commons declared that Britain had rights in Oregon which were "clear and unquestionable", and the Leader of

[4] James D. Richardson, *A Compilation of the Messages and Papers of the Presidents,* ([New York], 1910), III:2231.

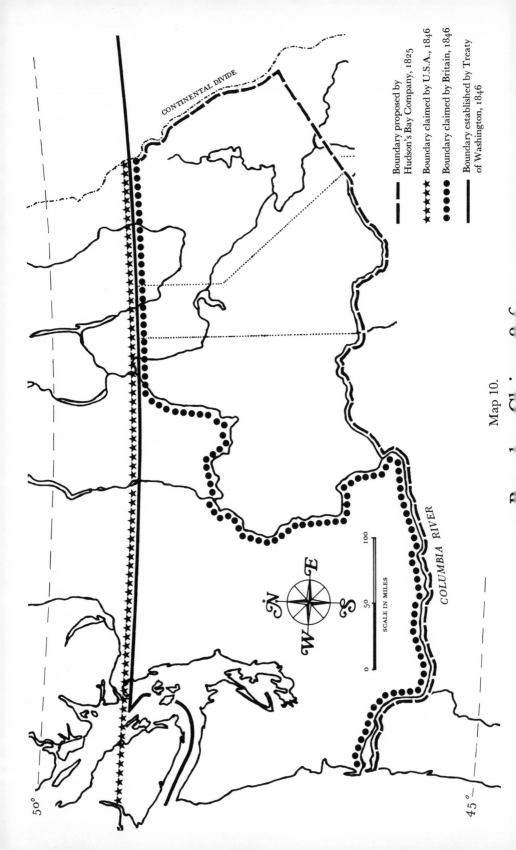

CONTINENTAL DIVIDE

Boundary proposed by
Hudson's Bay Company, 1825

★★★★★ Boundary claimed by U.S.A., 1846

●●●●● Boundary claimed by Britain, 1846

Boundary established by Treaty
of Washington, 1846

COLUMBIA RIVER

N
W   E
S

SCALE IN MILES

0   50   100

50°

45°

Map 10.

the Opposition associated himself with Peel's stand. As one exasperated observer remarked, the U.S. had no more rights or title to the lands north of the Columbia than she had to Siberia.[5] The remark was a little extreme, but it had some justification.

It is instructive to note a distinguished American historian's summation of the situation at this time existing in the so-called "Triangle" between the lower Columbia River, the Pacific and the 49th parallel.

North of the Columbia River . . . in the region really at issue, the total number of American settlers was eight. Seven of these with their families . . . had established themselves in October 1845, at the head of Puget Sound. At Jackson Prairie near the Cowlitz Landing was an Americanized Englishman. That was the extent of American occupation north of the Columbia; and of American commercial activity here, there was in 1846 none.[6]

On the other hand, within this triangle, the British had Fort Vancouver, populated by about 200 men with their wives and families, with a large adjacent area under cultivation; Fort Nisqually where 5800 sheep, 200 horses and 1850 cattle grazed over 167,000 acres; another farm at Cowlitz with 1500 head of livestock, where more than 10,000 bushels of grain were raised each year; the recently founded and thriving Fort Victoria, and Fort Okanagan. Also within the triangle was a French-Canadian village made up of some nineteen families close to the HBC's Cowlitz farm. To quote the American Merk once more:

Clearly British influence outweighed American in this contested area; and if occupation had determined its fate in 1846, it must inevitably have become British territory.[7]

Not occupation but the shameless threat of an unprovoked war of aggression was to secure this territory for the United States.

Even so, how did it happen that a British government, which in 1845 was as firm as any of its predecessors in insisting upon the Columbia River line, signed away the triangle the next year? For

[5] Anon., "Oregon", *Nautical Magazine* 15 (1846), p. 300.
[6] Merk, *Oregon Question*, p. 236.
[7] *Ibid.*, p. 238.

the answer we must turn to Lord Aberdeen, the British Foreign Secretary.

George Gordon, 4th Earl of Aberdeen (1784-1860) was in many ways a most attractive person, though a few found him cold and aloof. Deeply interested in all the arts, he won from the poet Byron the epithet of "Athenian Aberdeen". Even if he had not been the protégé of Pitt the Younger, he could have regarded a career in politics almost as his birthright if he had cared to claim it. In September 1813 Aberdeen had been appointed Ambassador to Austria, at that time Britain's ally in the Napoleonic Wars, and the youthful British Ambassador had accompanied Emperor Francis in the field. Thus he was an eyewitness of the Battle of Leipzig. The experience was a traumatic one which marked him psychologically for life. Many years later he informed the Russian Czar that he "had once seen forty thousand men dead or dying on the field of battle, and that he had solemnly vowed never to be connected with a Government engaged in war!"[8] There was nothing in any way hypocritical about that statement. His own description of himself was "a Minister of Peace, if ever there was one".[9] All of which was very admirable, but hardly fitted Aberdeen to be the Foreign Secretary of a great power.

In time Aberdeen would rise to be Prime Minister and that ultimate, most testing of offices, revealed weakness in the man. In some ways he was akin to the appeasers in the British Government who let Hitler have Czechoslovakia. As far as the Oregon triangle was concerned, he seems to have regarded it, like that portion of New Brunswick which he let the Americans have, as a "tract of barren pine swamp". President Polk and his Secretary of State, Buchanan, were fortunate in their adversary, if such a word may be applied to the studious, fastidious, pacifist and deeply humanitarian Aberdeen.

Before ever Polk delivered his notorious inaugural address, Aberdeen had decided, quite correctly, that despite all the 54°40' blustering, the U.S. would settle for the 49th parallel, and he had

---

[8] *The Croker Papers*, ed. L. J. Jennings (London, 1884), III:299.

[9] Lady Frances Balfour, *The Life of George Fourth Earl of Aberdeen* (London, n.d.) I:iv.

decided, if need be, to let her have it. Working deviously, almost in collaboration with the American ambassador, he set about persuading the British that the Columbia was not an important issue and that the Americans had a very good claim to it. Mounting a careful propaganda campaign, at first through Whig newspapers (a cunning tactic for a Tory minister), and then through *The Times* which was beholden to him, he gradually softened up the British public, winning it more and more over to his own conviction about the disputed territory — "Its real importance is insignificant".[10]

Aberdeen would not have been able to bring the British cabinet around to his point of view had it not been for Fort Victoria. The Hudson's Bay Company had thought it a very wise move to establish a new base at Fort Victoria, where its stores would be safe from any uprising by the American settlers, and whither supply ships could safely come without facing the hazard of the Columbia bar. But in reaching this decision, the HBC's Governor and Committee had robbed themselves of their strongest argument when urging Britain to support them on the Columbia. Fort Vancouver could no longer be presented as the indispensable depot, and the Columbia River, the "western St. Lawrence", accordingly seemed less indispensable as an artery for trade. Increasingly the British cabinet felt that, if they could save Fort Victoria for the HBC, they might be well advised to let Fort Vancouver and the Columbia go, rather than fight a war. So Aberdeen had his way.

In fairness to Aberdeen, it must be noted that he did what he could, through Pakenham, the British ambassador in Washington, to save as much as possible of the triangle. The Americans having urged that they needed ports on Puget Sound to compensate for the lack of harbours south of the Columbia, Aberdeen offered them free port privileges on the Sound. That offer was rejected. Then arbitration was offered. Aware of American republican prejudices, Aberdeen proposed that no European monarchy should be the arbitrator but rather the republic of Switzerland, or the free cities of Hamburg or Bremen. The Americans, knowing the weakness of their case, refused to go to arbitration. So Aberdeen prepared to capitulate.

[10] Aberdeen to Peel, 22 Oct. 1844, in R. C. Clark, ed., "Aberdeen and Peel on Oregon, 1844", *OHQ* 34 (1933):240.

He insisted upon only one thing — the boundary could follow the 49th parallel only to the sea, but then it must turn south through the Strait of Juan de Fuca, giving Britain access to the Strait of Georgia and the Fraser River, keeping Vancouver Island intact and British, and preserving for the HBC its depot at Fort Victoria. The concession was not a major one, and the United States Senate ratified the treaty by more than the required two-thirds majority.

> Intelligent students of American history today candidly admit that the American diplomats did exceedingly well in finally placing the line of the Canadian boundary at the 49th parallel of north latitude. . . . [11]

Such is the verdict, something of an understatement, by an American historian.

Other factors besides Aberdeen's pacificism entered into the ultimate settlement of the boundary issue. Britain as a whole did not want hostilities with the United States. The business community in London was determinedly against such a war, since it had been investing extensively in American state bonds and industrial stocks. The war, if it had to be fought, would have its outcome determined not in the West but in the East — and it was not certain that the Canadians could be counted upon, even though they had repudiated Mackenzie and Papineau when the latter had attempted rebellion a few years earlier. Moreover, some of the Métis (people partly of Indian and partly of French-Canadian descent) in the Red River district, could not be counted upon since they rather favoured annexation by the United States.

The Americans also had reasons for avoiding war if they could get a sizeable chunk of territory without one. A chief consideration was the war which the United States had already begun against her sister republic of Mexico. British Columbians who today feel sad when they think of what the United States took from them in 1846 may take consolation by comparing their loss with that suffered by the Mexicans. Mexico had no great European power to stand behind her. Fighting alone, she offered desperate resistance, culminating in the heroic defence of Chapultepec by the young officer

[11] T. C. Elliott, "David Thompson and the Columbia River", *OHQ* 12 (1911):203-204.

cadets of the Mexican Army. But the odds were hopeless. When the war ended, Mexico was stripped of two-fifths of her territory, the infamous Treaty of Guadalupe Hidalgo transferring to the Americans the present-day states of Utah, Nevada and California, as well as parts of Colorado, Wyoming, New Mexico and Arizona. Moreover, the Mexicans were forced to acquiesce in American annexation of Texas, which had been set up as an independent republic by rebellious American settlers.

In short, Canadians can assure themselves that, in an age when bellicose Americans were defining their boundaries as the Atlantic and the Pacific, the North Pole and Panama, they got off almost lightly. What saved them was the latent power of Britain represented in part by that little squadron based at Esquimalt harbour in 1846: H.M.S. *Herald*, H.M.S. *Cormorant*, H.M.S. *Fisgard*, H.M.S. *Pandora*. It is fitting that what was saved of Columbia should bear, as a memorial, the name of British Columbia.

By an irony of history, word of the signing of the Treaty of Washington reached London the day that the Peel Ministry lost office and Aberdeen ceased to be Foreign Secretary. His successor, the spirited Palmerston, would almost certainly have gone to war rather than concede the 49th parallel. Possibly, confronted by Palmerston, the Americans would have settled for the Columbia River line, but Polk would have had a hard time abandoning a cause to which he had so deeply committed himself. Had war come, the Americans might well have found themselves confronted by an Anglo-Mexican alliance. Even so, they might possibly have won ultimately — it never does to underestimate the energy, the imagination and the determination of the American people.

A greater threat, actually, than Polk's belligerence was the policy of "masterly inactivity" advocated by the brilliant American statesman Calhoun. He realized that if confrontation were avoided and nature simply allowed to take its course, the whole disputed area would in time become American because of the ultimate inpouring of an American population. In 1849 the California gold rush brought a torrent of newcomers from the eastern United States. In 1858 many of these same Americans streamed north to the Fraser River in another gold rush. Had the old co-dominion still existed, that American influx would almost certainly have resulted in the whole country going to the United States; but providentially the U.S. had in 1846 recognized by treaty the 49th parallel as its northern boundary, and that line held. Perhaps, paradoxically, we should be a little grateful to President Polk for prematurely forcing confrontation in 1846. Still, it is outrageous what the Americans extorted by threats and bluster. The Washingtonians of today are friendly and decent neighbours; but one must be haunted by a certain sadness when one thinks on what might have been. The blow was a grievous one.

Sound a brief lament for our lost kingdom: Willapa, Cowlitz, Chehalis, Nisqually, Puyallup, Rainier, Olympus, Nooksack, Stillaguamish, Skyhomish, Snoqualmie, Wenatchee, Chelan, Omak, Sanpoil — soaring mountains and winding waterways, pleasant valleys and high plateaus — a goodly, goodly land. Now forever lost.

Bibliography

1. *Bibliography of British Columbia*

Strathern, Gloria M. *Navigations, Traffiques & Discoveries 1774-1848: A Guide to Publications Relating to the Area now British Columbia.* Victoria, 1970. A detailed bibliographical description of 631 printed books in their various editions. Unfortunately periodical articles are not included.

2. *Manuscripts*

Those interested in relevant manuscripts in the Spanish and Mexican archives are referred to Warren L. Cook, *Flood Tide of Empire: Spain and the Pacific Northwest, 1543-1819* (New Haven, 1973), pp. 591-95.

A large number of libraries and archives contain manuscripts in English or French which are of interest to students of the early history of the Pacific North-west. The most important collections have already been noted in the "Acknowledgements" printed at the head of this volume. A few comments may be added here.

The paramount collection of manuscript material is that in the Hudson's Bay Company Archives, now in the keeping of the Provincial Archives of Manitoba. A complete set of microfilms of these manuscripts may be seen in the Public Archives of Canada, Ottawa. The PAC also contains a wealth of manuscript material of its own. One may cite, as examples, the Ermatinger Papers, the McLeod Papers, the Manby Journal of Vancouver's voyage, and the Warre Journal. The Provincial Archives of British Columbia, as might be expected, contains much material relating to the early period, although its real strength comes later.

The prime repository in Great Britain is, of course, the Public Record Office in London, particularly the records of the Admiralty, the Colonial Office and the Foreign Office. Papers relating to the early fur trading ventures based in India will be found in the India Office Library, and those relating to early botanical expeditions in the libraries of the Royal Botanical Gardens at Kew, and the Natural History Museum in Kensington.

Edward Bell's journal of the Vancouver expedition is in the Alexander Turnbull Library in Wellington, New Zealand. Only a portion of this was printed by Professor E. S. Meany and included in the 1957 edition of his *Vancouver's Discovery of Puget Sound.*

The most important of the American collections is that in the Bancroft Library of the University of California, Berkeley. Here are the materials which H. H. Bancroft, in preparation for his histories of the North-west Coast, obtained from various retired officers of the Hudson's Bay Company. Among the most valuable of these are:

Anderson, A. C., *History of the Northwest Coast*

Finlayson, Roderick, *History of Vancouver Island & the Northwest Coast*

Roberts, George B., *Recollections*

Tod, John, *History of New Caledonia & the Northwest Coast*

Tolmie, W. F., *History of Puget Sound & the Northwest Coast*

Typed transcripts of the above and of many other Bancroft items are to be found in the Public Archives of Canada.

3. *A Select Bibliography of Printed Materials*

Balfour, Lady Frances. *The Life of George Fourth Earl of Aberdeen.* London, n.d.

Bancroft, H. H. *History of British Columbia 1792-1887.* San Francisco, 1887.

———. *History of the Northwest Coast 1543-1846.* 2 vols. San Francisco, 1886.

———. *History of Oregon 1834-1888.* 2 vols. San Francisco, 1886-1888.

Beaglehole, J. C. *The Life of Captain James Cook.* Hakluyt Society. London, 1974.

Beaver, Herbert. "Experiences of a Chaplain at Fort Vancouver, 1836-1838". Ed. R. C. Clark, *OHQ* 39 (1938) :22-38.

Belcher, Edward. *Narrative of a Voyage Round the World Performed in H.M.S. Sulphur 1836-42.* London, 1843.

Bishop, Charles. *The Journal and Letters of Captain Charles Bishop on the North-west Coast of America . . . 1794-1799.* Ed. Michael Roe. Hakluyt Society. Cambridge, 1967.

Bishop, R. P. "Drake's Course in the North Pacific". *BCHQ* 3 (1939) :151-82.

Black, Samuel. *A Journal of a Voyage from Rocky Mountain Portage ... in Summer 1824.* Ed. E. E. Rich. HBRS 18. London, 1955.

Blanchet, F. N. *Historical Sketches of the Catholic Church in Oregon and the Northwest.* Ferndale, 1910.

[Blanchet, F. N. and Demers, M.] *Notices & Voyages of the Famed Quebec Mission to the Pacific Northwest.* Trans. C. Landerholm. Oregon Historical Society. Portland, 1961.

Bolton, H. E. *Fray Juan Crespi, Missionary Explorer on the Pacific Coast 1769-1774.* Berkeley, 1927.

Bridgwater, Dorothy. "John Jacob Astor Relative to His Settlement on Columbia River". *Yale University Library Gazette* 24 (1949): 53-54.

Campbell, Marjorie W. *The North West Company.* Toronto, 1957.

[Cardero, José] *A Spanish Voyage to Vancouver and the North-west Coast of America ... in the Year 1792. ...* Trans. C. Jane. London, 1930.

Chevigny, Hector. *Russian America: The Great Alaskan Venture 1741-1867.* London, 1966.

[Chimmo, William] *Euryalus; Tales of the Sea.* London, 1860.

Clark, R. C., ed. "Aberdeen and Peel on Oregon, 1844". *OHQ* 34 (1933):236-40.

Cline, Gloria. *Peter Skene Ogden and the Hudson's Bay Company.* Norman, Okla., 1974.

Cook, James. *The Journals of Captain James Cook.* Ed. J. C. Beaglehole. 3 vols. Vol. III: "The Voyage of the *Resolution* and *Discovery* 1776-1780". Hakluyt Society. Cambridge, 1967.

Cook, James, & King, James. *A Voyage to the Pacific Ocean. Undertaken, by the Command of His Majesty, for making Discoveries in the Northern Hemisphere.* Vols. I and II by Capt. James Cook, Vol. III by Capt. James King. London, 1784.

Cook, Warren L. *Flood Tide of Empire: Spain and the Pacific Northwest, 1543-1819.* New Haven, 1973.

Cox, Ross. *The Columbia River.* Ed. E. I. & J. R. Stewart. Norman, Okla., 1957.

Craig, Hardin, (Jr.), ed. "A Letter from the Vancouver Expedition". *PNWQ* 41 (1950):352-55.

Dee, H. D. "An Irishman in the Fur Trade: The Life and Journals of John Work". *BCHQ* 9 (1943):229-70.

Dixon, George. *A Voyage round the World; But More Particularly to the North-west Coast of America.* London, 1789.

Douglas, David. *Journal Kept by David Douglas during his Travels in North America 1823-1827.* London, 1914.

Douglas, James. "Douglas Expeditions, 1840-41". Ed. H. A. Leader. *OHQ* 32 (1931) : 1-23; 145-64; 262-78; and 350-72.

Drake, Sir Francis. *The World Encompassed by Sir Francis Drake.* Hakluyt Society. London, 1854.

Dunn, John. *History of the Oregon Territory and British North American Fur Trade.* London, 1844.

Elliott, T. C. "David Thompson, Pathfinder and the Columbia River". *OHQ* 12 (1911) : 195-205.

Ellis, W. *An Authentic Narrative of a Voyage Performed by Captain Cook and Captain Clerke ... During the Years of 1776, 1777, 1778, 1779, and 1780 ... 2 vols.* London, 1782.

Fleming, R. H., ed. *Minutes of Council Northern Department of Rupert Land, 1821-31.* HBRS 3. London, 1940.

Forsyth, J. "Documents Connected with the Final Settlement of the Nootka Dispute". *BCHA Second Annual Report* (1924), pp. 33-35.

Franchère, Gabriel. *Journal of a Voyage on the North West Coast of North America During the Years 1811, 1812, 1813 and 1814.* Ed. W. Kaye Lamb. Champlain Society 44. Toronto, 1969.

Fraser, Simon. *The Letters and Journals of Simon Fraser.* Ed. W. Kaye Lamb. Toronto, 1960.

Fry, Jack. "Fort Defiance". *The Beaver* (Summer 1967) : 18-21.

Galbraith, John S. "The Early History of the Puget's Sound Agricultural Company, 1838-43". *OHQ* 55 (1954) : 234-59.

———. *The Hudson's Bay Company as an Imperial Factor 1821-1869.* Berkeley, 1957.

Gough, Barry M. *The Royal Navy and the Northwest Coast of North America 1810-1914: A Study of British Maritime Ascendancy.* Vancouver, 1971.

Hargrave, James. *The Hargrave Correspondence 1821-1843.* Ed. G. P. Glazebrook. Champlain Society 24. Toronto, 1938.

Harlow, Vincent T. *The Founding of the Second British Empire 1763-1793.* 2 vols. London, 1964.

Harmon, Daniel W. *Sixteen Years in the Indian Country: The Journals of Daniel Williams Harmon 1800-1816*. Ed. W. Kaye Lamb. Toronto, 1957.

Helmcken, J. S. "Fort Rupert in 1850". *Victoria Daily Colonist*, 1 Jan. 1890, p. 4.

Howay, F. W. " 'The Ballad of the Bold Northwestman', An Incident in the Life of Captain John Kendrick". *WHQ* 20 (1929) : 114-23.

————. "Discovery of the North West Coast". *Annual Report of the Canadian Historical Association* (1926) : 88-94.

————. "An Early Account of the Loss of the *Boston* in 1803". *WHQ* 17 (1926) : 280-88.

————. "A List of Trading Vessels in [the] Maritime Fur Trade, 1785-1794". *Transactions of the RSC* (Section II, 1930), pp. 111-34.

————. "A List of Trading Vessels in the Maritime Fur Trade, 1795-1804". *Transactions of the RSC* (Section II, 1931) : 117-49.

————. "A List of Trading Vessels in the Maritime Fur Trade, 1805-1814". *Transactions of the RSC* (Section II, 1932) : 43-86.

————. "The Loss of the *Tonquin*". *WHQ* 13 (1922) : 83-92.

————. "An Outline Sketch of the Maritime Fur Trade". *Annual Report of the CHA 1932*, pp. 5-14.

————. "The Spanish Settlement at Nootka". *WHQ* 8 (1917) : 163-71.

————. "The Voyage of the *Hope* 1790-1792". *WHQ* 11 (1920) : 3-28.

————, ed. *Voyages of the "Columbia" to the Northwest Coast 1787-1790 and 1790-1793*. Massachusetts Historical Society. Boston, 1941.

Howay, F. W., & Scholefield, E. O. S. *British Columbia from the Earliest Times to the Present*. 4 vols. Vancouver, 1914.

Innis, Harold A. *The Fur Trade in Canada*. Revised ed. Toronto, 1956.

Jewitt, John R. *Narrative of the Adventures and Sufferings of John R. Jewitt*. New York, n.d.

Judson, Katharine B. "The British Side of the Restoration of Fort Astoria". *OHQ* 20 (1919) : 243-60 and 305-30.

Kane, Paul. *Paul Kane's Frontier*, including *Wanderings of an Artist among the Indians of North America*. Toronto, 1971.

Kime, W. R. "Alfred Seton's Journal: A Source for Irving's *Tonquin* Disaster Account". *OHQ* 71 (1970) :309-24.

Lamb, W. Kaye. "The Advent of the 'Beaver' ". *BCHQ* 2 (1938): 163-79.

——. "The Founding of Fort Victoria". *BCHQ* 7 (1943) :71-92.

——. "McLoughlin's Statement of the Expenses Incurred in the 'Dryad' Incident of 1834". *BCHQ* 10 (1946) :291-97.

Ledyard, John. *A Journal of Captain Cook's Last Voyage....* Hartford, 1783.

Lee, Jason. "Diary of Rev. Jason Lee". *OHQ* 17 (1916) :116-46; 240-66 and 397-430.

Lent, D. Geneva. *West of the Mountains: James Sinclair and the Hudson's Bay Company.* Seattle, 1963.

McCormac, E. I. *James K. Polk: A Political Biography.* Berkeley, 1922.

McDonald, Archibald. *Peace River. A Canoe Voyage from Hudson's Bay to Pacific by the Late Sir George Simpson ... in 1828.* Ed. Malcolm McLeod. Ottawa, 1872.

McKechnie, Dr. R. E. *Strong Medicine.* Vancouver, 1972.

Mackenzie, Sir Alexander. *The Journals and Letters of Sir Alexander Mackenzie.* Ed. W. Kaye Lamb. Hakluyt Society. Cambridge, 1970.

McLean, John. *John McLean's Notes of a Twenty-five Years' Service in the Hudson's Bay Territory.* Ed. W. S. Wallace. Champlain Society 19. Toronto, 1932.

McLoughlin, Dr. John. "Letter of Dr. John McLoughlin to *Oregon Statesman,* June 8, 1852". *OHQ* 8 (1907) :294-99.

——. *Letters of Dr. John McLoughlin Written at Fort Vancouver 1829-1832.* Ed. B. B. Barker. Oregon Historical Society. Portland, 1948.

——. *The Letters of John McLoughlin From Fort Vancouver to the Governor and Committee, First Series 1825-1838.* Ed. E. E. Rich. HBRS 4. London, 1941.

——. *The Letters of John McLoughlin From Fort Vancouver to the Governor and Committee, Second Series 1839-44.* Ed. E. E. Rich. HBRS 6. London, 1943.

——. *The Letters of John McLoughlin From Fort Vancouver to the Governor and Committee, Third Series 1844-46.* Ed E. E. Rich. HBRS 7. London, 1944.

Manning, W. R. "The Nootka Sound Controversy". *American Historical Association Annual Report, 1904*, pp. 283-478.

Meany, Edmond S. *Vancouver's Discovery of Puget Sound*. Enlarged edition. Portland, 1957.

Meares, John. *Voyages Made in the Years 1788 and 1789 from China to the North West Coast of America*. London. 1790.

Menzies, Archibald. *Menzies' Journal of Vancouver's Voyage, April to October 1792*. Ed. C. F. Newcombe. PABC Memoir 5. Victoria, 1923.

Merk, Frederick. *Fur Trade and Empire: George Simpson's Journal ... 1824-25*. Cambridge, Mass., 1968.

————. *The Oregon Question: Essays in Anglo-American Diplomacy and Politics*. Cambridge, Mass., 1967.

Miles, E. A. " 'Fifty-four Forty or Fight' — An American Political Legend". *Mississippi Valley Historical Review* 44 (1957) :291-309.

Morice, Rev. A. G. *The History of the Northern Interior of British Columbia*. Toronto, 1904.

Morton, A. S. "The North West Company's Columbian Enterprise and David Thompson". *Canadian Historical Review* 17 (1936) : 266-88.

Moziño, José Mariano. *Noticias de Nutka: An Account of Nootka Sound in 1792*. Trans. & ed. Iris H. Wilson. Toronto, 1970.

Nuttall, Zelia, ed. *New Light on Drake*. Hakluyt Society. London, 1904.

Ogden, Peter Skene. "Peter Skene Ogden's Notes on Western Caledonia". Ed. W. N. Sage. *BCHQ* 1 (1937) :45-56.

Oliver, E. H., ed. *The Canadian North-west, Its Early Development and Legislative Records*. 2 vols. Ottawa, 1914.

"Oregon". *Nautical Magazine* 15 (1846) :293-303.

Ormsby, Margaret A. *British Columbia: A History*. n.p., 1958.

Patterson, Samuel. *Narrative of the Adventures and Sufferings of Samuel Patterson*. Palmer, 1817.

Peña, Fray Tomas de la. "Diary of the Voyage ... in His Majesty's Ship called the *Santiago*". *Publications of the Historical Society of Southern California*, Vol. 2, Part 1 (1891) :111-43.

Pethick, Derek. *S.S. Beaver: The Ship that Saved the West*. Vancouver, 1970.

Portlock, Nathaniel. *A Voyage Round the World; But More Particularly to the North-west Coast of America.* London, 1789.

Purchas, Samuel. *Purchas His Pilgrimes.* London, 1625.

"Recollections of Six Months in Puget Sound". *Nautical Magazine* 21 (1852):244-49 and 314-18.

Rich, E. E. *The History of the Hudson's Bay Company.* HBRS 21 & 22. London, 1958 and 1959.

Rickman, John. *Journal of Captain Cook's Last Voyage.* . . . London, 1781.

Robertson, Colin. *Colin Robertson's Correspondence Book, September 1817 to September 1822.* Ed. E. E. Rich. HBRS 2. London, 1939.

Richardson, James D., ed. *A Compilation of the Messages and Papers of the Presidents.* 11 vols. New York, 1910.

Ross, Alexander. *Adventures of the First Settlers on the Oregon or Columbia River.* Ed. R. G. Thwaites. Cleveland, 1904.

―――. *The Fur Hunters of the Far West.* Ed. K. A. Spaulding. Norman, Okla., 1956.

Sage, Walter N. *Sir James Douglas and British Columbia.* Toronto, 1930.

Scholefield, E. O. S. "Simon Fraser". *Westward Ho! Magazine* 3 (1908):217-31.

Scott, L. M. "Report of Lieutenant Peel on Oregon in 1845-46". *OHQ* 29 (1928):51-76.

Scouler, John. "Journal of a Voyage to N.W. America". *OHQ* 6 (1905):54-75; 159-205; and 276-87.

Seemann, Berthold. *Narrative of the Voyage of H.M.S. Herald During the Years 1845-51.* 2 vols. London, 1853.

Simpson, Sir George. *London Correspondence Inward from Sir George Simpson 1841-42.* Ed. Glyndwr Williams. HBRS 29. London, 1973.

―――. *Narrative of a Journey Round the World.* 2 vols. London, 1847.

―――. *Part of Dispatch from George Simpson Esqr . . . to the Governor & Committee of the Hudson's Bay Company London.* Ed. E. E. Rich. HBRS 10. London, 1947.

Slacum, W. A. "Slacum's Report on Oregon, 1836-37". *OHQ* 13 (1912):175-224.

Smiley, H. D. "The Dalliance of David Thompson". *The Beaver* (Winter 1972) :40-47.

Smith, Dorothy Blakey. *James Douglas: Father of British Columbia.* Toronto, 1971.

Strange, James. *James Strange's Journal and Narrative of the Commercial Expedition from Bombay to the North-west Coast of America.* Madras, 1928.

Thom, Adam. *The Claims to the Oregon Territory Considered.* London, 1844.

Thompson, David. *David Thompson: Travels in Western North America 1784-1812.* Ed. V. G. Hopwood. Toronto, 1971.

———. *David Thompson's Narrative 1784-1812.* Ed. Richard Glover. Champlain Society 40. Toronto, 1962.

Thomson, George M. *Sir Francis Drake.* London, 1972.

Tolmie, W. F. *The Journals of William Fraser Tolmie: Physician and Fur Trader.* Vancouver, 1963.

Tyrrell, J. B. "David Thompson, A Great Geographer". *The Geographical Journal* 37 (1911) :49-58.

Vancouver, George. "Original Vancouver Letters". *WHQ* 18 (1927) : 55-57.

———. *A Voyage of Discovery to the North Pacific Ocean and Round the World.* 3 vols. London, 1798.

Wagner, Henry R. "Apocryphal Voyages to the Northwest Coast of America". *Proceedings of the American Antiquarian Society* 41 (1931) :179-90.

———. *Spanish Explorations in the Strait of Juan de Fuca.* Santa Ana, 1933.

Walbran, John T. *British Columbia Coast Names 1592-1906.* Ottawa, 1909.

Warre, H. J. "Secret Mission of Warre and Vavasour". *WHQ* 3 (1912) :131-53.

———. *Sketches in North America and the Oregon Territory.* London, 1848.

Wilkes, Charles. *Narrative of the United States Exploring Expedition During the Years 1838, 1839, 1840, 1841, 1842.* 5 vols. Philadelphia, 1845.

Wilson, Clifford. *Campbell of the Yukon.* Toronto, 1970.

Work, John. *The Journal of John Work, January to October, 1835.* Ed. H. D. Dee. PABC Memoir 10. Victoria, 1945.

Wrinch, Leonard A. "The Formation of the Puget's Sound Agricultural Company". *WHQ* 24 (1933) :3-8.

Zimmermann, H. *Zimmermann's Account of the Third Voyage of Captain Cook 1776-1780.* Alexander Turnbull Library Bulletin No. 2. Wellington, New Zealand, 1926.

Index

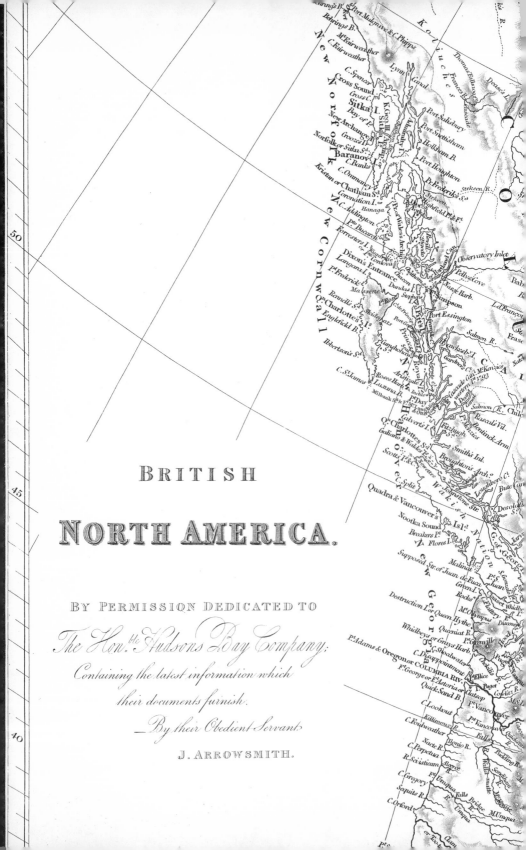

BRITISH

NORTH AMERICA.

BY PERMISSION DEDICATED TO

The Hon.ble Hudsons Bay Company;

Containing the latest information which

their documents furnish.

— By their Obedient Servant

J. ARROWSMITH.